SOVIET MILITARY POWER*

*The Pentagon's Propaganda Document, Annotated and Corrected

Also by TOM GERVASI

Arsenal of Democracy:
American Weapons Available for Export

Arsenal for Democracy II:
*American Military Power in the 80's
and the Origins of the New Cold War*

Arsenal of Democracy III:
America's War Machines

The Myth of Soviet Military Supremacy

Also from the DEPARTMENT OF DEFENSE

<table>
<tr><td rowspan="3">SOVIET
MILITARY
POWER</td><td>First Edition</td><td>September 1981</td><td>Fourth Edition</td><td>April 1985</td></tr>
<tr><td>Second Edition</td><td>March 1983</td><td>Fifth Edition</td><td>March 1986</td></tr>
<tr><td>Third Edition</td><td>April 1984</td><td>Sixth Edition</td><td>April 1987</td></tr>
</table>

SOVIET MILITARY POWER*

*The Pentagon's Propaganda Document, Annotated and Corrected

by TOM GERVASI

Design/art direction by DON DUFFY

Produced by BOB ADELMAN

VINTAGE BOOKS
A Division of Random House
New York

A Vintage Original, First Edition
January 1988

Library of Congress Cataloging-in-Publication Data
Gervasi, Tom.
Soviet military power.
1. Soviet military power.   2. Soviet Union—Armed Forces.
3. Soviet Union—Defenses.   4. Soviet Union—Military policy.
5. United States—Military policy.
I. Title.
UA770.G425 1988   355′.0332′47   87-40280
ISBN 0-394-75715-7 (pbk.)

Manufactured in Japan by Dai Nippon Printing Co., Ltd.
10   9   8   7   6   5   4   3   2   1

Typography: U.S. LITHOGRAPH, typographers
Production Coordinators:
Dayna Burnett and
Carol Woolworth

This book, a most complex task, would not be possible without
the selfless dedication, consummate professionalism and good
humor of the Pentagon Irregulars:
    Dayna Burnett, Theta Duffy, Don Duffy, Lynne Fink,
    Lisa Folsom, Wendy Gervasi, Glorya Hale, Arthur Hale,
    Susan Hall, Quentin Hughes, Jr., Mori Otaki,
    Karen Quinn, Michael Riesenberg, and Carol Woolworth.
We are indebted to our editors Jason Epstein, Linda Rosenberg,
Julie Grau and especially David Rosenthal for his wise counsel
and patience.
                                —TOM GERVASI AND BOB ADELMAN

INTRODUCTION

Several times over the past forty years a curious drama has repeated itself in our nation's political life. It has always begun with a military emergency.

Grim prophets have appeared to warn us that America's prestige and power were on a dangerous decline, or that we had neglected our military for too long, or that our defenses had eroded, leaving our security at grave risk, or that our lead in the arms race was rapidly diminishing, or that a window of vulnerability was opening, or a gap looming, or that the military balance (in some unspecified way) was shifting inexorably against us. The prophets always had the same solutions to recommend. To repair our defenses, regain our lead, or redress any adverse imbalance of power, a massive increase in military spending was needed. This increase was always granted.

Each time this drama played itself out, however, a growing number of Americans became disturbed by it. Some felt that the impending threats were not significant enough to require any response from the United States. Others, who shared these doubts about the gravity of the threat, feared that further increases in military spending might have devastating effects on our economy. They were always dismissed as purveyors of "gloom and doom."

Still, the prophets of military emergency were never dismissed. All who doubted their predictions were discredited as agents or victims of disinformation, despite the fact that not a single one of the emergencies they predicted ever materialized.

Over the years, these prophets achieved an unbroken record of false alarms. Each new prediction turned out to be a mistake. Though each mistake was always acknowledged, it was acknowledged only years after the mistake had been made. It turned out, each time, that there had never been a bomber gap, or a missile gap, or any other gap. Each new expansion of American military power to close these gaps had therefore been unwarranted. It was always impossible, however, to appreciate this fact until long after all of the money had been spent.

Thus does America's military-industrial complex periodically accelerate its growth. National debate on how to spend the money, let alone whether to spend it at all, is neatly circumvented. To preserve the illusion of democracy, the public must be given some reason for spending its money. So it is given lies. Though these lies are no more persuasive from one occasion to the next, they are important. They give people something to believe in. Many Americans prefer to believe what their government tells them rather than face the painful recognition that it is lying to justify misusing their money and that they are helpless to prevent it.

At no time in our history, though, have the lies been so numerous and the warnings so urgent as during the past seven years of the Reagan administration's tenure. President Reagan went so far as to say that the Soviets had achieved a "definite margin" of military superiority over the United States. In scale with this assessment was the administration's first budget request for an unprecedented peacetime program of $1.6 trillion in military spending in only five years. The administration's claim of Soviet military superiority was the only justification it ever offered for its program to "rearm America." In fact, it was also the only justification that it ever offered for *any* of its military policies, including its accelerated expansion of America's nuclear arsenal, its introduction of new nuclear weapons in Europe, its refusal to accept a bilateral nuclear weapons freeze or a comprehensive test ban, its negotiating habit of asking for much greater reductions in Soviet than in American arms, and its promotion of a costly program to develop new weapons in space—where they promise to be far more effective in an offensive role against Soviet satellites than in a defensive one against Soviet missiles.

To sell its military programs, the administration waged an intensive propaganda battle. News conferences, press briefings, and addresses by major administration officials were only a few of the platforms used to disseminate the lies. But the most effective tool was a new device of the Reagan administration's own invention, the publication of *Soviet Military Power*, which refined the techniques of selective emphasis and omission to focus almost exclusively on the Soviet military threat to the West without giving any but the most insignificant details of the much larger military threat the West continues to pose to the Soviet Union.

The administration published the first volume of *Soviet Military Power* in September 1981. Lavishly illustrated with charts and graphs, intelligence photographs—some of them newly declassified—of Soviet weapons, and full-color paintings of some weapons that did not yet exist and may never, the volume was manufactured at taxpayer expense, placed on sale at bookstores across the nation, and distributed free to the administration's most important audience, the domestic and international press. *The New York Times* reported its publication by noting that it contained "no new information, no conclusion," and "no systematic comparison with American forces." This was the only way it could convey what *The Times* called an "impression of relentless and almost overwhelming Soviet military power" that was "fully consistent" with "Reagan's charge in the 1980 presidential campaign that the Soviet Union had achieved military superiority over the United States."

Soviet Military Power has had considerable success. In March 1983 the administration published 300,000 copies of a new edition of *Soviet Military Power* at a cost of $585,000. Since then, an updated and expanded edition has appeared each year. The volume has grown in size from its original length of 100 pages to 160 pages in 1987. In response to growing criticism from members of Congress and the media, current volumes now include some comparisons of Soviet and American equipment in those few categories where a Soviet lead either actually exists or may be claimed to exist in the absence of any information to the contrary. But its authors continue meticulously to avoid any comparisons that would show the many leads and advantages the West continues to hold over the Soviet Union.

The contents of each new edition have been reported worldwide, and portions of each annual have been republished in newspapers, magazines, and books. So broad is its dissemination that it has even become regarded as an official source. For example, many publications now routinely report the range of the newly deployed Soviet AS-15 air-to-ground missile as 3,000 km because that is what *Soviet Military Power* has been claiming since it first reported the existence of this weapon. But the most successful tests the Soviets have had with the AS-15 have been at ranges of no more than 1,200 km. Even the London-based International Institute for Strategic Studies—a strong administration supporter—in its annual report, *The Military Balance, 1986–1987*, reports a range of only 1,800 km for the AS-15.

Even the most basic facts are distorted. We will read in *Soviet Military Power* that there are more than 5.8 million active uniformed military personnel in the Soviet armed services. In reality, there only 3.7 million; the rest are reservists. We will read that the Soviets have 211 army divisions; but only 54 of these are fully manned and fully equipped.

As on every other such occasion earlier in our history, this administration's assertions about Soviet military power are misleading and wrong. The Soviet Union remains a second-rate military power. It still lacks an intercontinental strategic bomber force, and would not have one for decades even if it decided to build one now. Due to geographic constraints, its fleet will never be assured of access to the open ocean and may always be limited to coastal operations. It lacks the capability to project military power beyond the Eurasian land mass and may never significantly develop that capability. While its army is the largest in the world, most of its equipment faces block obsolescence in the near future. It has few ready divisions; West Germany's army, though smaller, is much more powerful because it is far better equipped and benefits from higher levels of training and readiness. Considerations like these demonstrate how numbers alone don't really count.

While the Soviets have done all they could do to match Western levels of strength, they have failed to change the military balance. By every significant measure of comparison, the United States has always held, and continues to hold, a commanding lead in strategic power. Both the nuclear and conventional balances of power in Europe have always heavily favored NATO and continue to do so.

The actual facts are not in dispute; the administration cannot really deny them. It can only avoid mentioning them, misrepresent them, or, as it does frequently in this book, simply lie.

There are many purposes behind this annotated and corrected edition. The first and foremost is to find and expose the lies, correct the administration's exaggerations of the numbers and capabilities of Soviet weapons, and identify the hidden assumptions used to create incomplete and misleading comparisons of military power. What I have also tried to do is add all the pertinent information the administration has *excluded* on Western military capabilities so that honest and complete comparisons may be made of equivalent weapons and forces, thereby allowing the proper scale of Soviet military power to be judged in the full context of the real military balance.

The public information I have utilized to contradict and correct the administration's assertions is abundant. Among the key sources have been the CIA's annual reports to Congress, *Military Posture Statements* of the Joint Chiefs of Staff, sworn testimony from chiefs of the military services and Defense Department officials before the Armed Services and Appropriations Committees of Congress, the governments of other NATO nations (especially Canada and West Germany), and a variety of independent sources of information on military and technical affairs—for example, the International Institute for Strategic Studies in London, the Center for Defense Information in Washington, D.C., the Union of Concerned Scientists, the Federation of American Scientists, and the Stockholm International Peace Research Institute. Among the many books that were especially helpful, I would like specifically to mention the Jane's annual reference volumes on military equipment, as well as *Jane's World Armored Fighting Vehicles* by Christopher Foss, David Isby's *Weapons and Tactics of the Soviet Army* (MacDonald & Jane's, London, 1981), and *Soviet Military Aircraft* by Bill Sweetman (Presidio Press, 1981).

The edition of *Soviet Military Power* republished here is that issued in April of 1987. The corrected facts and figures apply to that time, not to any later time. This book is being published several months later, though none of the facts and figures have changed appreciably in the meantime. What cannot be changed is the fact that the administration lied when it lied. That is a matter of permanent record. It is time Americans looked at that record and learned a permanent lesson from it. It should not be possible, in the United States, for government and the private interests it serves to deceive the public in exactly the same way, for exactly the same purpose, over and over again. That these interests have been able over and over again to obtain control over vast amounts of the public wealth, and then misuse it when so many more urgent needs go unattended, is a national tragedy.

—TOM GERVASI
October 1987

SOVIET MILITARY POWER*

*The Pentagon's Propaganda Document, Annotated and Corrected

SOVIET
MILITARY
POWER

The United States Government has not recognized the incorporation of Estonia, Latvia, and Lithuania into the Soviet Union. Other boundary representations on the maps are not necessarily authoritative.

The illustrations of Soviet defense facilities and weapon systems included in this publication are derived from various US sources; while not precise in every detail, they are as authentic as possible. Satellite photographs of Soviet facilities were obtained commercially from the SPOT Image Corporation and EOSAT Inc.

President Reagan here portrays the Soviet Union precisely as he knows the rest of the world might portray the United States. It is characteristic of propaganda to project upon an adversary the mirror image of our own least admirable behavior. In fact, it is the United States which continues to secure for itself the military advantages over the Soviet Union, and thereby poses the larger threat; the United States which defines for itself the broadest set of "interests" throughout the world, in order to protect which it has forcibly intervened in the affairs of other nations far more times than any other government has; the United States whose intelligence community now spends more than $12 billion a year on operations and equipment, including the most sophisticated tools of espionage; and the United States whose current government has the most solidly documented record of state terror, from the mining of Nicaraguan harbors and the killing of Libyan civilians in the attempted assassination of Colonel Quaddafi to the daily murder of Nicaraguan peasants by the Contra "freedom fighters" this administration supports. Statements like President Reagan's, which focus only on the Soviet "reality," are designed to obscure these American realities, which then become more easily deniable, and eventually unthinkable.

This is meaningless. What if the USSR is merely catching up, as in nuclear submarines, with what the US produced in an earlier period? It is also misleading. The USSR has more missiles, but US strategic forces can deliver 5,100 more nuclear warheads to their targets than Soviet forces can. That's what counts more than anything else. Most of the figures given are also wrong, as noted.

The administration has given the public no credible evidence that our technology has been stolen. It has merely publicized a greater number of arrests and trials, and sought heavier sentences for espionage, to dramatize this threat and to create the impression that we are newly vulnerable to it.

Not new, but a conversion of the SS-13. The administration calls it the "SS-25" so that it will be regarded as a new missile. In that way, when the Soviets deploy the SS-X-24, we can complain that they have violated SALT II, which allowed each signatory only one new ICBM. Having already begun deployment of our new "Peacekeeper" (MX), we really will violate SALT II when we proceed with plans to deploy our new Midgetman. Of course, now we will say the Soviets violated this provision first. Having already violated other provisions of SALT II, the administration has declared it is no longer "bound" by the treaty. But it is still useful to charge violations in order to justify new deployments of our own.

PREFACE

"... the threat from Soviet forces, conventional and strategic, from the Soviet drive for domination, from the increase in espionage and state terror remains great. This is reality. Closing our eyes will not make reality disappear."

Ronald Reagan

In the military strategy and resulting weapons program flowing from its doctrine, the USSR has long followed the Leninist maxim that quantity has a quality of its own. To appreciate the commitment that the USSR makes to its armed forces, it is useful to start with a look at the weapon systems the Soviets are procuring for those forces and to place those figures alongside similar US procurement. For the decade 1977-1986, the USSR built 3,000 ICBMs and SLBMs, the US 850; the USSR 140,000 surface-to-air missiles, the US 16,200; the USSR 24,400 tanks, the US 7,100; the USSR 90 submarines, the US 43; the USSR 28,200 artillery pieces, the US 2,750.

Because of the large Soviet advantage in numbers of troops and weapons, the West has in the past relied upon superior technology to ensure the continuance of an effective deterrent. Each year, however, we confront a more technologically advanced Soviet Union, which has been aided by theft and legal acquisition of Western technology and growing sophistication of the USSR's own scientific knowledge. Our technological lead is being increasingly challenged.

Soviet Military Power 1987 reviews new developments in the USSR's armed forces over the past year and places these in the context of current doctrine and strategy. These developments again underscore that the USSR is building new generations of offensive strategic and theater nuclear forces, as well as conventional land, sea, and air forces and strategic defense forces, going far beyond legitimate requirements for defense. Among the more noteworthy Soviet military efforts for 1986 were the following:

- The USSR's newest class of strategic ballistic missile submarine, the DELTA IV, is preparing to put to sea on its first operational mission carrying in its missile bay 16 SS-N-23s, the Soviets' newest submarine-launched ballistic missile. Each SS-N-23 carries 10 MIRVed nuclear warheads and has greater accuracy than its predecessors.

- The USSR's first fifth-generation ICBM, the road-mobile SS-25, now numbers about 100 launchers, with additional support bases nearing completion.

- An extensive network of rail support facilities continues to take shape in preparation for the imminent deployment of the rail-mobile SS-X-24 ICBM. This missile, nearly the size of Peacekeeper, will be armed with 10 MIRVed nuclear warheads. Some of these new missiles will also be deployed in silos.

- Test flights have now begun for the follow-on missile to the SS-18 Mod 4 ICBM, a missile that will probably have greater throw-weight, carry at least 10 warheads, and have greater accuracy than its predecessor, increasing its effectiveness against US ICBM silos and other hardened targets.

Most of the "Leninist maxims" the administration quotes are taken from *The Blue Book of the John Birch Society.*

Wrong. The USSR built 1,186 ICBMs and SLBMs in this period.

Wrong. The US built 84,235 surface-to-air missiles for its own services alone, not counting export production.

Wrong. We outproduced the USSR in this period, with 12,655 M60 and M1 tanks, to their 9,370 T-72s (including the "T-80" variant).

Wrong. The USSR built 5,625.

Implies they are catching up, while we are standing still. We are not standing still. If we were, we would no longer claim they were trying to steal our technology.

Who defines what is "legitimate"? Why does the US now have over 38,000 nuclear warheads, when a few hundred would suffice for deterrence?

We continue to put new Trident submarines to sea, with much more accurate missiles.

Implies it can be launched from a road transporter. Not too likely for a Soviet ICBM.

In other words, they are trying to improve the SS-18 guidance. Our ICBMs remain the greater threat to hardened targets. Our best can strike within 300 feet of their aimpoints. Their best can strike within 850 feet.

Only 240 of these are deployed within range of Western Europe.

The Soviets certainly would like to improve the accuracy of the SS-20. This missile only can strike, at best, within 1,320 feet of its aimpoint. Our Pershing II, deployed within range of Moscow, can strike within 100 feet.

Don't count on it.

These are replacements for old FROGS and SCUDs. Overall numbers have not increased in Europe.

Still not operational.

Wrong. 1,200 km.

Our cruise missiles were first deployed in the air in 1981, on the ground in 1983 and at sea in 1984. Their range is 3,900 km, and will soon increase.

There is no evidence that even the 32 GALOSH missiles specially designed for this task can accomplish it.

Neither the BEAR J nor the MIDAS is yet operational. Only 3 of the CONDORs are in service. We have had 78 C-5As in service since the early 1970s, and have 16 C-5Bs on order.

The USSR now has only 30 BISON and 20 BADGER tankers for its strategic forces. We have 663 KC-135s and KC-10As. It will be many more years before the USSR will be able to extend the range of its bombers as we have.

We now have more than 2,000 MACH-2+ aircraft: 757 F-15 EAGLEs, 977 F-16 FALCONs and 300 F-14 TOMCATs. The USSR does not have 300 MiG-29 FULCRUMS. It has fewer than 30.

• The USSR, even though it has 441 SS-20 longer range intermediate-range nuclear force missile launchers already deployed, is vigorously pursuing test-firings of a still more accurate version of the SS-20 missile, which could become operational this year. Deployment continues for the newest generation SS-23 and SS-21 short-range ballistic missiles. Based on previous practice, tests of new follow-ons for these systems could begin soon.

• In strategic bomber developments, additional supersonic BLACKJACK bombers have joined the five aircraft that were reported last year to be undergoing flight-testing. More than 50 operational BEAR H bombers are now fitted with 3,000-kilometer-range, nuclear-capable AS-15 air-launched cruise missiles, and these bombers have routinely flown training missions against North America throughout 1986, approaching within 80 kilometers of the Alaskan coast.

• Along with the operational deployment of air-launched cruise missiles, the USSR is pursuing flight-testing of SSC-X-4 nuclear-capable ground-launched cruise missiles and SS-NX-21 nuclear-capable sea-launched cruise missiles from submarines.

• The USSR has begun operational deployment of an entirely new generation of mobile surface-to-air missiles, the SA-12A/GLADIATOR. The SA-X-12B/GIANT, a second missile for this new mobile missile system, is still under development and has the capability of intercepting cruise missiles, tactical ballistic missiles, aircraft at all altitudes, and it may have the potential to intercept some types of strategic ballistic missiles as well.

• In additional air developments, the naval aviation BEAR J communications relay aircraft became operational. The new MIDAS tanker aircraft also became operational, enabling the USSR to extend the range of its strategic bombers and eventually its supersonic fighter-interceptors. More than 300 of the Mach-2+ FULCRUM fighter-interceptors are now operational. Additional units of the CONDOR transport, with its 150-metric ton lift capacity, have emerged from the airframe plant at Kiev.

• The USSR's immense military industrial capabilities are mirrored in its naval construction program. To cite just a few examples, the third KIROV-Class nuclear-powered cruiser and the eighth SOVREMENNYY-Class guided-missile destroyer were launched; the second SLAVA-Class guided-missile cruiser became operational; the lead unit of the SIERRA-Class nuclear-powered attack submarine was assigned to operational forces; the second AKULA and SIERRA units began sea trials; the fourth DELTA IV- and the fifth TYPHOON-Class nuclear-powered ballistic missile submarines were launched; *Baku,* the fourth KIEV-Class carrier, entered sea trials; and fitting out proceeded on the 65,000-metric ton aircraft carrier *Leonid Brezhnev,* while construction continued on the second carrier of this class at Nikolayev Shipyard.

● Our military aircraft, many of them armed, do not simply approach within 80 kilometers of the Soviet coast. They cross right over that coast, into Soviet territory. Since 1950, we have deliberately flown hundreds of aircraft into Soviet airspace in a systematic provocation of Soviet air defenses, in order to monitor the results, learning all we could about their radar and interceptor capabilities, their communications and their chain of command. There is a price to pay for reckless endangerment. Before Korean Air Flight 7 was shot down in 1983, we had already lost at least 139 lives and 27 aircraft, including an EC-130 over Soviet Armenia, a U-2 over Sverdlovsk in the heart of the Urals, and an RB-47 over Sakhalin Island, all so that our Strategic Air Command could determine the best routes of attack for its bombers.

● The SA-12A has a speed of Mach 2.5 and a range of 70 km. Our PATRIOT surface-to-air missile, already deployed, has a speed of Mach 3.9 and a range of 400 km.

● Our shipyards are outbuilding Soviet yards. In the past year, we have added to our fleet two more OHIO class ballistic missile submarines, six more LOS ANGELES class attack submarines, two more TICONDEROGA class cruisers and five more PERRY class missile frigates. We plan to add two more aircraft carriers to the 14 now in service. The only aircraft the USSR can fly from its carriers is the Yak-36 FORGER, whose combat radius is 250 km. The combat radius of our carrier-based F-14 TOMCAT is 1,600 km. Our NIMITZ class carriers weigh over 90,000 tons and carry 86 aircraft each.

The US sustains a "flow of arms" to more than 100 nations in every hemisphere. This frequently produces ●
"hostile activities," as it has in Afghanistan, where we have supplied arms to the mullahs since 1973, six
years before Soviet troops were sent there; in Ethiopia, where we have armed separatist movements in
Eritrea and the Ogaden since a socialist regime took power; and in Angola, where we continue to arm
UNITA, the losers in a civil war whose winners are now internationally recognized as the legitimate government of that nation.

Secretary Weinberger here deplores the lack of "public debate and scrutiny on funding and other issues" ●
in the USSR. He purports to recognize that debate and scrutiny are "essential in free societies." This administration has no interest in debate and scrutiny. If it wanted public debate, we would have had a proper one
over its defense "buildup," and the radical shift in this nation's resources to pay for it, including devastating
cuts in public services and social programs, never would have taken place. It doesn't want "informed citizens," or it wouldn't be so busy misinforming them, as it does in this book. It certainly doesn't want its
citizens to "make the choices required for our defense." Polls have shown what choices we would have made.
A majority in this nation has wanted a nuclear freeze. We have not gotten it. A majority wants to cease
wasting money on "defensive" weapons based in space. We continue to waste it. This is not democracy. It is
also time we asked what sort of "freedom" this administration means to "safeguard." President Roosevelt
sought to guarantee four: freedom of speech and religion, freedom from fear and freedom from want. There
will be no freedom from fear as long as there are nuclear weapons, 17,000 more of which this administration
has built. There is no longer freedom from want for thousands of America's farmers whose mortgages are
being foreclosed; for 20 percent of our work force which can find no more than an hour or two of work a week
or none at all, or which has ceased believing it can find work; for the nation's three million homeless, its
20 million starving, or its 38 million living below the official poverty line. This administration came into
office proudly proclaiming: "There are no entitlements." It has shown that it means it.

The USSR renounced this prediction, made by the Comintern in 1917. It was Ronald Reagan who pre- ●
dicted in 1983 that the Soviet system would wind up "on the ashheap of history."

**In this summary of what appear to be the major "findings" in this year's edition of *Soviet Military
Power*, familiar patterns emerge. Soviet levels of arms production and military spending are exaggerated. Existing weapons are given improved capabilities that more nearly match our own.
Modifications of existing systems are described as "follow-on" systems to make them seem like
new ones, or are simply given new names. Systems not yet deployed are said to be. The imminent
deployment of many new systems is promised, when it may not occur for some years, if at all.
These misrepresentations are designed not only to "enhance" the Soviet threat but also to suggest
a Soviet initiative where we have already taken one or plan to take one. Often, then, when officials
misrepresent Soviet programs, they are in a very real sense describing our own.**

- Soviet production facilities for all types of ground force equipment continued to turn out modern T-80 tanks; nuclear-capable, self-propelled and towed 152-mm artillery pieces; and 220-mm multiple rocket launchers. They soon will begin series production of HAVOC and HOKUM attack helicopters.

- The USSR's research facilities continue to exploit new biological warfare technologies. New genetically engineered agents could be so impervious to treatment that only scientists with the knowledge of how the original mutation was developed could produce an effective prevention or cure.

Each of these developments, as well as other efforts by the USSR to enhance its military forces and its military-related space program, is reported in *Soviet Military Power 1987.*

This year's edition provides an updated report on the USSR's strategic defense program, a program that over the past 10 years has cost the Soviets the equivalent of some $200 billion for all types of defensive weapon systems and supporting subsystems. Over the past year, our monitoring has revealed the construction of three additional large phased-array ballistic missile warning and target tracking radars, beyond the six reported previously. The Soviets may even build one or two more such radars in the near future.

Appreciating the size of the Soviet Union's armed forces is not enough. We must also think critically about why the Soviets continue to devote such a large portion of their national resources — 15 to 17 percent of their Gross National Product — to supporting this military buildup. As free peoples, we must base decisions on our security, both national and collective, on a realistic understanding of the Soviet military threat. We do not have to look far to see evidence of that threat: to subjugated Eastern Europe, including Poland and the crushed Solidarity movement; to Afghanistan where, despite a sham withdrawal of some Soviet forces, the drive against the Afghans continues; to the flow of arms and hostile activities in our own hemisphere; to the support of state terrorism; and to Angola and Ethiopia, where Soviet surrogates are in combat.

As free peoples, we must understand that the Soviet political system — a system the Soviets proclaim will prevail over ours — fosters the growth of military power. It provides for long-term investments in research and development, as well as long-term decisions on the production and deployment of weapon systems, with none of the public debate and scrutiny on funding and other issues so essential in free societies. Against the background of the reality of this continuing Soviet challenge, *Soviet Military Power 1987* is published to report on the USSR's military developments. It is designed to assist informed citizens in free nations everywhere to make the choices required to provide for the defense and security necessary to safeguard freedom.

Caspar W. Weinberger
Secretary of Defense

March 1987

- There is no such thing as a "T-80." There is only a T-72 with armoured fabric side skirts and smoke grenade launchers. The administration promised, but never delivered, a very different tank, as we shall see.

- More of the mirror-image. It is the US which has begun military and open-air commercial tests of genetically engineered agents, despite the clear awareness shown here of their dangers.

- Research on an antiballistic missile (ABM) defense has certainly produced what John Pike of the Federation of American Scientists calls "an ABM gap," but that gap, he adds, is "in our favor," no matter how much money was really spent.

- Wrong. According to the CIA, Soviet defense spending has been increasing at an annual rate of 2 percent per year. It is now the equivalent of about $100 billion a year, and is 6 percent of Soviet GNP. Our defense budget has increased 100 percent since 1979. It now averages $300 billion a year. This and all other defense-related spending in the US now comprise 40 percent of all Federal spending and 9 percent of our GNP. Our GNP is about twice that of the Soviet GNP.

- Cited here are two of the five occasions on which the USSR has sent or used its military personnel abroad to impose or restore favorable political conditions. The US has done the same on more than 53 occasions since 1800.

- We await proof of Soviet support of state terrorism more credible than what Claire Sterling and others have thus far supplied.

● Here is the first of a number of illustrations in this book, each with an artist's "impression" of a weapon system newly deployed, about to be deployed or under development. The illustrations substitute for photographs, either because no such weapon system really is under development or being deployed, or because a photograph would reveal that what is being deployed looks nothing like this and has none of the new capabilities the administration has decided to say it has. Illustrations are effective in two ways. By depicting new Soviet weapons which do not exist and never may, they imply that such weapons already exist or soon will, and thereby literally make the Soviet threat "larger than life." This is useful whenever an undistorted view of existing Soviet weapons and forces might fail to persuade the public that any military expansion of our own is needed. Before the Reagan military "buildup" began, for example, the US and NATO already had on hand more than enough military power to meet any genuine threat from the USSR. Had this been apparent at that time, it would have taken more than an attempt on President Reagan's life to get the administration's first swollen defense budget through Congress. But the administration and its supporters had worked hard throughout its campaign for office to make the threat larger than life. By depicting very advanced weapons soon to emerge, these illustrations also promise an unending expansion of Soviet military capabilities, and thereby extend the threat to the future. Taken together with warnings of immutably hostile Soviet intentions, they create the sense of a permanent threat which can never subside but only increase, justifying a limitless expansion of military power of our own in reponse. This is the best way to guarantee a continuing growth of return on investment in defense manufacturing. That is all the Soviet threat has ever been about.

● A perfect example of how a misleading illustration can be used to "enhance" the threat occured in the 1981 edition of *Soviet Military Power*. It was an artist's "impression" of what the administration called the new Soviet "T-80 tank," which it promised would soon begin deployment. The tank in the illustration looked exactly like our own new M-1 ABRAMS tank, with its square turret and heavy compound armour. No photograph of the "T-80" appeared until the 1983 edition. The adminsitation described it as "the most modern Soviet tank," featuring "enhanced firepower," and warned that it would have a "significant" impact on NATO. But the tank in the photograph, with its familiar rounded turret, was a T-72. It looked nothing like our M-1 ABRAMS. It had no "enhanced firepower." It had the same 125mm gun all other T-72s had. Its only differences were the addition of armoured fabric sideskirts to give its suspension some protection from low caliber cannon fire,

and smoke grenade launchers—which most other tanks already had. The promised new tank which so much resembled our M-1 ABRAMS never appeared. In the USSR and most other nations, weapons development usually follows the slow, evolutionary course reflected in these minor modifications of the T-72. This is less true in the US, where weapons are often produced from completely new designs, like that for the M-1 ABRAMS, since this requires the greatest expenditure of our money in new capital outlays, thereby most rapidly increasing the profit margin for defense contractors. Profits, after all, are primarily what US corporations have obligated themselves to produce, whatever else they may produce.

● The USSR is not "quite unlike" other nations in seeking absolute security. Every nation seeks it. None will ever have it, until all agree to abandon the use of force in resolving their differences. Nor is the USSR unlike other nations in seeking to extend its political and economic influence throughout the world in every way it can. All nations do this too. But there is not a shred of evidence that the Soviet

government seeks world domination, or thinks of this as a feasible or even a desirable goal. In their effort to produce evidence, alarmists must continually revert to the 1917 Comintern prediction that communism would outlive capitalism as a political and economic system, and then they must add their own suggestion that implicit in this prediction was the Soviet goal of bringing about this outcome by force if necessary. Nothing of the kind was ever implicit in that prediction. The USSR has long ceased to think the prediction itself was realistic. The most recent Party Congress acknowledged that capitalism had proven to be a most "durable" institution, and that the two systems must learn to coexist. Nor does the pattern of Soviet military spending suggest a goal of world domination. Any military analyst who is not a beneficiary of defense spending, or paid by this administration, will point out that the Soviets spend little on power projection. The bulk of the effort is directed at defense of the homeland. It always has been. This is the response of a nation which has been repeatedly invaded. It was even invaded by the US and other Western powers in 1919. It lost 25 million people when it was invaded by the Germans in World War II. Its primary commitment is to ensure that this does not happen again.

● All military organizations, not only those in the USSR, are dedicated to "force modernization." If a new Soviet anti-aircraft gun system is truly under development, it will probably closely resemble the ZSU-23-4 SHILKA shown in the background above, or another of its predecessors. It is not likely to resemble the very modern system shown in the illustration's foreground—any more than a variant of the T-72 tank resembled the illustration of a "T-80" tank which appeared in the 1981 edition of this book. The weapon system featured in the illustration above closely resembles the West German GEPARD Flakpanzer. The illustrations in all editions of this book show weapons which invariably look more like Western systems than Soviet ones. Not only does this suggest that the Soviets have attained a comparable level of technological development. It may also be an effort to confuse the sequence of events: to suggest that the Soviets have attained this level first, and that our weapon systems, closely resembling those in these illustrations, are a response to theirs. This would help shift responsibility for initiatives that we have already taken in the arms race. The Soviets certainly are doing their best to close the technology "gap," but we have only widened it.

Chapter I

Soviet Policies and Global Ambitions

The major task assigned to the Soviet military, quite unlike that of other nations' militaries, is to achieve a force posture for the Soviet Union that provides for absolute security as it continues to seek world domination. The USSR's drive for absolute security, however, threatens to create absolute insecurity for its neighbors and other states, thereby resulting in heightened global tensions. Such a force posture is very costly to establish and maintain and places a heavy burden on national resources. Despite economic constraints, the Soviets continue to deploy materiel in large amounts, as well as to develop newer, more capable weapon systems. Moreover, Soviet plans and policies for the use of military power in both peace and war are continually adapted to respond to technological advances and changes in the political environment.

The Soviet deployment of survivable land-based and mobile theater and strategic nuclear forces has markedly increased the USSR's confidence that the West now faces tremendous destruction regardless of which side initiates nuclear strikes. These deployments exacerbate the strategic imbalance in ICBMs and confirm the Soviet advantage in the number of shorter range nuclear missiles, particularly in Europe. The Soviets view these developments as hastening the day when nuclear weapons might only be useful in deterring other nuclear weapons, rather than as a credible deterrent to conventional attack.

The ZSU-X is the USSR's newest antiaircraft system designed to operate with motorized rifle and tank divisions. The ZSU-X adds to the air defense coverage provided by highly effective surface-to-air missiles. This upgrade illustrates the Soviet military's dedication to force modernization programs that continually field more capable systems.

● In the first four pages of text in this book, this is the third time the Soviets have been accused of seeking world domination. That may seem stupid, when nothing supports this view. But propaganda is by nature stupid. That doesn't mean it isn't effective. It has been driving the arms race for 40 years. Repetition is one of its most effective techniques. Say something often enough, goes the rule, and eventually people will believe it.

● The mirror image again. The problem is much worse in the US. The authors clearly understand how serious a problem it can be.

● Let us hope the West appreciates that deterrence now works both ways.

● The USSR faces a worse strategic imbalance in SLBMs and weapons delivered by aircraft.

● The Soviet "advantage" in shorter range missiles is as meaningless as the much larger NATO "advantage" in artillery projectiles.

● This is meant to imply that when that day comes the West will be vulnerable to conventional attack. But despite some numerical advantages in equipment, the Warsaw Pact's conventional forces are not as strong as NATO's. The West, as we shall see, is not vulnerable to conventional attack.

The Naval Balance in the Atlantic and Mediterranean— 1987

	USSR	USSR & Allies	US	US & Allies
Aircraft Carriers	0	0	7	9
Helicopter & VSTOL Carriers	3	3	6	13
Major Combatants Over 2000 Tons	94	101	106	314
Major Combatants Under 2000 Tons	90	126	0	82
Attack Submarines	185	191	54	198
Naval Aircraft	854	955	1,016	1,686

The Soviet Baltic and Black Sea Fleets would have to pass, respectively, through the Danish and Turkish Straits, both under NATO control, and bound to be heavily mined and patrolled in time of war, to reach open ocean. The Northern Fleet would have to pass through gaps between Greenland, Iceland and Great Britain, also heavily guarded, to reach the Atlantic. These are crippling disadvantages.

Only 20 of these could participate in an immediate assault on the NATO Central Front. The rest would take between one and four months to mobilize and reach the battle area.

31, actually, including the 34th Guards Artillery Division at Potsdam.

This means 77 strategic ballistic missile subs have been added to make the submarine total as large as possible. But they are not attack submarines. Their warheads have been counted in the balance of strategic warheads added below.

As noted earlier, it isn't too likely that the USSR has "mobile" ICBMs which could be launched from a transport vehicle, as the silhouette shown here implies. The SS-4 and SS-20 missiles, and BADGER and BLINDER bombers, lack the intercontinental range to strike targets in the US. The BACKFIRE, as our State Department noted, is "neither equipped nor deployed" as a strategic bomber. None of these should be included with Soviet strategic systems. The only significant measure of strategic power is the number of warheads you can deliver to your opponent's homeland. This is shown at left.

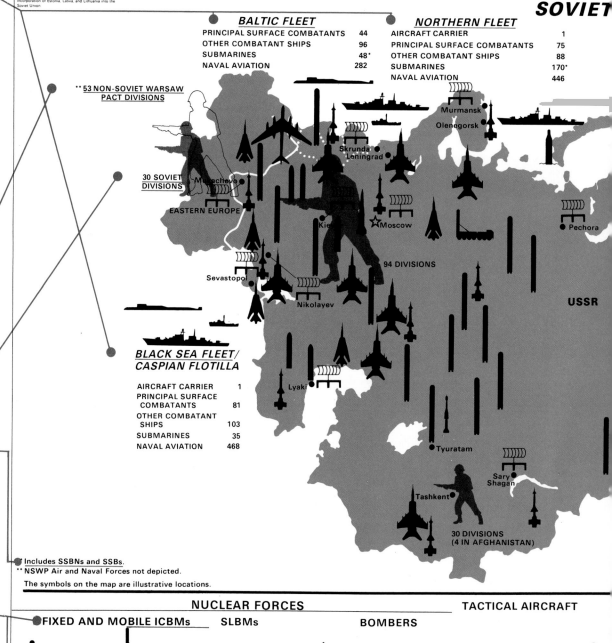

SOVIET

BALTIC FLEET
PRINCIPAL SURFACE COMBATANTS	44
OTHER COMBATANT SHIPS	96
SUBMARINES	48*
NAVAL AVIATION	282

NORTHERN FLEET
AIRCRAFT CARRIER	1
PRINCIPAL SURFACE COMBATANTS	75
OTHER COMBATANT SHIPS	88
SUBMARINES	170*
NAVAL AVIATION	446

** 53 NON-SOVIET WARSAW PACT DIVISIONS

30 SOVIET DIVISIONS
EASTERN EUROPE

Makhachevo
Skrunda
Leningrad
Murmansk
Olenegorsk
Moscow
Pechora
Kiev
94 DIVISIONS
USSR
Sevastopol
Nikolayev
Tyuratam
Lyaki
Sary Shagan
Tashkent
30 DIVISIONS (4 IN AFGHANISTAN)

BLACK SEA FLEET/ CASPIAN FLOTILLA
AIRCRAFT CARRIER	1
PRINCIPAL SURFACE COMBATANTS	81
OTHER COMBATANT SHIPS	103
SUBMARINES	35
NAVAL AVIATION	468

* Includes SSBNs and SSBs.
** NSWP Air and Naval Forces not depicted.
The symbols on the map are illustrative locations.

Boundary representations are not necessarily authoritative. The United States Government has not recognized the incorporation of Estonia, Latvia, and Lithuania into the Soviet Union.

NUCLEAR FORCES

FIXED AND MOBILE ICBMs
SS-11	440
SS-13	60
SS-17	150
SS-18	308
SS-19	360
SS-25	About 100

LRINF
SS-4	112
SS-20	441

SLBMs
SS-N-5	39
SS-N-6	272
SS-N-8	292
SS-N-17	12
SS-N-18	224
SS-N-20	80
SS-N-23	48

BOMBERS
BACKFIRE	290 *
BISON	15
BEAR	150
BADGER	272
BLINDER	135

* Including 130 in Soviet Naval Aviation.
Seven BLACKJACK in advanced flight testing.

TACTICAL AIRCRAFT

TACTICAL AIRCRAFT   5,200 ×

The Balance of Strategic Nuclear Warheads— 1987

	USSR	US
CARRIED BY LAND-BASED MISSILES	5,424	2,302
CARRIED BY SEA-BASED MISSILES	2,672	6,464
CARRIED BY LONG-RANGE BOMBERS	264	4,728
TOTAL DELIVERABLE WARHEADS	8,360	13,494

	USSR	USSR & Allies	US	US & Allies
The Naval Balance in the Pacific and Indian Ocean— 1987				
Aircraft Carriers	0	0	7	7
Helicopter & VSTOL Carriers	2	2	6	6
Major Combatants Over 2000 Tons	44	44	105	151
Major Combatants Under 2000 Tons	36	47	0	134
Attack Submarines	77	77	42	78
Naval Aircraft	461	461	1,016	1,350

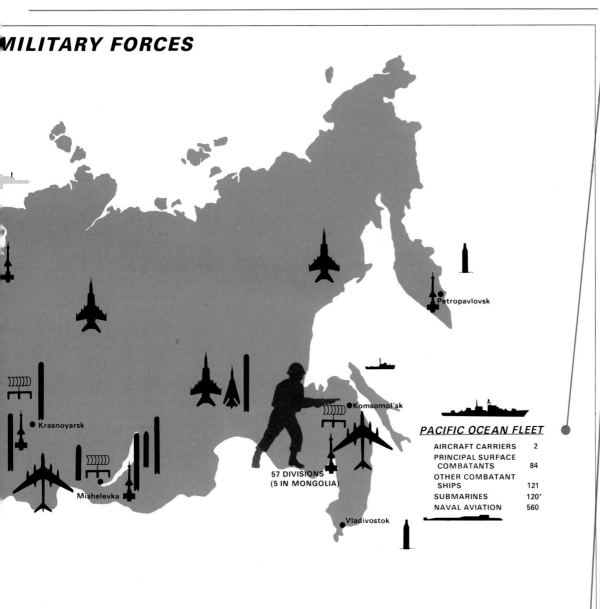

● Units of the Soviet Pacific Fleet based at Vladivostok would have to pass from the Sea of Japan through the Korean or Tsugaru Straits, or from the Sea of Okhotsk through the Kuril Straits, all heavily guarded by the US and its allies in time of war, to reach open ocean. Some units are based at Petropavlovsk, but this port is icebound six months a year.

The European, Middle Eastern and Asian land masses have been removed from this map, to give the false impression that Norway, Denmark, Greenland, Iceland, the United Kingdom, Greece, Turkey, the Korean Peninsula and Japan do not create choke points which bottle up the Soviet Fleets as they do.

● Only 138 of these vessels displace more than 2,000 tons. The US has 211 ships which do. Its allies have another 254. The West has an advantage of more than 3 to 1 in tonnage alone.

● These are missile patrol or gunboats even smaller than the Soviet Navy's frigates. None can operate at high speeds or use sonar or other equipment in the open ocean. They are restricted to coastal waters.

● To enlarge the category of "combatant craft," which includes minesweepers and coastal patrol vessels, the missile patrol and gunboats have been added in again, and counted a second time. Compare all this with the US Coast Guard's 2,493 gunboats, cutters and other craft.

● Our 53 largest replenishment ships displace a total of 1,413,000 tons. Their 85 largest displace 570,000 tons.

PACIFIC OCEAN FLEET

AIRCRAFT CARRIERS	2
PRINCIPAL SURFACE COMBATANTS	84
OTHER COMBATANT SHIPS	121
SUBMARINES	120*
NAVAL AVIATION	560

57 DIVISIONS (5 IN MONGOLIA)

GROUND FORCES*

MOTORIZED RIFLE DIVISIONS	150
TANK DIVISIONS	52
AIRBORNE DIVISIONS	7
STATIC DEFENSE DIVISIONS	2

* Totals exclude 5 mobilization divisions and 2 new Army Corps.

ˣ Force restructuring.

STRATEGIC DEFENSE FORCES

ABM/BMEW RADAR

INTERCEPTORS 2,250ˣ

ASAT

SAM** LAUNCHERS 9,000+

ABM LAUNCHERS 100

**In USSR only — does not include Soviet Strategic SAMs (SA-2/3/5) in Mongolia or with Groups of Forces.

NAVAL FORCES

AIRCRAFT CARRIERS	4
PRINCIPAL SURFACE COMBATANTS	284
OTHER COMBATANT SHIPS	408
COMBATANT CRAFT	765
AUXILIARIES	300
SUBMARINES	373
NAVAL AVIATION	1,756

Chapter 1 Soviet Policies and Global Ambitions

● Only 27 of these could take part in an immediate assault on NATO's Central Front. Ten more, including all airborne units, could join battle within 72 hours. Another 5 could mobilize and reach the front in 10 days, another 10 within 30 days at the soonest. After that, at least three more months would elapse before additional Soviet divisions could be made available. NATO, with ample warning time to bring more troops into place before combat began, would continue to reinforce more quickly, and never lose its significant edge in combat troop strength.

● Wrong. 1,315 helicopters and fixed-wing aircraft. All but 84 helicopters and 39 VSTOL aircraft are land-based.

● Includes 77 ballistic missile submarines with nuclear weapons dedicated to the strategic role, and 174 obsolete diesel electric boats, 34 of them no longer in service. Of the remainder, 23 are new diesel electric boats with low speed and short range. None of the nuclear boats is yet a match in speed and diving depth to its Western counterparts.

Disingenuous discussions of this sort, which seem to speculate about possible changes in Soviet thinking, abound in the book. They are here merely to provide a context in which to repeat, as often as possible, the basic false premises that justify official US policy. The false premise in this paragraph is that the Soviets have the "preponderance of power in conventional forces," and that consequently NATO has to rely "on nuclear weapons to deter a major conventional attack." This has always been our rationale for keeping nuclear weapons in Europe. Yet NATO has always had, and continues to have, more than sufficient conventional power to deter a conventional attack. Our real reasons for placing nuclear weapons in Europe are different. They comprise a fourth strategic force, in addition to longer-range weapons counted under the SALT Treaties, with which to threaten the Soviet homeland from forward bases to which the Soviets have no counterpart. They also make Europe a nuclear target, creating an atmosphere of emergency in which support for official policy becomes patriotic and dissent disloyal. This helps to enforce a political consensus in support of US military goals.

All nuclear weapons create a "non-use" environment.

No evidence exists to suggest that an effective defense against ballistic missiles can ever be developed. The USSR certainly cannot expect this. We are well ahead of them in research, and have nothing to show for it.

The mirror image again. This is precisely what Caspar Weinberger promised US forces would be prepared to do.

These problems are real in the USSR, but far more serious in the US, where we spend 3 times as much on the military, absorbing even a greater share of a larger GNP. Again, the authors show they are well aware of the adverse effects of excess military spending on the domestic economy. But again, they treat these problems as though they were unique to the USSR, giving no hint that they are much more serious at home. We deny our own truth by projecting it abroad.

Just as the Pentagon is reluctant to alter its procurement procedures, with the result that in 1981 and 1982 it wasted, according to the Grace Commission, $92 billion in defense outlays.

One interpretation of these developments is that nuclear deterrence of a Warsaw Pact conventional attack may be diminishing. A second interpretation is that while the Soviets believe the fear of vast devastation might eventually prevent both sides from using nuclear weapons, and thus both sides would avoid such a conflict, they still think such a war is possible. In the Soviet view, their preponderance of power in conventional forces means the West must rely to a significant extent on nuclear weapons to deter a major conventional attack.

The Soviets systematically work on the problem posed by the conventional and nuclear forces equation. On the one hand, they are developing formidable nuclear weapons that help to create a "non-use" environment since these weapons are so destructive. Moreover, they are modernizing existing defenses and developing advanced defenses against ballistic missiles. On the other hand, they are developing, modernizing, and fielding conventional forces that would enable them to prevail in a non-nuclear environment. Essentially, while the Soviets might strive to create a global situation favorable to the employment of their conventional forces, they currently plan and develop a well-balanced force posture that would, in their view, enable them to fight and prevail over their adversaries at any level of conflict.

Domestic Policy

In domestic policy, the Communist Party of the Soviet Union's (CPSU's) major challenge is to revitalize the flagging Soviet economy and lay the base for future military expansion. Soviet economic growth slowed from an annual average rate of 5 percent in the 1960s to 2 percent in the early 1980s. During this period, military spending grew faster than the overall economy because of the leadership's strong commitment to military power. As a result, the military's share of the Gross National Product (GNP) increased from some 12-14 percent in 1970 to 15-17 percent by the mid-1980s. The concomitant deprivation of civil investment is a primary factor behind the country's aging and inefficient industrial base, and the neglect of Soviet living standards is a major reason for chronically low labor motivation and productivity in the USSR.

In response to these problems, General Secretary Mikhail Gorbachev has introduced an ambitious series of programs to stimulate economic growth. These policies do not represent a fundamental alteration of the Soviet central planning system. They are designed to raise capital and labor productivity through improvements in the management and worker incentive systems and, most important, through a major technological renovation of the country's industrial base. The Soviet 12th Five-Year Plan (FYP), for 1986-90, calls for extensive replacement of obsolescent machinery and equipment. The focal point of investment is the machinery-producing sector — the source of new capital stock, consumer durable goods, and military weapons and equipment. Civil machinery-producing ministries are slated for an 80-percent increase in investment in the next 5 years. This investment should redress the past concentration on military industrial ministries, which now account for almost 60 percent of total output and investment in the machinery-producing sector.

The Soviet goal is a more modern, productive economy that will support advances in military technologies and generate sufficient growth for military outlays to increase without absorbing an ever larger share of GNP. The improved economic performance in 1986 provided a good start, but whether the program will really take hold remains questionable. Measures taken so far, such as tightening worker discipline and increasing managerial accountability, address the most accessible targets in the program to raise productivity. It will be more difficult to achieve the assimilation of advanced, high-quality machinery — which is to provide more than two-thirds of planned productivity increases — and to overcome impediments to growth such as high raw material costs and skilled labor shortages. Moreover, rapid technological innovation and efficient management are likely to be hindered, as in the past, by the central planning system that the leadership is reluctant to alter fundamentally. If progress toward the more efficient and productive use of resources proves insufficient, then sustaining high growth rates will become increasingly difficult.

Other initiatives undertaken by the leadership reflect a desire to reform the Soviet system within the existing framework. The dominant theme of Soviet social policies is the need for greater discipline and order. This theme has taken the form of a renewal of the labor discipline campaign popularized under Andropov

According to the CIA, the Soviet economy has grown at an average annual rate of 4.7 percent since 1950, and the military's share of Soviet GNP has remained at about 6 percent throughout this period. Inflated estimates of that share have resulted from repeated reinterpretations of CIA data. Reinterpretation is fundamental to propaganda. Facts must be adjusted to create a "reality" consistent with official statements. Thus, in 1976 George Bush, then CIA director, convened a special "B Team" of such fair-minded men as Richard Pipes, Paul Nitze and Daniel O. Graham to "reassess" the agency's estimate of Soviet military spending. First they discarded the CIA's estimate of Soviet GNP, and produced a much smaller figure, thereby raising the share of GNP absorbed by military spending from 6 to 13 percent. Next they substituted the larger figure they had earlier discarded for GNP, and calculated 13 percent of that. They declared this to be the real level of Soviet military spending. It doubled the CIA's estimate. Sophistry of this sort helped President Reagan claim, in 1981, that the Soviets were spending more on the military than we were.

Arms control is a difficult subject to touch upon in this book. The authors acknowledge that Moscow has made "a wide range of arms control proposals," but they cannot explain why we haven't accepted any of them. Moscow has said it would cease all nuclear tests, remove all nuclear weapons from Europe, abide by the ABM Treaty, adhere to SALT II, and forgo placing weapons in space, if we would but do the same. Instead, this administration has abandoned SALT II and declared its space weapons program "non-negotiable." It continues to avoid a Euromissile agreement it once claimed it wanted, and it now plans to undermine the ABM Treaty. All the authors can do is suggest that the Soviet proposals are "designed to pressure the US" into agreements we do not want. The administration can only say that we do not want such agrements because they "freeze existing inequities" favoring the USSR. Its only rationale for every one of its military programs and policies has been this claim that such inequities exist. Were there any truth to this claim, we would feel none of the "pressure" the Soviets place upon us to demonstrate our commitment to arms control. We would be placing that pressure on them.

and a crackdown on corruption and alcohol abuse. Gorbachev's attack on corruption and inefficiency within the Party elite is part of a larger effort to transform the Party into a more dynamic organization that can better control the development of Soviet society.

Foreign Policy

In foreign policy, the new leadership has retained long-term Soviet objectives and strategies, although it appears to be acting with greater vigor and, in some cases, greater effectiveness. The Party leadership remains committed to the long-term objective of establishing the USSR as the dominant world power. The USSR's relationship with the US has remained a central issue in Soviet foreign policy, particularly the strategic equation. The main goal of the Soviet arms control strategy is to control the pace of force modernization in the West, as well as to block certain programs such as the Strategic Defense Initiative (SDI) and other US military modernization plans. To achieve these objectives, Gorbachev has given new emphasis to the Soviet Union's policy of trying to pressure the US to soften its negotiating positions in the arms talks. He has intensified the USSR's campaign to divide the US from its allies, floating a wide range of arms control proposals designed to pressure the US to accept an arms agreement beneficial to the USSR.

The Soviet policy toward Eastern Europe follows established patterns. Gorbachev has emphasized closer economic ties within the socialist community, particularly in the scientific and technical areas. He has also increased pressure on East European leaders to move ahead with economic improvements intended to make the socialist system work better, to supply better quality goods to the USSR, and to foster modernization of Pact members' military forces.

The policies of the General Secretary toward the Third World reflect a continuing commitment to destabilizing Western-oriented states and to supporting Soviet allies with military and economic assistance. He is vigorously pursuing policies established by his predecessors.

As with domestic policy, Gorbachev has tried to portray his approach to Soviet diplomacy as a new era in the USSR's foreign policy. This approach is more stylistic than substantive. It largely reflects the new leadership's more sophisticated use of propaganda and the foreign news media to influence international public opinion.

The Role of the Military

In the Leadership Structure

The Soviet strategic decisionmaking process is dominated by the Party leadership but influenced by top military leaders. The strategic decisions that result from that process — how to prosecute the war in Afghanistan, for example — are Party decisions. Military professionals certainly play an important role in the strategic decisionmaking process by providing information, assessing alternatives, developing contingency plans, and making recommendations. The dominant players, however, are the most influential Party leaders who sit on the Defense Council.

The Defense Council, the highest decisionmaking body for all aspects of national security policy, conveys the Party's wishes on all defense, budgetary, organizational, and senior personnel matters. It is composed primarily of Party leaders and is chaired by General Secretary Gorbachev.

Marshal of the Soviet Union (MSU) Sergey Sokolov, Minister of Defense, is the only military member of the Defense Council. MSU Sergey Akhromeyev, Chief of the General Staff, probably serves as the Secretary of the Defense Council and participates in its activities. Their participation works two ways. First, it allows top military leaders to express their ideas and concerns in the key national security decisionmaking body. Second, military representation provides the Defense Council with the capability to ensure that direct action is taken on its decisions.

The standing of the military within the overall Soviet leadership has been somewhat reduced in recent years. One example is Defense Minister Sokolov's continued status as a candidate member rather than a full member of the Politburo. While some ministers of defense under Stalin and Khrushchev had to wait several years to achieve full Politburo membership, the trend during the Brezhnev years was to accord the minister of defense full membership. Since Sokolov has apparently been passed over for full membership on several occasions, the leadership might wish to retain a slightly less powerful figure in charge

● Repetition at work. This is the fourth assertion in only six pages of text that the Soviets seek world domination. Have any readers been persuaded yet?

● Reinterpretation at work. Hunger, poverty and political repression can never be the cause of discontent and instability in the world. Only Soviet subversion can cause instability. This is especially true, the administration would have us believe, among "Western-oriented states." These states, of course, are part of the "free" world. The "free" world, in turn, comprises those states which oppose communism and, largely because they do, receive US aid and guarantees of US military "protection." How repressive such states may be is quite beside the point.

● Reinterpretation again. Moscow does not embarrass us in the court of world opinion by demonstrating that we have no genuine interest in arms control. It merely makes "more sophisticated use of propaganda." How this succeeds, of course, cannot be explained.

● The military is also subordinate to civilian authority in our own system.

● Wrong. General Dimitri Yazov is Minister of Defense.

● There is no reason why arms agreements "beneficial to the USSR" cannot be equally beneficial to us. But the implication here is that such agreements would favor the USSR, and therefore must be avoided. How does the Soviet proposal for a comprehensive test ban favor them, when we have exploded 765 nuclear devices to their 564? How can a ban on space weapons favor them when they have placed no weapons in space? If they were ahead of us in developing such weapons, we would be the ones trying to "block" their progress, and insisting at Geneva that all such weapons be banned. If they were ahead of us in any field of military development, we would be the ones making the "wide range" of proposals to "control the pace" of their force modernization. We are not the ones. Then we are ahead in all these fields. The administration knows this perfectly well, but lies to create the impression the reverse is true. This justifies administration programs to accelerate the pace of our own force modernizations, in order to multiply military advantages we already have, and provides an excuse to avoid arms agreements which would bring these programs —and the arms race—to a halt.

When Mathias Rust, a very young and inexperienced West German pilot, who had logged only 25 hours of solo flight time but nevertheless had prepared his Cessna 172 aircraft for an unusually demanding flight, removing its passenger seats and replacing them with long-range fuel tanks, took, for reasons yet unexplained, and about which our press displays not a hint of curiosity, the extraordinary risk of being shot out of the sky by flying from Helsinki straight across the Finnish border into Soviet territory and onwards for 400 miles to Moscow, there to land, on May 28, 1987, in Red Square, where it just so happened that an American tourist was on hand with videocamera to record the event on tape of exceptional quality, which quickly found its way onto Western European and American television, Soviet authorities were understandably embarrassed. The result was that two of the gentlemen listed below, Defense Minister *Sergei Sokolov* and Air Defense Marshal *Alexander Kodunov*, are no longer in office. Both were relieved for negligence in allowing Mr. Rust to get so far. Marshal Sokolov has been replaced by General Dimitri Yazov.

These policymaking groups are similar in composition to our own National Security Council and the smaller decisionmaking bodies within it. Our Director of Central Intelligence, roughly the counterpart to the Chairman of the KBG, is always a member of these groups or represented in them as are the President, the Secretary of Defense and other civilians. Many members, especially in the current administration, are selected, if not for their party affiliation, then for their strong ideological views which, ever more frequently, go hand in hand with their affiliation.

We have here an organization not unlike our Joint Chiefs of Staff. There are differences, of course. We do not have a separate military service for landbased missiles or aerospace defense, both of which functions are handled by our Air Force. The Soviets do not have a separate Marine Corps. Why should they? They have 18,000 Naval Infantry. We have 196,200 Marines.

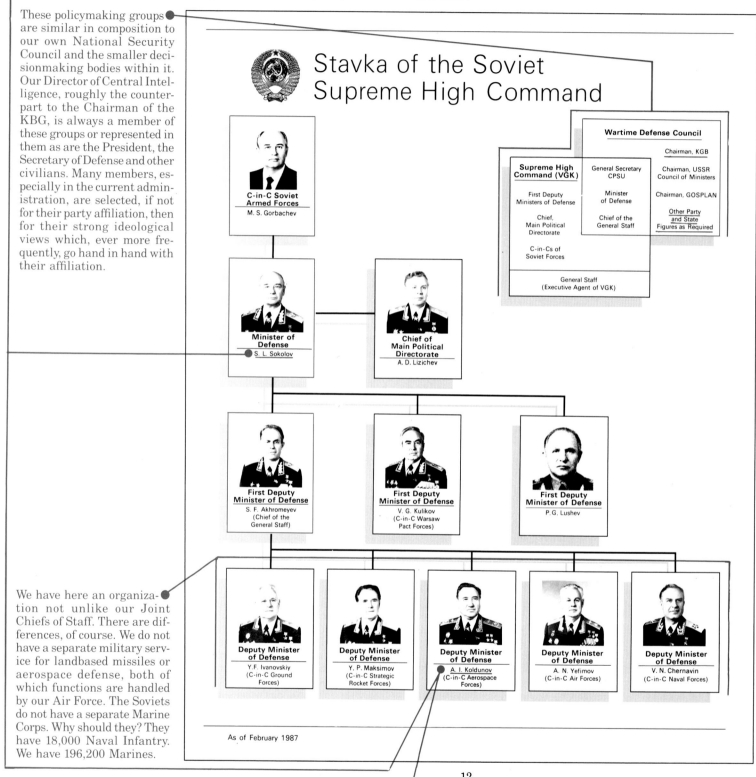

Stavka of the Soviet Supreme High Command

C-in-C Soviet Armed Forces
M. S. Gorbachev

Wartime Defense Council

Chairman, KGB

Chairman, USSR Council of Ministers

Chairman, GOSPLAN

Supreme High Command (VGK)

First Deputy Ministers of Defense

Chief, Main Political Directorate

C-in-Cs of Soviet Forces

General Secretary CPSU

Minister of Defense

Chief of the General Staff

Other Party and State Figures as Required

General Staff (Executive Agent of VGK)

Minister of Defense
S. L. Sokolov

Chief of Main Political Directorate
A. D. Lizichev

First Deputy Minister of Defense
S. F. Akhromeyev
(Chief of the General Staff)

First Deputy Minister of Defense
V. G. Kulikov
(C-in-C Warsaw Pact Forces)

First Deputy Minister of Defense
P. G. Lushev

Deputy Minister of Defense
Y.F. Ivanovskiy
(C-in-C Ground Forces)

Deputy Minister of Defense
Y. P. Maksimov
(C-in-C Strategic Rocket Forces)

Deputy Minister of Defense
A. I. Koldunov
(C-in-C Aerospace Forces)

Deputy Minister of Defense
A. N. Yefimov
(C-in-C Air Forces)

Deputy Minister of Defense
V. N. Chernavin
(C-in-C Naval Forces)

As of February 1987

Kodunov remained in office after Korean Air Flight 7 was shot down in the night in 1983. Moscow apparently judged that his command had done what it had to do, just as Israel judged it had done what it had to do when it shot down a Libyan airliner straying over the Sinai in 1973, and killed all 110 persons aboard. Israel incurred none of the global condemnation the Reagan administration quickly organized over the Korean Air incident, and used to raise support for new missile deployments. Not until five weeks after Ronald Reagan insisted the Soviets had known they were attacking a civilian plane did US officials admit the Soviets probably could not have known this. But Mathias Rust flew in from Finland in broad daylight. The Soviets could not this time hand Washington another opportunity to build anti-Soviet feeling by shooting him down. The solution was to force him to land. But Rust's prop-driven Cessna had an airspeed of 138 miles per hour. Soviet jet interceptors would have stalled at that speed, so could not keep a tight formation to guide him down. The likelihood of a Soviet blunder under these circumstances could not have been greater had the whole affair been arranged by Western intelligence.

The United States has threatened forcible intervention too. Massive and almost continuous US troop exercises in Honduras have been threatening Nicaragua for the past four years. The Soviet Union has sent combat troops beyond its own borders to intervene forcibly in the affairs of other nations on four occasions in its history. The United States has openly intervened with force on twenty-eight occasions since 1900, and on fifty-three occasions since 1800. The USSR has only intervened in the affairs of bordering nations. The United States has intervened in the Middle East, Asia and the Pacific, and through-out South America, Central America and the Caribbean. With other Western powers, we even invaded Russia in 1920, to support Admiral Kolchak's unsuccessful effort to overthrow the Bolshevik regime, a regime we had recognized at the Treaty of Brest-Litovsk in 1918. Since this really happened, but a Soviet invasion of the United States has never occurred, propaganda efforts like the films *Red Dawn* and *Amerika* characteristically portray a reversal of the truth. In frequency and scale, no other nation existing today has a record of forcible intervention and disrespect for sovereignty approaching ours.

of defense. This break with recent practice may also be perceived as a reduction in the status of the armed forces within Soviet decisionmaking circles.

Currently, the professional military are assuming a more visible public role as spokesmen for Soviet military and foreign policies. The policy decisions that affect the armed forces, however, will continue to mirror the preferences of the Party elite.

In Power Projection

Because of the USSR's limited ability to provide large amounts of economic aid, and because of disenchantment in other nations with Soviet-style socialism as a political system, the Soviets rely heavily on the military for projecting national power. The USSR accomplishes political goals through the presence of military forces in other countries, global air and naval deployments, port calls, demonstrations of force, and exercises. This reliance is also visible through military assistance programs and the use of top armed forces leaders in a diplomatic capacity.

To gain influence over politically volatile situations in other countries, the Soviets have occasionally resorted to military force. They may use threats of forceful intervention, as in Poland in 1981; actually intervene, as in Afghanistan in 1979; or base forces in a country to ensure political stability, such as the Soviet Groups of Forces in East Germany, Poland, Czechoslovakia, and Hungary. Permanent Soviet bases have also been established overseas; one of the most notable is at Cam Ranh Bay in Vietnam.

Soviet air and naval deployments are also used to project national power. Since 1970, the USSR has deployed BEAR aircraft from the Kola Peninsula to Cuba. In Angola, the Soviets maintain and operate CUB transport aircraft supporting counterinsurgency operations against the National Union for the Total Independence of Angola. Soviet naval deployments are used to show the flag in the Caribbean and occasionally in the Gulf of Mexico, and to exercise with Cuban Navy and Air Force units. Soviet naval ships also conduct port calls at Havana, Cienfuegos, Mariel, and periodically at ports in eastern Cuba.

The Soviets stage large military exercises in the USSR and in non-Soviet Warsaw Pact countries to show their strength. These exercises demonstrate actual military capabilities and, in maneuvers held outside the Soviet Union, the cooperation of the host countries.

The USSR delivers more military assistance than economic aid to Third World countries in seeking to acquire influence. Military assistance is more useful because it can be closely controlled and supervised, and it provides an expansionary potential for use against states abutting Third World clients.

Military assistance is tailored not only to appeal to the customer but to create a dependence that is militarily, politically, and economically costly to break. The recipient often is made to rely on the Soviet Union for training and advisers, logistics support, spare parts, and repairs. Advisers and technicians deliver, assemble, and maintain purchased equipment, and they supervise training and the construction of military facilities.

The growing complexity of modern weapons has given the Soviets the opportunity to send an increasingly large number of advisers to client countries in the Third World. Advisers can influence the military and foreign policies of host countries by providing personal and interservice linkages that complement and shape overt ties. They can spot talented and politically impressionable individuals and single them out for special instruction and political indoctrination in the USSR, where training of foreigners includes large doses of Marxist-Leninist ideology. The influx of advisers also provides cover for members of the KGB and GRU. Moreover, the umbrella of military aid can cover the use of Cuban and East German proxy forces for security functions, training, overseeing combat operations, and even the actual employment of combat forces, most recently demonstrated in Afghanistan.

Soviet military representatives are also used in a diplomatic capacity. High-level Ministry of Defense officials, such as Sokolov and Akhromeyev, are used as spokesmen for the government. In July 1986, Sokolov headed a high-level military delegation to Finland. He was accompanied on this reciprocal country visit by Air Forces Commander in Chief (CINC) Marshal Alexsandr Yefimov, Navy CINC Fleet Admiral Vladimir Chernavin, and General Staff arms control expert Colonel General Nikolay Chervov. This visit also demonstrates the use of the military in a diplomatic capacity and the military's endorsement of Gorbachev's policies.

As militarism rises here at home, we, too, hear military men promoting the administration's views ever more frequently. Gen. Bernard Rogers tells us about the Soviet conventional threat. Gen. James Abrahamson tells us about the Soviet space threat.

Soviet influence in the world has been declining. In the past few decades, the USSR has lost influence in Albania, Algeria, Bangladesh, China, the Congo, Egypt, Ghana, Guinea, India, Indonesia, Iraq, Mali, North Korea, Somalia, Sudan, North Yemen and Yugoslavia. The USSR retains significant influence in only 18 countries today.

The US provides more military than economic aid too. In this administration's first 5 years, the US government sold a total of $61.3 billion in arms and approved another $6 billion in commercial sales. It provided $34.4 billion in International Security Assistance in the same period. Soviet arms sales and military aid in this period amounted to just over half the combined US total.

Our advisers provide cover for the CIA, the DIA, the NSA, the INR, the ONI, the AFI, and ASA, the CIC.

The United States has kept forces based in Germany and Japan since the end of World War II. The USSR maintains or has access to 80 military bases beyond its national borders, only 13 of which are outside the Warsaw Pact area. Beyond our national borders, we maintain or have access to 967 military bases, 730 of which are outside the NATO area, and more than 1,300 other military installations. The Soviet intervention in Afghanistan involves 118,000 Soviet troops. Our intervention in Vietnam involved more than 500,000 American troops. Apart from its troops in Afghanistan, and those in support of the Warsaw Pact and Mongolia, the USSR has 22,650 military personnel stationed in 28 countries as combat troops, technicians or advisers. The US, apart from its troops in support of NATO, has 168,590 military personnel stationed in 62 countries abroad as combat troops, technicians or advisers. The US conducts military maneuvers in support of mutual defense pacts with 43 nations around the world. US naval maneuvers are more dangerous than Soviet maneuvers. Those conducted by our Sixth Fleet in Libya's Bay of Sidra have twice to date resulted in the destruction of Libyan air and naval units.

Fewer than 30 MiG-29s have been delivered to the Soviet Air Force. The MiG-29 will not be replacing the MiG-23, which will remain in inventory for a long time. The MiG-29 is not nearly as capable in speed, range, agility or load capacity as our F-14, F-15, or F-16 aircraft or even our older generation F-4 PHANTOM.

The USSR's new, highly capable MiG-29/FULCRUM is replacing older MiG-23/FLOGGERs.

In August 1986, the military presented Soviet proposals on arms control issues to the Conference on Confidence and Security Building Measures and Disarmament in Europe. Akhromeyev made a proposal to allow onsite inspection — including aerial inspection — to assure compliance with the notification and verification provisions of a prospective agreement. Akhromeyev also played a prominent role in the October meeting between President Reagan and General Secretary Gorbachev in Reykjavik. The use of Akhromeyev in this capacity, instead of one of the civilian negotiators, once again demonstrates Soviet use of the military in roles the West generally reserves for diplomats. Akhromeyev's visit to Turkey a month later is also believed to have been mainly diplomatic, as an effort to improve Soviet-Turkish relations that have been strained since the Soviets invaded Afghanistan.

In National Economics

Soviet military leaders realize that the armed services will be the ultimate beneficiary of successful industrial modernization and have voiced their support for it. They are aware that economic revitalization will ease resource constraints and accelerate the introduction of new technology, setting the stage for more rapid military modernization in the 1990s. The areas targeted for priority development in the 12th FYP — computers, electronics, instruments, machine tools, and robots — are key to future state-of-the-art weapons production as well as to higher capital and labor productivity in the whole economy.

In the short term, however, Gorbachev's industrial modernization plans will involve increased demands for many of the same resources that could be used to produce weapons. Thus, short-term fluctuations may occur in the rate of growth of Soviet military spending over the next few years. Nonetheless, the achieved level of military expenditures is so large that the Soviets have a formidable base from which to continue to modernize their armed forces. Because of substantial investment in military industry over the past decade, the plant ca-

These are certainly logical priorities to select for the purposes of this fantasy, since they represent areas in which we are decades ahead of the Soviets. It should be noted, however, that while such areas may be key to future "state-of-the-art" weapons production, they may not be key to reliable weapons production. Computers and robots are key to "labor productivity" only if the workers they replace are given other work to perform. This does not seem to be happening in the US.

14

The West does nothing of the kind. What about General Edwin L. Rowny, delegate to the Geneva arms negotiations? General Alexander M. Haig, Secretary of State? General Vernon A. Walters, Ambassador to the United Nations? Our top diplomatic posts have been held by military men. We may retire them from the military, and dress them in civilian clothes to make them seem more like diplomats. But to this administration, it is largely their experience in the military which has qualified them for the job.

Soviet military spending is another theme which receives the repetition treatment in this book. By itself, this statement is not incorrect. The level of military spending in the USSR is "large." However, it is not nearly "so large" there as it is in the US. When the authors speak of this level as a "formidable base," of course, they are getting out of line again.

● Here is a glib turn of phrase. Do the authors mean some of the most advanced weaponry yet produced in the Soviet Union, or some of the most advanced weaponry yet produced? Guess which meaning they want to imply. We need only remember that the most advanced weaponry yet produced is far more advanced than any weaponry yet produced in the Soviet Union. For the foreseeable future, this state of affairs is not likely to change.

● The ultimate mirror image. If there is any statement in this book which best applies to the United States, which best sums up the most serious problem our society faces today, and which best explains why books like this one are written, in an effort to create a false rationale for prolonging that problem, this is it.

pacity exists to turn out most of the military hardware projected for the remainder of the 1980s, including some of the most advanced weaponry yet produced.

In the 1990s, a successful economic revitalization program could have a profound impact on the military. If the Soviets achieve at least partial success in industrial modernization and can sustain accelerated growth, the economic base for military modernization — most importantly in sophisticated, high-technology systems — will be strengthened substantially. If economic progress proves insufficient, however, the leadership will face difficult choices in the late 1980s between larger investments in the economy and larger investments in future military programs. If past national strategy is a guide to the future, the Soviets can be expected to place military power as the first priority.

Soviet Doctrine and Strategy

To the Soviets, military doctrine is concerned with the essence, purpose, and character of a possible war and the preparation of the country and its armed forces for war. Military strategy deals with defining the essential tasks of the armed forces; carrying out measures to equip and train the armed forces; preparing the economy and the population for war; identifying potential adversaries and assessing their capabilities; and determining the size and composition of military forces necessary to wage war. The actual practice of preparing the country and its armed forces for war, as well as training troops for strategic, operational, and tactical combat, is encompassed in Soviet military art — to include the effective application of military power to achieve political goals.

Soviet military writings state that a future war would be a decisive clash on a global scale between two diametrically opposed socioeconomic systems — socialism and capitalism. The idea of only two camps means that a world war would be a coalition war. The Soviets believe that an outcome favorable to their interests depends on complete unification of the political, economic, and military forces of all countries within the socialist coalition. To this end, the Soviets have concentrated on developing and implementing a single strategic policy for the entire Warsaw Pact forces. Marshal Viktor Kulikov, CINC of the Warsaw Pact, has referred to his command as a unified combat formation.

As cohesiveness is seen by the Soviets as indispensable to the Warsaw Pact's preparing for and actually conducting coalition warfare, so potential strains within the NATO Alliance are seen as a source of great vulnerability to the West. The military principles governing the conduct of coalition warfare constitute a key element in Soviet strategy, a strategy aimed at dividing and destroying an enemy coalition while enforcing Warsaw Pact unity.

The Soviets now believe that a world war could be waged for an extended period with conventional weapons only. Although general nuclear war is not considered inevitable, with their current force balance, the Soviets would be prepared to wage such a war if a conventional conflict were to escalate to the use of nuclear weapons.

The Soviets recognize the catastrophic consequences of global nuclear war. Nonetheless, they seek to survive and prevail in such a conflict. In a global war, they plan to eliminate the enemy's nuclear forces and the related command, control, and communications capability; to seize and occupy vital areas on the Eurasian landmass; and to defend the Soviet state from attack. In their concept, a future war will consist of strategic attack and defense operations and campaigns in continental and oceanic theaters conducted in accordance with a common goal and strategy. They have developed formidable strategic attack forces consisting of ground- and sea-based missiles and long-range bombers. These are complemented by a widespread strategic defense effort. This element includes a large national air defense system, the world's only operational antiballistic missile system, and an intensive program to ensure the survivability of the Party, the state, military forces, industrial infrastructure, and essential working population through hardening, dispersal, and mobility.

Although strategic nuclear and strategic defense forces would play the dominant role in a nuclear war, the Soviets recognize the crucial function of combined arms warfare in seizing and occupying their ultimate objectives. They believe that a world war could be relatively brief or develop into a protracted conflict. Great importance is attached to the initial phase because it would largely determine all subsequent actions. This belief accounts for the extraordinary attention paid to the overall mobilization capability and to the perceived requirement for a rapid transition of high-level

● The first false note in this passage. The Soviet military can no more believe than our military does that a conventional war can be long fought without risking escalation to nuclear war. That is why even conventional combat between Soviet and US forces anywhere in the world poses too great a risk, and must be avoided with the same care taken to avoid nuclear war.

● We return to the Weinberger edict to prevail. In fact, the sheer insanity of possessing nuclear weapons requires doctrine to justify their existence. Military planners duly set about creating this, as though it were possible to "survive and prevail" in such a war. Most sane military men—and most military men are sane on both sides of the Teflon Curtain—know this is quite impossible.

● It is doubtful that Soviet doctrine calls for eliminating enemy command and control. This would only make it impossible to negotiate an end to war by eliminating anyone who could negotiate.

● That word "formidable" again. We must remind ourselves: not nearly so formidable as our own forces.

● The only reason the Soviets have "the world's only operational" ABM system is because we dismantled the more advanced one we had built in 1975, recognizing that ABM systems were tactically obsolete.

● Like so many other passages in this book, these several paragraphs, purporting to explain Soviet doctrine and planning, perfectly mirror our own doctrine and planning. Simply substitute "Americans" for "Soviets" and "NATO" for "Warsaw Pact," and it reads like a text from one of our own war colleges, outlining the same objectives and principles, and recognizing the same risks. What better model do the authors have to follow? It is all they really know.

● US efforts to ensure the survival of our own leadership, which under the Reagan administration would be composed almost exclusively of members of one political party, are enshrined in Presidential Directive 58 and other documents. There is no "dispersal" or "mobility" for the Soviet population. According to the CIA, the Soviets would suffer "over 100 million prompt casualties" in a nuclear exchange.

While the Soviet Union has divided its territory and adjacent areas into separate theaters of military operations, the United States has divided the whole world into separate military commands. Our Central Command (CENTCOM), for example, is responsible for military operations in the Middle East and Asia, and has the authority to assemble a force of up to 294,000 troops, 600 combat aircraft and three naval carrier battle groups and one surface action group for that part of the world, which is not adjacent to any part of the Untied States. This administration no longer refers to these combat units as our Rapid Deployment Force, perhaps because that title implies some of the recklessness that has characterized so many of our previous deployments, and perhaps because it demonstrates a clear redundancy in force structure. For more than a century, after all, we have had a rapid deployment force called the US Marine Corps.

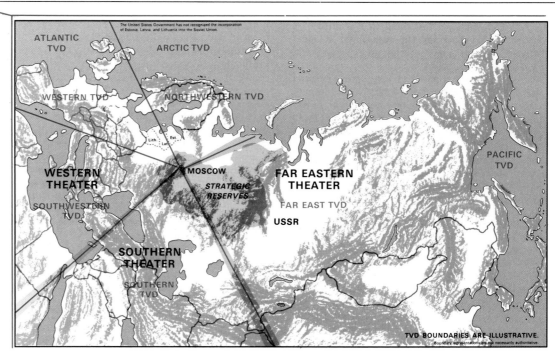

political-military control organs from a peacetime to a wartime footing to take maximum advantage of the initial period of a war.

Soviet doctrine envisions that a war with the West would be wide in scope and waged over vast territories. Such a war would be characterized by an absence of continuous fronts, by rapid and sharp changes in the strategic situation, and by deep penetrations into rear support areas of the forces involved. Forces would rely on mobility to maneuver and to wage an intense struggle to seize and maintain the initiative. The Soviets emphasize the primacy of the offensive, stating that military and political objectives are ultimately achieved only through aggressive and continuous offensive actions. Defensive actions are, however, receiving increasing emphasis in Soviet strategy. These would be innovative operations undertaken either to support nearby offensive operations or to create favorable conditions for resuming the offensive.

The Soviets believe that victory in war is possible only through the combined and coordinated efforts of all services and troop branches. As a result, Soviet military strategy, which views warfare as a series of interdependent, large-scale operations, is the same for all the

services. The concept of combined arms warfare specifies that the services and independent units must be under a single commander.

Although the Soviets envision that hostilities may be conducted in three theaters of war — Western, Southern, and Far Eastern — the theater of military operations geographical concept (*Teatr Voennykh Deistvii,* abbreviated TVD) is the focus of planning and control for major theater strategic military actions. The TVD concept has also been translated as theater of military operations (TMO), theater of military action (TMA), and theater of strategic military action (TSMA). Each TVD can extend a thousand kilometers or more in both depth and width. Military assets vary within a TVD and are usually determined by political objectives and enemy strength. For strategic actions, plans are formulated for the full spectrum of combat throughout the entire area.

Soviet planning for the Western Theater, encompassing all of Europe, envisions three continental TVDs — Northwestern, Western, and Southwestern — and two oceanic TVDs, Arctic and Atlantic. This organizational concept enables military planners to work out the strategy and tactics to achieve political objectives in a given geographic region, taking into

The discussion of Soviet doctrine and strategy continues here, and continues to employ vague generalities, envisioning a world war "waged over vast territories," with abrupt changes in the "strategic situation," so that it sounds exactly like any other nation's military doctrine and strategy. Yet the words have been chosen with some care. While the Eurasian land mass certainly encompasses "vast territories," there are territories equally vast that it does not encompass. Use of the phrase implies the Soviets are capable of fighting a conventional war that is truly world-wide in scope, and thereby obscures the real limits of Soviet military power. The Soviet Fleet is incapable of operating effectively far beyond Soviet coastal waters. The Soviets lack the ability to project substantial conventional power far beyond the Eurasian land mass. The first false note is the remark that defensive action "is receiving increasing emphasis in Soviet strategy," as though it had not received such emphasis before. This obscures, and is intended to obscure, the fact that defense of the homeland has always been, and continues to be, the primary objective of Soviet strategy.

● On the maps on this and the following page, a total of 211 Soviet Army divisions is listed, together with 53 divisions in other Warsaw Pact armies. In fact, the Soviets have 185 divisions, only 119 of which are within potential reach of Western Europe. Only a third of these, or 42 divisions, could fully mobilize within less than a month's time. Most of the remainder would take from three to four months. The waves of reinforcing divisions alarmists always portray, following right on the heels of the initial Warsaw Pact attack, would not be there. Only 27 Soviet divisions are in position to participate, with 20 other Warsaw Pact divisions, in an immediate attack on NATO's Central Front. NATO would have 8 to 15 days of warning time before that attack began, in which to bring in massive reinforcements. By the time an attack of 47 Warsaw Pact divisions could begin, NATO would have the equivalent of 55 divisions waiting for it. Most NATO divisions are also 50 percent larger than Soviet divisions. NATO's advantage in manpower is therefore substantial. In an effort to obscure these realities, some NATO governments have misrepresented the manpower balance with counts of troops "in place" in Europe. One of

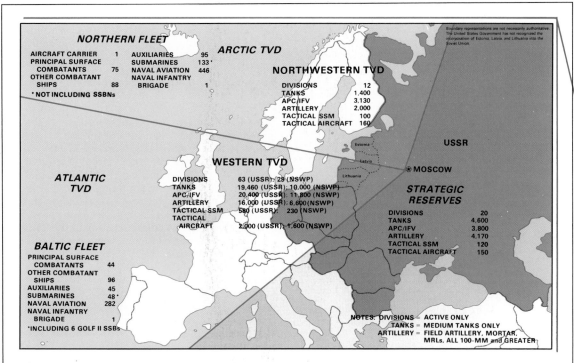

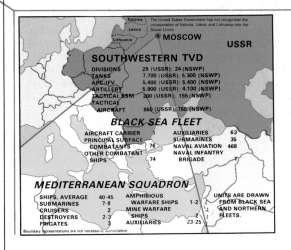

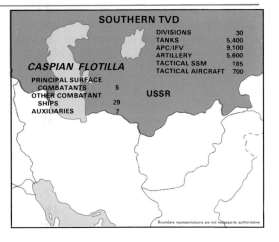

● The primary principle of propaganda is emphasis. We speak only of what we wish to focus your attention upon, and we speak of it as though it existed in a vacuum, unaffected by conditions in the real world. On these maps, the numbers of Soviet naval vessels and army divisions are listed along with some of their equipment, as though the threat they presented were absolute, unconstrained and undeterred by the existence of other armies and navies, or by other factors. The second principle of propaganda is repetition, which serves to reinforce emphasis. This is the second time in this book that Soviet naval vessels and army divisions have been listed in this way. For the balance of naval power throughout the Atlantic and Mediterranean, and for an understanding of the difficulties Soviet vessels would face in attempting to reach open ocean from their principal bases, see the commentary on page 8.

consideration the capabilities of the missiles, aircraft, ships, and ground forces at their disposal. The same planning process is used in the Southern and Far Eastern Theaters. While a strategic operation within the TVDs may be conventional only, contingency nuclear strike planning is conducted at all levels.

The contemporary Soviet concept of theater strategic military actions has expanded in scope and complexity. They now plan for a theater operation to consist of several fronts conducting dynamic, fast-moving operations to seize strategic ground objectives located 600 to 800 kilometers away. Front offensive operations would be combined, coordinated operations to include air, antiair, assault (airborne, amphibious, or joint), and naval forces.

If a war escalates to the nuclear level, Soviet doctrine calls for the massive use of nuclear weapons to preempt an imminent,

these, frequently quoted by the Reagan administration, reports 742,000 NATO and 960,000 Warsaw Pact troops in Central Europe. This counts all the Warsaw Pact's combat and support troops in the region, but only a portion of NATO's support troops. It excludes 58,000 French troops in place in West Germany, and 411,000 British, French and US troops which are not in place there but would arrive in the region, to round out and reinforce existing units, well before combat began. On the other hand, this count includes 45,000 Polish, Czech and East German troops which could not be mobilized in time to join an initial attack force, and 150,000 Soviet troops stationed not in Europe but in the Soviet Union, most of them so distant from the battlefield that they could not reach it until at least 10 days after the attack had taken place. In fact, by the time an immediate attack could be launched in this region, 1,298,000 NATO troops would be facing 766,000 troops of the Warsaw Pact. There would never be a time, in successive stages of mobilization and reinforcement, when the Warsaw Pact could bring more troops into battle than NATO would already have opposing them.

● This is a reprise of US strategic policy, from Secretary Weinberger's vision of a nuclear war fought over a "protracted period" right down to plans for a massive first strike to preempt an enemy attack. The US has always accused the USSR of having such plans, and has always denied having such plans of its own, claiming that it believed striking first was morally indefensible. But in fact, the US has been planning for a first strike since September 19, 1945, when the Joint Chiefs of Staff, in a top secret directive, JCS 1496/3, officially adopted the policy of "striking the first blow" in a nuclear war. The directive warned that "we cannot afford, through any misguided and perilous idea of avoiding an aggressive attitude, to permit the first blow to be struck against us," and required that, in the event of crisis, commanders make "all preparations to strike the first blow," a blow which should "overwhelm" the enemy and "destroy his will and ability to make war before he can inflict significant damage upon us." Official US policy has not changed since that time. Under Secretary of Defense Richard DeLauer remarked in 1981 that our Trident II D-5 missile had been designed with "a preemptive capability."

Doctrine may seem inconsistent which plans both for "protracted" nuclear war and for a first strike, as though no war could be protracted after a first strike. This presupposes that the first strike will have been successful, eliminating the adversary's retaliatory capability. Nuclear conflict might also begin with a protracted war, escalating slowly to a massive first strike intended to terminate hostilities. US doctrine certainly plans for all these contingencies, while Soviet force structure and weapons development indicate that the primary focus of Soviet doctrine is on denying us a first strike capability and retaining their retaliatory capability, thus preserving deterrence.

The USSR is wholly incapable of achieving any one of these purported aims. Its first real aim in a global war would be to protect the Soviet homeland, by protecting its retaliatory forces, and so deterring US strikes on Soviet territory.

large-scale enemy attack. The Soviets would employ ground, Strategic Rocket Forces (SRF), naval, and aviation systems in a coordinated strike against targets throughout the depth of enemy territory. Following nuclear exchanges, the Soviets anticipate that combat at all levels would continue, possibly for a protracted period. Their doctrine stresses the reconstitution of remaining forces and the continuation of the offensive where possible, despite heavy losses and widespread devastation.

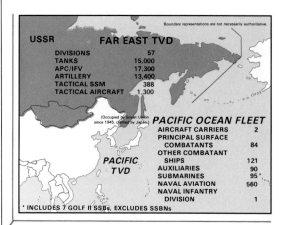

Specific Soviet aims in a global war would be to:

- defeat European NATO forces at any level of conflict, occupy NATO countries, and use Europe's surviving economic assets to assist Soviet recovery;
- neutralize the US and its allies by disrupting and destroying their military forces;
- deter China's entry against the USSR, and if deterrence fails, neutralize Chinese capability to interfere with the USSR, while avoiding land war in Asia;
- limit damage to vital Soviet political, military, and economic structures; and
- dominate the postwar world in which socialism would become the basic politico-economic system in all nations.

From an internal viewpoint, the CPSU leadership would seek to maintain its control over the government, civilian population, military, police, and internal security organs. Efforts would be made to minimize losses to the Soviet leadership, essential scientific and technical personnel, the general population, and the economy. Repair and recovery operations would be organized to deal with war-related damage.

Soviet Armed Forces Structure

Supreme leadership of the USSR's Armed Forces is vested by the Soviet Constitution in the CPSU and in the highest bodies of the Soviet government — the Presidium of the Supreme Soviet and the Council of Ministers. Party dominance of the armed forces is assured through its decisionmaking authority and power over personnel appointments. Party control of the military, however, is assisted by the Defense Council.

Direct control and administration of the daily activities of the armed forces is entrusted to the Ministry of Defense (MOD), headed by MSU Sokolov. As Minister of Defense, Sokolov is charged with maintaining the condition and overseeing the development of the armed forces. This responsibility includes officer recruitment and conscription of enlisted personnel; equipping the forces with weapon systems and military materiel; developing military strategy, operational art, and tactics; training the forces; and ensuring high standards of military discipline and political loyalty. Sokolov is also responsible, in coordination with local government organizations, for the civil defense program.

The MOD Collegium functions as a consultative body and policy review board. Chaired by the Minister, the Collegium discusses and resolves issues connected with the development of the armed forces, their combat and mobilization readiness, and the effectiveness of military and political training. Membership includes the deputy ministers of defense, the Chief of the Main Political Directorate, and other top military leaders.

The Minister of Defense exercises control of the armed forces through first deputy ministers and deputy ministers of defense. The first deputy ministers are as follows: MSU Sergey Akhromeyev, Chief of the General Staff since September 1984; MSU Viktor Kulikov, Commander in Chief of the Warsaw Pact Forces since 1977; and Army General Petr Lushev. Five of the 11 deputy ministers are CINCs of the services — Strategic Rocket Forces, Ground Forces, Navy, Aerospace Forces, and Air Forces.

The five service CINCs are responsible for

● For the balance of naval power throughout the Pacific and Indian Ocean, and for an understanding of the difficulties Soviet naval vessels would face in attempting to reach the open ocean from their principal bases in wartime, see the commentary on page 9.

● Europe after a global war would have no assets to assist Soviet recovery. This fantasy is based on the simplistic notion that to the victor go the spoils. If there is ever another global war, there will be no victors, and no spoils.

● Our own military forces receive political training too. They are taught to defend freedom. Freedom is a geographical term, designating certain areas of the world. The US and 43 other nations with which we hold mutual defense pacts, many of them ruled by repressive regimes, all live within freedom's embrace. The rest of the world is either not free or struggling to remain free but threatened by Soviet subversion. When we place combat troops on foreign shores, with or without invitation, as we have done in Korea, Vietnam, Laos, Cambodia, Lebanon, Cuba, the Dominican Republic, Grenada and Honduras, we do so not to preserve our sphere of influence but to preserve freedom, protecting it from Soviet subversion. Whenever the starving or the oppressed take up arms in desperation, anywhere within freedom's domain, we know they are Communists, the enemies of freedom. When weapons are raised against leftist regimes, we know they are raised by freedom fighters, even if the fighters only fight because we pay them. This is what we teach not only to our military, but to hundreds of thousands of foreign military, foreign police and foreign labor union leaders trained in the United States.

● peacetime administrative management, including combat and political training of the forces. Direct leadership of the Armed Forces is the responsibility of the Supreme High Command (*Verkhovnoye Glavnokomandovaniye,* abbreviated VGK). The General Staff serves as operational staff and executive agent for the VGK. Six other deputy defense ministers are in charge of civil defense, rear services, the main inspectorate, construction and billeting, personnel, and armaments.

The most important element in the Defense Ministry for peacetime forces management, as well as for wartime control of operational formations, is the General Staff, headed by Marshal Akhromeyev. As the central military staff organ, the General Staff exercises operational control over the armed forces. It is responsible for coordinating the activity of the main staffs of the 5 services, the staffs of 16 military districts, 4 groups of forces, 4 fleets, rear services, civil defense forces, and the main directorates of the Defense Ministry.

The General Staff coordinates military planning, advises the Defense Council on military policy, develops military strategy for approval by the Defense Council, and directs functions common to all the services. The major responsibilities of the General Staff in peacetime are to ● ensure that military forces reach and sustain a high level of combat readiness and to prepare strategic operation plans in the event of war. During wartime, the General Staff would be the primary organization to implement operational orders of the VGK.

Territorially, the USSR is organized into 16 military districts (MDs). An MD is a high-level administrative command element that contains military units up to army level, training institutions, recruitment and mobilization offices or military commissariats, and other military establishments. A primary mission of the military district commander is to train military units so that they have a high level of combat readiness.

Other important responsibilities include registration and induction of draftees, mobilization, civil defense, and premilitary and reserve training. In war, certain military districts, such as those on the USSR's periphery, could generate fronts or other operational field forces, either singly or in combination. Soviet units stationed in Eastern Europe are organized into four groups of forces, located in Poland, East Germany, Czechoslovakia, and Hungary.

Military districts and groups of forces are subordinate to the Ministry of Defense. They contain their own staff elements responsible for political affairs, personnel administration, training, rear services, construction and billeting, and civil defense. Each MD and group of forces command staff has officers who serve as chiefs of their respective service components. Soviet naval forces are assigned to four fleets, all of which have command and staff organizations and relationships similar to those of military districts.

In wartime, non-Soviet Warsaw Pact (NSWP) forces are planned to come under Soviet command. In peacetime, NSWP plans, doctrine, tactics, training, force structure, and readiness are shaped according to Soviet dictates. This policy seeks to guarantee that the coalition will act as a single body. In terms of a wartime strategy, the Soviet objective of dismantling NATO and maintaining the cohesion of the Warsaw Pact will be of primary importance. For the East European member states, this means that the Soviets will subordinate East European national interests, particularly in war, to Soviet-defined policies.

Wartime Command and Control

The Soviets believe in a rapid and efficient transformation of their peacetime national security organization into an operational command capable of achieving all major political and military objectives in a general war. To this end, they have established peacetime national security and high-level military organizations that closely approximate the anticipated wartime structure. These peacetime organizations expect to shift their activities to wartime operations with minimal organizational disruption and little augmentation in membership. Party and state control would be maintained through the relocation of high-level officials to hardened emergency facilities.

In war, the Defense Council probably would be expanded to include additional representatives of the highest Party, state, and military leadership. It would function similarly to the World War II State Defense Committee, ensuring centralized political and economic direction of the entire war effort.

General Secretary Gorbachev would function as wartime Defense Council Chairman and exercise direct leadership of the Soviet Armed Forces as Supreme Commander in Chief of

---

● They haven't achieved a very high level of readiness. The readiness rate of the Soviet ICBM force in peacetime is 30 percent, compared with a 98 percent readiness rate for our own ICBM force. Only 15 percent of the Soviet ballistic missile submarine fleet is on patrol at any one time, compared with 66 percent of our ballistic missile submarine fleet at all times. Of the Soviet Army's 185 divisions, only 54 line divisions are fully equipped and at a high state of readiness, capable of reaching full strength within a week after mobilization. The bulk of the remainder could not be deployed until three or four months after mobilization, and have only half their required equipment at best. Despite the large numbers of Soviet reserves alarmists like to cite, the Soviets have no more than 50 reserve formations, only 20 of which have cadres of more than 300 men. None of these units could be deployed until six months after mobilization. All would field obsolete equipment, much of it of World War II vintage.

The *Brezhnev*, shown below as it may look when completed, is about two thirds the size of our own aircraft carriers, most of which are ships of 80,000 or 90,000 tons. The Soviet carrier does not even attempt to match our capabilities. When it enters service, it will not carry high-performance aircraft like our A-6 INTRUDER, whose combat radius is 1,450 km, or our F-14 TOMCAT, whose combat radius is 1,600 km. The only fixed-wing aircraft the Soviets have developed for carrier use, and which they now use on 30,000 ton carriers like the *Kiev*, is the Yak-36 FORGER, whose engines use vertical thrust to take off and land, and whose combat radius is 250 km. While the *Breshnev* will raise the number of aircraft in the Soviet fleet, it will not extend the fleet's strike range. Even our 40,000-ton *Tarawa* class amphibious assault ships carry aircraft with greater range. Our AV-8B HARRIER, operating from the *Tarawa's* flight deck, has a combat radius of 1,200 km. If the Soviets decided today to build aircraft carriers as large as ours, it would take decades before they could build as many as we already have, and decades more to equip them with comparable aircraft.

This is an artist's conception of the *Leonid Brezhnev*, formerly known to US intelligence analysts as *Black Com 2*. It is still under construction at Yard 444 in Nikolayev on the Black Sea, and probably will not enter service until the mid-1990s—somewhat later than the caption here suggests. It will carry a mix of about 60 helicopters and Yak-36 aircraft.

The lead unit of the USSR's 65,000-metric ton aircraft carrier class — now fitting out at Nikolayev Shipyard, with sea trials anticipated in 1989 — will mark an evolutionary advance in Soviet naval capabilities over currently operational 37,100-metric ton KIEV-Class carriers.

the VGK and head of its General Headquarters (*Stavka*).

The Ministry of Defense Collegium would probably provide the foundation for the wartime *Stavka* VGK, which would include, in addition to the General Secretary, the Minister of Defense, the Chief of the General Staff and other first deputy ministers of defense, the Chief of the Main Political Directorate, and the five Armed Forces Commanders in Chief.

The General Staff would serve as operational staff and executive agent for the *Stavka* VGK.

In 1985, Samuel Loring Morison, a civilian photo interpreter for the Navy, and the US editor of *Jane's Defence Weekly*, was convicted of espionage and sentenced to two years in prison for sending *Jane's* 3 classified photos of the *Brezhnev* under construction, taken from a KH-11 satellite 504 miles overhead. Clearly, espionage was not Morison's purpose. Nor were any secrets revealed. The government did not even suggest any hostile power had seen the photos, which never left *Jane's* until the British government returned them to the US. But prosecutors insisted that reproductions of the photos in *Jane's* constituted a "potentially" damaging disclosure of information, revealing the high resolution of the KH-11's imagery. They revealed nothing of the kind. The reproduction screen had eliminated the finer details in the photos. The Soviets already knew the KH-11's resolution was less than 1 inch. KH-11 photos were published by Iran in 1981. The photo of a BACKFIRE bomber on page 61 of the 1981 edition of this book was taken by a KH-11. High officials leak information of this kind with impunity whenever it suits them, and only claim "damage" when other leaks do not suit them.

Working in conjunction with the main staffs of the five services, the Main Operations Directorate of the General Staff would draft plans for strategic operations for consideration by the *Stavka* VGK. Once approved, these plans would be issued to operational commanders as orders of the VGK. This group would ensure timely and precise execution of the VGK military campaign plans by the operational commands.

To ensure centralized control of strategic planning and decentralized battle management of the armed forces, the Soviets in wartime would employ intermediate High Commands of Forces in TVDs that would be subordinate to the VGK and would be responsible for directing the efforts of subordinate formations. Commanders for four of the probable TVD High Commands are MSU Nikolay Ogarkov, Army General Ivan Gerasimov, Army General Mikhail Zaytsev, and Army General Ivan Voloshin. In certain circumstances, the VGK might create High Commands for independent strategic directions (that is, a major axis or avenue of attack not already under the control of a High Command in a TVD).

A wartime coalition command structure also has been created for the quick transformation of the Warsaw Pact into an effective military alliance capable of operating as an extension of the Soviet Armed Forces. Since the late 1970s, the Soviets have introduced and institutionalized measures aimed at modernizing the Warsaw Pact's unified command structure. The integration will be achieved through <u>the complete wartime subordination of the armed forces of the non-Soviet Warsaw Pact countries to the High Commands</u> of Forces (HCF) in the Western and Southwestern TVDs. These commands provide a key link between the supreme military authority vested in the VGK and the fronts, fleets, and armies operating within the TVDs.

In keeping with the Soviet concept of combined arms operations, the TVD HCF not only has the assets available in the ground forces but also the naval and air assets. In the Western and Southwestern TVDs, some if not all of the armed forces of the non-Soviet Warsaw Pact states operating there will be subordinate to the Soviet HCF. This subordination reflects the belief that a cohesive, well-equipped, and well-trained alliance, employing the best strategy and tactics and controlled by a superior command, can defeat any coalition force.

Military Modernization

In his pragmatic approach to Soviet power politics, General Secretary Gorbachev has vigorously supported the military modernization efforts instituted by his predecessors. Quantity, quality, and diversity continue to be stressed in Soviet weapon programs. Gorbachev's approach to arms control allows the USSR to appear flexible and reasonable while it fields large quantities of increasingly sophisticated weapons. He continues to support the military's expensive policy of <u>making up in quantity that which is lacked in quality</u>. Pursuit of this policy has resulted in <u>the accumulation of military equipment far in excess of what one might reasonably expect for defensive purposes</u>. Indeed, this practice is facilitated, to a large extent, by internal characteristics of the Soviet political system, characteristics not found in Western democratic nations. <u>The closed nature of the Soviet state means that it can be unresponsive to public opinion</u> and that any public restraint on the small number of men who rule the USSR is virtually non-existent. Thus, the Soviets are able to sustain their long-term arms buildup programs unaffected by public opinion and to employ their military forces in wars of aggression, such as in Afghanistan, with little concern for public reaction.

The Soviet Union's strong commitment to and reliance on the military as the prime instrument of national power is described in detail in the following chapters. As derived from their doctrine and strategy, the Soviets have established a large offensive strategic and theater nuclear force, a comprehensive strategic defense program, a general-purpose force for all types of warfare, a highly developed combat support structure, and an expanding research and production base that gives primacy to military needs.

This is not unlike the command structure of the NATO Alliance, most of whose nations subordinate their military commands to the Supreme Allied Commander, Europe (SACEUR), who up to this time has always been an American.

In 1983, when the CIA presented an estimate of Soviet military spending over the previous 7 years that was only half what the Reagan administration was quoting (and still quotes), it told the Joint Economic Committee of Congress that its estimate was "based on evidence that the Soviet Union has been producing less military equipment than was expected."

When this administration cannot shape public opinion to its liking, the American state seems quite unresponsive to public opinion too. When the public and Congress would not approve aid to the force of Contra "freedom fighters" it had created in Central America, the administration found secret and illegal ways to make sure that its will was done. Nor is it any more responsive to world opinion, having declared itself exempt from the rulings of the World Court after that body condemned the US mining of Nicaragua's harbors as a unilateral act of war.

Repetition is also served by these running heads, which reinforce the claim of Soviet "global ambitions."

Much of this chapter, outlining Soviet military organization and doctrine, emphasizes Soviet intentions over Soviet capabilities. This is a useful exercise for the propagandist. If Soviet military capabilities pose no threat which cannot be easily met with forces already at hand in the West, and higher levels of defense spending in the West are therefore unwarranted, the propagandist who cannot obscure these truths can always change the subject and turn to Soviet intentions. Ignoring what may be learned of actual Soviet intentions from official statements, arms proposals and other diplomatic initiatives, or from the structure of Soviet military forces, the skilled propagandist can refer to any Soviet transgression on record, whether real or imagined, and take it as the model of what we may always expect in the future from the USSR. He may ask: How many more Afghanistans will there be? This creates the sense of a permanent threat against which we must continue to arm ourselves, even though we are already armed to the teeth. The permanent threat of hostile Soviet intentions, however slim the evidence for this, creates the most reliable basis for our permanent war economy.

An illustration, purportedly of the new Soviet BLACKJACK, which very much resembles our own new B-1 bomber. From KH-11 satellite photography, we know that the actual BLACKJACK prototype has much more angular lines than the aircraft shown here, as well as a completely different frontal view. But this illustration follows the familiar pattern of making new or forthcoming Soviet weapons look more like our own, in order to create the false impression that our design is inspired by theirs, and that we are building our bombers only because they built theirs, so reversing the truth of the action-reaction cycle. There are only a few prototype BLACKJACKS now flying. The bomber is not yet in production. Our B-1 bomber, on the other hand, became operational in 1985. Twenty-six B-1s now comprise the 96th Strategic Bomb Wing at Dyess Air Force Base in Texas. We plan a total of 100 B-1s. The Soviets have no more than a token bomber force, mostly comprised of aging BEARs, which are prop-driven. Their bomber force presently can deliver no more than 264 nuclear weapons to their targets. Our bomber force can deliver a total of 4,728 nuclear weapons to their targets with an accuracy which

exceeds even the most accurate Soviet missiles. Much has been made of the "formidable" Soviet air defenses, through which Mathias Rust so blithely flew his Cessna 172 in 1987. According to the Congressional Budget Office, even under wartime conditions 95 percent of our strategic bombers could be fully alerted before an attack began, 73 percent could survive an attack even if it came from Soviet submarines at close range, and as many as 75 percent of these could penetrate Soviet air defenses and deliver their weapons to their targets in the Soviet Union. Not that they need go so far. Armed with cruise missiles, whose current range is 3,900 km and will soon increase to 4,800 km, they.can fly to the perimeter of Soviet territory, launch their missiles and return home. We didn't need a new B-1 bomber to do this. We could have hired People's Express. Our B-52s are more than adequate for the task. We are building new bombers anyway, and will follow the B-1 with a new "Stealth" bomber. It would take thirty years for the Soviets to build a bomber force with capabilities comparable to those our Strategic Air Command now has, let alone those it will have. It's unlikely that they will even try to do this.

Chapter II

Forces for Nuclear Attack

Despite the USSR's recently renewed interest in and emphasis on arms control, Soviet production of newer, more lethal strategic nuclear weapons continues. Even as the Soviets proceed with deployment of the SS-25 mobile intercontinental ballistic missile (ICBM), two new strategic ballistic missile submarines, and the flight-testing of a new strategic bomber, they are developing another generation of air-, sea-, and ground-launched nuclear-capable cruise missiles. The AS-15 air-launched cruise missile is already operational on over 50 BEAR H bombers, and the SSC-X-4 ground-launched and SS-NX-21 sea-launched cruise missiles may become operational this year. These developments, along with the greater improvements in the accuracy, survivability, and lethality of the USSR's short-range ballistic missile force, underscore the Soviet Union's commitment to modernizing its large nuclear arsenal.

The overall direction of Soviet strategic nuclear force development and associated command, control, and communications is toward a completely integrated force. All elements of their "triad" may eventually have a hard-target-kill potential. These developments are consistent with Soviet military doctrine.

The Soviet Union now has about 10,000 deployed intercontinental strategic nuclear weapons (missile warheads and bombs) and by 1990 is likely to have about 12,000. While the Soviets would not necessarily expand their

---

Additional BLACKJACK long-range strategic bombers emerged from the airframe plant at Kazan in 1986. The USSR's continuing introduction of new generations of strategic offensive nuclear forces, including these cruise missile carriers, as well as mobile ICBMs, and more accurate submarine-launched missiles, contribute to the growing challenge to US deterrent forces.

● Despite the Reagan administration's professed interest in arms control, in the past two years we have deployed a new strategic bomber, the B-1, several new ballistic missile submarines, and one new ICBM, the MX, while preparing to deploy another, the MIDGETMAN.

● Remember, we have only the administration's word that the SS-25 is "mobile."

● We first deployed cruise missiles in the air in 1982, on the ground in 1983 and at sea in 1984.

● The AS-15 has a range of only 1,200 km. The current range of our cruise missiles is 3,900 km, and this will be increased to 4,800 km.

● No Soviet weapon has yet achieved sufficient accuracy to ensure a hard-target kill. They must still plan for cross-targeting with weapons of very large yield, for a reasonable assurance of destruction. Several US weapons, including all our cruise missiles, the PERSHING II, most air-delivered weapons, the MX missile and all of our MINUTEMEN equipped with the Mk-12A re-entry vehicle, can now achieve a hard-target kill.

● Wrong. They currently can deliver 8,360 strategic warheads and bombs.

● Not nearly as much as we contribute to the growing challenge to Soviet forces.

The Soviets can increase their number of deliverable strategic warheads somewhat by increasing the numbers of bombers and submarines available to deliver them. But they could not achieve the capacity to deliver this many nuclear weapons without first improving the miniaturization of their weapon components, so that a greater number of them might fit more easily on existing ICBMs. They could not attempt to use smaller weapons until they had achieved higher levels of accuracy, so that weapons of smaller yield could still be capable of the same level of destruction. They are several years behind us in miniaturization and accuracy. The weapons they developed would still have to run through the entire testing cycle. The US, on the other hand, will have the capacity to deliver 20,000 strategic nuclear weapons within the next three years.

"Probably" is the applicable word here. The most accurate SS-18 currently can strike within 850 ft of its aimpoint at best. Compare that with our MINUTEMAN III, which can strike within 490 ft, and our MX, which can strike within 300 ft.

The mention of "rail-mobile" here is meant to prepare the public for our own plans for a "rail-mobile" MIDGETMAN.

We have an ELF system. Therefore we must say they have one for all their ballistic missile submarines. But they don't.

But it barely ever made its debut.

The BEAR H is prop-driven, and much too slow to survive existing US air defenses. If the Soviets ever build enough BLACKJACKs, we will set up an air defense missile system. We had such systems in the 1950s and 1960s, though at that time we didn't really need them.

Only 240 of these are actually within range of Western Europe.

We have already deployed such weapons. The Soviets were bound to follow suit.

The use of nuclear weapons for this purpose risks escalation to global nuclear war. If we are talking of conventional weapons, then NATO can do with aircraft what the Soviets are here said to plan with short-range ballistic missiles, and NATO can do it better.

---

intercontinental attack forces significantly in the absence of arms control constraints, they have the potential to deploy between 16,000 and 20,000 strategic nuclear weapons by 1996. Moreover, this force will be significantly more flexible, survivable, and effective. Thus, both quantitatively and qualitatively, the Soviets will enhance their first-strike capability and their ability to fight a protracted nuclear war through the deployment of more accurate and survivable systems.

In the land-based force, the development of the hard-target-kill SS-18 follow-on and a silo-based SS-X-24, both probably more accurate and reliable than current systems, will significantly increase the lethality of the USSR's force. The rail-mobile SS-X-24 and the road-mobile SS-25 will provide the Soviets with highly survivable systems for protracted operations. Indeed, the SS-25 may be the perfect reserve weapon for such a war. It has a single reentry vehicle and is thus easily retargeted.

Perhaps the most notable growth will take place in the submarine ballistic and cruise missile force. By 1995, this force will grow from roughly 20 percent of today's Soviet strategic nuclear warheads to over 30 percent of an expanded force. This future submarine force will be quieter, more responsive because of better communications, and more effective. Supported by an extremely-low-frequency communications system, the DELTA IV could be almost as responsive as an ICBM for destroying time-critical targets. Submarine-launched cruise missiles will provide the Soviets with yet another weapon for US early warning and command-and-control systems to track.

Strategic aviation is making a strong comeback in the Soviet Union. The BACKFIRE, the BEAR H, and in the near future, the BLACKJACK, will provide the Soviets with the ability to attack the US through multiple avenues. The Soviets will have the capability with the BEAR H and the BLACKJACK to launch hundreds of difficult-to-detect, hard-target-kill AS-15 cruise missiles. Moreover, the BLACKJACK will be able to conduct reconnaissance and strike operations in a nuclear war lasting beyond an initial missile exchange. Additionally, the Soviets are significantly upgrading the communications support to these forces.

With the mobile SS-20 intermediate-range ballistic missile, each with three independently targetable warheads, the Soviets have maintained their nuclear strike capability against both the European and Asian theaters. At the same time, the mobility inherent in the SS-20 design has afforded a level of undetectability and survivability unmatched in previous systems. The system also has an inherent refire capability. Of the 441 SS-20 launchers now operational in the force, approximately two-thirds face NATO from the western USSR, and the remainder are deployed in the Soviet Far East. Instead of increasing the size of the already large SS-20 force, the Soviets will quite likely strive for better accuracy, nuclear lethality, and survivability. These technical improvements are already being integrated in a new, improved version of the SS-20 that could become operational in 1987.

In addition to the threat posed by the SS-20 ballistic missile force, the Soviets continue development of a new class of mobile land-attack cruise missile — the SSC-X-4 ground-launched cruise missile and the SS-NX-21 sea-launched version. When deployed later this decade, these missiles will add yet another dimension to the Soviet longer range intermediate-range nuclear forces (LRINF) threat to NATO and Asia. The new generation of cruise missiles will quite likely complement both Soviet bombers and SS-20s in the continental theaters surrounding the USSR, compounding an already difficult air defense environment in wartime target areas. Potential accuracy improvements in future cruise missile design will allow targets to be struck with greater precision than ballistic missiles are currently capable of attaining. Cruise missile deployment will also free a significant number of Soviet theater bombers now allocated for nuclear strikes to carry out missions such as attacks with chemical and improved conventional munitions.

The Soviet Union is also making substantial strides in improving its sizable shorter range ballistic missile force. This force, which numbers more than a thousand launchers, is expected to grow steadily in the near term. The implications for the US and its allies reside not only in the numbers and the improvements that are forecast for missile accuracy and warhead options, but also in the potential employment of these missiles. The Soviet commander will be able to launch a devastating attack to the depth of the theater rear. The accuracy of the missiles and the potential of non-nuclear warheads will allow a reduced number of missiles to strike any single target with the same confidence of destruction formerly associated with significantly larger numbers of the older systems, and this combination could allow the Soviets to do so without crossing the nuclear threshold.

Soviet literature reflects an understanding of the need for target acquisition, analysis, and strike weapons to attack reserves; command, control, and communications structures; and the logistics infrastructure in a highly responsive manner. The constantly improving accuracy and warhead capability of the shorter range missile, its short flight time, and its relative invulnerability in flight make it an ideal strike weapon. The Soviets are expected to seek further refinements in targeting for these missiles. These weapons will remain a potentially devastating force against the West.

Nuclear Doctrine and Strategy

Soviet leaders since the 1960s have followed a consistent policy for the development of forces for nuclear attack. The Soviet leadership, however, recognizes the devastating consequences of a general nuclear war. In a nuclear war, Soviet strategy would be to destroy enemy nuclear forces before launch or inflight to their targets; to reconstitute the USSR, should nuclear weapons reach the Soviet homeland; and to support and sustain combined arms combat in several theaters of military operations. Several overarching strategic wartime missions would require:

- disruption and destruction of the enemy's essential command, control, and communications capabilities and reconnaissance means;
- destruction or neutralization of enemy nuclear forces on the ground or at sea before they could be launched; and
- protection of the Soviet leadership and cadres, military forces, military and economic assets necessary to sustain the war and, to the extent possible, the general population.

Strategic and theater forces and programs in place or under active development designed to accomplish these objectives include:

- hard-target-capable ICBMs, new submarine-launched ballistic missiles (SLBMs), LRINF ballistic missiles, and land-based cruise missiles;
- shorter range INF (SRINF) and short-

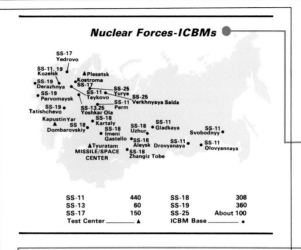

Nuclear Forces-ICBMs

SS-11	440	SS-18	308
SS-13	60	SS-19	360
SS-17	150	SS-25	About 100
Test Center ▲		ICBM Base ●	

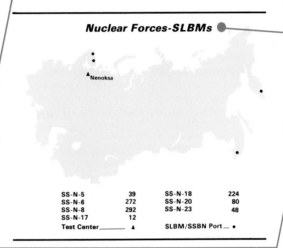

Nuclear Forces-SLBMs

SS-N-5	39	SS-N-18	224
SS-N-6	272	SS-N-20	80
SS-N-8	292	SS-N-23	48
SS-N-17	12		
Test Center ▲		SLBM/SSBN Port ●	

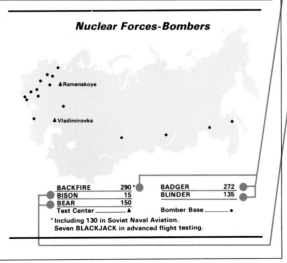

Nuclear Forces-Bombers

BACKFIRE	290*	BADGER	272
BISON	15	BLINDER	135
BEAR	150		
Test Center ▲		Bomber Base ●	

* Including 130 in Soviet Naval Aviation.
Seven BLACKJACK in advanced flight testing.

Not nearly so devastating as what the West poses for the East. NATO can now deliver 8,584 nuclear weapons to their assigned targets in Eastern Europe. The Warsaw Pact, by contrast, can deliver 3,217 nuclear weapons to their targets.

This gives the number of ICBMs the Soviets possess, but not the number of warheads these missiles carry. They currently carry 5,424 warheads. Our ICBM force carries 2,302 warheads.

We should be grateful that someone does.

The number of SLBMs is given here, but again, not the number of warheads they carry. The Soviet SLBM force currently carries 2,672 nuclear warheads. Our submarine force carries 6,464 warheads.

Options for which we have planned as well.

Listed here are two bombers, the BADGER and the BLINDER, which lack the range to strike targets in the United States. Also listed is the BACKFIRE bomber, which our State Department has declared is "neither equipped nor deployed" as a strategic bomber.

The BISON and the BEAR are the only bombers in the Soviet intercontinental strike force. They currently carry a total of 264 nuclear weapons. Our bombers, as noted earlier, now carry a total of 4,728 nuclear weapons.

Neither superpower can ever be assured of achieving any of these objectives, but we are well ahead of the Soviets in the effort to achieve them.

The purpose of this illustration and the one below is to dramatize the administration's claim that the Soviets have deployed "mobile" ICBMs. Since we plan to deploy our own "mobile" ICBMs, it is quite in keeping with our standard practice to claim that the Soviets deployed one first. Every time we have taken any major new step in the arms race, we have always claimed that the Soviets took it first. In fact, we have always taken it first. While the Soviets tested the first ICBM, even in this case we were the first to deploy an operational ICBM, and had several ATLAS missiles deployed before the Soviets could deploy their first four SS-6 missiles. We deployed the first multiple warheads in 1970. The Soviets followed in 1975. We had the first cruise missiles in 1982. The Soviets have now begun deploying the first of theirs. The record of history, if history survives so long, will probably show that we deployed the first mobile ICBM too, if a mobile ICBM proves feasible at all.

These, especially, in this list of Soviet capabilities "under development," will be under development for a very long time indeed. The Soviets are far from achieving effective operational systems.

This is a remarkable acknowledgement, after all the claims to the contrary by The Committee on the Present Danger, that the Soviets have no more of a solution to the problem of civil defense than any other nation has, or ever can have.

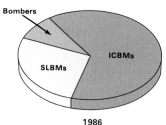

Soviet Intercontinental Attack Forces
Warhead Mix

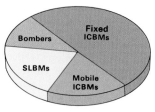

* Estimates based on current trends.

1986   Mid-1990s*

range nuclear forces (SNF) systems deployed with combat troops;
- bombers and air-launched cruise missiles (ALCMs) designed to penetrate US and allied defensive systems;
- large numbers of land-attack and antiship cruise missiles on various platforms;
- antisubmarine warfare (ASW) forces to attack Western nuclear-powered ballistic missile submarines (SSBNs) and protect Soviet SSBNs;
- air and missile defenses, including early warning satellites and radars, interceptor aircraft, surface-to-air missiles (SAMs), antiballistic missile (ABM) radars and interceptors, and some antiaircraft artillery;
- antisatellite weapons;
- passive defense forces, including civil defense forces and countermeasures troops and equipment devoted to confusing incoming aircraft;

- hardened facilities numbering in the thousands, command vehicles, and evacuation plans designed to protect Party, military, governmental, and industrial staffs, essential workers and, to the extent possible, the general population; and
- varied and redundant communications networks.

Supporting a land war in Eurasia and eliminating the US capacity to fight and support a conflict would require the capability to employ theater and strategic forces over a variety of ranges and the destruction of:
- military-associated command-and-control assets;
- war-supporting industries, arsenals, and major military facilities;
- ports and airfields in the US and along air and sea routes to European and Asian theaters of war; and
- satellite surveillance sensors, ground-

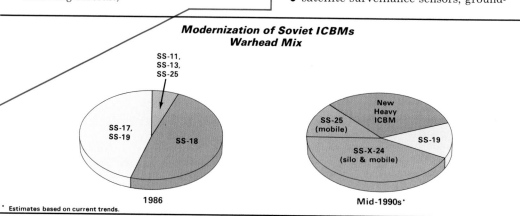

Modernization of Soviet ICBMs
Warhead Mix

* Estimates based on current trends.

1986   Mid-1990s*

On page 28 of the 1983 edition of this book, a map appeared showing coverage by Soviet over-the-horizon radar, which seemed to extend for several thousand miles right across the United States. This map was withdrawn from subsequent editions of *Soviet Military Power*. There is a reason. When Korean Air Lines Flight 7 was shot down in 1983, President Reagan immediately called this the "Korean Airlines massacre," and his administration busied itself trying to pursuade

the world that this proved that the Soviets were more barbaric than the nation which had committed the massacres at My Lai, Kent State, Attica and Wounded Knee. Many Americans, however, were wondering why the US government had not tried to warn KAL-7 back on course. A variety of US radars were operational that evening in the area. One of these, an over-the-horizon backscatter (OTH-B) radar

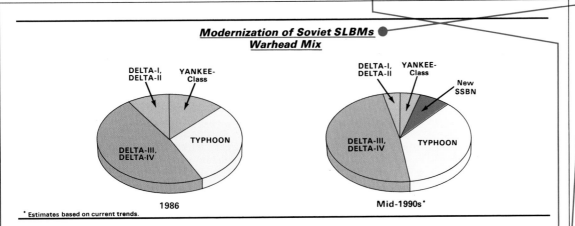

Modernization of Soviet SLBMs Warhead Mix

DELTA-I, DELTA-II
YANKEE-Class
DELTA-III, DELTA-IV
TYPHOON

1986

DELTA-I, DELTA-II
YANKEE-Class
New SSBN
DELTA-III, DELTA-IV
TYPHOON

Mid-1990s*

* Estimates based on current trends.

● This seems a reasonably accurate prediction of the Soviet SLBM warhead mix by the late 1990s, if the new Soviet ballistic missile submarine shows up on time.

based surveillance sensors, and related communications facilities.

Soviet nuclear forces are designed and personnel are trained to fulfill their missions under all circumstances. Soviet leaders appear to believe that nuclear war might last weeks or even months, so they have included this possibility in their force planning. Despite their public rhetoric alleging their commitment to no first-use of nuclear weapons, the Soviets have developed extensive plans for using nuclear weapons first to preempt any use by other states.

The keys to a successful first use of nuclear weapons would be accurate intelligence on enemy intentions and the effective coordination of the strike. Meeting these demands in war requires reliable command, control, and communications under all conditions.

A launch-under-attack circumstance would place great stress on attack warning systems and launch coordination. To meet the demands

of a launch-under-attack contingency, the Soviets have established an elaborate warning system. Satellite, over-the-horizon radar, and other early warning systems have been built to provide the USSR with the capability to assess accurately and to respond effectively to any nuclear attack. These warning systems could give the Soviets time to launch their forces very quickly.

Follow-on strikes would require the survival not only of major weapons but also of command, control, and communications systems. The Soviets have invested heavily in providing this survivability. The SS-17, SS-18, and SS-19 ICBMs are housed in the world's hardest operational silos. Silo deployment has been adopted for ABMs as well. To increase its survivability, the Soviets designed the SS-20 LRINF missile to be mobile. The mobile SS-25 ICBM is being deployed and the development of the mobile SS-X-24 continues. The SA-X-12B/GIANT, with some capability

● When it became obvious that the greater accuracy of our missiles produced a larger window of vulnerability for the USSR, much was made of the hardness of Soviet missile silos, presumably to offset the advantage it was becoming only too clear that we had always held. Our missile silos are hardened to withstand 2,000 lbs per square inch of atmospheric blast overpressure. According to Herbert Scoville, 3,000 lbs per square inch is the maximum possible hardness that may be attained with reinforced concrete structures. Many of our weapons now have sufficient accuracy to excavate and vaporize their targets, no matter how hardened these may be. The Soviets have not yet developed weapons which can do the same. Eventually, however, they probably will.

● Repetition here again reinforces our claim that the Soviets have "mobile" ICBMs.

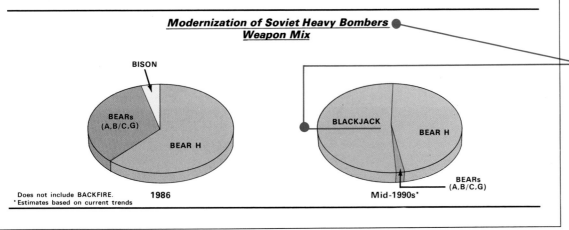

Modernization of Soviet Heavy Bombers Weapon Mix

BISON
BEARs (A,B/C,G)
BEAR H

1986

BLACKJACK
BEAR H
BEARs (A,B/C,G)

Mid-1990s*

Does not include BACKFIRE.
* Estimates based on current trends

● It will take several years for the Soviets to produce enough BLACKJACK bombers to play the major role suggested here in their strategic bomber force, and it will take several more years before they have developed cruise missiles with ranges to match our own. Their current AS-15 missile has a range of only 1,200 km. Our current cruise missiles have a range of 3,900 km.

(continued from above)

Chapter II Forces for Nuclear Attack

called *Cobra Talon*, located on the island of Shemya in the Aleutians, was able to track Flight 7 through its entire journey into Soviet air space from 575 miles off Shemya's coast to a distance of 2,070 miles. Since we had not warned the aircraft, the administration took the position that we had not been monitoring its course, and that even if we had been, we would have been unable to contact the aircraft —though any airline pilot will tell you that worldwide ground-to-air communications are routine. The administration went further, pretending that *Cobra Talon* didn't even exist, and that our first two

over-the-horizon radars, one of them in Washington and the other in Maine, would not be operational until 1986. Some civilian analysts pointed out that according to *Soviet Military Power* the Soviets had already had such radars in 1983, but that every year since 1981, Under Secretary of Defense for Research and Engineering Richard DeLauer always told Congress that the US was well ahead of the USSR in radar sensor technology. To obscure this inconsistency, later editions of this book still claim that the Soviets have over-the-horizon radar, but no longer dramatize this claim with illustrations.

It is extremely unlikely that the Soviets have any solution to this problem. We are still trying to solve it ourselves.

We, too, have a fleet of "looking-glass" aircraft and other airborne command posts, including four modified Boeing 747s, designated E-4B Airborne National Command Posts (ABNCP).

In wartime conditions it will be next to impossible for the Soviets to disperse these boats. Almost all of them will be bottled up in sanctuaries close to their home ports. Even in these sanctuaries, they could be hunted down by US attack submarines and other ASW forces.

Given the levels of radiation produced by even a limited nuclear exchange, it would be impossible to decontaminate missile silos or any other areas exposed. According to our Strategic Air Command, Soviet reload missiles would not be compatible with "existing silo launchers." Our Defense Department has estimated that "reloading a significant fraction of the ICBM force" might take the Soviets up to several weeks. The Defense Intelligence Agency estimates that reloading missiles at sea as well, would be "unlikely, if not impossible" during a nuclear war.

against strategic ballistic missiles, is also mobile. The launch-control facilities for offensive missiles are housed in very hard silos or on off-road vehicles. Communications are redundant and hardened against both blast and electromagnetic-pulse damage. Higher commands have multiple mobile alternate command posts available for their use, including land vehicles, trains, aircraft, and ships. Bombers are assigned dispersal airfields. Operational ballistic missile submarines will be dispersed while being protected by surface, air, and submarine forces, while those not ready for deployment could be hidden in caves or submerged in deep fjords just off their piers.

The belief that a nuclear war might be protracted has spurred Soviet emphasis on nuclear weapon system survivability and sustainability. For their ICBM, LRINF, SRINF, SNF, SLBM, and air defense forces, the Soviets have stocked extra missiles, propellants, and warheads throughout the USSR. Some ICBM silo launchers could be reloaded, and provisions

have been made for the decontamination of those launchers. Plans for the survival of necessary equipment and personnel have been developed and practiced. Resupply systems are available to reload SSBNs in protected waters.

As part of these ambitious development and deployment programs, the Soviets continue to modernize all elements of their nuclear attack forces. At the same time, the leadership has been directing a campaign to support and to encourage antinuclear movements in the West to influence, delay, or frustrate Western nuclear force programs.

Soviet and US Intercontinental Attack Forces

Intercontinental Ballistic Missiles

The operational Soviet ICBM force consists of some 1,400 silo and mobile launchers, aside from those at test sites. Some 818 of the silo launchers have been rebuilt since 1972. Nearly half of these silos are new versions of the

An SS-18 follow-on ICBM has been flight-tested. These new missiles are likely to have greater throw-weight, have at least 10 warheads, and be more accurate than the SS-18 Mod 4.

The Soviets cannot expect to destroy even a single US ICBM in its silo, let alone 1,000 of them. Our MINUTEMAN force has a readiness rate of 98 percent compared with the Soviet ICBM readiness rate of 30 percent. One disadvantage the Soviets face is that given the ample warning time we would have in which to confirm an impending attack, we could launch all of our MINUTEMEN before the earliest Soviet warheads arrived to destroy them. Moreover, a variety of random and systematic uncertainties will always bedevil planners contemplating the use of nuclear weapons. Will all of the boosters burn for the required time, bringing their missiles to the necessary height, so that they can release their post-boost vehicles at the proper altitude?

original designs and have been reconstructed or modified in the past 7 years. These silos contain the USSR's most modern deployed MIRVed ICBMs — the SS-17 Mod 3 (150 silos), the SS-18 Mod 4 (308), and the SS-19 Mod 3 (360). Deployment of these most recently modified ICBMs began just 8 years ago.

The highly accurate SS-18 ICBMs carry larger MIRVs than the Peacekeeper, the most modern deployed US ICBM. The SS-18 Mod 4 carries at least 10 MIRVs. It was designed to attack and destroy ICBMs and other hardened targets in the US. The SS-18 Mod 4 force currently deployed has the capability to destroy 65 to 80 percent of US ICBM silos using two nuclear warheads against each. Even after this type of attack, more than 1,000 SS-18 warheads would be available for further strikes against targets in the US. The SS-19 Mod 3 ICBM, while less accurate than the SS-18, has significant capability against all but hardened silos. It could also be used against targets in Eurasia. Although the SS-17 is somewhat less capable than the SS-19, it has similar targeting flexibility.

The remaining Soviet ICBM silos are fit-

US and Soviet ICBM Launcher and Reentry Vehicle (RV) Deployment 1971-1987

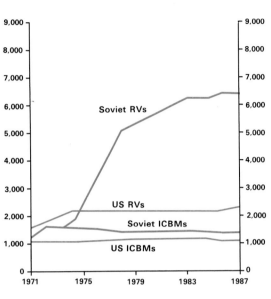

The Soviet ICBM force currently carries about 1,000 fewer RVs than this number. The number shown here is based on the assumption that all Soviet ICBMs have been fitted with multiple warheads to the maximum extent possible. In fact, many Soviet ICBMs are still fitted with single warheads. The administration has done its best to suppress this fact. Nevertheless, Defense Intelligence Agency officials acknowledge that some Soviet ICBMs "are still configured to carry single warheads," and that current force loading is actually below the estimate shown here, "taking into consideration actual single warhead deployments." They add that this information has been omitted from annual editions of *Soviet Military Power* due to "space considerations."

The most accurate SS-18 ICBM the Soviets have currently can strike within no fewer than 850 ft of its aimpoint at best. Our MX, which the administration insists on calling the "Peacekeeper," can strike within only 300 feet. Soviet ICBMs carry larger warheads than ours do in an effort, albeit an unsuccessful one, to accomplish with greater megatonnage and a higher release of energy what they cannot achieve with inferior accuracy. Even then, their planners must cross-target two warheads on each US missile silo, which still achieves only theoretical destruction.

Will polar magnetism or unpredictable changes in weather move whole flights of missiles off course? Will a mote of dust on an accelerometer throw a reentry vehicle many miles from its intended target? How many of the warheads will actually detonate? How many will suffer from "fratricidal" effects, their circuitry melted and fused or their reentry vehicles blown off course by the explosions of others? In short, how many of the opponent's missiles would remain unharmed, to inflict unacceptable levels of damage in retaliation? Such uncertainties can never be resolved, and they are what will always guarantee deterrence.

● The charts below show many more Soviet ICBM types than American types. This suggests that the Soviets have many more ICBMs than we do. For once, the suggestion is not untrue. They have 394 more ICBMs. Most of the Soviet ICBMS appear to be larger than ours. That, too, is true. Does this mean they are better missiles? No. It means the Soviets are behind us in three critical areas: miniaturization, accuracy, and fuel efficiency. To compensate for their inferior accuracy, the Soviets have had to build larger warheads with greater explosive yields. To throw the greater weight of those warheads over the distances required, and to do this with less efficient fuel, they have had to build larger rocket casings to hold greater volumes of fuel. Most Soviet missiles, in fact, are liquid-fueled. This means that they must be fueled up before launch and defueled again when taken off alert. The fuel is much too volatile and dangerous to remain standing in the rocket for extended periods of time. There have been several serious accidents, the most publicized of which have taken place

Wrong. 15,000 km. ●

Wrong. 12,900 km. ●

Wrong. 10,700 km. The MX ● could have had a range of 11,600 km as planned, but it carries ten Mk 21 reentry vehicles, each of which weighs 822 lbs. The weight of all ten violates Salt II by exceeding that treaty's maximum allowable throwweight of 7,939 lbs, and also reduces the missile's range.

More repetition to reinforce ● the belief in a mobile Soviet ICBM, thereby justifying deployment of our own—if we can ever develop a mobile ICBM sufficiently accurate to make the exorbitant costs worthwhile.

Looks like a photograph, ● doesn't it? Quite a beautiful job, really. But in this case seeing *isn't* believing. It doesn't exist now and it never may.

● Here is a hint that other Soviet ICBMs don't use solid fuel, without any discussion of the significant implications of that fact. Actually, the Soviet SS-13 uses solid fuel, and it will probably turn out that the SS-25 is merely a modification of the SS-13, minimal enough to qualify it under SALT II, as a modification of an old missile rather than as a completely new missile.

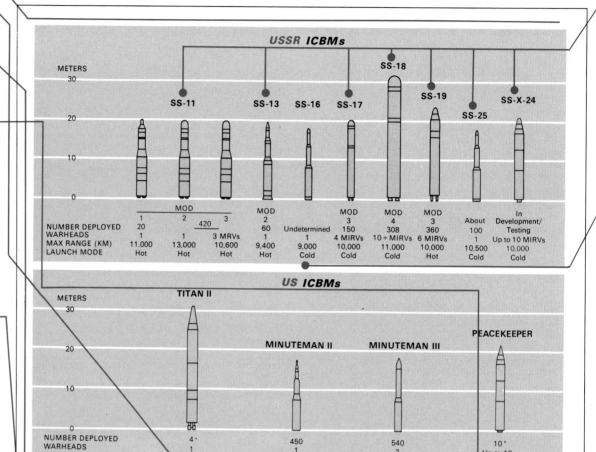

USSR ICBMs

	SS-11 Mod 1	SS-11 Mod 2	SS-11 Mod 3	SS-13 Mod 2	SS-16	SS-17 Mod 3	SS-18 Mod 4	SS-19 Mod 3	SS-25	SS-X-24
NUMBER DEPLOYED	20	420		60	Undetermined	150	308	360	About 100	In Development/ Testing
WARHEADS	1	1	3 MRVs	1	1	4 MIRVs	10 + MIRVs	6 MIRVs	1	Up to 10 MIRVs
MAX RANGE (KM)	11,000	13,000	10,600	9,400	9,000	10,000	11,000	10,000	10,500	10,000
LAUNCH MODE	Hot	Hot	Hot	Hot	Cold	Cold	Cold	Hot	Cold	Cold

US ICBMs

	TITAN II	MINUTEMAN II	MINUTEMAN III	PEACEKEEPER
NUMBER DEPLOYED	4 *	450	540	10 *
WARHEADS	1	1	3	Up to 10
MAX RANGE (KM)	12,000	12,500	11,000 +	11,000 +
LAUNCH MODE	Hot	Hot	Hot	Cold

* As of early 1987

ted with SS-11 Mod 2/3s and SS-13 Mod 2s. These older types of ICBMs are housed in less-survivable silos and are considerably less capable. Nonetheless, their destructive potential against softer area targets in the US and Eurasia is significant in terms of many of the Soviet requirements outlined above.

The most recent development in the Soviets' operational ICBM force was the deployment of the road-mobile SS-25 missile. The SS-25 is about the same size as the US Minuteman ICBM. It carries a single reentry vehicle and is being deployed in a road-mobile configuration similar to that of the SS-20. As such, it will be highly survivable with an inherent refire capability. Bases for the SS-25 are operational and consist of launcher garages equipped with sliding roofs and several support buildings to

Deployment of the rail-mobile SS-X-24, expected soon, will provide the Soviets with yet another new, highly survivable ICBM.

(continued from above)

aboard Soviet submarines in international waters—like the one referred to in the caption to the photo on page 34 of this book. We have had our own accidents with the liquid fuels used for the Titan II, now going out of service. This is why we use solid fuels. Obviously we could have built much larger rockets had we chosen to do so. We didn't need to. Another significant difference between the two ICBM forces which is rarely mentioned, is that because the Soviets rely so much on liquid fuels, they cannot launch most of their ICBMs upon confirmed warning of an attack, as we can. The time it would take for them to prepare for launch exceeds the time it would take for our warheads to reach the Soviet silos. The most important characteristic of these weapons, their accuracy, has not been included on these charts, of course, because our accuracy so much exceeds theirs. The current levels of US and Soviet ICBM accuracy are in the commentary on the previous page.

● All of the ranges given are wrong. Here are the correct ones: for the SS-11 Mod I, 9,600 km. For the SS-11 Mod II, 9,000 km. For the SS-11 Mod III, 8,800 km. For the SS-13 Mod II, 8,000 km. For the SS-17 Mod III, 8,800 km. For the SS-18 Mod IV, 8,800 km. For the SS-19 Mod III, 8,000 km. For the SS-25, probably 9,000 km. No one really knows what the range of the SS-X-24 will be. The Soviets certainly have a design specification down on paper, and if it has ever been read aloud by a human voice, we might know what it is. But we will only be certain of the range after tests are completed.

● The SS-16 ICBM has been included here as an old opportunity for threat enhancement. Note that the number deployed is undetermined, since we are not prepared to prove that any are deployed at all. In 1977 alarmists made much of the possibility that the Soviets could overnight expand their ICBM force by adding a third stage to their SS-20 intermediate range ballistic missile. No evidence exists that any such weapon was ever deployed, or ever will be.

The mobile SS-25 marks a Soviet decision to make the ICBM component of their strategic forces more survivable.

house the requisite mobile support equipment.

Deployment programs for all of the currently operational silo-based Soviet ICBMs are essentially complete. The command, control, and communications system that supports the Soviet ICBM force is modern and highly survivable, and the reliability of the ICBMs themselves is regularly tested by live firings, including some from operational complexes.

Some silo-based ICBMs in the current force that are not replaced with modified or new ICBMs will, in accord with past practice, be refurbished to increase their useful lifetime and reliability. During this process, some system modifications could also be made.

Force Developments. Soviet research and development on ICBMs is a dynamic process involving several programs. Deployment of the SS-25 marks a significant point of departure in Soviet ICBM developments, featuring solid-propellant missiles and mobile basing modes. Modernized versions of or new replacements for the SS-18 are likely to be deployed in existing silos through the end of the century. Indeed, one new ICBM to replace the SS-18 has entered flight test.

The Soviets appear to be planning on new solid-propellant ICBMs to meet many future mission requirements. They already have two new solid-propellant ICBMs — the single-warhead, mobile SS-25 described above, now being deployed, and the SS-X-24. The SS-X-24 — about the same size as the US Peacekeeper —

is <u>well along in its flight-test program</u>. The SS-X-24 deployment in a rail-mobile mode is expected to begin in 1987, with silo-based deployment soon thereafter.

Follow-on missiles to the SS-X-24 and SS-25 are anticipated. Both of these missiles are likely to have better accuracy and greater throw-weight potential than their predecessors. The SS-25 follow-on could be developed as a MIRV. Such a development would further expand the already large warhead inventory possessed by the Soviets. By the mid-1990s the current Soviet ICBM force will have been almost entirely replaced with new systems.

Submarine-Launched Ballistic Missiles

The Soviets maintain the world's largest ballistic missile submarine force. As of early 1987, the force numbered 61 SSBNs carrying 916 nuclear-tipped missiles. The missile total does not include the six accountable missiles deployed on a GOLF III ballistic missile submarine (SSB) or the six on a HOTEL III SSBN. Neither total includes the 13 older GOLF II-Class SSBs with 39 missiles, which are currently assigned theater missions. Twenty-one SSBNs are fitted with 352 MIRVed SLBMs. These 21 units have been built and deployed within the past 10 years. Two-thirds of the ballistic missile submarines are fitted with long-range SLBMs, including those equipped with

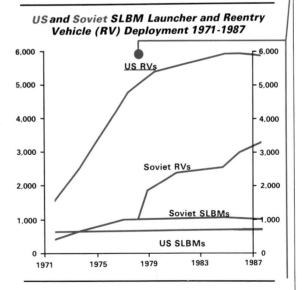

US and Soviet SLBM Launcher and Reentry Vehicle (RV) Deployment 1971-1987

● Again, reinforcement for the administration's claim that the Soviets have a mobile ICBM. The equipment in the illustration looks more like the launch system for the SS-20 ICBM. Even the SS-20 must use pre-prepared sites. It requires several hours of preparation before it can be launched.

● The SS X-24 has just begun its flight test program.

● Don't hold your breath.

● But not the world's largest force of submarine-based ballistic missile warheads.

● The administration was reluctant to make any comparisons between US and Soviet equipment at all, until it found ways of obscuring the most significant data. It finally began to add such comparisons to *Soviet Military Power*, after early editions received criticism because they did not give such comparisons. It must be especially painful to acknowledge, in this particular graph, that we have such a clear numerical lead over the Soviet Union. But even here the administration hedges on the truth. The number of US SLBM warheads shown, about 5,800, represents a standard means of misrepresenting our actual lead. It acknowledges the addition of only half of the 1,200 warheads added to the fleet in 1980, when the number of warheads on each POSEIDON missile was increased from 10 to 14. It also slightly exaggerates the number of Soviet warheads. Currently, the US has 6,464 sea-based warheads, the Soviet Union 2,672.

Chapter II Forces for Nuclear Attack

● Note that the "launch mode" is specified instead of such niggling details as accuracy or type of fuel. This is another opportunity for threat enhancement. Alarmists have made a great deal of the fact that some Soviet missiles were launched "cold" out of their silos by compressed air, before the rocket booster began to burn, which

was said to save much damage to the silos, since presumably they could be much more easily reloaded with more missiles of the same type—if any happened to exist. For the Pentagon's only assessment of the likelihood that missile silos could be quickly reloaded in a nuclear war, see the commentary on page 28.

A very nice photo. Compliments to our intelligence community, whose managers say that we cannot adequately verify arms treaties and who say this whenever we are offered a treaty we never had any intention of signing.

Five TYPHOON boats have been launched, but only four are operational.

Five of the TYPHOON-Class SSBNs have been launched. Armed with 20 SS-N-20 submarine-launched ballistic missiles, each unit can strike targets in the US from home waters.

Nuclear Submarine-Launched Ballistic Missiles

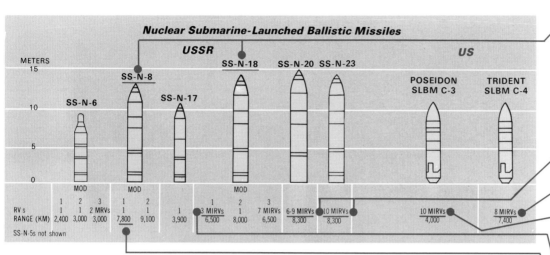

USSR

SS-N-6 · SS-N-8 · SS-N-17 · SS-N-18 · SS-N-20 · SS-N-23

US

POSEIDON SLBM C-3 · TRIDENT SLBM C-4

METERS: 15, 10, 5, 0

	SS-N-6			SS-N-8		SS-N-17	SS-N-18			SS-N-20	SS-N-23	POSEIDON SLBM C-3	TRIDENT SLBM C-4
MOD	1	2	3	1	2		1	2	3				
RVs	1	1	2 MRVs	1	1	1	3 MIRVs	1	7 MIRVs	6-9 MIRVs	10 MIRVs	10 MIRVs	8 MIRVs
RANGE (KM)	2,400	3,000	3,000	7,800	9,100	3,900	6,500	8,000	6,500	8,300	8,300	4,000	7,400

SS-N-5s not shown

MIRVed missiles, thereby allowing the submarines to patrol in waters close to the Soviet Union and be protected from NATO submarine warfare operations. Moreover, the long-range missiles would allow the Soviets to fire from home ports, if necessary, and still strike targets in the US.

Five units of the modern Soviet ballistic missile submarine class, the TYPHOON, have already been launched. Each TYPHOON carries 20 SS-N-20 solid-propellant, MIRVed SLBMs. The TYPHOON is the world's largest submarine, with a displacement approximately one-

Modern SSBN Force Levels

US 8 OHIO

USSR: 23 DELTA, 9 YANKEE, 4 TYPHOON

US: 28 LAFAYETTE, BEN. FRANKLIN, JAMES MADISON

USSR: 16 DELTA, 9 YANKEE

Boundary representations are not necessarily authoritative. The United States Government has not recognized the incorporation of Estonia, Latvia, and Lithuania into the Soviet Union.

Nuclear-Powered Ballistic Missile Submarines

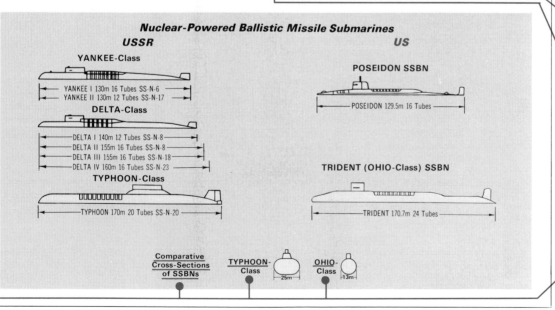

USSR

YANKEE-Class
- YANKEE I 130m 16 Tubes SS-N-6
- YANKEE II 130m 12 Tubes SS-N-17

DELTA-Class
- DELTA I 140m 12 Tubes SS-N-8
- DELTA II 155m 16 Tubes SS-N-8
- DELTA III 155m 16 Tubes SS-N-18
- DELTA IV 160m 16 Tubes SS-N-23

TYPHOON-Class
- TYPHOON 170m 20 Tubes SS-N-20

US

POSEIDON SSBN
- POSEIDON 129.5m 16 Tubes

TRIDENT (OHIO-Class) SSBN
- TRIDENT 170.7m 24 Tubes

Comparative Cross-Sections of SSBNs

TYPHOON-Class 25m · OHIO-Class 13m

● No evidence exists that either the SS-N-8 Mod II or the SS-N-18 Mod II is currently deployed, or ever has been deployed. The ranges shown for these mythical missiles are also way out of line for liquid-fueled rockets of this size.

● Wrong. 7,400 km.

● Wrong. 7,800 km.

● Wrong. 14 MIRVs. This change was publicly announced in 1980, and it has been repeatedly confirmed by Navy officials in sworn testimony before Congress. The range given is also wrong. The correct range is 4,600 km. If the missile carried only 10 MIRVs, the range would be 5,100 km.

● Wrong. 3,100.

● Wrong. 5,500 km.

● Again, five units have been launched, but only four are operational.

● The Soviet missile boats would not necessarily be protected. US attack submarines can follow them right into port. In 1973, a US submarine entered Murmansk harbor, placed a hydrophone on a Soviet submarine just so we could hear what the Soviets were hearing, and left undetected.

● Remember the obvious: if we had wanted to build the world's largest submarine, we would have done so.

This is the result of the Soviet use of liquid fuels. See the commentary on bottom of page 30.

Wrong. 7,400 km.

By which time we will have more TRIDENT submarines operational.

We don't yet know whether it will be more accurate than the SS-N-18. The SS-N-18, in any case, is not terribly accurate. It can strike at best within no fewer than 4,617 ft of its aimpoint. Our Trident I C-4 can now strike within 750 ft of its aimpoint.

Eventually they may. But given current levels of Soviet SLBM accuracy, that time is a long way off. In the meantime, our TRIDENT II D-5, soon to be deployed, will already have a hard-target-kill capability. In fact, as noted earlier, it has been designed with a "preemptive capability." It will be able to strike within only 300 ft of its aimpoint.

Again, the mirror image of our own ELF communications system, and of our TACAMO aircraft—which have been relaying communications to and from submerged submarines for the past twenty years, and are now being replaced by newer aircraft.

The YANKEE-Class SSBN that sank off Bermuda in October 1986 as a result of an explosion in one of its missile tubes served as a reminder of the constant SLBM threat to the US.

third greater than that of the US Ohio-Class. It can operate under the Arctic Ocean icecap, adding to the protection afforded by the 8,300-kilometer range of its SS-N-20 SLBMs. Two or three additional 25,000-metric ton TYPHOONs are probably under construction and will be operational by the early 1990s.

The Soviets since 1978 have removed 15 YANKEE I units from service as ballistic missile submarines by dismantling their launchers. These units were removed as newer submarines were produced in order for the overall Soviet SSBN force to stay within the 62 modern SSBN/950 SLBM limits established in 1972. Some have been reconfigured as attack or long-range cruise missile submarines.

In a widely reported accident, the Soviets lost a YANKEE-Class SSBN in the Atlantic near Bermuda in October 1986. The ship suffered serious structural damage as a result of an explosion, presumably of volatile missile fuel. The loss of this unit had a negligible impact on Soviet strategic forces.

Force Developments. The Soviets have launched four units of a new class of SSBN, the DELTA IV, that are fitted with the SS-N-23 SLBM. This large, liquid-propelled SLBM will have greater throw-weight, carry more warheads (10 rather than 7), and be more accurate than the SS-N-18, which is currently carried on the DELTA III-Class SSBN. Up to two more DELTA IVs are under construction. A new class of submarines is likely to enter the force in the early 1990s.

Wrong. The AS-15 has a range of only 1,200 km.

This statement creates the impression that most of these aircraft are tankers, when they are not. The Soviets have only 30 converted BISONs and 20 converted BADGERs to serve as tankers. It is the US Strategic Air Command that has 663 tanker aircraft.

BEAR H bombers, which carry the 3,000-kilometer-range AS-15 cruise missile, have been intercepted by Canadian CF-18s while on training missions against North America.

It is really a medium-range cruise missile, isn't it? As noted above, its range is only 1,200 km.

The Soviets will probably begin flight-testing a modified version of the SS-N-20. Additionally, based on Soviet practice, a modified version of the SS-N-23 will probably be developed early in the next decade. The modified versions of these SLBMs are likely to be more accurate and possess greater throw-weight than their predecessors, and they may eventually provide the Soviets with hard-target-capable SLBMs.

To ensure communications reliability, the Soviets have deployed an extremely-low-frequency (ELF) communications system that will enable them to contact SSBNs under most operating conditions. Additionally, they have a specially equipped BEAR airframe, the BEAR J, that can perform a similar mission using VLF communications.

Strategic Aviation

The five air armies subordinate to the Supreme High Command (VGK) that contain the Soviet strategic bombers and strike aircraft are Smolensk, Legnica, Vinnitsa, Irkutsk, and Moscow.

The strike assets of the air armies include some 165 operational BEAR and BISON bombers, 160 BACKFIRE bombers, 405 medium-range BLINDER and BADGER bombers, and over 450 shorter range FENCER aircraft. The Soviets have allocated these aircraft among five air armies to cover specific theaters of military operations (Europe, Asia, and the US) and yet retain the flexibility to reallocate aircraft as necessary during wartime.

The Moscow air army contains the intercontinental BEAR and BISON bombers that could be made available for maritime and Eurasian missions, further underscoring the flexibility of Soviet strategic aviation forces.

Some 130 BACKFIRE and 240 BLINDER and BADGER bombers are in Soviet Naval Aviation. Moreover, some 530 tanker, reconnaissance, and electronic warfare aircraft are in the air armies and Soviet Naval Aviation.

The Soviets are upgrading their long-range bomber force. The new BEAR H bomber, carrying the AS-15 long-range cruise missile, became operational in 1984. Over 50 of these aircraft are now in the inventory. BEAR H bombers have been observed in training flights simulating attacks against North America.

BEAR H is the first new production of a strike version of the BEAR airframe in over

The numbers are all correct, but only the first two bomber types, the BEAR and the BISON, are deployed by the Soviets as intercontinental strategic bombers. That is because only these first two types have the range to fly to the United States and return. The other four bomber types are indeed included by the Soviets in what they call "strategic" aviation forces, and that may be the poor excuse for including them here. But none of the other four has sufficient range to be of use as an intercontinental bomber. That includes the BACKFIRE, which has a much shorter range than we have long pretended.

The BEAR shown here is one of but two bomber types the Soviets now deploy with sufficient range to enable them to fly intercontinental missions and return home. The other bomber type is the BISON, almost all of which have now been retired. Consequently, the Soviet intercontinental bomber force is almost entirely comprised of various models of the BEAR. Note from the photograph that the BEAR is a propeller-driven aircraft. Its top speed is 515 miles per hour. Aside from some improvements in avionics, this is basically World War II technology. It is certainly no challenge for the F-15s, F-106s and F-4s of the US Aerospace Defense Command and our Air National Guard.

As noted earlier, we will not need to add antiaircraft missiles to our air defenses until the Soviets have deployed a number of BLACK-JACK bombers, and until they have developed cruise missiles of much greater range. As things stand, our interceptors, all of them refuelable by air, would shoot down aircraft faster than the BEAR well beyond the range of the cruise missiles these bombers currently carry. To send a force of BEARs to the United States on a strike mission would therefore be futile and suicidal. This is so obvious that alarmists insult our intelligence when they tell us otherwise. So far there has never been a genuine Soviet bomber threat to the United States.

More than 50 of the BEAR H manned strategic bombers, initial launch platforms for the USSR's nuclear-armed air-launched cruise missiles, are now operational with Soviet strategic aviation.

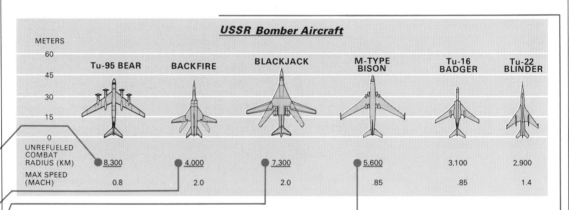

USSR Bomber Aircraft

METERS	Tu-95 BEAR	BACKFIRE	BLACKJACK	M-TYPE BISON	Tu-16 BADGER	Tu-22 BLINDER
UNREFUELED COMBAT RADIUS (KM)	8,300	4,000	7,300	5,600	3,100	2,900
MAX SPEED (MACH)	0.8	2.0	2.0	.85	.85	1.4

Wrong. 6,270.

Wrong. 2,890.

We don't yet know what the range of this aircraft will be. The range shown could be correct.

Wrong. 4,860.

Wrong. 3,780.

15 years. Additionally, the Soviets are reconfiguring older BEAR aircraft, which carry the subsonic AS-3 air-to-surface missile (ASM), to carry the newer supersonic AS-4. About 40 of these reconfigured aircraft, known as BEAR Gs, are operational.

The Soviets continue to produce the BACK-FIRE, the most modern operational bomber in their inventory, currently at a rate of about 30 per year. Some are used to form new active units; others are used as replacements in existing units. The production rate is likely to be maintained at least through this decade. Several modifications have been made and more

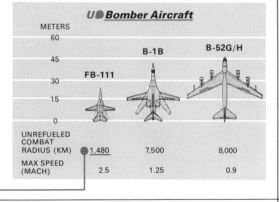

US Bomber Aircraft

METERS	FB-111	B-1B	B-52G/H
UNREFUELED COMBAT RADIUS (KM)	1,480	7,500	8,000
MAX SPEED (MACH)	2.5	1.25	0.9

This chart gives the impression that more Soviet than American bomber types are deployed in the strategic role, by including two aircraft, the BADGER and the BLINDER, which haven't the range for that role, as the range shown for the aircraft on this chart demonstrates, a third, the BACKFIRE, which our government has acknowledged is "neither equipped nor deployed" as an intercontinental bomber, and a fourth, the BLACKJACK, which is not yet deployed at all. Why not in that case include our own Stealth bomber, which is also not yet deployed, and our many other bombers—the F-4,

A-6, A-7 and F-16 to name only a few—which also lack intercontinental range? They do not appear here. A significant capability not included on either of these charts is the load capacity of the aircraft shown. The BEAR can carry only 25,000 lbs, the BISON only 10,000 lbs, our FB-111 37,500 lbs, and our B-52 70,000 lbs. This is why our bomber force can now carry more than 4,700 nuclear weapons, while Soviet bombers of intercontinental range currently carry no more than 264.

(continued above, page 37)

● This is a particularly flagrant misrepresentation. The authors had an especially difficult problem here, because the US lead in numbers of weapons carried by bombers is so immense. So they decided not to count numbers of nuclear weapons, and to count only bombers. But even by this measure, the US number is still greater than the Soviet one. How to keep the line representing the Soviet Union ascendant over the line representing the U.S.? To the 165 BEAR and BISON bombers which make up the Soviet intercontinental strike force, they added 160 BACKFIRES—even though the text right above this graph quietly admits that without a refueling probe, which the

BACKFIRE does not now have, the aircraft cannot be used against the continental US. Yet even after this force of BACKFIREs has been added in, the line representing the number of US bombers still remains ascendant over the dotted one representing the USSR. So the authors have added in another 160 BACKFIREs to achieve a solid line well above ours. So that all seems on the up and up, they have carefully acknowledged at the bottom of the graph that the BACK-FIRE has been included in these calculations, and have further noted that the dotted Soviet line excludes aircraft assigned to Naval Aviation. This is all to suggest that, in the view of the authors, there are

---

are likely to be made to upgrade performance. The BACKFIRE can perform various missions, including nuclear strike, conventional attack, antiship strike, and reconnaissance. Its low-altitude dash capabilities make it a formidable platform to support military operations in Europe and Asia. Additionally, the BACKFIRE can be equipped with a probe to permit inflight refueling so that it can be used against the continental US if sufficient tankers are available.

Force Developments. The BLACKJACK, a new long-range bomber larger than the US B-1B, is still undergoing flight-testing. The BLACKJACK will probably be faster than the B-1B and may have about the same combat radius. The new bomber will be capable of carrying cruise missiles, short-range missiles, bombs, or a combination of each, and could be operational as early as 1988. It will probably be used first to replace the much less capable BISON bomber and then the BEAR A bomber.

The Soviets have started deploying the MIDAS, an aerial-refueling tanker version of the CANDID transport aircraft. The new tanker will probably be used to support defensive as well as offensive operations and will significantly expand the ability of the Soviets to conduct longer range missions.

The BLACKJACK bomber, still undergoing flight-testing, will also carry nuclear-armed AS-15 cruise missiles for its strike and reconnaissance role in a nuclear war.

Long-Range Cruise Missiles

The AS-15, a small, air-launched, subsonic, low-altitude cruise missile, became operational in 1984. It is similar in design to the US Tomahawk and has a range of about 3,000 kilometers. It is currently deployed with the BEAR H and is expected to be carried on the BLACKJACK when that aircraft becomes operational. The BEAR H and eventually the BLACKJACK, in combination with the AS-15, provide significantly increased Soviet capabilities for strategic intercontinental air operations.

A sea-launched version and a ground-launched version of the AS-15 are under development. The ground-launched cruise missile variant, the SSC-X-4, will probably become operational this year. Its mission will be to support theater operations in the Eurasian theater because the Soviets are unlikely to deploy it outside the USSR and because its range is too short for intercontinental strikes. The SSC-X-4 is being developed as a mobile system and will probably follow operational procedures similar to those for the SS-20 LRINF system.

The sea-launched variant, the SS-NX-21, is small enough to be fired from standard Soviet torpedo tubes. VICTOR and specially configured YANKEE submarines are the most likely launch platforms for the SS-NX-21; other less likely candidates are the AKULA and SIERRA. The SS-NX-21 is expected to become operational soon and could be deployed on submarines that will patrol off the US.

In addition to the SS-NX-21 small, long-range cruise missile system, a larger sea-launched cruise missile is under development. This missile, designated the SS-NX-24, has been flight-tested from a specially converted YANKEE-Class nuclear-powered cruise missile

● This is a useful official admission that the BACKFIRE is *not* currently equipped with a probe to permit inflight refueling, and so cannot now be used against the continental US. Nor, in any case, would sufficient tankers be available to the Soviets for a very long time. Whenever these observations were made in the past, alarmists would retreat to their fallback position that BACKFIREs might be sent on a one-way suicide mission, or land in Cuba to refuel after striking targets in the US—as though Cuban airfields would remain operational for more than ten minutes under such circumstances.

● Wrong. 1,200 km.

● It was noted earlier that until the Soviets have built many BLACKJACKs, and deployed cruise missiles with much greater ranges, they will continue without any significant intercontinental strike capability in their bomber force.

● Our ground-launched and sea-launched Cruise missiles are already deployed and have ranges of up to 3,900 km.

● Our ground-launched missile has been operational for four years. It was deployed in Europe in 1983.

● In addition to two classes of submarine, our sea-launched cruise missile is now being deployed on IOWA Class battleships, LONG BEACH, CALIFORNIA, VIRGINIA and TICONDEROGA Class cruisers, and SPRUANCE and BURKE Class destroyers.

● Not yet.

● It will take several years before the Soviets can build enough tankers to expand their capabilities in this way. Currently they have only 50 tankers converted from other aircraft. Our Strategic Air Command has 663 tankers.

US and Soviet Intercontinental-Capable Bombers *

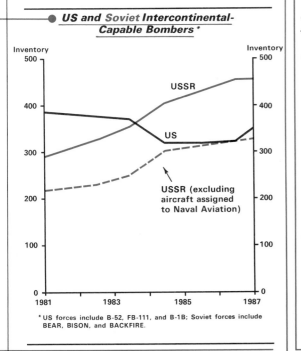

Inventory
500 — 400 — 300 — 200 — 100 — 0

Inventory
500 — 400 — 300 — 200 — 100 — 0

USSR

US

USSR (excluding aircraft assigned to Naval Aviation)

1981   1983   1985   1987

* US forces include B-52, FB-111, and B-1B; Soviet forces include BEAR, BISON, and BACKFIRE.

two more or less "legitimate" ways of looking at the number of Soviet intercontinental bombers: by including all BACKFIREs in the Soviet inventory, or by excluding those BACKFIREs assigned to Naval Aviation while keeping the rest. In fact, no BACKFIREs at all should be included in a count of Soviet "intercontinental-capable" bombers, since none of them is capable of this mission without the refueling probes and tankers which the authors themselves just got through admitting they lack. A corrected graph would show the U.S. line where it is, and the Soviet line tapering off between 100 and 200. The tech-

nique used here is to be very straightforward about how you have achieved your misrepresentation, to create the false impression that since nothing is hidden it must be a legitimate way of representing things. Note, too, that the BADGER and BLINDER have been excluded from this graph. Why, then, were they included on the chart on the previous page? Of course, that chart did not have the heading "Intercontinental-Capable Bombers." It only had the heading "Bomber Aircraft." It is this sort of evasiveness in which propagandists take great pride.

Long-Range Cruise Missiles

	USSR					US		
	SS-NX-21*	AS-15	SSC-X-4*	SS-NX-24*	GLCM**	ALCM	TOMAHAWK GLCM	TOMAHAWK SLCM
WARHEADS	1	1	1	—	—	1	1	1
RANGE (KM)	3,000	3,000	3,000	—	—	2,500	2,500	2,500

*In development
** Possible development

Wrong. 1,200 km.

Wrong. 3,900 km. It is standard practice for the propagandist to represent the opponent's weapons as having the greater range, though our weapons were deployed five years before theirs.

Our sea-launched cruise missile was deployed, with nuclear warheads, on LOS ANGELES Class attack submarines off Soviet coasts in 1984.

attack submarine (SSGN). It could become operational by 1988. A ground-based version of this missile may be developed.

These cruise missiles will be equipped with nuclear warheads and will be capable of attacking some hardened targets. Future variants could be accurate enough to permit the use of conventional warheads, depending on munitions developments and the types of guidance systems incorporated in their designs.

US Forces

In measuring and evaluating the continuing progress being made by the USSR's strategic forces, readers may wish to consider the status of US forces, the modernization of which is discussed in Chapter VIII. By mid-1987, US strategic deterrent forces will consist of:

- 22 MX Peacekeepers;
- 978 Minuteman ICBMs;
- (The Titan force will be retired by mid-1987);
- B-52 bombers:
  — 98 B-52Gs with ALCMs
  — 69 B-52Gs without ALCMs, with gravity bombs and short-range attack missiles (SRAMs)
  — 46 B-52Hs with ALCMs, gravity bombs, and SRAMs
  — 50 B-52Hs with gravity bombs and

The new AKULA-Class nuclear attack submarine, now deployed in the Pacific, is a possible launch platform for the 3,000-kilometer-range SS-NX-21 cruise missile.

Not likely to be more than 1,200 km, over the first few years of deployment.

38

In deference to much criticism over the lack of information about US forces in previous editions of this book, the authors here provide some, but only of the least useful kind for comparative purposes. Listed are the numbers of bombers and missiles in US strategic forces today, but not the numbers of warheads, bombs and other nuclear weapons they all carry. According to our Defense Department, "the most significant measure of strategic strength" is the number of individual nuclear weapons a strategic force can carry, not the number of missiles and bombers in that force. US strategic forces currently can carry a total of 13,494 nuclear weapons to their targets in the Soviet Union. Soviet forces currently can carry a total of 8,360 such weapons. By the beginning of next year, US strategic forces will be able to deliver a total of 16,477 nuclear weapons to their targets, while Soviet forces will be able to deliver 8,856. What this means is that we will be able to attack almost twice as many targets in the Soviet Union as the Soviets can attack in the United States. The greater accuracy and reliability of our weapons also increases the likelihood that they will destroy their targets.

SRAMs (scheduled for ALCM conversion);

- 56 FB-111 bombers plus some 5 aircraft undergoing maintenance and modification;
- 54 B-1B bombers;
- 448 Poseidon (C-3 and C-4) fleet ballistic missile launchers; and
- 192 Trident (C-4) fleet ballistic missile launchers.

The historic and continuing objective of US strategic forces is deterrence of nuclear and conventional aggression against the US, its allies, and friends. This policy has preserved peace since World War II and is based on the conviction widely held in the US that no winners would emerge from a nuclear conflict.

The US does not have a strategic first-strike policy. Moreover, the US has no plans to adopt a first-strike policy. Rather, our deterrence policy seeks to maintain the situation in which any potential aggressor sees little to gain and much to lose by initiating hostilities against the US or its allies.

To realize these deterrence objectives requires the development, deployment, and maintenance of strategic forces whose size and characteristics clearly indicate to an opponent that politico-military objectives cannot be achieved through employment of nuclear weapons or through political coercion based on nuclear advantages. In the Strategic Defense Initiative, the US is now investigating the potential over the long term of basing deterrence increasingly on defensive systems.

Soviet and US Non-Strategic Nuclear Forces

Longer Range Intermediate-Range Nuclear Forces

The Soviets began a vigorous effort to modernize and expand their intermediate-range nuclear force in 1977 with the deployment of the first SS-20 LRINF missiles. Because each SS-20 is equipped with three MIRVs, Soviet LRINF missile warheads have more than doubled since

There are 441 SS-20 mobile LRINF launchers now operational. Test flights continue on an even more accurate SS-20 follow-on missile.

Yes, we do. For documented proof of this, see the commentary on page 18. A direct denial of the truth is often the best indicator of what the truth is. Nixon: "I am not a crook." Johnson: "We seek no wider war." Reagan: "There ain't no smoking gun."

The SS-20 was intended as a replacement for earlier SS-4 and SS-5 missiles. Indeed, all of the SS-5s and many of the SS-4s have now been withdrawn.

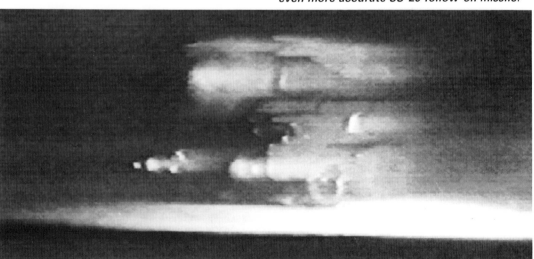

Chapter II Forces for Nuclear Attack

The coverage shown suggests that the SS-20 has a range of about 5,000 miles. This is wrong. The SS-20 currently deployed has a range of 3,700 km. If a version of the missile with a single warhead were deployed, it would have a somewhat longer range, but the bar charts below, indicating a great many more reentry vehicles than missiles, show that the authors agree that the type of SS-20 deployed by the Soviets is the Mod 2, with three separate warheads, which has a total throwweight of 1,590 lbs. and accordingly a lower range.

If it were difficult to detect it would be difficult to count. And yet we count it.

Only 240 of these are deployed within range of Western Europe.

Come, now: right on the road? In fact, the SS-20 must be launched from carefully prepared positions, and none of these is going to be right on the road.

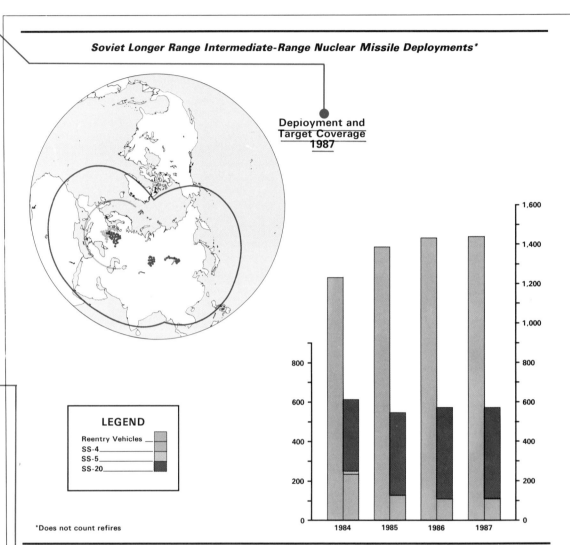

Soviet Longer Range Intermediate-Range Nuclear Missile Deployments*

Depioyment and Target Coverage 1987

LEGEND
Reentry Vehicles ___
SS-4 _____
SS-5 _____
SS-20 _____

*Does not count refires

1977. The SS-20s also have significantly greater range and accuracy and a much shorter reaction time than the missiles they have replaced.

The Soviets have deployed 441 SS-20 launchers west of the Urals and in the Soviet Far East. During 1984, the Soviets began construction of more bases for the SS-20 than in any other year. Some of this construction was to assist the relocation of SS-20 units that had been displaced from their former bases. The former SS-20 bases have now been converted to accommodate the SS-25 mobile ICBM.

The mobility of the SS-20 system, unlike the older, fixed-based SS-4, allows it to operate under both on- and off-road conditions. As a

result, the survivability of the SS-20 is greatly enhanced because of the difficulty in detecting and targeting this system when it is field deployed. Further, the SS-20 launcher can be reloaded and refired, and the Soviets stockpile refire missiles. The Soviets are flight-testing an improved version of the SS-20, which is expected to be more accurate than its predecessor.

In addition to the SS-20s, the Soviets maintain 112 SS-4 LRINF launchers. All of these are located in the western USSR opposite European NATO.

NATO's initial deployment of Pershing IIs and ground-launched cruise missiles (GLCMs) began in Europe in late 1983. The number

40

● In a nuclear war, the highest probability is that few mobile launchers like the SS-20, and few aircraft, surface ships, missile silos, artillery pieces or other types of launcher will survive long enough to be reloaded, and that few command centers will have the information needed to redirect such forces to remaining secondary targets, let alone the means to communicate with them. Soviet planners cannot have thought it any more sensible than American planners have to build large numbers of reload weapons whose prospects for use are so poor. This statement therefore is not likely to be true.

● Here is one of the Reagan administration's most infamous misrepresentations of the balance of military power, the one on which it based its "zero-option" proposal in 1981. Missing, then and now, from NATO's arsenal of "longer-range intermediate-range" nuclear missiles are the French land-based S-3, the French sea-based M-20 and M-4, the British POLARIS S-3 and, most important of all, 896 POSEIDON warheads carried by missiles aboard four POSEIDON submarines specifically assigned to the Supreme Allied Commander, Europe (SACEUR), for NATO use. That these boats and their missiles are counted as strategic systems under the SALT II counting rules does nothing to change the fact that they are assigned to SACEUR. At the time of the "zero-option" proposal, and prior to deployment of our Cruise and PERSHING II, NATO had a total of 1,058 "longer-range intermediate-range" nuclear missile warheads, the Warsaw Pact 887. Today, NATO has 1,750 "longer range intermediate range" nuclear missile warheads in the European theater; the Warsaw Pact, 946. By

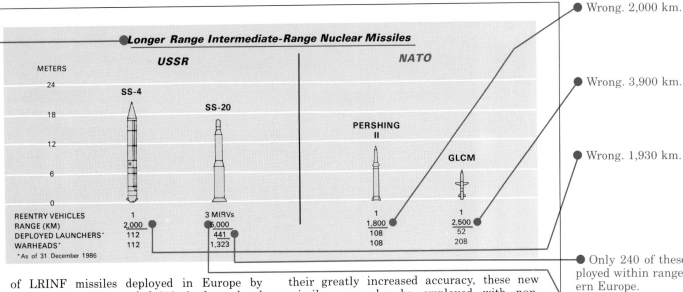

Longer Range Intermediate-Range Nuclear Missiles

	USSR		NATO	
	SS-4	SS-20	PERSHING II	GLCM
REENTRY VEHICLES	1	3 MIRVs	1	1
RANGE (KM)	2,000	5,000	1,800	2,500
DEPLOYED LAUNCHERS*	112	441	108	52
WARHEADS*	112	1,323	108	208

*As of 31 December 1986

METERS: 24, 18, 12, 6, 0

● Wrong. 2,000 km.

● Wrong. 3,900 km.

● Wrong. 1,930 km.

● Only 240 of these are deployed within range of Western Europe.

● Wrong. 3,900 km.

● Only when enough of these new guns and howitzers are deployed. Presently, there are fewer than 4,000 nuclear-capable artillery tubes, most of them of 152 mm, in the entire Soviet inventory.

● The missions for which these missiles have been designed are assigned by NATO to aircraft. NATO has a force of nuclear-capable aircraft three times the size of the Warsaw Pact's, and so powerful that it is barely mentioned in this book. NATO's aircraft assigned to the nuclear strike role can deliver more than 2,500 nuclear weapons to their targets with great precision, while the Warsaw Pact can deliver 450 at most.

of LRINF missiles deployed in Europe by 31 December 1986 totaled 316 single-warhead missiles on 160 launchers. These consist of 108 Pershing II missiles on 108 launchers and 208 GLCMs on 52 launchers.

Other Nuclear Forces

In 1985, a brigade in the Belorussian Military District became the first operational unit ● to receive the SS-23 shorter range INF missile. The SS-23, with its 500-kilometer range, is a marked improvement in range and accuracy over the 300-kilometer SS-1c/SCUD B surface-to-surface missile it is replacing. If the SS-23 follows the same sequence of deployment seen with the SCUD B, the western military districts will receive it first, followed by the Group of Soviet Forces, Germany.

● The SCALEBOARD, another Soviet SRINF system, has a range of 900 kilometers. Each front commander also may have a brigade of 12 to 18 new SCALEBOARD launchers available, which are more accurate than the older SCALEBOARDs they replaced.

Over 60 SCALEBOARD launchers are opposite European NATO. In 1984, the Soviets forward-deployed the SCALEBOARD ballistic missile to Eastern Europe. These front-level weapons, which normally accompany Soviet combined arms formations, are now in position to strike deep into Western Europe. Forty SCALEBOARDs are along the border with China. A battalion is opposite Southwest Asia and eastern Turkey, and one battalion is maintained in strategic reserve. Because of their greatly increased accuracy, these new missiles can also be employed with non-nuclear warheads.

Soviet armies and fronts have missile brigades equipped with 12 to 18 SS-1c/SCUD launchers. More than 500 are located opposite European NATO, and over 100 are along the border with China and in the Far East. Additionally, about 75 are opposite Southwest Asia and eastern Turkey, with over 25 launchers held in strategic reserve.

Various SNF consist of tube artillery and missiles of much shorter range than INF. These SNF assets are available to the Soviet division commander. The most prominent such system at division level is the unguided free-rocket-over-ground (FROG), which is deployed in a battalion of four launchers. The Soviets are replacing FROGs with the more accurate, longer range SS-21s in some divisions opposite NATO. About 500 FROG and SS-21 launchers are opposite NATO. Another 215 FROG launchers are opposite China and in the Far East; some 100 are opposite Southwest Asia and eastern Turkey; and about 75 are in strategic reserve.

Nuclear-capable artillery tubes are also available to front commanders. Three newer self-propelled, nuclear-capable artillery pieces are being added to the inventory: a 152-mm gun (which also has a towed version), a 203-mm gun, and a 240-mm mortar. When fully deployed, these new nuclear-capable artillery tubes plus older 152-mm howitzers that are also capable of firing nuclear rounds will exceed 10,000.

The Soviet Union will maintain its substan-

leaving the French, British and POSEIDON missile warheads off its balance sheet of missiles in the European theater, the administration created the false impression that NATO suffered an adverse imbalance of power which the new missiles, the Cruise and PERSHING II, presumably would redress. The Soviets rejected our proposal, as most experts had predicted, and as the administration had expected, clearing the way for deployment of our new missiles, which have only added to the enormous numerical advantage NATO enjoys. The Soviets have since determined that the PERSHING II is a threat to the USSR, capable of striking command posts in Moscow within only six minutes after launch. They want it removed, and so make the same proposal we made in 1981, exempting French and British missiles, and US sea-based missiles from negotiations. We will either have to agree, or demonstrate conclusively that we never wanted our offer accepted and never proposed it in good faith. So far, we have raised every possible objection. The final one is likely to be over verification.

It seems that the authors have given up even on partial and incomplete comparisons. No mention is made here of NATO's PERSHING I, HONEST JOHN, LANCE or PLUTON missiles.

Wrong. 55 km.

Wrong. 350 km.

Wrong. 160-270 km.

The key phrase here is "in an Advance." Were there no "advance," then neither would there be the coverage shown. One might as easily produce a map showing the "coverage" of anything from our Cruise missile to our shorter-range LANCE in an "advance" clear across the Soviet Union. That would no more show what targets such weapons can hit *prior* to an "advance" than this map does.

This advantage is not that substantial. NATO currently holds a total of 407 battlefield-range launchers whose missiles can be equipped with nuclear warheads, while the Warsaw Pact holds 579.

Wrong. NATO continues to hold a sizable numerical as well as qualitative advantage in INF aircraft. See the comment on the preceding page.

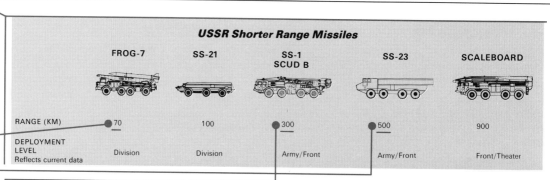

USSR Shorter Range Missiles

	FROG-7	SS-21	SS-1 SCUD B	SS-23	SCALEBOARD
RANGE (KM)	70	100	300	500	900
DEPLOYMENT LEVEL Reflects current data	Division	Division	Army/Front	Army/Front	Front/Theater

SCALEBOARD Coverage from the USSR and Eastern Europe

Potential SS-23 and SCALEBOARD Missile Coverage in an Advance Across Europe

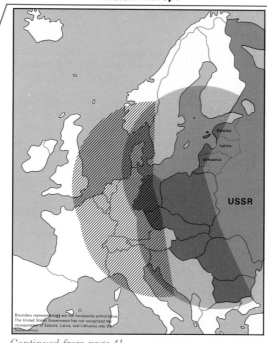

Continued from page 41

tial numerical superiority in shorter range INF and SNF systems while improving the qualitative characteristics of its forces. The USSR also has a significant numerical advantage in INF aircraft and is reducing the qualitative advantage NATO has held. This development is taking place despite NATO's INF aircraft modernization program, in which older aircraft are being replaced by the F-16 and Tornado.

Force Developments. As in all other nuclear attack forces, the Soviets will probably continue to seek ways to improve the capabilities of their tactical missiles and nuclear

artillery. These improvements will be accomplished through incremental modernization of existing systems as well as through the introduction of entirely new systems.

The Soviets probably will also work to upgrade their shorter-range ballistic missile force. Advancements in warhead capabilities, accuracy, and reliability are likely and tests could begin soon. Combined arms commanders would then have enhanced non-nuclear targeting options and more flexible and survivable ballistic missile assets. These systems will be capable of delivering nuclear, chemical, or conventional

42

● According to the text on page 41, the Soviets will not have 10,000 nuclear-capable gun tubes until a great many more 203 mm and 240 mm weapons are deployed. Currently, most Soviet nuclear-capable artillery tubes are towed or self-propelled 152 mm howitzers and guns. Many other standard Soviet artillery pieces, including the self-propelled 122mm howitzer, are not nuclear-capable.

● The balance has actually widened in NATO's favor. NATO currently deploys in Europe a total of 3,032 nuclear capable artillery pieces, the Warsaw Pact 1,165.

All of the 10,000 self-propelled and towed 152-mm howitzers and guns, now operational with the USSR's ground forces, are nuclear capable.

warheads closer toward the forward edge of the battle area and to greater depth within the military theater of operation.

The US SNF is made up of Lance tactical missiles and nuclear artillery. Although SNF artillery was once an area of NATO advantage, the balance has shifted in favor of the Soviets in recent years.

Sea-Based Forces. The Soviets operate 13 GOLF II-Class ballistic missile submarines equipped with 3 SS-N-5 SLBMs each. Six GOLF IIs are assigned to the Baltic, where they pose a threat to most of Europe, while the remaining seven are based in the Sea of Japan, where they can be employed against targets in the Far East.

The Soviet Navy also maintains an extensive sea-based non-strategic nuclear force comprising both antisurface warfare (ASUW) and antisubmarine warfare (ASW) as well as land-attack systems. The Soviets maintain an in-

ventory of nuclear-armed torpedoes as well as ASW depth bombs; the newest versions of both entered service in the early 1980s. The Soviet Navy also deploys an extensive array of ASUW and ASW cruise missile systems, ranging from the SS-N-3 to the newer SS-N-19 and SS-N-22; the latter two were also introduced in the early 1980s. Some 288 surface warships, 340 submarines, and about 30 other combatant ships carry at least one of these systems.

US sea-based non-strategic programs include continued production of the Tomahawk nuclear-armed land-attack cruise missile and development of a nuclear depth/strike bomb (NDSB). The Tomahawk provides increased range over carrier aircraft and allows dispersal of nuclear strike assets over a large number of naval platforms. The NDSB, combining land-attack and ASW features in a single bomb, will replace the aging nuclear bombs currently fulfilling this mission.

● Here is a disingenuous little paragraph meant to create the impression that the weapons covered are the extent of America's response. In fact, the US Navy deploys a wide variety of nuclear-armed antiship missiles, land-attack missiles, antiaircraft missiles, depth bombs, and antisubmarine torpedos and has done so for several decades.

● No mention is made here of the threat to Eastern Europe and the Soviet Union from French, British and US submarines.

Chapter II Forces for Nuclear Attack

We now enter the realm of pure fantasy. Represented in the illustration shown here are some of the components of a space-based antiballistic missile defense system. It is extremely unlikely that such a system will ever be built, because it is extremely unlikely that it would ever be able to fulfill its ostensible mission of shooting down ballistic missiles. Such weapons, among them lasers, particle beams and hypervelocity rockets, might much more easily be effective against satellites, and this is the real threat posed by current research on such systems. But to be effective against missiles, large numbers of weapons would have to be lifted into space, at an exorbitant cost, and kept there. They would have to draw on immense supplies of power not presently available. To be able to hit anything, they would need optically perfect focusing mirrors, which have never been produced. They would need absolute precision in aiming, over distances of several thousand km, which has never been achieved. They would need a battle management system of flawless efficiency, which would instantaneously select the nearest new target for each weapon each time. The system would have to function automatically, with no time for human intervention. Its computers would require up to one million lines of error-free programming which could never be fully tested except under battle conditions. Consequently, we would never be able to trust that the program was reliable. These requirements are so far beyond the reach of foreseeable technology that almost all of the nation's scientists not paid by the Reagan administration, including nearly the entire memberships of the National Academy of Sciences, the Federation of American Scientists, the Union of Concerned Scientists and the American Physics Society, have declared that the project is simply not feasible. An experienced propagandist might dismiss all this, saying that learned bodies have been wrong before, and claiming there was once a time when scientists believed an intercontinental ballistic missile could never be built. It isn't all that clear whether there was ever such a time. The idea of a rocket spanning the continents seems to have occurred even to Sir William Congreve in the early 1800s. There certainly was a time, however, when men believed it might be possible to turn lead into gold—and this seems to be the mentality to which the Reagan administration now urges a return. President Reagan takes visible pride in asserting his individual right to believe in whatever he wishes, but it becomes a very public matter when he imposes that belief on the US taxpayer with a program of twenty-six billion dollars, which would be much better spent on domestic social needs, than for research on a series of weapons that hold absolutely no promise for making us more safe, but which are likely to make us less so. President Reagan's sincerity must also be questioned. When he announced his plan to spend our money in this way, he declared: "Our moral imperative is to work with all our power for that day when the children of the world can grow up without the fear of nuclear war." Yet the program he has launched does not even attempt to dispel that fear. He does not propose a defense against nuclear weapons. He proposes a defense against ballistic missiles. This would do nothing to eliminate the threat from cruise missiles, from nuclear weapons delivered by bombers, or from clandestine nuclear weapons broken down into components, and then secretly brought into a country and reassembled. Even this limited defense is an imperfect one. Physicist Edward Teller, who pursuaded the President to adopt it, himself acknowledges: " I do not believe we can look forward, in the foreseeable future, to a one hundred percent perfect defense." When it became clear that this system did not guarantee protection of our cities, the administration dropped its pretense that the system could, and retreated to its fallback position that the system was still needed anyway in order to "strengthen deterrence," by making the results of a Soviet attack "too unpredictable." The re-

sults of a Soviet attack are already too unpredictable. See the commentary on page 29. If we were to carry out a first strike, however, we might believe that such a system could be used effectively in conjunction with it. Though our shield in space would be highly imperfect, we might still believe it could absorb the much lighter, retaliatory attack the Soviets would launch after being first struck. In short, the shield helps the swordsman, and becomes part of an offensive weapons system. Once all this became apparent, the administration could no longer pretend its system was meant to dispel the fear of nuclear war. So it has returned to the time-honored method of justifying new military programs: the claim that the Soviets are developing the same weapons, too. That is why this entire chapter is here. As we read it, however, it would be well to remember that, while the Soviets are certainly engaged in research on lasers and particle beam weapons, as we have been for many years, it is they, not we, who have proposed banning all weapons in space. We could agree to do so, and dispense with all of this right now. Then why haven't we done so?

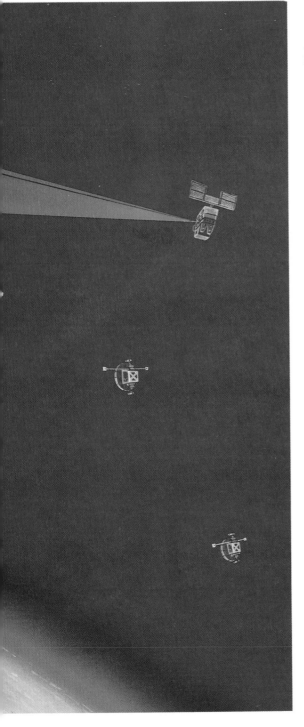

Chapter III

Strategic Defense and Space Operations

Since World War II, the Soviets have pursued wide-ranging strategic defense programs in a clear and determined effort to blunt the effect of any attack on the USSR. These programs are reflective of Soviet military doctrine, which calls for equal attention to defensive as well as offensive capabilities. <u>The USSR today maintains the world's only operational antisatellite (ASAT) and antiballistic missile (ABM) defense systems.</u> This two-layer ABM strategic defense system has been continually improved over the past 2 decades.

As early as 1965, the Soviets were writing about an anti-space defense mission, which they described as a component of their strategic defense program. To the Soviets, the main purpose of an anti-space defense would be to destroy space systems in orbits that were being used by the enemy for military purposes. The principal means of destruction would be special aircraft and vehicles controlled either from the ground or by crews onboard a space vehicle.

During the past decade alone, the Soviets allocated resources equivalent to <u>approximately $400 billion to both strategic offensive and defensive programs</u> in almost equal amounts — about $20 billion per year for each program. During the same time, the cost of Soviet military space programs approached $80 billion.

Soviet writings on the nature of future war suggest that strategic defenses will be expand-

While publicly opposed to the US Strategic Defense Initiative, the Soviet Union is forging ahead with research and development of land-, air-, and space-based ballistic missile defenses. <u>The Soviets already have ground-based lasers that can damage satellites,</u> and by the year 2000, other systems could be used for defense against ballistic missiles.

The USSR did not have its ASAT system "operational" until 1981. It is a primitive system, effective only against satellites in their lowest orbits, at altitudes of no more than a few hundred km. More than half the tests of this system have been failures. The US, on the other hand, first deployed an ASAT system in 1964, and kept it operational at Johnston Island and Kwajaleia Atoll in the Pacific until 1975. We are ready to deploy a new ASAT system, which will be capable of destroying satellites at altitudes of several thousand km. There is no evidence that the Soviet ABM system can protect Moscow from a missile attack. In tests, the system has hit its targets fewer times than our own SPARTAN and SPRINT missiles have. We have also designed the Mk 500 MARV (Maneuvering Reentry Vehicle) and Mk 600 PGRV (Precision Guided Reentry Vehicle), specifically in order to defeat such ABM systems. We abandoned our own more sophisticated ABM system in 1975, when we realized that ABM systems could be easily and cheaply defeated by adding greater numbers of warheads and decoys to the attacking force. The most effective use of the Soviet ABM system would be against components of our "defensive" shield in space, if we ever actually did build one.

We don't really know how much the Soviets have spent on these programs. As we have seen, the administration exaggerates Soviet military spending anyway, so there is good reason to believe that the actual amounts spent are smaller. It doesn't really matter, since we are ahead of the Soviets in every critical area of this technology.

In 1975, one of our MIDAS satellites was illuminated, with minimal damage, by a bright flash of light from the Soviet Union. Alarmists were quick to jump on this as evidence of a Soviet military laser. Most experts believe it was a gas fire.

● Of course the USSR has this network. It needs it. We would have built one too had we needed it. But we did not. It is we who have the powerful strategic bomber force, capable today of delivering more than 4,700 nuclear weapons to their targets in the Soviet Union. The Soviets do not have such a force. Since the end of World War II, the Soviets have faced a powerful US bomber force. In 1945, we had almost 4,000 B-29 bombers capable of delivering nuclear weapons to the Soviet heartland from a chain of bases virtually surrounding the USSR. Then we built the B-32, the B-36, the B-45, the B-47, the B-50, the B-52, the B-58, the B-66 and the FB-111. In all, we built more than 8,000 aircraft of ten types, while the Soviets built only 210 long-range bombers, none of which has posed any real challenge for US air defenses.

---

ing to include defense against cruise missiles and precision-guided conventional munitions that could be targeted against Soviet strategic forces in any protracted conventional war. As a result of this view of global conventional war fought under the constant threat of escalation to the use of nuclear weapons, the Soviets are likely to continue to enlarge their strategic defense and space operations beyond the extensive structure and investment existing today.

In addition to its ABM system, the USSR has a multifaceted operational strategic air defense network that dwarfs that of the US, as well as a wide-ranging research and development program in both traditional and advanced defenses. This active program employs various weapon systems to protect territory, military forces, and other key assets throughout the USSR. Moreover, the Soviets' passive program includes civil defense and structural hardening to protect important political, economic, and military leaders and facilities.

Recent activities in the Soviet strategic defense program are as follows:

- upgrading and modernizing the operational ABM defense, which is around Moscow;
- continued construction of a large phased-array radar (LPAR) at Krasnoyarsk for ballistic missile early warning and tracking, in violation of the ABM Treaty;
- construction of three additional LPARs, bringing the number to nine;
- further modernization of strategic air defense forces;
- construction of a new over-the-horizon radar in the Soviet Far East for detecting long-range aircraft operating over the Pacific Ocean;
- continued extensive research into and development of advanced technologies for ballistic missile, ASAT, and air defense, including laser, particle beam, and kinetic energy weapons; and
- improving passive defenses by constructing and maintaining deep underground bunkers and blast shelters for key personnel and enhancing the survivability of some offensive systems through mobility and hardening.

Since the beginning of the nuclear age, the Soviets have placed great importance on limiting the amount of damage the USSR would suffer to key targets in a global war. They have organized and structured their strategic defense forces accordingly. For example, the National Air Defense Forces, which include missile and space defense, became an independent service in the late 1950s and have generally ranked third in prominence within the military, following the Strategic Rocket Forces and the Ground Forces. During the 1960s, the Soviets established the strategic defense missions for ASAT operations and ABM defense.

Soviet strategic defense forces play a role equal to that of offensive forces. In the event of war, nuclear or conventional, Soviet offensive forces are to:

- destroy or neutralize as much of the enemy's air and nuclear assets as possible on the ground or at sea before they are launched; and
- destroy or disrupt enemy air and nuclear-associated command, control, and communications.

Soviet defensive efforts, designed to enhance the credibility of offensive forces, are to:

- intercept and destroy surviving retaliatory weapons — aircraft and missiles — before they reach their targets; and
- protect the Party, state, military forces, industrial infrastructure, and essential working population with active and passive defense measures.

As in a conventional conflict, if a war escalates to the use of strategic nuclear weapons, Soviet military doctrine calls for their forces to seize the initiative. Passive and active defensive systems would try to negate much of the US and allied capability for retaliation. The Soviet military holds defense from nuclear attack as a key, integrated component of their military strategy. From this Soviet perspective, any measures the West would take to defend itself are seen as potentially denying the achievement of key objectives within Soviet war-fighting strategy. For these reasons, the Soviets strenuously oppose the US Strategic Defense Initiative (SDI). At the same time, with consistency and vigor, the Soviets maintain their balanced offensive-defensive strategy in order to fulfill their strategic objectives.

Ballistic Missile Defense

Since 1978, the Soviets have been expanding and modernizing the ABM defenses at Moscow. The single-layer system includes 16 (originally 64) reloadable above-ground GALOSH launchers and the DOG HOUSE and CAT HOUSE

● The Soviets have no civil defense. See commentary at bottom right of page 15.

● We are back to reciting the obvious. These are the objectives of any military organization, including our own.

● This seems to be our own perspective as well. When asked how he would feel about a Soviet "defensive" system of weapons in space, Defense Secretary Weinberger called this "one of the most frightening prospects" imaginable. The Soviets are also aware that we could use our own "defensive" system most successfully to attack satellites rather than ballistic missiles, destroying their early warning and communications satellites as part of a coordinated plan for a first strike.

● According to the ABM Treaty, radars "for early warning of strategic ballistic missile attack" should be located only "along the periphery" of a nation's territory and "oriented outward." According to the CIA, the radar under construction at Krasnoyarsk is "not well designed" for ballistic missile early warning and tracking because it operates at the wrong frequency, has only a single face which is "not at the optimal angle to perform a battle management function," is not "hardened" as battle management radars are, is undefended by interceptor missiles and "does not cover the path of incoming US ICBMs because it is too far east and pointing in the wrong direction." If all that is so, then the radar certainly cannot be used effectively for ballistic missile early warning and tracking. But the radar is located 750 km from the Soviet border with Mongolia. The US, however, is also building similar radars in Thule, Greenland and Flyingdales in the United Kingdom. By no stretch of the imagination can these be considered located "along the periphery" of US "national territory." If they turn out to possess all the necessary capabilities for missile early warning and tracking, then they would appear to be the much larger violation of the ABM treaty than the radar at Krasnoyarsk.

This looks exactly like our SAFEGUARD ABM system, employing long-range exoatmospheric SPARTAN and short-range endoatmospheric SPRINT missiles, which we first deployed at Grand Forks, North Dakota, in 1974, but deactivated the following year, after a long public debate, when scientists and the military finally agreed that all ABM systems were technically obsolete because an attacker could always add more warheads and decoys to overwhelm such a defense more rapidly and economically than the defensive system itself could be expanded. A heavier attacking force would remain a simple and effective countermeasure to any defensive system we ever built in space. Another effective countermeasure would be to attack our defenses directly, as the Soviets could do with the very missiles being described here. The GALOSH would be far more effective against satellites than missiles.

A new component of the USSR's strategic defense capability is the GAZELLE silo-based missile. This missile, probably armed with a nuclear warhead, is modernizing Moscow ABM defenses.

Do the Soviets have over-the-horizon radars? Have they had them for a very long time? If so, is it possible that we did not deploy the first of ours until 1986, even though the Under Secretary of Defense for Research and Engineering has consistently reported us "ahead" of the Soviets in radar technology? See commentary at top of page 27.

battle management radars south of Moscow. The four firing complexes consist of TRY ADD tracking and guidance radars and four exoatmospheric interceptors (nuclear-armed, ground-based missiles designed to intercept reentry vehicles in space shortly before they reenter the Earth's atmosphere).

The new Moscow ABM system will be a two-layer defense composed of silo-based, long-range, modified GALOSH interceptors; silo-based, probably nuclear-armed GAZELLE high-acceleration endoatmospheric interceptors (designed to engage reentry vehicles within the atmosphere); and associated engagement, guidance, and battle management radar systems, including the new PILL BOX large, four-sided, phased-array radar at Pushkino north of Moscow. This modernization will bring Moscow's ABM defenses up to 100 operational ABM launchers, the limit permitted by the 1972 ABM Treaty. The new system could become fully operational in the late 1980s.

The current Soviet ICBM launch-detection satellite network can provide as much as 30 minutes' tactical warning and can determine the general origin of the missile. Additionally, two over-the-horizon radars that are directed at US ICBM fields could give about 30 minutes' warning.

The next layer of ballistic missile detection consists of 11 large HEN HOUSE ballistic missile early warning radars at 6 locations on the periphery of the USSR. These radars can confirm the warning from the satellite and over-the-horizon radar systems, characterize the size of an attack, and provide target-tracking data in support of antiballistic missile forces. The Soviets have improved the capabilities of the HEN HOUSE radars since the signing of the ABM Treaty.

Although the Soviet Union continues to maintain and upgrade its older network of ballistic missile detection and tracking systems, including launch-detection satellites and over-the-horizon radars, it is deploying a new series of LPARs.

The addition of three radars in the western USSR will form almost a complete circle of LPAR coverage around the USSR. These radars provide significantly improved target-

Over-the-horizon radars would not be effective beyond 3,300 km. Where would these Soviet radars be sited, even if they did exist?

This is a precise description, with names changed, of the ABM system we built and then deactivated in North Dakota, for the reasons noted in the commentary above. More mirror-imaging.

● Here is a demonstration of the principle of emphasis. All that you see are Soviet radars. This may give the impression that only the Soviets have such radars. A splendid map could be drawn of the US radar system, stretching from Scotland to Hawaii, including the 12 large phased-array radars of our Ballistic Missile Early Warning System, the four large phased-array radars of our PAVE PAWS system, the 75 radars of our DEW Line and North Warning System, our Pe-

rimeter Acquisition Radar Attack Characterization System, the three radars of our Navy's Space Surveillance System, the 16 radars of our Air Force Spacetrack and other systems, and, of course, our over-the-horizon backscatter radars. All of these are already fully operational, whereas the Soviet system shown here, as the text below acknowledges, will not be operational until the mid-1990s at the earliest.

Note that Soviet over-the-horizon radars are not shown on this map. For the reason why, see the commentary on the previous page and on page 27.

This radar has been emphasized in an attempt to advance the administration's argument that it fills an important "gap" in Soviet defenses. However, the Krasnoyarsk radar does not cover the path any incoming US missiles would follow.

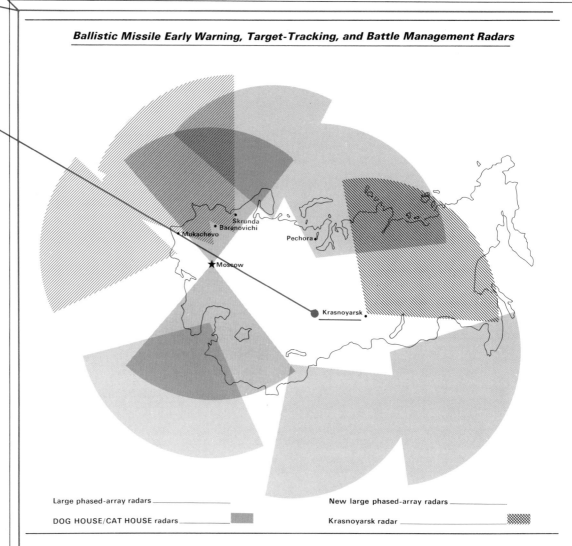

Ballistic Missile Early Warning, Target-Tracking, and Battle Management Radars

Large phased-array radars _____   New large phased-array radars _____
DOG HOUSE/CAT HOUSE radars _____   Krasnoyarsk radar _____

tracking and -handling capabilities and add a redundancy in coverage over the existing HEN HOUSE network. In conjunction with the HEN HOUSE radars, the LPAR near Krasnoyarsk in Siberia, when fully operational, will close the final gap in the Soviet ballistic missile early warning radar coverage. <u>The entire network could become fully operational in the mid-1990s.</u>

    The US and USSR, in signing the ABM Treaty, recognized the need for ballistic missile early warning radars while seeking to prevent their use for a nationwide antiballistic missile system. The ABM Treaty restricts the place-

ment of ballistic missile early warning radars to the periphery of national territory and oriented outward. In that way, the desirable and legitimate goal of early warning could be advanced while minimizing the danger that the radar's target-tracking and impact-prediction capabilities could be used for effective nationwide ABM battle management.

    The Krasnoyarsk radar, essentially identical to the other large phased-array radars that the Soviets have acknowledged to be for ballistic missile detection and tracking, <u>violates the 1972 ABM Treaty.</u> The radar is not located on the periphery of the USSR and pointed out-

See commentary on page 46.

• Having prosecuted one government employee for "espionage" after he had given three classified satellite photographs to the press rather than to a foreign government, the administration now wants to be careful that it is not accused of using a double standard by publishing classified satellite photographs in this book, as it used to do. See the commentary on page 20. Consequently, any photographs here that can be identified as having been taken from a satellite have been purchased from a commercial firm and credited accordingly. In this case, the image is from the French SPOT satellite. Its resolution is about 10 meters. The administration does not want commercial satellite photography to improve too much. In July, 1987, it issued regulations giving the Departments of State and Defense the right

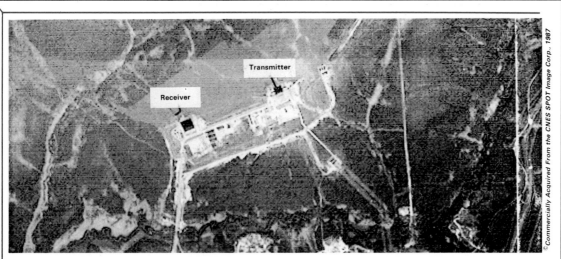

©Commercially Acquired From the CNES SPOT Image Corp., 1987

The Pechora large phased-array radar (LPAR), for ballistic missile detection and target tracking, is one of nine LPARs currently under construction.

ward, as required for early warning radars. It is some 750 kilometers from the nearest border — Mongolia — and it is oriented not toward that border, but across approximately 4,000 kilometers of Soviet territory to the northeast.

The Soviet Union claims that the Krasnoyarsk radar is designed for space tracking rather than for ballistic missile early warning, and therefore does not violate the ABM Treaty. Its design and orientation make clear that this radar is intended for ballistic missile detection and target tracking in the LPAR network.

HEN HOUSE Radars

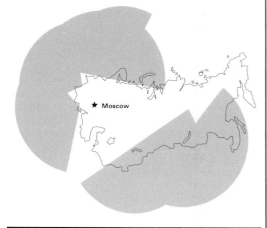

★ Moscow

The growing network of large phased-array radars, of which the Krasnoyarsk radar is a part, is of particular concern when linked with other Soviet ABM efforts. These radars take years to construct and their existence could allow the Soviet Union to move quickly to deploy a nationwide ABM defense. The degree of redundancy being built into their LPAR network is not necessary for early warning. It is highly desirable, however, for ballistic missile defense.

During the 1970s, the Soviets developed components that could be integrated into an ABM system that would allow them to construct individual ABM sites in months rather than the years required for more traditional ABM systems. The development and testing of the components represent a potential violation of the ABM Treaty's prohibition against the development of a mobile land-based ABM system or components. By using such components along with the LPARs, the Soviets could strengthen the defenses of Moscow and defend targets in the western USSR and east of the Urals.

The Soviet Union has conducted tests that have involved air defense radars in ABM-related activities. The large number, and consistency over time, of incidents of concurrent operation of ABM and SAM components plus Soviet failure to accommodate fully US concerns, indicate the USSR probably has violated the Treaty's prohibition on testing SAM

• If you think this is redundancy, see the commentary on our own radar network on page 48.

• If the administration had the least bit of evidence of any such thing, you may be sure it would be published here. It isn't.

• A little vague here, aren't we?

• Again, if there were real evidence, it would be here. But it is useful to seem uncertain. This supports the administration's claim that our verification capabilities are inadequate.

• See commentary on page 46.

to veto license applications for private ownership of satellites capable of producing high-resolution photographs. Applicants must disclose the resolution of their equipment. So long as this is acceptable to the government, they will be allowed to operate and sell their images. The administration says its concern is that commercial photographs whose resolution is too high will reveal military secrets. Whose military secrets? Does this mean that Soviet technology is so backward that they cannot photograph US military equipment with a resolution as high as commercial firms are capable of achieving? Or does it mean that when commercial firms begin photographing Soviet military equipment and Soviet military deployments, it will soon become evident that the administration has vastly exaggerated the quantities of such equipment, and that it has no evidence to support its claims of Soviet arms treaty violations?

● Another demonstration of emphasis. One might as easily produce a chart showing French developments in these areas of technology and this might produce a considerable amount of agitation over how far the French had gotten in these fields. Let us bring the matter into focus: according to Richard DeLauer, Under Secretary of Defense for Research and Engineering, out of the twenty most important technology areas, the US is ahead in fifteen and the Soviets are ahead in only one. Far from losing our lead, DeLauer acknowledges that we have been expanding it. According to John Pike of the Feder-

ation of American Scientists: "The Soviets are five years behind us on lasers, five to ten on sensors, and at least a decade on computerized battle management." The lightly shaded areas in the chart below mean nothing. They indicate research which every developed nation has under way. The darker shaded areas, according to the authors, indicate that the Soviets have achieved operational systems, which are in their deployment phase. In some of these cases, they have indicated deployment before it took place. In all of these cases, we deployed our own systems long before they deployed theirs.

As the authors quietly ● note at the bottom of this chart: "The Soviet direct ascent" ASAT capability *is* the original Moscow ABM system. This is an important acknowledgment that any space defense system we ever built could be directly attacked. The time graph in the chart, however, indicates that the system was first deployed in the early 1960s. In fact, the Soviet GALOSH was first deployed in 1968. We deployed our first direct ascent ASAT system in 1964.

Can we call this an opera- ● tional system, when more than half of its tests have failed?

Through the 1960s and ● 1970s, we spent an average of half a billion dollars a year on research of this kind until the Reagan administration began spending more.

Not too likely, when the ● missile specifically designed for this mission, the GALOSH, can hit satellites more easily than it can hit ballistic missiles.

No such defense is possi- ● ble. The Soviets probably know this. If they didn't know it, they would have built a great many more missiles than the few they placed around Moscow in 1968. Yet no other missiles of this type can be found.

If they are really investing ● so much, why haven't they drawn ahead of us? Why would they want to acquire our technologies? See the commentary above.

Perhaps it would cost this ● much under a free enterprise system, but even if it did, it would not be "considerably larger" than the annual cost of the US laser program in recent years.

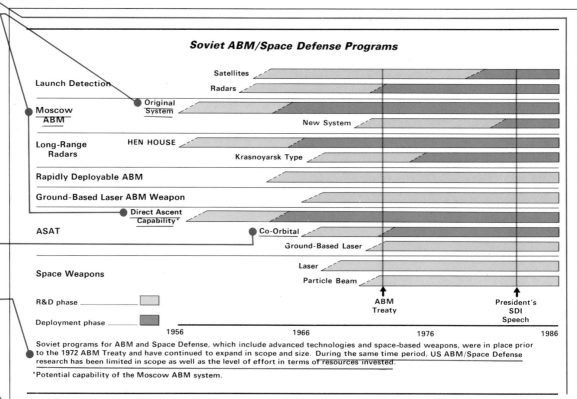

Soviet ABM/Space Defense Programs

Launch Detection — Satellites / Radars

Moscow ABM — Original System / New System

Long-Range Radars — HEN HOUSE / Krasnoyarsk Type

Rapidly Deployable ABM

Ground-Based Laser ABM Weapon

ASAT — Direct Ascent Capability* / Co-Orbital / Ground-Based Laser

Space Weapons — Laser / Particle Beam

R&D phase _____

Deployment phase _____

1956   1966   1976   1986

ABM Treaty   President's SDI Speech

Soviet programs for ABM and Space Defense, which include advanced technologies and space-based weapons, were in place prior to the 1972 ABM Treaty and have continued to expand in scope and size. During the same time period, US ABM/Space Defense research has been limited in scope as well as the level of effort in terms of resources invested.

*Potential capability of the Moscow ABM system.

components in an ABM mode. Additionally, the SA-10 and SA-X-12B/GIANT systems may have the potential to intercept some types of strategic ballistic missiles. Both systems are expected to have widespread deployment. The technical capabilities of these systems highlight the problem that improving technology is blurring the distinction between air defense and ABM systems. This problem will be further complicated as newer, more complex air defense missile systems are developed.

Taken together, all of their ABM and ABM-related activities indicate a significant commitment to enhancing the strategic defenses of the USSR and suggest that the Soviets may be preparing an ABM defense of their nation.

Advanced ABM Technologies

In the late 1960s, the USSR initiated a substantial research program into advanced technologies applicable to ballistic missile defense systems. This effort covers many of the same technologies currently being explored for the US SDI but involves a much greater investment of plant space, capital, and manpower. The

USSR will undoubtedly increase its efforts to acquire Western technologies associated with space and the SDI program.

Laser Weapons

The USSR's laser program is considerably larger than US efforts and involves over 10,000 scientists and engineers as well as more than a half-dozen major research and development facilities and test ranges. Much of this research takes place at the Sary-Shagan Missile Test Center, where ABM testing also is conducted. At Sary-Shagan alone, the Soviets are estimated to have several lasers for air defense and two lasers probably capable of damaging some components of satellites in orbit, one of which could be used in feasibility testing for ballistic missile defense applications. The Soviet laser weapons program would cost roughly $1 billion a year in the US.

Scientists in the USSR have been exploring three types of lasers that may prove useful for weapons applications — the gas-dynamic, the electric discharge, and the chemical. They have achieved impressive output power

These passages are quite significant when read as a revelation of our own intent. That is how propaganda can usually be read. All three passages acknowledge that Soviet research and development of lasers, particle beam weapons and kinetic energy weapons, the three basic types of weapon proposed for our own "defensive" shield in space, will have to continue for a number of years before an operational *antiballistic missile* system could be deployed, but all three specifically warn that each type of weapon could be developed into an *antisatellite* system much sooner. Consequently, the first threat of a "defensive" shield in space, like the one we and not the Soviets propose, is to satellites, not ballistic missiles. The administration likes to cite Soviet opposition to our plans for such a shield, which it claims

levels with these lasers. The Soviets are possibly exploring the potential of visible and very-short-wave-length lasers. They are investigating the excimer, free-electron, and x-ray lasers, and they have been developing argon-ion lasers.

The Soviets appear generally capable of supplying the prime power, energy storage, and auxiliary components for their laser and other directed-energy weapons programs. They have probably been developing optical systems necessary for laser weapons to track and attack their targets. They produced a 1.2-meter segmented mirror for an astrophysical telescope in 1978 and claimed that this reflector was a prototype for a 25-meter mirror. A large mirror is considered necessary for a long-range space-based laser weapon system.

The USSR has progressed in some cases beyond technology research. It has ground-based lasers that have some capability to attack US satellites and could have a prototype space-based antisatellite laser weapon by the end of the decade. Additionally, the Soviets could have prototypes for ground-based lasers for defense against ballistic missiles by the late 1980s and could begin testing components for a large-scale deployment system in the early 1990s.

The remaining difficulties in fielding an operational laser system will require more development time. An operational ground-based laser for defense against ballistic missiles probably could not be deployed until the late 1990s or after the year 2000. If technological developments prove successful, the Soviets might be able to deploy a space-based laser system for defense against ballistic missiles after the year 2000. The Soviets' efforts to develop high-energy air defense laser weapons are likely to lead to ground-based deployments in the early 1990s and to naval deployments in the mid-1990s.

Particle Beam Weapons

Since the late 1960s, the Soviets have been exploring the feasibility of using particle beams for a space-based weapon system. They may be able to test a prototype space-based particle beam weapon intended to disrupt the electronics of satellites in the 1990s. An operational system designed to destroy satellites could follow later, and application of a particle beam weapon capable of destroying missile boosters or warheads would require several additional years of research and development.

Soviet efforts in particle beams, particularly ion sources and radio-frequency accelerators for particle beams, are impressive. In fact, much of the US understanding of how particle beams could be made into practical weapons is based on published Soviet research conducted in the late 1960s and early 1970s.

Radio-Frequency Weapons

The USSR has conducted research in the use of strong radio-frequency (high-power microwave) signals that have the potential to interfere with or destroy critical electronic components of ballistic missile warheads or satellites. The Soviets could test a ground-based radio-frequency weapon capable of damaging satellites in the 1990s.

Kinetic Energy Weapons

The Soviets also have research programs underway on kinetic energy weapons, which use the high-speed collision of a small object with the target as the kill mechanism. In the 1960s, the USSR developed an experimental "gun" that could shoot streams of particles of a heavy metal, such as tungsten or molybdenum, at speeds of nearly 25 kilometers per second in air and more than 60 kilometers per second in a vacuum.

Long-range, space-based kinetic energy weapons for defense against ballistic missiles probably could not be developed until at least the mid-1990s. However, the Soviets could deploy in the near term a short-range, space-based system for space station defense or for close-in attack by a maneuvering satellite. Current Soviet guidance and control systems are probably adequate for effective kinetic energy weapons use against some objects in space, such as satellites.

Computer and Sensor Technology

Advanced technology weapons programs — including potential advanced defenses against ballistic missiles and ASATs — are dependent on remote sensor and computer technologies, areas in which the West currently leads the Soviet Union. The Soviets are devoting considerable resources to acquiring Western know-how and to improving their abilities and expertise in these technologies. An important part of that effort involves the increasing exploitation of open and clandestine access to Western technology. For example, the Soviets operate a well-funded program through

Not really. Only research for the Radio Frequency Quadrupole (RFQ). According to Rand Corporation physicist Nikita Wells, the Soviets are now behind us in RFQ research.

Our research in both these areas started way before theirs and has progressed far beyond theirs. Little of promise has emerged.

Disinformation. Nothing suggests that an optically perfect mirror of this size could ever be built. Where did the Soviets make this claim? And please, no forgeries this time, like the ones prepared in 1981 to "prove" a flow of arms from Nicaragua into El Salvador, or the ones now being prepared to back up Oliver North's testimony that "young Nicaraguan children" use textbooks in which they "learn how to count by counting grenades and AK-47s."

No laser has yet been built with sufficient power to do any damage to even the most delicate objects at orbital range. Laser energy diffuses and its intensity rapidly diminishes as it spans greater distances.

All that will probably prove successful are demonstration models, which the Soviets don't need. But we need them, in order to gain public support for expanded investment in space. We will demonstrate at very short range what never would work over the vast distances required for an effective laser weapon. If necessary we will cheat. We recently used a laser to explode a TITAN rocket casing. What we did not tell the public was that the rocket casing had been filled with compressed gas.

(continued from above)

51

is an antiballistic missile shield, as proof that the Soviets believe it will be effective against ballistic missiles, in order to persuade us that we should believe it too. But since the administration here acknowledges that such weapons will be effective much sooner against satellites, it is fully aware, and would prefer us not to be aware, that *this* is a powerful reason for Soviet opposition. As noted earlier, the simplest and most effective use of our "defensive" shield in space would be to destroy Soviet early warning and communications satellites while our cruise missiles, flying beneath the search lobes of Soviet coastal and long-range radars, destroyed those radars, so the Soviets would have no means of knowing when the missiles of a US first strike had been launched, and so could do nothing to prepare for it. Of course, the administration has publicly assured the world that this is not our intention. If you lived in the USSR, would you accept the reassurances of a self-declared adversary?

Here is another one of those direct denials. They are a dead giveaway. As the art of propaganda becomes progressively more refined, its practitioners will have to learn to be more sophisticated than this. In fact, we don't really know how extensive the Soviet program is, but our own program is certainly "comparable" to what the authors here *say* it is. The details of Presidential Directive 58, providing for the dispersion and relocation of federal officials, are highly classified. Nevertheless, enough information has become available about our Federal Relocation Arc, our Unified Vaults & Storage system, and our Alternate Capitol at Mount Weather in the Blue Ridge Mountains, to give us an idea of the very comprehensive plans our government has drawn up and the enormous investment of our money it has made, in order to protect federal, state and local officials. This planning began in 1954. Additional alternate capitols and other command centers, as well as a variety of underground storage facilities, have since been selected, built, hardened, fully stocked and permanently staffed. All this involves much more than 1,500 shelters and 175,000 people.

These third parties haven't been very successful, however. According to John Pike of the Federation of American Scientists: "We're sitting here with something like 140 installed supercomputers, and they've got one that's considered to be at the very low end of the spectrum."

So have we.

We, too, maintain reserves of strategic materials.

There is little such protection. According to the CIA, "the Soviets would suffer over one hundred million casualties in a nuclear exchange," and the bulk of the general population, far from having access to blast shelters or other facilities, "must rely on evacuation from urban areas for its protection." So much for the "massive" Soviet civil defense program.

More repetition to reinforce our "mobility" claim.

We have done the same. We are designing weapons for World War IV, even though Albert Einstein probably came closest to the truth when he said that if World War IV is ever fought, "it will be fought with bows and arrows."

See commentary on page 51.

Then you may be sure that it is a high priority US objective, too.

third parties for the illegal purchase of US high-technology computers, test and calibration equipment, and sensors.

Passive Defenses

A key element of Soviet military doctrine calls for passive and active defense to act together to ensure wartime operations and survival. The Soviets have undertaken a major program to harden military assets to make them more resistant to attack. Included in this program are their ICBM silos, launch facilities, and some command-and-control centers.

The Soviets provide their Party and government leaders with hardened alternate command posts located well away from urban centers — in addition to many deep underground bunkers and blast shelters in Soviet cities. This comprehensive and redundant network, patterned after a network designed for the Soviet Armed Forces, provides more than 1,500 hardened alternate facilities for more than 175,000 key Party and government personnel throughout the USSR. In contrast, the US passive defense effort is far smaller and more limited. It is in no way comparable to the comprehensive Soviet program.

Elaborate plans also have been made for the full mobilization of the national economy in support of a war effort. Reserves of vital materiel are maintained, many in hardened underground structures. Redundant industrial facilities are in active production. Industrial and other economic facilities are equipped with blast shelters for the work force, and detailed procedures have been developed for the relocation of selected production facilities. By planning for the survival of the essential work force, the Soviets hope to reconstitute vital production programs using those industrial components that could be redirected or salvaged after an attack.

Additionally, the USSR has greatly emphasized mobility as a means of enhancing the survivability of military assets. The SS-20 and SS-25 missiles, for example, are mobile. The deployment of the rail-mobile SS-X-24 is expected soon. The Soviets are also developing an extensive network of mobile command, control, and communications facilities.

Antisatellite Operations

The Soviets continue to field the world's only operational ASAT system. It is launched into an orbit similar to that of the target satellite

The Soviets' operational antisatellite system attacks other satellites in orbit by maneuvering a conventional warhead within range and destroying its target with a multi-pellet blast.

and, when it gets close enough, destroys the satellite by exploding a conventional warhead. The Soviet co-orbital antisatellite interceptor is reasonably capable of performing its missions, and thus it is a distinct threat to US low-altitude satellites.

Other Soviet systems have ASAT capabilities. The nuclear-armed GALOSH ABM interceptor deployed around Moscow has an inherent ASAT capability against low-altitude satellites. The Sary-Shagan lasers may be capable of damaging sensitive components onboard satellites. Although weather and atmospheric beam dispersion may limit the use of ground-based laser ASATs, such systems would quite likely have the major advantage of being able to refire and therefore to disable several targets.

During the next 10 years, the Soviets are likely to retain their current ASAT-capable systems while moving aggressively ahead in developing and deploying new ASAT systems. Their large-scale ballistic missile defense research and development efforts in laser, particle beam, radio-frequency, and kinetic energy technologies may also soon provide them with significant ASAT capabilities.

The development of a space-based laser ASAT that can disable several satellites is probably a high-priority Soviet objective. The Soviets may deploy space-based lasers for antisatellite purposes in the 1990s, if their technological developments prove successful. Space-based laser ASATs could be launched on demand, or maintained in orbit, or both. By storing a

This unreliable system, which has failed in more than half of its tests, was declared operational by the Soviets in 1981. Our tests of a similar system relying on coorbital impact go back to the US Navy's Project Blackeye in 1961. We abandoned this technique in favor of a direct ascent system, which first became operational in 1964. The Soviet GALOSH ABM system, which the authors here again rightly acknowledge has an inherent ASAT capability, was not deployed until 1968. Our newest ASAT system, now ready for deployment, is the Vought Miniature Homing Vehicle, which would be launched by an F-15 aircraft at a height of over 100,000 feet and, using infrared sensors, would home in on a collision course with satellites at much higher orbits than those the Soviet ASAT system has occasionally been able to hit.

• Correct, and alarmists make much of it. The Soviets, for example, conducted 98 space launches in 1985, the US 17. However, the higher Soviet launch rate, according to our Defense Department "is necessitated primarily by the shorter system lifetimes and poorer reliability of most Soviet satellites." The average US photoreconnaissance satellite lasts for at least three years. The Soviet reconnaissance satellite lasts for no more than three weeks. Alarmists don't tell you about that. All of this is certainly expensive for the Soviets. That, along with the propensity of the authors to exaggerate, could account for the higher figures quoted in this book for the Soviet investment in space. Nevertheless, the Soviets must feel that they have no choice but to try to catch up with us. Consequently, on their behalf, the authors here promise future Soviet satellites whose, "lifetimes and survivability" are expected to increase.

laser ASAT in orbit, the Soviets could reduce the time required to attack a target. This option would decrease the warning time available to the target needed to attempt countermeasures. The Soviets are also developing an airborne laser whose missions could include ASAT, and limited deployment could begin in the early 1990s.

Space Operations

The Soviets operate about 50 types of space systems for military and civilian uses. These systems include manned and man-associated spacecraft; space stations; reconnaissance vehicles; launch-detection satellites; and navigational, meteorological, and communications systems.

The USSR conducts approximately 100 space launches annually. Some launches have put as many as eight satellites in orbit from one launch vehicle. The number of active, usable satellites the Soviets maintain in orbit has increased from about 120 in 1982 to about 150 in 1986.

At least 90 percent of the launches and satellites are military related and support both offensive and defensive operations. The USSR tries to mask the true nature of most of its space missions by declaring them as scientific. Because the 1967 Outer Space Treaty requires nations to register space launches with an agency of the United Nations, the Soviets acknowledge most of their space launch activity. Few details, however, are provided. The results and data of these missions are rarely published or disclosed except for some aspects of the manned program. Throughout, the Soviets steadfastly maintain they have no military space program.

The military emphasis is expected to continue in the years ahead. Of the approximately 200 operational Soviet satellites projected to be in orbit by the mid-1990s, about 150 will most likely have purely military missions, such as ocean reconnaissance, electronic intelligence, imagery reconnaissance, and special communications. Another 40 could support joint military-civilian functions, such as providing communications, navigation, and weather data. The manned program will fulfill both military and civilian missions. The approximately 10 remaining satellites could include interplanetary probes and other scientific missions.

The lifetimes and survivability of Soviet satellites are expected to increase in the next 10 years because of the incorporation of more sophisticated technology and the placement of satellites at higher altitudes. These moves would increase the satellites' fields of view and would make them less vulnerable to an ASAT attack.

Military Support From Space

Under cover of their COSMOS designator, the Soviets continue to develop and deploy space systems designed to support military operations on Earth. They now operate several types of space-based reconnaissance systems. Two of these, the radar ocean reconnaissance satellite and the electronic-intelligence ocean reconnaissance satellite, are used to locate naval forces that could be targeted for destruction by antiship weapons launched from Soviet platforms. The US has no comparable capability. Moreover, the Soviets actively practice their detection and targeting techniques, routinely launching these satellites to monitor both Soviet and NATO naval exercises.

The Soviets continue to expand an already mature satellite reconnaissance program. Several enhancements, such as incorporation of a data-relay satellite system, could improve the timeliness of their satellite reconnaissance data. Demonstrations of flexibility and versatility in launching and deploying their surveillance systems have continued, and the Soviets are capable of redirecting them for worldwide missions as situations dictate. Meanwhile, the satellite imagery reconnaissance capability has been refined, and space-based electronic-intelligence assets are being upgraded.

Deployment continues of the Soviet space-based global navigation satellite system known as GLONASS. This system will probably be capable of providing highly accurate positioning data to Soviet military and civilian users by the end of this decade. GLONASS is the Soviet version of the US NAVSTAR global positioning system (GPS). In fact, the Soviets acquired data on digital signal processing from GPS documents for inclusion in GLONASS. The GLONASS is being placed in a GPS-like orbit. Based on the 9 to 12 satellites announced for the system, GLONASS would have a worldwide, two-dimensional capability. If the Soviets want GLONASS to provide worldwide, three-dimensional navigation updates, they would need to orbit 18 to 24 satellites.

The Soviets are increasing the number and

• Such an act, by either superpower, would be tantamount to preparation for war, and could not be tolerated. Immediate demands would be made that it be withdrawn, or it would be immediately destroyed with all of the consequences that might ensue. This should drive home how the Soviets view our plans for a "defensive shield" in space.

• Have you noticed that everything is going to begin in the early 1990s? This is the fourth time in two pages of text that such promises were made. Next we shall have the "mid-1990s." What we seem to have established here is a permanent floating threat.

• The mirror image again. This is a good description of our own NAVSTAR Global Positioning System (GPS), the primary components of which are already operational in space, enabling the MX and TRIDENT II D-5 reentry vehicles to strike within 300 ft of their aim points.

• Well, that's more than it seems we've planned to do.

• This is the only reason why the US public learns what little it does about our own space launch capabilities, which are otherwise kept highly secret.

• The bulk of NASA's activities have always been military-related too, and today this agency is completely subordinate to the Department of Defense. All future shuttle flights are likely to be for military missions. Our space shuttle was primarily designed for this purpose.

• Another false denial. We launched our Naval Ocean Surveillance Satellite (NOSS), using active imaging radar, in December, 1977. We launched our Radar Ocean Reconnaissance Satellite (RORSAT) using improved radar, in April, 1983. In the intervening period we improved the system's imagery from a resolution of about one foot down to six inches. Under project White Cloud, we launched our ELINT Ocean Reconnaissance Satellite (EORSAT), which could record any signal broadcast on the oceans, in December, 1971. We have launched several improved systems since.

• Well, at least it has been refined to the extent that the Soviet commercial firm Soyuzkarta is now offering satellite photographs worldwide with resolutions as low as 6 meters, whereas the resolution of the French SPOT system is 10 meters, and that of the American LANDSAT system is only 30 meters. For the reason why the administration is reluctant to have photographs of higher resolution circulating, see the commentary on page 49. The current resolution of our own KH-11 satellite is less than one inch.

● Here is a remarkable assertion that the Soviets do not yet have this capability. We live in an age of instantaneous global communication. A television studio in Boston links up in "real time" with a television studio in Moscow—a city well beyond line of sight. The Olympics are televised live throughout the world. Are we to believe that radio cannot do what television does, even though its signals are much less complicated? One detects a certain caginess on the part of the authors, who undoubtedly remember that the Reagan administration took the position that it had no means of communicating directly or indirectly with Korean Airlines Flight 7 on the night of

● Our first space shuttle launch came in 1981. Once again, we are well ahead of the USSR.

● Our MIDAS (Missile Defense Alarm System Satellite), with infrared sensors to detect missile launches from rocket exhaust plumes, was launched into geosynchronous orbit in May, 1960.

● What sort of advantage would this be? Our satellites do not malfunction as often as Soviet satellites do, and don't need to be replaced as quickly. The main reason the Soviets need a robust space launch program is that the satellites they send up come back down so quickly. See commentary on page 53.

● Not really. The Saturn V was more powerful, with a takeoff weight almost half again as large as that of the SLW.

● If it really was possible, as the administration would have us believe, for the superpowers to build large directed-energy weapons and place them on battle stations in space, what would a small manned spacecraft be doing flying around in this kind of environment? How would it go about conducting "space station defense" when these beam weapons would be destroying each other with rapid bursts of energy, lethal over distances of thousands of kilometers, in a matter of seconds? Real Buck Rogers stuff.

variety of their communications satellites. They have filed their intent with the International Frequency Registration Board to place almost 100 individual communication payloads in more than 25 positions in the geostationary orbit belt. Some of the satellites are expected to be used to relay data between two ground sites, including ships, or between a satellite and ground sites. The Soviets demonstrated this capability by using a data-relay satellite to transmit television reports from the MIR (Peace) space station to the ground. By using such satellites, the Soviets would be able to communicate between ships, other satellites, and ground stations that are not within line of sight of each other. This technique increases the timeliness of these communications.

The Soviets will continue deploying their current launch-detection satellite network. They are probably working on a system for space-based detection of US submarine-launched ballistic missiles (SLBMs), as well as European and Chinese missile launches. Although the USSR's land-based ballistic missile defense radar network permits detection of SLBM launches, a space-based geosynchronous launch-detection satellite system could significantly increase warning time. The Soviets probably have the technical capability to deploy an operational satellite system by the end of the decade.

New Space Launch Systems

The success of the Soviet space program is due largely to its versatile and reliable inventory of space launch vehicles (SLVs) and to its space launch and support facilities. About every third day, the Soviets launch a satellite, using one of eight types of operational SLVs. The USSR's impressive ability to launch various boosters and to orbit payloads quickly would give the Soviets a distinct operational military advantage in any crisis. Most malfunctioning satellites could be rapidly replaced, and additional satellites could be launched to cover new or expanding crisis areas. Nonetheless, the use of vehicles and satellites in surge launches could have a negative short-term effect by reducing rapidly their total number of available launchers and satellites. The Soviets are already expanding their extensive family of SLVs with new expendable launch vehicles and reusable manned spacecraft. The expected deployment of the medium-lift Titan IIIC-Class SL-X-16, the heavy-lift Saturn V-Class SL-W, a

shuttle orbiter, and a space plane will increase the number and payload weight of satellites the Soviets will be capable of orbiting.

The SL-W heavy-lift vehicle will be used to launch the Soviet space shuttle orbiter. Launch pad compatibility testing of an orbiter attached to the SL-W vehicle may already have taken place, and a launch could come in 1987 or 1988. Soviet orbiter development has been heavily dependent on US orbiter propulsion, computer, materials, and airframe design technology. By using US technology and designs, the Soviets were able to produce an orbiter years earlier, and at far less cost, than if they had depended solely on their own technology. Money and scientific expertise could thus be diverted to other areas.

The location of the main engines at the base of the SL-W rather than on the orbiter gives the SL-W added versatility as a heavy-lift vehicle because it can launch heavy payloads other than the orbiter. The SL-W will be able to place payloads of over 100,000 kilograms into low Earth orbit, a figure comparable to the discontinued Saturn V. Potential payloads include modules for a large space station, components for a manned or unmanned interplanetary mission, and perhaps directed-energy ASAT and ballistic missile defense weapons.

The SL-X-16 booster is capable of placing a payload of more than 15,000 kilograms into low Earth orbit. This capability fills a gap in the current SLV inventory for an economical means of launching medium-weight payloads. A payload candidate for the SL-X-16 is the space plane, a different program than the space shuttle. A subscale version of this vehicle has been flight-tested in orbit and a full-scale version could be in production. This small, manned spacecraft could be used for quick-reaction, real-time reconnaissance missions, satellite repairs and maintenance, crew transport, space station defense, satellite inspection and, if necessary, negation. The SL-X-16 has been flight-tested, placing at least three payloads into orbit, and will soon be fully operational. The Soviets are not expected to launch the space plane until they have had sufficient experience with the SL-X-16. Testing of a full-scale space plane could begin in the late 1980s.

When these two systems become operational, the Soviets will have 10 types of expendable launch vehicles, 4 of which will be man-associated, and 3 different manned space ve-

(continued from above)

August 31, 1983, even if it had monitored the aircraft wandering off course, which it claimed it had not. In this way, the administration disclaimed any responsibility for its failure to warn the airplane back on course. In fact, any of those who did monitor Flight 7 that evening had only to pick up the telephone. Global radio and telephonic communications have been routinely relayed in real time by satellite since the fourth Early Bird was orbited in April, 1965. In addition to the fleet of INTELSATS and other civilian satellites, the US military keeps more than forty communications satellites of various kinds in orbit for the instantaneous relay of high frequency radio, telephone, television, or digital satellite imagery to ground stations all over the world.

hicles — SOYUZ-TM (an improved SOYUZ-T crew ferry vehicle), the shuttle, and the space plane. The combination of these systems will give the Soviets even greater versatility and redundancy to conduct and to augment military operations in space.

Manned Operations

Despite a minor setback in late 1985, the Soviets made considerable progress toward achieving a permanent, militarily significant, manned presence in near-Earth orbit during 1986. Although forced to curtail a manned mission on their SALYUT-7/COSMOS-1686 space station complex in November 1985 when one of their cosmonauts became ill, the Soviets still launched the core vehicle of a modular space station in February 1986. MIR, as designated by the Soviets, is an impressive advancement over SALYUT-7, having enhanced solar energy and electrical power systems, greater computer capabilities, and individual "cabins"

for crewmembers. Most significant, while SALYUT-7 had only two docking ports, MIR has six — one rear axial docking port, one forward axial port, and four forward lateral ports.

The MIR core vehicle is essentially a habitation and flight control center. Most of the cosmonauts' military and scientific work will take place in specially outfitted space station modules. These modules will provide the Soviets with greater flexibility in performing missions such as reconnaissance, targeting, and military-related R&D, as well as research in fields such as astrophysics, biology, and materials processing.

With the launch of MIR, the space station module, and SOYUZ-TM, the Soviets are well on their way to fulfilling their goal of establishing a permanent manned presence in space. The modular space station will probably house 3 to 12 cosmonauts. In the early-to-mid 1990s, the Soviets should be able to construct

These are exactly the missions for which we have been using our own space shuttle flights. The *Columbia*, for example, took remarkable radar images of the topographical structure *beneath* the Sahara Desert. It is likely that future US shuttle flights will be devoted more to military than nonmilitary research.

We could have done the same, had we chosen to do so. We did not choose to do so. In the 1970s, the US turned away from prolonged manned space flight. While we might still launch our own space station in the next decade, this is not a high priority on our military agenda. Our equipment in space is much more sophisticated than Soviet equipment, and can do pretty much what we want it to do without human supervision.

Note how much the Soviet shuttle represented here and on the following page resembles our own. Lest any readers be confused by this, and think that our shuttle design may have been inspired by the Soviet design, and that consequently the Soviets are ahead of us in some significant manner, they need only remember that our shuttle first flew in 1981, while the Soviet shuttle has not flown yet. Americans are not likely to learn what the Soviet shuttle really looks like until the Soviets release photographs of the completed vehicle, at which point there will no longer be any purpose in denying the public photographs we already have of whatever has been constructed.

Here is one prediction which came true. The Soviets flight-tested their heavy-lift launch vehicle, though without the shuttle, in May, 1987.

The first flight test of the heavy-lift launch vehicle, without the shuttle, may come in 1987.

Our Saturn V vehicle, ● which carried our *Apollo* lunar landing module in 1973, had 2,700,000 kg of lift-off weight and 3,400,000 kg of thrust.

One recalls rather a lot of ● publicity over the US lunar landings in the late 1960s and early 1970s. Did we dream up the entire program just to flaunt American technical prowess? Doubtful. Both nations have every right to be proud of their accomplishments in space. The Soviets, or course, have had failures rather more serious than the "minor setback" referred to on the previous page. They have had terrible tragedies, some comparable to our own *Challenger* disaster, and some much worse. The only reason the American public doesn't know about these failures is that our government, which certainly knows about them, doesn't publicize them. Doing so would undermine its claim that the Soviets are "ahead."

We were already doing this ● twenty years earlier.

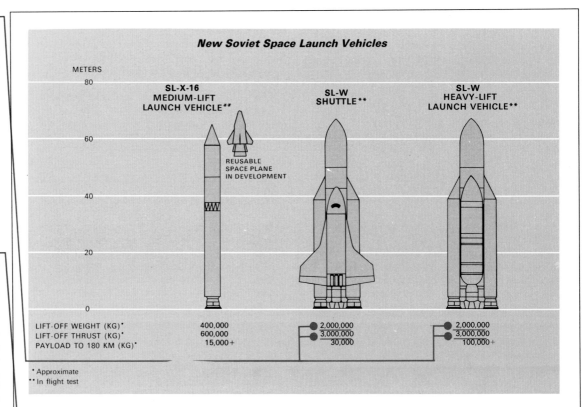

New Soviet Space Launch Vehicles

METERS

	SL-X-16 MEDIUM-LIFT LAUNCH VEHICLE**	SL-W SHUTTLE**	SL-W HEAVY-LIFT LAUNCH VEHICLE**
LIFT-OFF WEIGHT (KG)*	400,000	2,000,000	2,000,000
LIFT-OFF THRUST (KG)*	600,000	3,000,000	3,000,000
PAYLOAD TO 180 KM (KG)*	15,000 +	30,000	100,000 +

REUSABLE SPACE PLANE IN DEVELOPMENT

* Approximate
** In flight test

a very large modular space station. They have discussed ultimately housing up to 100 cosmonauts in this large space complex.

In March 1986, SOYUZ T-15 carried the first crew to MIR — mission commander Colonel Leonid Kizim and civilian flight engineer Vladimir Solovyov. These cosmonauts were in orbit for only 125 days, a short mission by Soviet standards, and they returned to Earth in July. Nonetheless, it was the most widely publicized Soviet manned space flight in 1986. Key events were often announced in advance and some events were televised live. These unprecedented developments were, in part, an effort to publicize Soviet accomplishments.

The mission was significant in an operational sense, however, because Kizim and Solovyov conducted the first manning and checkout of MIR, the initial use of a data-relay ● satellite to communicate with them, and the first station-to-station crew transfers. In early May, Kizim and Solovyov departed MIR aboard SOYUZ T-15 and docked with the SALYUT-7/COSMOS-1686 complex. After conducting numerous experiments and two sessions of ex-

travehicular activity, the cosmonauts returned to MIR in late June and to Earth in mid-July.

In other significant developments, the USSR announced that international crew visits to the MIR complex will start in the fall of 1987, beginning with a Syrian cosmonaut. A Frenchman and a Bulgarian are scheduled to visit MIR on separate flights during 1988, and the Soviets are evidently discussing similar missions with other countries. At least one such mission a year can be expected during MIR's lifetime.

The Soviet manned space program occupies a unique position in the USSR's space efforts. It is heavily publicized to demonstrate the ● peaceful nature and technological superiority of the USSR's space efforts. Visits to the Soviet space station by foreign cosmonauts and the long missions by Soviet cosmonauts have been reported with great fanfare in the nation's news media. Nonetheless, the Soviets have made a strong commitment to using the manned space program to accelerate their drive to achieve space superiority.

Soviet literature reports that the military

● What technological superiority? According to Dr. Robert Cooper, Director of our Defense Advanced Research Projects Agency, "We are clearly ahead of the Soviets in overall space technology." The Soviets cannot match the flight of our *Voyager*. They cannot match the capabilities of our satellites. While over the past decade they have averaged over 90 space launches each year, and we have averaged 22, both nations now have about 120 operational satellites in orbit. According to NASA Administrator James Beggs, the high Soviet launch rate demonstrates "a weakness rather than a strength. It means their satellites are less sophisticated than ours and require replacement more often. They don't have the life that ours do and they are not multi-purpose as many of ours are. This is not a numbers game. This is a capabilities game. We are more capable than they are in most areas and just as capable in many others. We also spend our space money more efficiently." In view of this, if the Soviets really were spending more money in space than we were, one could see why. See, as well, the commentary on page 50.

It is also an effort that is needed for precise navigation. Our NAVSTAR/GPS (Navigation System using Timing and Ranging) (Global Positioning System) satellites use atomic clocks with rubidium-atom oscillators accurate to within one-millionth of a second. Their UHF signals travel at the speed of light. A receiver, whether it is aboard a ship, an aircraft or a ballistic missile reentry vehicle, can measure its range from each NAVSTAR/GPS satellite by measuring the time lapse between the signal's transmission and its receipt. By triangulating its range from three such satellites simultaneously, the receiver may determine its own position in three dimensions to within ten feet, and its own velocity to within one-tenth of one mile per hour. That is how our MX warheads are able to strike within three hundred feet of their aimpoints. The Soviets have nothing like this level of accuracy, any more than they have such means of achieving it. The accuracy needed to aim directed energy weapons, however, would be even greater than this.

● An excellent photograph. Compliments to our National Reconnaissance Office— whose existence our government still does not acknowledge.

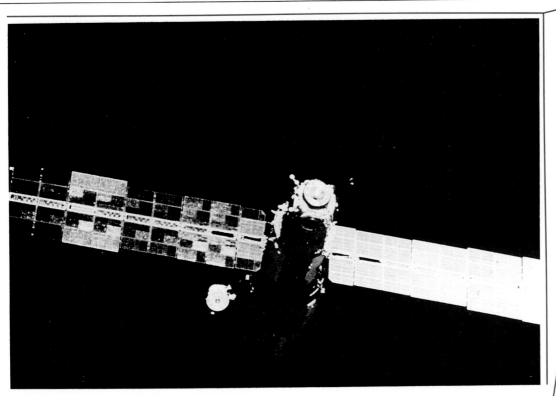

The MIR space station was launched in February 1986, providing the core-vehicle habitat and flight control center for a modular space complex.

● These are all areas in which our own astronauts have experimented and will continue to experiment in future shuttle flights. Every one of these is also an area in which we are years ahead of the Soviets.

applications of remote sensing, oceanography, meteorology, and geodesy have been the focus of repeated cosmonaut investigations. Even subjects such as astronomical observations, also performed by cosmonauts, have military uses. Such investigations, for example, can provide data useful for maintaining the orientation of certain equipment to an accuracy of a few arc-seconds, a capability needed to aim directed-energy weapons.

The ability to rendezvous and manually dock with uncooperative spacecraft, which Soviet cosmonauts demonstrated in 1985 and 1986, also has military applications. Cosmonauts use a laser rangefinder, a night vision device, and an optical sight while performing this operation. The Soviets state that this procedure will allow the rescue of cosmonauts stranded in orbit, but it could also be useful for repairing friendly satellites and for inspecting and disabling enemy satellites.

Conducting materials-processing experiments is an important cosmonaut function that has both civilian and military applications. Soviet efforts in this field, however, have concentrated on the production of substances with militarily significant applications regarding the development of semiconductor devices, infrared and optical detectors, and electro-optical systems.

Another crucial cosmonaut activity is Earth observation, which has implications for reconnaissance and targeting applications. The Soviets report that their cosmonauts have used visual observations, cameras, radars, spectrometers, and multispectral electro-optical sensors in their observations from SALYUT space stations. These experiments suggest the Soviets are evaluating their ability to locate, identify, and track targets from outer space as the first step toward designing a space weapons platform for use against targets in space and on Earth. Such a platform may eventually be used for ASAT and ballistic missile defense

● Shades of Buck Rogers again. You cannot simply dock with any spacecraft and board it. This is not the Barbary Coast. Hatches must be specifically designed and precision-engineered for compatibility with docking equipment. Any two nations will build docking ports of different dimensions and sizes, unless they do otherwise by prearrangement.

Eventually, Soviet radar will have some capability to distinguish moving objects from background "clutter," which is what is meant by a "look-down" capability. But they don't have it now and it will be quite some time before they do. In the chart on this page, the authors are trying to suggest that Soviet radar has already advanced to this point, by acknowledging that some Soviet radars do not have a look-

down capability, while pretending that others do. According to our own Department of Defense, even the radar dome aboard the Soviet Tu-126—the Soviet attempt at a counterpart to our E-2C HAWKEYE and E-3A AWACS airborne early warning radar aircraft—is "ineffective over land" and "marginally effective" over water. Our E-2C HAWKEYE, operating at an altitude of 30,000 feet, can track as

The MiG-31/FOXHOUND is one of the newest generations of supersonic interceptors with a look-down/shoot-down capability against aircraft penetrating at low altitudes.

At a fraction of the cost this administration is determined to continue wasting on its "defensive shield" in space, we could engage with the Soviets in a joint manned mission to Mars. That is the real road to a peaceful, safer world.

operations as well as for space station defense.

The most ambitious space goal the Soviets have set is a cosmonaut mission to Mars. To undertake such a mission, the Soviets would need to lift very heavy components into low Earth orbit and to assemble them there. The SL-W will give them that capability. They would have to sustain cosmonauts in orbit for at least a year. A manned mission to Mars is a major reason for the long stays Soviet cosmonauts

have undertaken on SALYUT stations. The cost of such a mission would be tremendous, but the Soviets would most likely expend the funds. Although very challenging, the Soviets could launch a manned mission to Mars in the first decade of the 21st century and probably could conduct a non-stop fly-by mission to Mars before the end of this century.

Space Program Costs

The high priority the Soviets are giving to their space program is reflected in the rapid overall growth of the program — a program that is absorbing a large share of the nation's most advanced and productive technology. Since 1980, the estimated dollar costs of the Soviet space effort have more than doubled, owing largely to programs for the manned space stations, new launch vehicles, supporting facilities, and the shuttle orbiter. The projected rate of growth in the space program, driven by the ambitious space-based manned program and future communications satellites, is expected to outpace overall trends in both military spending and GNP well into the future.

Air Defense

The USSR continues to modernize and expand what is already the most extensive strategic air defense network in the world. The

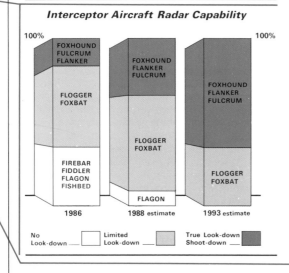

Interceptor Aircraft Radar Capability

100%   100%

1986: FOXHOUND FULCRUM FLANKER / FLOGGER FOXBAT / FIREBAR FIDDLER FLAGON FISHBED

1988 estimate: FOXHOUND FLANKER FULCRUM / FLOGGER FOXBAT / FLAGON

1993 estimate: FOXHOUND FLANKER FULCRUM / FLOGGER FOXBAT

No Look-down   Limited Look-down   True Look-down Shoot-down

As noted earlier, they are the only ones who need such a network, since we are the only ones with a strategic bomber force that threatens it.

(continued from above)

many as 300 separate targets at once, and can fully interpret 30 of them, measuring the dimensions of each, computing its altitude, speed and directional bearing and visually displaying this information in digital and alphanumeric form in the aircraft's operational center. Our E-3A AWACS, operating at 40,000 feet, can track as many as 600 targets simultaneously and can fully interpret more than 240

of them. Both of our aircraft have target detection ranges of more than 400 km. The Hughes AN/APG-63 radar aboard our F-15 EAGLE aircraft has a target detection range of more than 160 km, and can "look down" detect, identify and "lock on" to targets flying in ground clutter at speeds of Mach 2 and at altitudes of no more than 15 meters off the ground.

● Here is yet another small deception. To create the quick impression that the Soviets have more interceptor aircraft than we do, the authors have shown every possible type of aircraft the Soviets might use for air defense, while showing only those US aircraft specifically assigned to our Aerospace Defense Command. What gives the deception away is the term "North American" to describe US aircraft, and the inclusion of the Canadian CF-18. Thus, if questioned, the authors could assert that they meant only to represent those aircraft assigned to the defense of the North American continent. In fact, a number of other US aircraft would certainly play a role in

● Wrong. 740. ● Wrong. 650. ● Wrong. 1,300. ● Wrong. 1.13. ● Wrong. 2.2. ● Wrong. 930. ● Wrong. 4 AAMs. ● Wrong. 1,650.

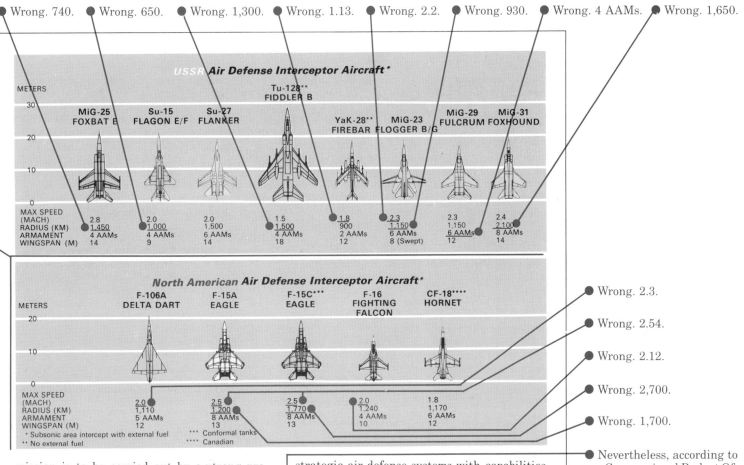

USSR Air Defense Interceptor Aircraft *

	MiG-25 FOXBAT E	Su-15 FLAGON E/F	Su-27 FLANKER	Tu-128** FIDDLER B	YaK-28** FIREBAR	MiG-23 FLOGGER B/G	MiG-29 FULCRUM	MiG-31 FOXHOUND
MAX SPEED (MACH)	2.8	2.0	2.0	1.5	1.8	2.3	2.3	2.4
RADIUS (KM)	1,450	1,000	1,500	1,500	900	1,150	1,150	2,100
ARMAMENT	4 AAMs	4 AAMs	6 AAMs	4 AAMs	2 AAMs	6 AAMs	6 AAMs	8 AAMs
WINGSPAN (M)	14	9	14	18	12	8 (Swept)	12	14

North American Air Defense Interceptor Aircraft *

	F-106A DELTA DART	F-15A EAGLE	F-15C*** EAGLE	F-16 FIGHTING FALCON	CF-18**** HORNET
MAX SPEED (MACH)	2.0	2.5	2.5	2.0	1.8
RADIUS (KM)	1,110	1,200	1,770	1,240	1,170
ARMAMENT	5 AAMs	8 AAMs	8 AAMs	4 AAMs	6 AAMs
WINGSPAN (M)	12	13	13	10	12

* Subsonic area intercept with external fuel
** No external fuel
*** Conformal tanks
**** Canadian

● Wrong. 2.3.
● Wrong. 2.54.
● Wrong. 2.12.
● Wrong. 2,700.
● Wrong. 1,700.

mission is to be carried out by a strong pre-positioned national air defense force established in peacetime according to a unified concept and plan. The leadership appears to be in constant search for the optimum organizational structure of the air defense assets.

Major organizational changes instituted in 1980 transferred control of air defense aircraft, SAMs, and radars from national air defense authorities to local military district commanders. This change was probably implemented to provide battlefield commanders with greater flexibility. Even after reorganizing, the Soviets appeared to be dissatisfied with their air defense structure.

More recent shifts are apparently resubordinating surface-to-air missiles and aircraft back to the national air defense forces. The rationale may involve a desire for greater centralized control over weapons rather than the flexibility of the local commander in making certain decisions.

The Soviets have deployed a large number of strategic air defense systems with capabilities against aircraft flying at medium and high altitudes. They are now in the midst of a major effort to improve their capabilities against aircraft and cruise missiles that operate at low altitudes.

This effort includes upgrading their early warning and surveillance systems; deployment of more efficient data-transmission systems; as well as development and initial deployment of new aircraft, associated air-to-air missiles, SAMs, and airborne warning and control system (AWACS) aircraft.

Currently, the Soviets have more than 9,000 strategic SAM launchers, nearly 5,000 tactical SAM launchers (excluding handheld), and some 10,000 air defense radars. Approximately 2,250 air defense forces interceptor aircraft are dedicated to strategic defense. An additional 2,100 interceptors assigned to Soviet Air Forces could be drawn upon for strategic defense missions. Collectively, these assets present a formidable defense barrier.

● Nevertheless, according to our Congressional Budget Office, 75 percent of all the bombers we flew to the Soviet Union would be able to penetrate Soviet air defenses and deliver their weapons to their targets.

● As noted above, additional US aircraft, including our carrier-based F-14s and F-18s, could be drawn on for strategic defense.

● Are the authors chuckling here? One of the reasons why the Soviets may be dissatisfied is that, somehow or other, their air defenses continue to be penetrated, whether by Korean Airlines Flight 7 or by Mathias Rust in his Cessna 172.

(continued from above)

defending our territory if it were attacked, including the Vought A-7s and F-4 PHANTOMs of our Air National Guard. The A-7 has a combat radius of 1,150 km. The F-4 has a combat radius of 1,600 km and is capable of a speed of Mach 2.43. These aircraft should have been included here, but they are missing, as is our own FA-18, as well as our carrier borne F-14 TOMCAT—whose combat radius is 1,600 km and whose speed is Mach 2.34. The Soviets have more aircraft assigned to the defense of their territory than we have to ours, although some Soviet aircraft like the MIG-29 are available only in small numbers. But the Soviets also have a larger territory to defend than we do, and most of all, a much larger threat to defend it against. Nor do the listed capabilities of the aircraft shown take into account the much greater maneuverability and higher load capacities of US aircraft, their more efficient ratios of thrust to weight, the much greater sophistication of their electronics, or the much higher levels of US pilot training and readiness.

As yet, Soviet fighter aircraft have neither look-down radar nor multiple-target engagement capabilities. See the commentary on page 58.

At present, they have fewer than 30.

The FLANKER may begin deployment by the end of this year at the earliest. Again, the authors are pushing things a bit with another premature deployment date.

So far, only a few FULCRUMs carry the AA-10, since the other aircraft is not yet deployed.

It appears to be only a very slight improvement over the primitive Tu-126 MOSS which preceded it. The Soviets are still using these aircraft to fill in gaps in their ground radar network.

Another premature deployment date. None of these is yet operational.

For air defense, but not for ballistic missile defense. The US has the world's most extensive system for that.

They would not stop most of our bombers. See the commentary on the preceding page.

See the commentary on pages 27 and 48.

Since Soviet missiles specifically designed for this purpose, like the GALOSH, have seldom been able to hit such targets in tests, it isn't too likely that a missile designed merely to hit aircraft is going to do any better.

Aircraft

The most capable Soviet air defense interceptor aircraft, the FOXHOUND, has a look-down/shoot-down and multiple-target engagement capability. Over 150 FOXHOUNDs are now operationally deployed at several locations from the Arkhangelsk area in the northwestern USSR to the Soviet Far East. Thus far, the FOXHOUND has been dedicated to homeland air defense. Two new fighters, the FLANKER and the FULCRUM, also have look-down/shoot-down capabilities and are designed to be highly maneuverable in air-to-air combat. The Soviets have deployed approximately 300 FULCRUMs to operational regiments in theater forces and are expected to introduce this aircraft into the homeland defense interceptor role in the future. They also have begun deploying the longer range FLANKER, both to strategic aviation and into air defense interceptor units in the USSR.

These three aircraft are equipped with three new air-to-air missiles. The FOXHOUND carries the long-range AA-9, and the FULCRUM and the FLANKER carry the medium-range AA-10 and the short-range AA-11. All can be used against low-flying targets.

The USSR also is deploying the MAINSTAY AWACS aircraft, which will substantially improve Soviet capabilities for airborne early warning and air battle management, especially against low-flying aircraft. The MIDAS, a tanker variant of the CANDID, is being introduced into the Soviet aircraft inventory and will be used in support of the strategic bombers and various air defense elements, including the new MAINSTAY.

Radars

The Soviets maintain the world's most extensive early warning system for air defense. It comprises a network of ground-based radars linked operationally with those of their Pact allies. As previously noted, more than 10,000 air surveillance radars provide virtually complete coverage at medium-to-high altitudes over the USSR and, in some areas, well beyond its borders. Three operational over-the-horizon radars for ballistic missile detection could provide additional long-range warning of the approach of high-flying aircraft. A new over-the-horizon radar under construction in the Far East will provide long-range detection of aircraft from the Pacific Ocean.

The USSR also has an active research and development program designed to improve its air surveillance network. In 1983, the Soviets began to deploy two types of air surveillance radars that will enhance Soviet capabilities for air defense, electronic warfare, and early warning of cruise missile and bomber attacks. The Soviets are also continuing to deploy improved air surveillance data systems that can rapidly pass data from outlying radars through the air surveillance network to ground-controlled-intercept sites and SAM command posts.

Surface-to-Air Missiles

Soviet strategic surface-to-air missiles provide low-to-high altitude barrier, area, and terminal defenses under all weather conditions. Five systems are now operational: the SA-1, SA-2, and SA-3, and the more capable SA-5 and SA-10. Over the years, the Soviets have continued to deploy the long-range SA-5 and have repeatedly modified this system. Further deployments and upgrades are probable in order to enhance the SA-5's capability to work with the newer SA-10. The even more capable all-altitude SA-X-12B/GIANT will soon become operational, thus further enhancing Soviet strategic defenses.

The SA-10 offers significant advantages over older strategic surface-to-air missile systems, including multitarget handling and engagement characteristics, a capability against low-

The SA-X-12B/GIANT, now in development, can intercept aircraft, cruise missiles, and tactical ballistic missiles and may have the potential to intercept some types of strategic ballistic missiles.

• The reason why these missiles would hit so few of our bombers is that we have gone to considerable expense to equip the bombers with highly sophisticated electronic countermeasures, capable of jamming or otherwise confusing missile homing mechanisms as well as ground acquisition and tracking radars. Aboard our B-52s you will find the Sanders Associates AN/ALQ-100 series of false target generators, which return signals at the identical frequencies being used by Soviet radars, but at a higher strength than the real returning signals, so that those are drowned out. This gives Soviet ground controllers the impression that the aircraft is either well ahead of its actual position or behind it. We have spent several billion dollars on equipment of this kind. We systematically monitor Soviet radio frequencies and signal strengths, noting any changes so that we may adjust our equipment accordingly. This is why most of our bombers could easily penetrate Soviet air defenses and fly on to hit their intended targets. The Soviet air defense network, in any case, is rapidly becoming obsolete,

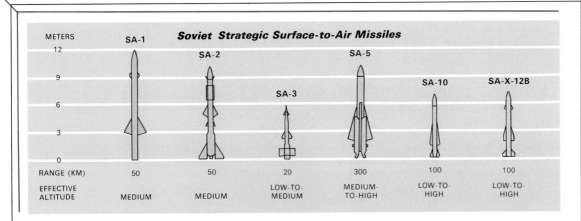

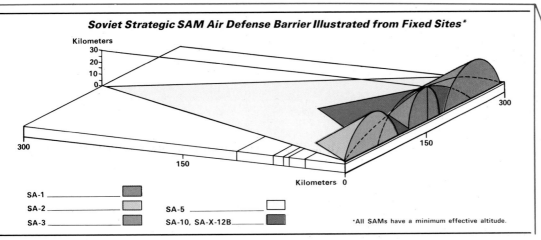

altitude targets with small radar cross-sections such as cruise missiles, a capability against tactical ballistic missiles, and possibly a potential to intercept some types of strategic ballistic missiles.

The first SA-10 site became operational in 1980. Over 80 sites are now operational and work is progressing on at least another 20 sites. Nearly half of these sites are located near Moscow. This emphasis on Moscow as well as the deployment patterns noted for the other SA-10 sites suggest a first priority on terminal defense of command-and-control, military, and key industrial complexes.

In keeping with their drive toward mobility as a means of weapons survival, the Soviets have deployed a number of mobile SA-10 systems. This version, designated SA-10b, could be used to support Soviet theater forces and to permit periodic changes in the location of SA-10 sites within the USSR to counter the various kinds of US retaliatory forces more effectively.

The Soviets also have begun deploying another important mobile SAM system, the tactical SA-12A/GLADIATOR, and are flight-testing an even more capable, longer range, higher altitude complement, the SA-X-12B/GIANT. The SA-12 missile system is capable of intercepting aircraft at all altitudes as well as cruise missiles and tactical ballistic missiles.

• As previously noted, the SA-X-12B may have the potential to intercept some types of strategic ballistic missiles. This SA-X-12B capability is a serious development because this system is expected to be deployed widely throughout the USSR. It could, if properly supported, add a measure of point-target defense coverage for a nationwide ABM deployment.

(continued from above)

61

now that we have deployed cruise missiles with ranges of 3,900 km. These missiles are much more difficult to shoot down than aircraft are. They have very small radar cross-sections, and they fly beneath the search lobes of most radars. The best way to find and destroy them is from above. But until the Soviets can develop an effective look-down radar for their aircraft, they will be almost defenseless against such weapons. The authors keep telling us the Soviets already have such radar, precisely so that they will not have to acknowledge that the entire Soviet air defense system is virtually obsolete.

You would have thought that Mathias Rust never would have been able to fly his Cessna 172 through all of this. And yet, it happened.

• The SA-10 is now being advertised with this capability, too. See the commentary on the preceding page.

This looks very much like
our own M-110 self-propelled
203 mm howitzer. For the reason why there is such a close
resemblance, see the commentary on page 6.

The important word here is "contiguous." It has been placed at the end of the sentence, however, so that the reader will gain a quick impression that the Soviets are prepared to fight on five separate continents. They are not so prepared, lacking the capability to project sufficient power for that purpose. The focus of their military planning is on operations across the Eurasian land mass. As for the two oceanic theaters of military operations, they are barely prepared at all. See the commentary on pages 8 and 9.

Chapter IV

Forces for Theater Operations

During a global war with the US and its allies, the Soviets are prepared to conduct large-scale offensive operations in the five continental and two oceanic theaters of military operations (TVDs) that are contiguous to the USSR or its Warsaw Pact allies. They are also prepared to conduct more limited operations in the other TVDs.

Despite their overwhelming superiority in numbers, the Soviets are concerned that fundamental changes in the nature of theater warfare, particularly in the crucial Western TVD opposite NATO's Central Region, may call into question their capability to attain victory by rapid offensive operations. These changes include:

- Growing technological sophistication and lethality of NATO conventional weapon systems, including aircraft and cruise missiles; armor and anti-armor; and artillery, missile, electronic warfare, and command, control, communications, and intelligence systems. The Soviets are especially concerned with emerging high-technology, deep-strike weapons that they refer to as "reconnaissance-strike complexes." They view the combination of emerging systems — the Joint Surveillance and Target Attack Radar System

The Soviet Union is proceeding with the development and deployment of new conventional deep-strike capabilities, including improved artillery. The 203-mm self-propelled gun, shown in foreground, has a range of 30 kilometers and is capable of firing nuclear rounds. The capabilities of this gun, together with even larger MRLs — including one in development that is about 280-mm — and 240-mm mortars, in background, demonstrate the Soviet drive to increase long-range firepower.

The Soviets do not have numerical superiority in most categories. They and their Warsaw pact partners have fewer combat troops, fewer major surface combatant ships, and fewer deliverable nuclear warheads than NATO. In those few categories where the Soviets have more equipment, as in numbers of tanks, this purported advantage is more than offset by the fact that there would seldom, if ever, be any place on the NATO battlefield where it could be brought to bear, as well as by NATO's immense qualitative advantages. NATO, for example, has many more advanced tanks than the Warsaw Pact has.

The technological sophistication and lethality of NATO's conventional weapons systems has been growing ever since NATO was formed in 1949.

Wrong. 18 km. Its US counterpart, our M-110A2 203 mm self-propelled howitzer, has a range of 35 km. With a rocket assisted projectile, it has a range of 40 km. Characteristically, the authors here endow a Soviet weapon with a capability only ours has. This reversal of truth occurs so frequently that you can almost predict what our newest weapons can do by paying close attention to what we say the newest Soviet weapons can do.

There is little similarity between our new AirLand Battle doctrine and Soviet doctrine, but then, there is little similarity between our new doctrine and any other doctrine. It is frought with contradictions. The AirLand Battle handbook, *US Army Field Manual 100-5,* acknowledges that we have arrived at an age of increasing sophistication and lethality on the battlefield, "when battle demands better and more effective command and control." At the same time, *Field Manual 100-5* emphasizes "securing and retaining the initiative and exercising it aggressively" as the primary mission of US forces. "To preserve the initiative," the *Manual* adds, "subordinates must act independently within the context of an overall plan.... They must deviate from the expected course of battle without hesitation.... They

---

Wrong. As yet, the Soviets have very limited look down radar capabilities. See the commentary on page 58.

This is a doctrine for public consumption. It is meant to imply that large waves of Soviet reinforcements would follow an initial Warsaw Pact attack. But the only follow-on forces we would see would be those which made up that initial attack, the major portion of which would have to follow *behind* the leading units due to the limited frontage available on the NATO battlefield.

Another mirror image, this time of our Multiple Launch Rocket System, (MLRS), which is far more capable and devastating. More than 300 units of our MLRS have now been deployed.

Almost true, but only for the newest models. The M-1976, for example, has a range of 27 km. Earlier versions of the 152 mm gun, like the D-1 and D-20, have ranges, respectively, of 12 and 18 km, and are still in service. Our M-198 155 mm howitzer has a range of 34 km.

Wrong. 18 km. See the commentary on the preceding page.

(continued from above)

(JSTARS), the Joint Tactical Fusion Program (JTFP), and the US Army's Tactical Missile System (ATACMS) — as having the potential to affect their offensive capabilities as a result of increased lethality. They believe these developments could extend devastating conventional strikes into the deep rear areas and to key theater targets such as command posts, logistics facilities, and follow-on forces.

- US and NATO development of deep-attack doctrines such as the US Airland Battle and the NATO Follow-on Forces Attack concepts. These developments are viewed by the Soviets as a reflection of NATO's determination to employ technologically advanced forces in offensive maneuvers and deep strikes to wrest the initiative away from the Warsaw Pact and carry the war into Pact territory. The Soviets interpret these emerging US and NATO doctrines as the equivalent of their longstanding doctrine of deep operations.

- A shift in the traditional Soviet expectation that a theater or global conflict would be of short duration. They now believe that both sides possess enormous military capabilities that cannot be rapidly destroyed, even in nuclear conditions; thus, they foresee prolonged theater campaigns. The operations may begin with a bitter struggle to seize the initiative, encompassing extreme destruction and mass casualties, and may spread to a multi-theater conflict.

To achieve victory under these conditions, the Soviets believe that forces equipped with large quantities of weaponry are required. These forces must be capable of attaining overwhelming superiority on the battlefield, coping with expected heavy losses resulting from attrition, and ensuring a continuous supply of fresh forces and equipment for prolonged theater operations.

The desire to be able to conduct high-speed, offensive operations despite NATO developments of deep-attack doctrines and supporting weapon systems is also influencing Warsaw Pact planning. Soviet planners now envision a combat environment with large-scale enemy ground offensives. They also expect that key rear area facilities will be subjected to large-scale attack by air forces, cruise missiles, and

---

"reconnaissance-strike complexes." To ensure their high-speed offensive capability, the Soviets are working on these developments:

- Enhancements in air and air defense capabilities to include deployment of late-model aircraft such as the FULCRUM and the FLANKER air superiority fighters. These aircraft are equipped with true look-down/shoot-down radar and advanced air-to-air missiles and can engage low-flying aircraft and cruise missiles. The Soviets are also deploying the highly mobile SA-11 surface-to-air missile (SAM) in large numbers in the ground forces. This system provides air defense against high-performance aircraft operating at low-to-medium altitudes as well as cruise missiles. The Soviets have also begun deployment of the SA-12A long-range mobile SAM system. This system provides defense against all types of aerodynamic vehicles, including cruise and some tactical ballistic missiles.

- Development and deployment of their own conventional deep-strike capabilities. Some of the more significant Soviet systems are:
  — The BM-27 220-mm multiple rocket launcher system, which can fire salvos of 16 rounds of high-explosive, improved conventional munitions (ICM), mines, or chemical rounds over a distance of 40 kilometers.
  — Highly accurate short-range ballistic missiles capable of delivering nuclear, chemical, high-explosive, or ICM warheads as well as mines. These missiles include the SS-21 system, now deployed in large numbers in Soviet and non-Soviet Warsaw Pact (NSWP) forces. It is very accurate and has a range of 80 to 100 kilometers. The SS-23, with a range of 500 kilometers and an accuracy similar to the SS-21, is also being deployed.
  — Tube artillery systems of increased range and accuracy which include late-model 152-mm towed and self-propelled (SP) versions with a range of 28 kilometers and 203-mm SP guns, with a range of 30 kilometers.
  — Long-range FENCER light bombers, which are continuing to be deployed in large numbers and which are ca-

---

will take risks and the command must support them." In fact, the *Manual* urges: "Our operations must be rapid, unpredictable, violent, and disorienting." The results of this advice may be too violent, unpredictable and disorienting for our own forces. Large numbers of men and vast amounts of equipment may be consumed for purposes which higher command never intended. The doctrine presupposes that aggressiveness will solve everything, when discipline, planning and precision are equally important. It weakens command and control, even while it acknowledges that these links must be improved. Essentially, it is nothing more than a military articulation of right wing brutishness. It is doubtful the Soviets take it very seriously. They have always known that we intended air strikes deep in their rear, because NATO has always planned for these.

There are few, if any, places on the NATO battlefield where the Soviets might achieve a sufficient concentration of forces to break through NATO's defense. "Overwhelming" superiority is an unattainable goal. We are not talking here of the open fields of France, across which the German *Panzer* divisions maneuvered so easily in 1940. We are talking of the middle of Germany itself. It is mountain-ous, densely forested terrain, laced with rivers. The attack across the North German Plain, which alarmists always envisage, is extremely unlikely. There are the Harz Mountains. There is the dense urban sprawl around Hannover. There is the Lüneberger Heath. These obstructions would make the rapid movement of armored forces impossible. The best the Soviets might do is attack along the Göttingen

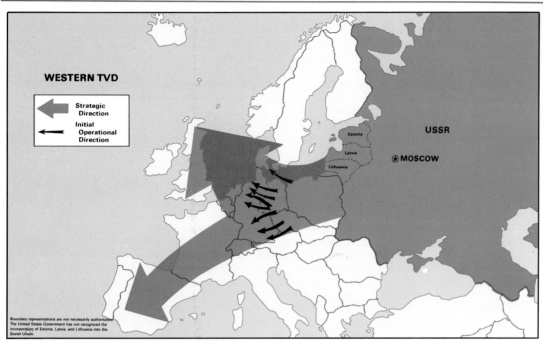

● Imagine opening a book and seeing the arrows going the other way, thrusting deep into the Soviet Union. The average American or West European reader would feel surprised and quite possibly indignant, finding it a complete misrepresentation of our intentions. That is how the average Soviet citizen would feel opening this book to this page. But this is powerful propaganda, immediately imprinting on our memory the vision of one possibility, without imprinting the reverse possibility, and so reinforcing allegations of Soviet intent made repeatedly, without any evidence to support them, in the first chapter of this book. Indeed, images like the ones below are so deeply ingrained in the American psyche that if the propagandists can ever be silenced, it will take several decades of raising clear-sighted new generations to erase all our artificial fears and suspicions of the USSR. This probably could not happen until major forces in our society shifted us away from the war economy which all this propaganda exists to sustain. Aside from the absence of any evidence that the Soviets even desire what is shown on these maps, they could never achieve it in any case. In this sense, the maps suggest an impossibility. See the commentary on the preceding page and on pages 17 and 19.

pable of penetrating deep into NATO airspace with a wide variety of precision-guided weapons.

● Continued development of the concept and capabilities for deep operations. Soviet theater war-fighting strategy is centered on deep strikes and offensive maneuvers to seize the initiative and shift the focus of theater operations deep into NATO's rear. This strategy involves an air operation including air, missile, and artillery strikes, as well as special operations forces strikes to gain nuclear and conventional fire superiority and paralyze the enemy's command and control. It would be complemented by a persistent ground advance supported by heavy firepower and exploited by Operational Maneuver Groups as well as airborne, airmobile, and amphibious forces attacking NATO's rear area.

● Emphasis on coalition warfare. The USSR's allies are significant components of Soviet military power in the Western and Southwestern TVDs opposite NATO's Central and Southern Regions, respectively. Under Soviet command in wartime, a result of the establishment of the

High Command of Forces in the TVDs, NSWP forces would be called upon to participate in and would be critical to the success of Soviet plans for early offensive operations within the TVDs. NSWP armies are generally well trained and well disciplined, but their willingness to support Soviet aggression against NATO territory, and forces capable of retalia-tion, is not a certainty. While equipped

● It is so far from a certainty that most NATO commanders believe Soviet forces are stationed in East European countries primarily to ensure internal order.

● More truisms and generalities.

Chapter IV Forces for Theater Operations

Corridor towards the Ruhr, through the Fulda Gap towards Frank-furt, or along the Hoff Corridor. But these corridors are narrow and do not allow for flanking movements. Advancing Warsaw Pact units could do nothing else but line up behind each other for the attack. This makes it virtually impossible to achieve the necessary ratio of superior force to break through the defense. The entire Northern and Central European front is only 725 km long. NATO has a full brigade to cover every 11 km of that front, and another brigade in reserve for every two brigades at the front. Reinforcements from Great Britain, France and the US would expand that force to the equivalent of 55 divisions before the first Warsaw Pact units could attack. It is simply too powerful a defense. Alarmists merely exploit public ignorance of these facts.

Most of the other Warsaw Pact nations have fewer than 100 T-72s. Older T-54s and T-55s make up the bulk of their tank inventories. Bulgaria, the German Democratic Republic and Romania still operate large numbers of World War II vintage T-34s.

In the air forces of all six of the other Warsaw Pact nations, there are fewer than 300 FLOGGER Gs. Czechoslovakia has just twelve FROGFOOTs and Hungary 15. The bulk of the remaining combat aircraft flown by these nations is made up of older MiG-21s and even older MiG-17s.

Had there been greater military potential in this technology, which we developed long before the Soviets did, we would have built more of these vehicles for ourselves.

There is no T-80. There is only a slight modification of the T-72, with no greater combat capability. See the commentary on page 6.

What this means is that almost half the Soviet tanks in Hungary are older models.

As noted earlier, our shipyards are outbuilding Soviet yards.

There is nothing particularly advanced about these aircraft. Their combat radius is only 250 km.

---

largely with older models of weapons and materiel, their ability to contribute to offensive operations is being improved by selective modernization of key components. This effort includes the acquisition of numerous late-model T-72 tanks and the enhancement of their large T-55 fleet with armor upgrades, better fire control systems, and improved automotive characteristics. Late-model aircraft such as the FLOGGER G, FROGFOOT, and FITTER K are also being acquired.

Regional Trends

NATO Europe

Soviet forces in the three TVDs facing NATO Europe (the Northwestern, Western, and Southwestern) are the most numerous and modern of the Soviet theater forces. This emphasis reflects Soviet assessments that the decisive arena of conflict between the US/NATO and the USSR/Warsaw Pact will take place on the European Continent, particularly in the Western TVD. In that TVD, the large ground force structures continue to receive the highest priority for modernization. For example, the deployment of the Soviets' newest tank, the T-80, proceeds at a high rate. More than 1,500 of them have been assigned to units. Nearly 75 percent of the 19,000 Soviet tanks in the theater are T-64/72/80 models.

Moscow continues to enhance its conventional and nuclear fire support. In 1985, the Soviets deployed their first SS-23 brigade to the Western TVD. Moreover, the SS-21 is replacing the FROG at division level. Virtually all of the approximately 130 SS-21 transporter-erector-launchers now deployed have been assigned to the Western TVD. About 100 are forward deployed with the Soviet and NSWP forces in East Germany and Czechoslovakia.

Air defense improvements include the first deployment of the SA-12A system. The SA-11 continues to be deployed and is replacing the SA-4 system in army-level SAM brigades.

The flanking Northwestern and Southwestern TVDs, which are oriented against NATO's Northern and Southern Regions, have lower priority for modernization. In the Southwestern TVD, tank modernization is nonetheless proceeding in Soviet forces in Hungary and the southern USSR. Well over half the Soviet tank inventory in the TVD comprises T-64/72 mod-

els. Bulgaria is also undergoing an ambitious program to upgrade its forces with the T-72 and an upgraded T-62.

The structure and operations of the Baltic Fleet as well as that of the Black Sea Fleet and the Caspian Flotilla, are heavily influenced by their relatively small primary operating areas. The Soviets continue to construct modern patrol combatants as well as air-cushion and wing-in-ground (WIG) effect craft that are well suited to operating in these restricted waters.

The Soviets lead the world in the production and utilization of military air-cushion vehicles (ACVs). A POMORNIK-Class amphibious version, the largest naval ACV ever built, has joined the Baltic Fleet, and additional units are under construction. These ACVs will add a significant dimension to the Soviets' capability to conduct amphibious operations in Eurasian coastal areas. Additional units of the AIST-Class ACV are also being produced. Another ACV, the PELIKAN-Class, is probably under construction in the Black Sea area and is apparently designed for a coastal minesweeping role.

The Soviets are also continuing to investigate various WIG designs. The ORLAN-Class WIG is designed primarily for amphibious operations. Units will quite likely be assigned to the Black Sea or Baltic Fleets, where their troop capacity and high speed could be used effectively in amphibious operations. An anti-surface warfare version WIG is also expected.

In the Baltic Sea, construction of the SOVREMENNYY- and UDALOY-Class guided-missile destroyers proceeds. The ninth SOVREMENNYY was launched in early 1987 while the ninth UDALOY was being fitted out.

In early 1986, a squadron of FENCER E fighter-bomber reconnaissance variants was delivered to the Baltic Fleet Air Force — the initial deployment of the FENCER within Soviet Naval Aviation. Although mainly for maritime reconnaissance, the FENCER E can be armed with a variety of air-to-surface ordnance.

In the Black Sea, the second SLAVA-Class guided-missile cruiser became operational in 1986 and the fourth KIEV-Class guided-missile aircraft carrier commenced sea trials. The first of a new class of aircraft carrier built at the Nikolayev shipyard began fitting out. A second is under construction. The new carrier's air wing will quite likely include at least 45 advanced vertical and/or short takeoff and land-

---

The authors here rely on a series of exaggerations which have been hammered into the common wisdom over time. The Soviets do not have anywhere near as many as 19,000 tanks in their Western TVD. They have, at most, 8,550 tanks assigned to front-line divisions stationed in Eastern Europe, including these tanks. They could not bring into Europe more than 18,230 tanks from all their TVDs, even after four months of mobilization and reinforcement. The entire Soviet production to date of T-64 and T-72 tanks, including the "T-80" variant, is 16,870. Some of these tanks have been exported. Others are assigned to Soviet units outside the Western TVDs.

ing (VSTOL) aircraft as well as antisubmarine warfare (ASW) and reconnaissance helicopters. It will be equipped with modern surface-to-air missiles, multiple Gatling guns, and possibly antiship missiles.

In this fleet's air force, a missile air regiment previously equipped with the BADGER was reequipped with the BACKFIRE C. This assignment was the first of the newest BACKFIRE variant with a slightly improved range within Soviet Naval Aviation.

Developments in the Northern Fleet have consisted mainly of upgrades to its imposing force of both strategic and general-purpose submarines. In addition to two new classes of nuclear-powered ballistic missile submarines, it is receiving new general-purpose submarines. Improved propulsion, sensor, and conventional and nuclear weapon systems, in combination with advances in submarine quieting techniques, have provided the Soviets with more formidable antisubmarine and antisurface warfare assets than were previously available.

The second unit of the SIERRA-Class of nuclear-powered attack submarines (SSNs) is on sea trials. The MIKE SSN will quite likely be used for R&D and testing of advanced submarine systems. OSCAR-Class nuclear-powered cruise missile submarines (SSGNs) continue to be built, and the fourth unit began sea trials in 1986. The Northern Fleet received two modern KILO-Class diesel attack submarines during 1986, the first to join this Fleet. The KILO is a quiet, medium-range, diesel-electric submarine well suited for patrols in coastal and open-ocean waters. Construction of the KILO continues at three shipyards, and additional units are certain to join the western Soviet fleets as well as selected NSWP navies. To date, Poland and Romania have each received one KILO.

Since 1978, the Soviets have dismantled 15 YANKEE-Class SSBNs. Three of the dismantled YANKEEs have been reconfigured as unique units — two SSNs and an SSGN. The Soviets are beginning series conversion on the reconfigured class of YANKEE SSN.

The Soviet Air Force in the Western Theater of War opposite all of NATO Europe has been substantially altered over the past decade to enhance its deep-strike capability. The long-range FENCER fighter-bomber has been the most important element of this capability. The recent introduction of the long-range

FLANKER air superiority fighter into Soviet forces adds an entirely new escort force for attacks into NATO's rear areas. FENCER aircraft continue to be produced, with further enhancements being incorporated over time.

The smaller, shorter range FULCRUM counterair fighter also continues to join tactical air force units, replacing the older, much less capable FLOGGER-series aircraft. The FULCRUM incorporates a high-visibility cockpit, good maneuverability, and new-design weapons and fire control systems. Within the last year, two Soviet regiments in East Germany converted to the advanced FULCRUM. The pace of the conversion demonstrates the Soviet commitment to reequipping their forces with sophisticated fighters. Seven Soviet Air Force regiments now have FULCRUMs operationally assigned, five of which are located in the west opposite NATO. One Soviet regiment, located in Hungary, began equipping with the FULCRUM during 1986.

Soviet Air Force tactical force structure emphasis, however, has been shifting from air superiority toward ground-attack roles. The number of theater and front-level ground-attack regiments opposite NATO has increased from 26 to 43 since 1978, while the number of fighter-interceptor units has declined by 14 percent. Continuing current practice, the Soviet fighter pilots are training for both a counterair and a secondary ground-attack role. Secondary ground-attack mission training is also expected

Strategic Direction
Initial Operational Direction
Likely Axis

USSR

Estonia
Latvia
Lithuania

NORTHWESTERN TVD

Boundary representations are not necessarily authoritative. The United States Government has not recognized the incorporation of Estonia, Latvia, and Lithuania into the Soviet Union.

● The Soviets are building these submarines in very small numbers. They are not nearly as quiet as ours. See the commentary on page 81.

● These developments have no effect on the military balance in the air. US and other NATO aircraft are far more capable. See the commentary on pages 59 and 78.

● As the Soviets change their tactics, they must change the type of aircraft suited to them. Most Soviet aircraft are designed only to perform a single role, while most NATO aircraft perform multiple roles. NATO has the greater flexibility.

So far, such variants have not been deployed. The aircraft remain restricted to a single role.

Sea-denial operations could be conducted much more easily against the Soviet Pacific Ocean Fleet. See the commentary on page 9.

This creates the impression that the Soviets have forcibly occupied Etorofu *without* Japanese consent. Their deployment of additional aircraft here follows a reassessment of gaps found in their air defense system by Korean Air Lines Flight 7. Note that this satellite photo is carefully credited to the French firm of SPOT. For the reason why the authors of this book have switched from military to commercial satellite photography, see the commentary on pages 20 and 49.

to be given to FULCRUM and FLANKER pilots. The FLANKER and FULCRUM should be reasonably effective in ground attack as well as air combat if the crews are adequately trained. Ground-attack variants of FULCRUM and FLANKER may be developed and deployed in the near future.

Far East

The Far Eastern Theater of War encompasses the continental Far East TVD directed against China as well as the Pacific Ocean TVD aimed mainly at the US and Japan. It is second in priority for the Soviet planner after the Western Theater of War.

The Pacific Ocean Fleet is a well-balanced naval force that includes considerable strategic strike, antisurface, and antisubmarine warfare assets. Its primary wartime mission is to be prepared to conduct strategic strikes. To accomplish this mission, the fleet has to protect its ballistic missile submarines by establishing and maintaining control of contiguous sea areas, including the Sea of Okhotsk, the Sea of Japan, and the Western Bering Sea. Protecting these sea areas would be crucial to the seaward defense of the Soviet Far East, particularly

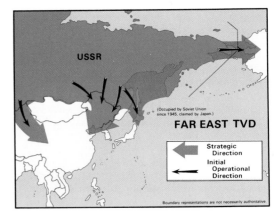

its important naval bases, from sea-based attack. To support sea control efforts, the Pacific Ocean Fleet would conduct sea-denial operations out to hundreds of nautical miles from the shore.

Since November 1985, three new principal surface combatants were transferred to the Pacific Ocean Fleet. These ships were a KIROV-Class nuclear-powered guided-missile cruiser, a SOVREMENNYY-Class guided-missile destroyer, and an UDALOY-Class guided-missile

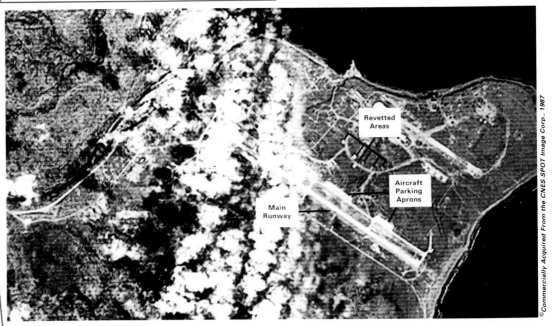

The Soviets have modernized their military capabilities on the Japanese Northern Territories island of Etorofu with the deployment of MiG-23/FLOGGERs.

©Commercially Acquired From the CNES SPOT Image Corp., 1987

destroyer — the first of their classes to be assigned to the Pacific Ocean Fleet. Their assignment to the Fleet upgrades the Soviet capabilities in antisurface and antisubmarine warfare (ASW) and the transfer of additional units of each class will continue to enhance these capabilities. As many as two KIROV cruisers, five SOVREMENNYYs, and four UDALOYs may eventually be assigned to the Fleet.

The second AKULA-Class nuclear-powered attack submarine began sea trials, and the eighth KILO-Class diesel-powered attack submarine designated for Soviet use was launched in 1986. Following sea trials, both are expected to join the Pacific Ocean Fleet. The KILO has the potential to become a popular export submarine to Third World nations, as already evidenced by the sale of a KILO to India.

A sea-based combat helicopter, the HELIX B, is now entering Soviet Naval Aviation and could be used with Soviet Naval Infantry units in the Pacific Fleet. Its primary functions are the delivery of precision-guided weapons and target designation. It can be deployed aboard the IVAN ROGOV-Class ships or other helicopter-capable combatants. The air assault and fire support features of the HELIX B will improve Soviet capabilities for conducting amphibious operations.

The Soviet Navy has maintained a continuous presence in the Indian Ocean since 1968, primarily to support the USSR's foreign policy and to counter Western navies operating in the region. Soviet naval force levels peaked in the region in 1980 in response to the Iranian and Afghan crises, but since then Soviet naval activity in the Indian Ocean has steadily declined to its mid-1970s level. This decline is due largely to the change in regional tensions affecting the US and USSR.

The Soviets began deploying naval forces to the South China Sea in 1979 as Sino-Vietnamese relations deteriorated into open border conflict. Cam Ranh Bay quickly became the focus of Soviet activity in the South China Sea and is now the site of the largest concentration of Soviet naval units and aircraft deployed to a naval facility outside the Warsaw Pact. This concentration includes submarines with supporting surface combatants and a composite naval air unit of BADGER strike and combat support aircraft, BEAR D reconnaissance and BEAR F antisubmarine aircraft, and an

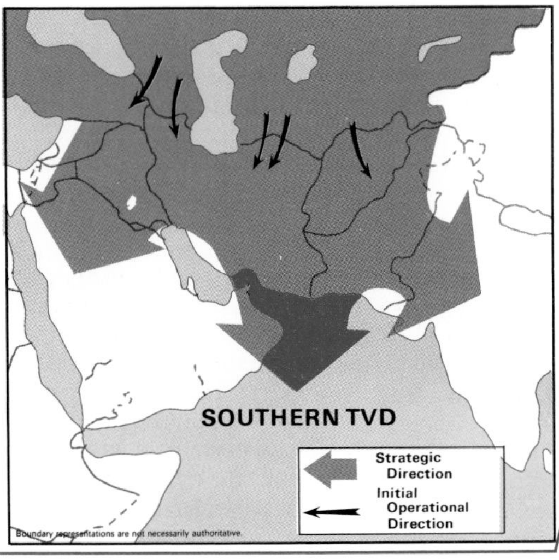

SOUTHERN TVD

Strategic Direction
Initial Operational Direction

Boundary representations are not necessarily authoritative.

air defense force of FLOGGERs. Cam Ranh Bay-based operations include intelligence collection against China and US naval activity in the region. Construction work indicates the Soviets view Cam Ranh Bay as a permanent installation that now serves as their most significant forward base in the South China Sea area.

Ground and air forces in the Far East during 1986 maintained the pattern of incremental growth and selective equipment modification established during the past 10 years. Soviet ground units on the Chukotsk Peninsula opposite Alaska continue to be expanded and reorganized into a coastal defense division. Ground forces on the Sino-Soviet border and in Mongolia are expanding, modernizing, and improving their readiness and sustainability. General Secretary Gorbachev's July 1986 Vladivostok speech offered the possibility that some Soviet forces would be withdrawn from Mongolia. It may reflect confidence that their forces and capabilities have been built up to such an extent that limited withdrawals can be made with little risk to overall military capabilities. As was also noted in the Western TVD, the air force structure in the Far East has been reconfigured to emphasize deep-strike operations. The number of ground-attack regiments has increased from 15 to 21 since 1978.

Southwest Asia

Forces in the Southern TVD are oriented against Southwest Asia, including Iran,

Chapter IV Forces for Theater Operations

This is one more effort to update the Soviet tank threat. That threat suffered a serious setback when it was discovered that a new Soviet "T-80" tank, which the administration had promised would pose a major threat to the West, did not exist. All that developed was a minor modification to the T-72. Another setback occurred when the Israelis released photographs showing the holes their tanks had blown through Syrian T-72s. A further setback occurred when experts revealed that the armor on the glacis plate of our old M-60 tank is 250mm thick while the heaviest frontal armor on the T-72 is 210mm thick. Alarmists had somehow to resurrect the threat, so they published this photo of the Soviet T-72, whose sideskirts make it what the administration calls the "T-80," draped with reactive armor, and Army General Robert J. Sunell told *The New York Times* that Soviet use of reactive armor "seriously changes the military balance. We've put too many of our eggs into such missiles as the TOW, and now we have a threat they will not meet." In fact, reactive armor, invented by the Israelis and tested in the US long before the Soviets began using it, has only a limited effect in dispersing the energy of man-portable

That is all they can do. It is all the Wehrmacht could do in the Balkans. It is all the British can do in Northern Ireland. It is all the French could do in Algeria and all the US could do in Vietnam. It is all we will ever be able to do in Central America, if we insist upon doing it.

Nevertheless, other such units are there, and count in the force total cited here.

If this were true, the administration would prove it by identifying the units in question. It has not done this.

This is true only of Soviet divisions stationed in Eastern Europe, and it may not be true even of all of them.

Afghanistan, Pakistan, and eastern Turkey. This theater currently has low priority for Soviet planners. Most of the developments center on the Soviet army in Afghanistan. After 7 years of combat, Soviet forces remain relatively limited in number and mission. Instead of seeking a direct military victory over the Mujahideen, the Soviets have focused on securing urban areas and lines of communication, while conducting mobile search-and-destroy operations against selected resistance forces.

The war itself is deadlocked. In an effort to change the situation, the Soviets have equipped their forces with the latest infantry fighting vehicles, heavy artillery, armored helicopter gunships, and close air support fixed-wing aircraft. In his Vladivostok speech, Gorbachev announced an intention to withdraw six regiments from Afghanistan. In October 1986, the Soviets, with much publicity, withdrew some forces. The actual withdrawal operation, however, was a sham. It consisted largely of forces such as tank and air defense units that are of little use in Afghanistan. Indeed, some of the units withdrawn were introduced into the country shortly before October for the purpose of the pullout. Soviet forces in Afghanistan now consist of about 116,000 personnel.

In this theater, Soviet tactical aviation has grown from about 540 aircraft in 1978 to 700 today. Reflecting trends observed in other theaters, ground-attack regiments have increased from 3 to 11. One fighter regiment is equipped with the FULCRUM.

Ground Force Developments

Reflecting its position as a continental land power, the USSR has traditionally fielded large, well-equipped ground forces. Current Soviet theater war-fighting concepts stress the need to expand and modernize these forces.

A typical Soviet tank division has raised its artillery and armored personnel carrier (APC)/infantry fighting vehicle (IFV) holdings 87 and 73 percent, respectively, since 1976. Division personnel strength has grown 17 percent, while

The box-like appendages around the turret of this T-80 tank are reactive armor. Exploding reactive armor dissipates the force of incoming antitank rounds, further protecting against the West's antitank capabilities.

(continued from above)

antitank rockets, like the US M-47 DRAGON or the Soviet RPG-7, and some types of high explosive tank ammunition. It would have no effect against the depleted uranium shells of our GAU 8/A 30mm gatling gun mounted on our A-10 aircraft, our air-delivered Rockeye cluster munitions, our Copperhead laser-guided artillery projectile, or any of the heavier antitank missiles, including the TOW, which make up the bulk of NATO's inventory of such weapons. Among our most effective antitank weapons is the tank gun. The *Times* article suggests that "reactive armor can be beaten" only by projectiles that travel a mile a second, and asserts that such projectiles only became available a few years ago with the advent of the smooth-bore 120mm tank gun. However, the standard NATO M-68 105mm tank gun, in service for decades, has long been equipped with several types of ammunition which travel a good deal faster, including the M-774 and M-833 projectiles. These weapons will continue to pose a devastating threat to Soviet tanks, with or without reactive armor, as will the TOW missile, whose warhead, on impact, creates a thick jet of molten copper moving at 27,000 feet per second.

tank holdings — more than 300 tanks — have remained constant. In motorized rifle divisions, APC/IFV and artillery holdings have increased 44 and 57 percent, while personnel has grown 12 percent. Tank strength, at approximately 250, has held steady. In the 1980s, two more artillery divisions have formed, and the number of non-divisional artillery brigades and regiments increased 20 percent. Many artillery units are expanding from 54-gun regiments to 96-gun brigades. Additionally, seven air assault brigades formed.

The Soviet Ground Forces now consist of 211 active and 5 inactive mobilization-base divisions. Of the active divisions, 150 are motorized rifle, 52 are tank, 7 are airborne, and 2 are organized for static defense. Two additional formations have been expanded into Unified Army Corps. These corps are about twice the size of divisions and are well suited to function as Operational Maneuver Groups to execute deep operations in the enemy rear area.

During peacetime, Soviet forces are maintained at varying levels of readiness. Forty percent of the divisions are kept at what the Soviets consider ready levels — that is, manned at 50 percent or higher of wartime authorized strength. The remaining divisions are considered not ready and are manned at a level below 50 percent. Upon implementation of their na-

tional mobilization plan, these divisions could be brought to full wartime manning levels in about a week. The divisions would, however, require time to train the newly mobilized re-

240-mm mortar (top), 152-mm howitzer

● Again, only in Soviet divisions stationed in Eastern Europe.

● The Soviets have a total of 185 divisions. See the commentary on page 17.

● No photograph is shown of this weapon, because there are so few to photograph.

● To appreciate how low these levels of readiness are, see the commentary on page 19.

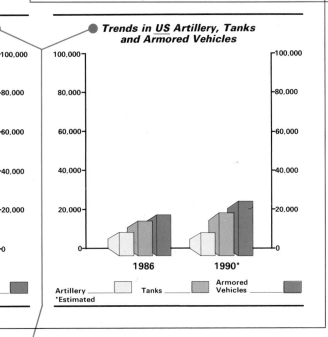

Trends in Soviet Artillery, Tanks and Armored Vehicles

Trends in US Artillery, Tanks and Armored Vehicles

Artillery | Tanks | Armored Vehicles
*Estimated

71

Chapter IV Forces for Theater Operations

● There are several distortions in these charts. First of all, they should compare NATO equipment holdings with those of the Warsaw Pact, rather than US and Soviet holdings. NATO, for example, has a total of 35,000 tanks; not merely the 15,000 US tanks shown here. While the Soviets do have the number of tanks shown here, they could only bring into battle in Central Europe a total of 18,230 tanks. NATO, as a whole, could bring in more tanks than that—a total of 18,717, though the Warsaw Pact, as a whole, could bring in a total of

24,523 tanks. Static comparisons of equipment in inventory have no significance. Comparisons of equipment which could actually be engaged in combat have some significance. But if static comparisons are going to be used, then we ought to get them right. The US, in addition to its 15,000 tanks, is not going to have 24,000 other armored vehicles in 1990. We have that number now. The Soviets do not now have 78,000 armored vehicles as shown. They have 56,000. The projections for Soviet inventory four years hence are absurd.

Currently deployed with Soviet Army units are about 2,000 of the 2S1, 1,300 of the 2S3; 1,000 of the 2S5; 1,200 of the M1976; 200 of the 2S7; and about 80 2S4s. The Soviets still field a number of older artillery types, including the 180mm and 130mm guns. Few of these are nuclear-capable, and most are obsolete. See the commentary on page 43.

Wrong. 27,000.

Wrong. 18,000.

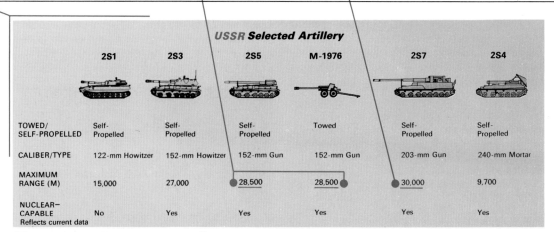

	2S1	2S3	2S5	M-1976	2S7	2S4
TOWED/ SELF-PROPELLED	Self-Propelled	Self-Propelled	Self-Propelled	Towed	Self-Propelled	Self-Propelled
CALIBER/TYPE	122-mm Howitzer	152-mm Howitzer	152-mm Gun	152-mm Gun	203-mm Gun	240-mm Mortar
MAXIMUM RANGE (M)	15,000	27,000	28,500	28,500	30,000	9,700
NUCLEAR–CAPABLE	No	Yes	Yes	Yes	Yes	Yes

USSR Selected Artillery

Reflects current data

Wrong. 30,000.

Wrong. 35,000-40,000.

Wrong. 34,000.

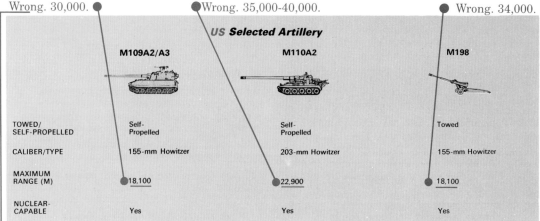

US Selected Artillery

	M109A2/A3	M110A2	M198
TOWED/ SELF-PROPELLED	Self-Propelled	Self-Propelled	Towed
CALIBER/TYPE	155-mm Howitzer	203-mm Howitzer	155-mm Howitzer
MAXIMUM RANGE (M)	18,100	22,900	18,100
NUCLEAR–CAPABLE	Yes	Yes	Yes

This is close to the true figure. How careless, then, to exaggerate that figure so much in the bar charts on the preceding page. One of the major hazards of lying has always been the difficulty of being consistent.

The 203-mm 2S7 self-propelled gun can fire nuclear and conventional rounds to a range of at least 30 kilometers.

servists. <u>The preparation of these troops for offensive operations could be accomplished in less than 60 days.</u>

Airborne divisions consist of three parachute regiments and supporting arms and services. Each parachute regiment has over 100 BMD armored vehicles, giving them excellent mobility, firepower, and protection.

Soviet Ground Forces also have an extensive array of non-divisional units, including tactical surface-to-surface missile (SSM), artillery, and air defense. Overall, the force contains over 53,000 main battle tanks, 59,000 APCs/IFVs, 29,000 artillery pieces, about 11,000 mortars, 7,000 multiple rocket launchers (MRLs), 4,800 SAM launchers (excluding the thousands of SA-7, -14, and -16 handheld systems), 12,500 antiaircraft artillery (AAA) pieces, 1,600 SSM launchers, 4,400 helicopters, and more than 2 million personnel. In peacetime, the force is subordinate to the 16 military districts in the USSR, 4 groups of forces in Eastern Europe, and an army each in Afghanistan and Mongolia. Airborne forces not in Afghanistan are subordinate to the airborne headquarters in Moscow. In wartime, the Soviets can field 27 combined arms and tank armies and 10 army corps (small armies, not including the 2 Unified Army Corps).

Wrong. Not before 120 days. See the commentary on page 19.

Again, several US artillery types, including the M-101, the M-102 and the M-114, are not included in this chart. The purpose of representing fewer US types, of course, is to make the US look weaker. The US hasn't as many guns as the Soviets have, but all of the US guns are superior in range, accuracy and rate of fire to their Soviet counterparts. In all, the US has about 5,500 guns and howitzers, including the M-101, M-102 and M-114. We have about 2,200 M-109s and 1,000 M-110s. About 500 M-109s and 500 M-110s are deployed with US forces in Europe, where another 1,500 of these weapons are deployed by our NATO allies. NATO would bring into battle about 20,000 major artillery pieces of all types.

Wrong. 30 MT.

Wrong. ● 1,400 mps.

Wrong. 780 mps.

Wrong. 60 kph.

There is no such tank. There is only a variant of the T-72, which looks like this. See the commentary on page 6.

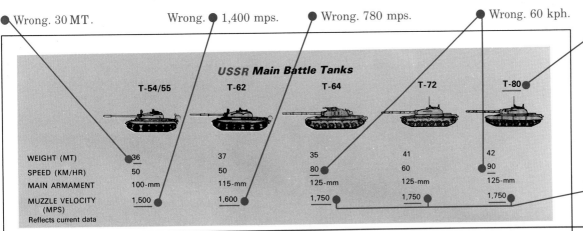

USSR *Main Battle Tanks*

	T-54/55	T-62	T-64	T-72	T-80
WEIGHT (MT)	36	37	35	41	42
SPEED (KM/HR)	50	50	80	60	90
MAIN ARMAMENT	100-mm	115-mm	125-mm	125-mm	125-mm
MUZZLE VELOCITY (MPS)	1,500	1,600	1,750	1,750	1,750

Reflects current data

Wrong. 1,600 mps.

These howitzers are not nuclear-capable.

Self-propelled 122-mm howitzers fire to a maximum range of 15 kilometers.

US *Main Battle Tanks*

	M-60A1/3	M-1/M-1A1 ABRAMS
WEIGHT (MT)	51	55
SPEED (KM/HR)	50	70
MAIN ARMAMENT	105-mm	105-mm/120-mm
MUZZLE VELOCITY (MPS)	1,500	1,500/1,660

Wrong. 1,870 mps.

Wrong. 1,870/1,700 mps.

Where are the other NATO tanks, the *Chieftains*, the *Leopards*, the AMX-30s and M-48s? This comparison is meant to obscure the fact that if Soviet tanks went to battle in Europe, they would face not only US tanks but all these other tanks too.

Quite impossible. See the commentary on pages 17, 49, and 64.

It threatens nothing of the kind. See the commentary on page 70.

Not very effective. See the commentary on page 70.

Any missile which gets through the gun barrel of this variant of the T-72 is headed in the wrong direction.

At the outset of war, the Soviets and their Pact allies can form at least 15 fronts and still maintain a strategic reserve. The front is the basic combined-arms strategic formation with which the Soviets conduct theater operations. It contains two to five armies, a large tactical aviation element, and an extensive support structure. Up to four first-echelon fronts may be organized within a TVD.

Ground Force Equipment

Armor

Late-model T-64/72/80 tanks constitute about one-third of the USSR's tanks. Older T-55 and T-62 tanks comprise most of the remainder. Several thousand additional older model tanks currently not in the active inventory could also be outfitted with reactive armor and would thereby be made effective against modern antitank weapons. The late-model tanks feature increased firepower, with a 125-mm main gun and improved fire control systems, including a laser rangefinder on some versions. Both the T-80 and a variant of the T-64 can fire an antitank guided missile through the main gun. Survivability has been increased through the use of improved armor incorporating laminates, composites, or reactive features. The development and extensive deployment of reactive armor capable of defeating relatively inexpensive antitank weapons threatens to shift fundamentally the conventional force balance.

Most of the USSR's APC/IFV inventory consists of the BTR-60 wheeled APC and the tracked BMP IFV, both of which are fully amphibious. The BTR-80, which is a follow-on to the BTR-70 and BTR-60, is being fielded in limited numbers. It has a more powerful engine, more dependable drive train, and better off-road performance. The improved BMP-2 is augmenting and replacing the BMP. It has a 30-mm rapid-fire gun in place of the 73-mm gun on the original version and carries the AT-5 antitank guided missile (ATGM). In addition to the BTRs and BMPs, the Soviets have fielded the BMD with airborne and air assault units and a number of light-ground-pressure vehicles such as the GT-T/MT-LB series for use in areas of poor trafficability.

The more important measurements of capability are missing here. NATO tanks are better armored. Their turrets turn more quickly, their guns elevate and depress to greater angles, they carry more ammunition, fire it more quickly, at higher muzzle velocities, to greater distances and consequently with more lethal effect than the best of their Soviet counterparts do. While the Warsaw Pact could eventually bring as many as 24,500 tanks into Central Europe, and NATO no more than 18,700, all but 1,200 of NATO's tanks are superior to anything the Soviets can build, and fewer than 5,000 tanks in the Warsaw Pact's force would even be a match for them.

If it were not possible for NATO aircraft to evade, jam, confuse and deceive these radars, or to destroy them with anti-radiation missiles specially designed for this purpose, like our AGM-45A SHRIKE or our AGM-88A HARM, this illustration would be impressive.

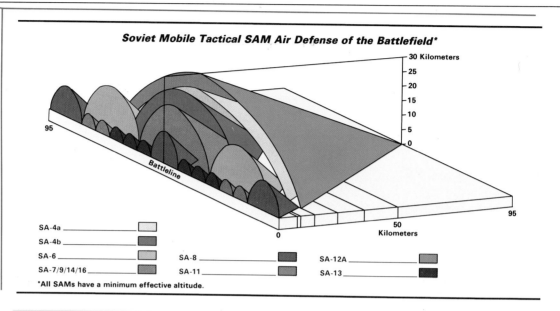

Soviet Mobile Tactical SAM Air Defense of the Battlefield*

SA-4a
SA-4b
SA-6   SA-8   SA-12A
SA-7/9/14/16   SA-11   SA-13

*All SAMs have a minimum effective altitude.

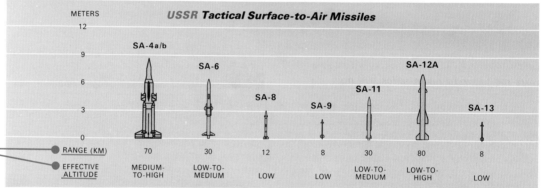

USSR *Tactical Surface-to-Air Missiles*

	SA-4a/b	SA-6	SA-8	SA-9	SA-11	SA-12A	SA-13
RANGE (KM)	70	30	12	8	30	80	8
EFFECTIVE ALTITUDE	MEDIUM-TO-HIGH	LOW-TO-MEDIUM	LOW	LOW	LOW-TO-MEDIUM	LOW-TO-HIGH	LOW

The speeds of these missiles, and the types of homing mechanisms they use, are among the important capabilities not listed here. The Soviet SA-12A, for example, has a speed of Mach 2.5, while our PATRIOT has a speed of Mach 3.9.

Shorter Range Missiles

Deployment of the Soviets' newest shorter range INF missile system, the SS-23, began in 1985. This system, which is still seen only in limited numbers, has a longer range and better accuracy than the older SCUD, which it is expected to replace. A more accurate version of the SCALEBOARD also has been deployed. Further, Soviet armies and fronts now have missile brigades equipped with SS-1c/SCUD missile launchers. At division level, the dominant short-range weapon, the unguided free-rocket-over-ground (FROG), is being replaced by the more accurate, longer range SS-21 missile. Owing to increased accuracy, the new generation of short-range missiles can be employed effectively with chemical as well as

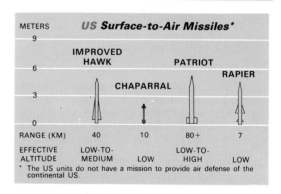

US *Surface-to-Air Missiles**

	IMPROVED HAWK	CHAPARRAL	PATRIOT	RAPIER
RANGE (KM)	40	10	80+	7
EFFECTIVE ALTITUDE	LOW-TO-MEDIUM	LOW	LOW-TO-HIGH	LOW

* The US units do not have a mission to provide air defense of the continental US.

improved conventional warheads. Deployment of these missiles therefore will give the Soviets a formidable conventional deep-strike system.

Wrong. Fewer than 30. The authors appear to be using the floating decimal point.

More than 300 MiG-29/FULCRUMs, armed with beyond-visual-range, long-range and short-range air-to-air missiles, are now operational with Soviet forces.

Fire Support

Soviet artillery units are being modernized through the acquisition of newer, primarily self-propelled models with improved range, accuracy, warhead lethality, mobility, and survivability. All 152-mm and larger caliber artillery weapons being acquired by the Soviets are nuclear capable.

Air Defense

Because of their continuing concern about the threat of NATO aerodynamic systems to their ground forces, the Soviets have put increasingly heavy emphasis on their traditionally strong commitment to ground force air defense. This structure consists of a dense array of mobile SAMs, antiaircraft guns, and handheld SAMs. The SA-11 and SA-12A systems are replacing the SA-4 in non-divisional air defense units. The 57-mm gun, still deployed at division level in many low-priority Soviet and NSWP units, is gradually being replaced by the SA-6 and -8 SAMs. At regimental level, a newer gun system, the ZSU-X, is beginning

to supplant the ZSU-23/4. The SA-14 and new, highly accurate SA-16 handheld SAMs are replacing the SA-7 in tactical units.

Equipment Deployment Patterns

Soviet equipment design, production, and deployment philosophies reflect the USSR's twin requirements for modernity and massive force structure. The Soviet industrial base can produce large amounts of equipment incorporating the latest technology. However, older items are maintained in units where the latest pieces may not be available. The acquisition of new items of equipment initiates a "trickle-down" process. High-priority formations such as Soviet forces in the Western TVD are usually the first to receive modern equipment. As their older materiel is replaced, it is sent to other TVDs, to reserve stocks, or to lower priority units in the USSR's interior. This equipment

All of those now being *acquired* may be, but only a portion of those still being *used* are nuclear-capable. See the commentary on page 43.

We still wait to see what this really looks like. See the commentary on pages 6 and 7.

For a better idea of how much equipment, new or old, the Soviet Army really has, see the commentary on page 19.

The M-46 has a maximum range of 27 km. How effective is that against an opponent whose howitzers can rain down counterbattery fire from distances of 35 and 40 km?

To appreciate how formidable they would be, see the commentary on page 19.

Another premature deployment date. The FLANKER is not yet operational. This is a photograph of one of the prototypes.

may replace older equipment but may also be used to form new units or to expand others. For example, non-divisional artillery assets located in the interior of the USSR are being expanded significantly with older artillery such as the 1950s-era 130-mm long-range M-46 field gun. This effective and reliable gun is being supplanted by late-model 152-mm weapons in high-priority artillery organizations. Large numbers of older but still highly capable guns and howitzers are thus available to equip other ground force units.

The ground forces include numerous units with varying capabilities provided by equipment from different eras. However, their capabilities are shaped by the Soviets to meet specific wartime requirements. Thus, Soviet forces planned for early offensive operations against NATO in the Central Region are well equipped with late-model weapons. Units assigned to other theaters, such as the Far East or Southern TVDs, facing less technologically advanced adversaries may be equipped with older weapons. Units in the interior of the USSR that would be used later in a conflict also often have older equipment. Nonetheless, they would have formidable capabilities when employed as fresh forces late in a war against an enemy that is exhausted or has experienced heavy losses.

Air Force Developments

The Soviet Air Forces (SAF) are a crucial element of the USSR's theater force structure. The Soviets are developing aircraft and munitions capable of both offensive deep-strike operations as well as defensive missions. The SAF is now organized to furnish dedicated support to all levels of command, from the maneuver division to the Supreme High Command (VGK).

The SAF includes three major combat components: Strategic Air Armies, Air Forces of the Military District and Groups of Forces, and Military Transport Aviation (VTA). The five Strategic Air Armies subordinate to the VGK created in 1980 as part of the reorganization of the air forces provide centrally controlled forces for support of theater strategic operations. Of these, the Moscow Air Army has the broadest responsibility, primarily for intercontinental operations. Some of the approximately 165 assigned BEAR and BISON heavy bombers may conduct land attacks and maritime strikes in support of the continental and oceanic TVD operations. The other four air armies — Smolensk, Legnica, Vin-

The USSR is deploying the new Su-27/FLANKER fighter-interceptor, with its increased capabilities against low-flying aircraft and cruise missiles, to operational bases.

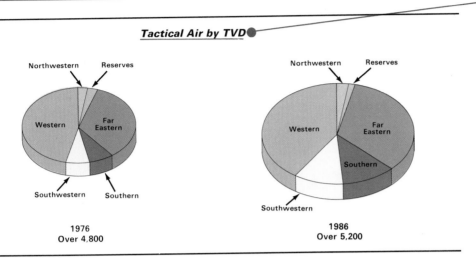

Tactical Air by TVD

1976
Over 4,800

1986
Over 5,200

● The number of Soviet tactical aircraft has certainly grown, but the number of NATO aircraft has grown faster, and is now larger. The number of aircraft assigned to the four Soviet Tactical Air Armies stationed in East Europe has remained constant over the past decade at fewer than 2,000.

nitsa, and Irkutsk — constitute the principal deep-strike component of the theater forces. They are equipped with about 565 BACKFIRE, BADGER, and BLINDER medium bombers and over 450 FENCER fighter-bombers. Some 250 FLOGGER, FISHBED, and FLANKER fighters provide force protection. About 20 percent of the bombers and fighter-bombers are assigned to the Irkutsk Air Army and are dedicated to operations in the Far East TVD. The remainder operate in the Western and Southern Theaters of War.

The 20 air forces in the groups of forces and military districts of the USSR, Mongolia, and Afghanistan constitute the second major component of SAF. They include over 5,000 fighters, fighter-bombers, reconnaissance, and electronic-countermeasures aircraft. Fighters and fighter-bombers are organized into divisions or independent units subordinate directly to the military districts or groups of forces. In wartime, these will be organized as the Air Forces of the Fronts.

The Soviet helicopter force is growing in numbers and capability. Helicopters are assigned at front, army, and division level, and they provide the maneuver division commander with dedicated aviation support. This force has virtually doubled in both quantity and effectiveness since 1979, thereby freeing fixed-wing aircraft to participate more extensively in theater air operations. Continued deployment of the FROGFOOT close air support aircraft will further this trend.

VTA, the third operational element of SAF,

primarily provides airlift for the Soviet airborne forces. It also furnishes air logistics support for deployed Soviet and allied armed forces and supports Soviet political and economic interests, especially in the Third World. The VTA forces consist of almost 400 CANDID and COCK medium- and long-range transports based in the western USSR and 200 CUB medium-range transports located primarily along the southern and Far Eastern periphery of the Soviet Union.

In addition to the VTA, the VGK air armies and the air forces of the military districts/

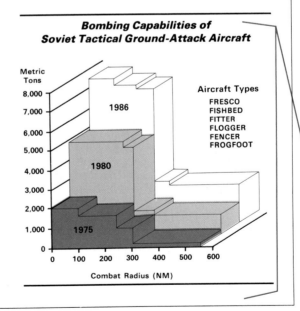

Bombing Capabilities of Soviet Tactical Ground-Attack Aircraft

Metric Tons

Aircraft Types
FRESCO
FISHBED
FITTER
FLOGGER
FENCER
FROGFOOT

Combat Radius (NM)

● It's impossible, of course, to tell from this chart which aircraft fly how far with what. In fact, only one of these aircraft, the FROGFOOT, may be able to carry more than 4,000 kg—or 4 metric tons— of ordnance under the best conditions. All would carry much less under combat conditions.

Chapter IV Forces for Theater Operations

● There has been a little cheating here. The authors are announcing that some of our aircraft could fly at greater distances if they carried less, but they have cut the combat radius *and* the load capacity of these aircraft at the same time. Shown in the margins are the actual distances these aircraft can fly and the actual loads they can carry to those distances. They are capable of even greater loads.

The F-111, for example, can carry 15,000 kg of munitions, the F-4 PHANTOM and A-10A 7,500 kg each. In the Soviet chart, on the other hand, most of the aircraft were given greater distances than they could fly with the loads shown. These have been corrected. Some of the Soviet aircraft could carry at most another 1,000 kg of weight, but only to lesser distances. It should be evident from all of this that

● Wrong. Mach 2.2   ● Wrong. 930 km.   ● Wrong. Mach 1.6   ● Wrong. Mach 1.8   ● Wrong. 480 km.   ● Wrong. 740 km.   ● Wrong. 500 km.

● Wrong. 1,100 km.

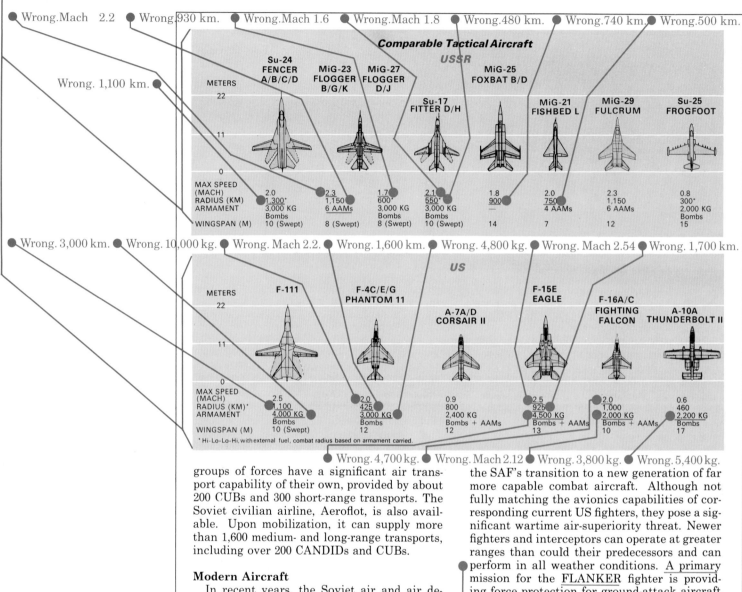

● Wrong. 3,000 km.   ● Wrong. 10,000 kg.   ● Wrong. Mach 2.2.   ● Wrong. 1,600 km.   ● Wrong. 4,800 kg.   ● Wrong. Mach 2.54   ● Wrong. 1,700 km.

● Wrong. 4,700 kg.   ● Wrong. Mach 2.12   ● Wrong. 3,800 kg.   ● Wrong. 5,400 kg.

groups of forces have a significant air transport capability of their own, provided by about 200 CUBs and 300 short-range transports. The Soviet civilian airline, Aeroflot, is also available. Upon mobilization, it can supply more than 1,600 medium- and long-range transports, including over 200 CANDIDs and CUBs.

Modern Aircraft

In recent years, the Soviet air and air defense forces have experienced modest numerical growth while dramatically increasing their capabilities through acquisition of aircraft with improved range, payload, and avionics.

Fighters. The FULCRUM and FLANKER aircraft have a true look-down/shoot-down radar, enabling them to engage low-flying aircraft or cruise missiles. Both carry the beyond-visual-range AA-10 and the short-range AA-11 air-to-air missiles. These aircraft, together with the FOXHOUND interceptor, mark

● True? Not true. See the commentary on page 58.

● This aircraft is not yet deployed.

the SAF's transition to a new generation of far more capable combat aircraft. Although not fully matching the avionics capabilities of corresponding current US fighters, they pose a significant wartime air-superiority threat. Newer fighters and interceptors can operate at greater ranges than could their predecessors and can perform in all weather conditions. A primary mission for the FLANKER fighter is providing force protection for ground-attack aircraft on deep strikes. The smaller FULCRUM will contest air superiority closer to the ground battle and in defense of Warsaw Pact airspace. The FLOGGER is by far the most numerous fighter-interceptor and is likely to remain in the force in sizable numbers through the mid-1990s. Other fighter-interceptors include the FOXBAT, FISHBED, and FLAGON. Almost 500 late-model FISHBEDs are operational but are being replaced — along with older FLOGGER B models — as the deployment of FULCRUMs

most US aircraft can carry much greater loads over much greater distances. Significant capabilities are also missing from these charts. Our F-15, for example, has a thrust-to-weight ratio of 4.1 to 1, the highest ratio for any aircraft in the world. As a result, it can pull a turn of more than 14 degrees per second. Our A-10 can spend an hour and forty-eight minutes of time over its target. Finally, important

aircraft are missing from this chart, including our carrier-based A-6 INTRUDER, which can carry up to 8,000 kg of ordnance, and has a potential combat radius of 1,400 km. Where are all of NATO's other aircraft—the JAGUAR, the TORNADO, the BUCCANEER, the F-104, British and West German F-4 PHANTOMS, and various models of the French MIRAGE?

Not yet deployed in 1987.   Wrong. 295 kph.   Wrong. 60.   Wrong. 320 kph.   Wrong. 340 km.

Wrong. 290 kph.

Wrong. 288 km.

Wrong. 270 kph.

Wrong. 530 km.

Wrong. 330 km.

Wrong. 15.

Wrong. 320 kph.

Wrong. 55.

Wrong. 320 kph.

Wrong. 335 km.

Wrong. 300 kph.

Wrong. 44.

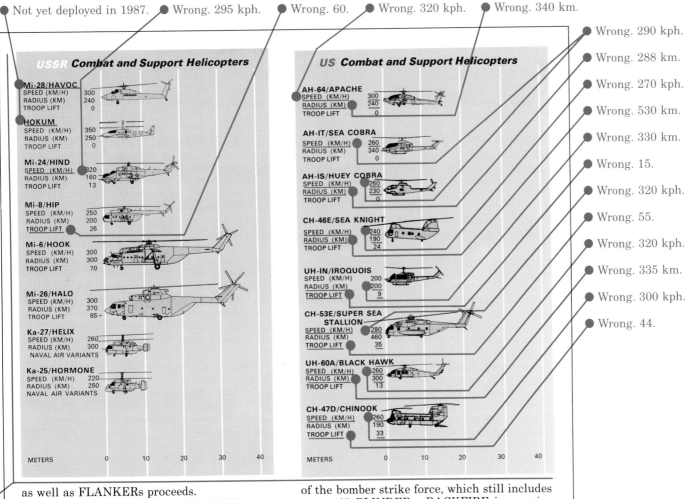

as well as FLANKERs proceeds.

Although the FITTER and FLOGGER constitute the bulk of the tactical ground-attack force, the Soviets have almost 800 FENCER fighter-bombers — the best deep-interdiction aircraft in their tactical inventory. The FENCER has twice the combat radius of the FITTER while carrying a comparable payload. The FENCER can carry about 3,000 kilograms of bombs 1,500 kilometers. The FENCER can also carry new tactical air-to-surface missiles such as the AS-10, -11, -12, -13, and -14 that provide some hard-target-kill capability and improved survivability. Additionally, the new long-range navigation system and electro-optics weapons delivery systems enable Soviet aircraft to penetrate enemy airspace at night or during poor weather with great precision.

Bombers. In the Soviet bomber force, the BACKFIRE is steadily replacing the BADGER. BACKFIRE now comprises nearly 30 percent of the bomber strike force, which still includes some 135 BLINDERs. BACKFIRE is superior to BADGER and BLINDER in combat radius, survivability, and weapon versatility.

Transports. In VTA, the CANDID continues to replace the CUB at a rate of about 30 per year. CANDID now accounts for almost 60 percent of the nearly 600 aircraft in the VTA force. The CANDID can carry twice the maximum payload more than three times as far as the older CUB. In addition to 340 CANDIDs and 200 CUBs, the VTA inventory includes about 55 COCK aircraft, the only Soviet transport currently able to carry out-sized cargo such as main battle tanks or large missiles. Production and deployment of the CONDOR transport — capable of a 150-metric ton payload, almost twice that of the COCK — will substantially upgrade VTA's heavy-lift capability. The CONDOR should begin arriving in VTA units in 1987.

Only three of these aircraft are in service.

These capabilities continue to elude the Soviet Air Force. Most US and NATO aircraft, on the other hand, can fly in poor weather and at night.

No, it can carry that weight for only 1,100 km. On the preceding page, the authors themselves say it can carry that weight for 1,300 km..

79   Chapter IV Forces for Theater Operations

More deception. Placing the helicopters compared here in profile helps to conceal the higher lift capacity of our wider-bodied aircraft. This impression is reinforced by listing fewer troops than some of our helicopters can carry. Our CH-53E SUPER SEA STALLION carries not 35 but 55 troops, and our CH-47D CHINOOK carries not 33 but 44 troops. To sustain the illusion that so many Soviet helicopters are larger than ours, the authors have also had to eliminate the largest of our helicopters, the CH-54 TARHE, which can lift 45 combat troops.

We built more than 100 TARHEs, and have more than 60 in service today, whereas the Soviets have only 18 of their Mi-26 HALOs. While they have about 470 Mi-6 HOOKs, we have more than 450 SUPER SEA STALLIONs *and* more than 450 CHINOOKs. Note, also, that two of the Soviet helicopters listed are not yet deployed in 1987, and that most of the US helicopters have somewhat higher speeds and ranges than the authors gave.

The U.S. helicopter force is the larger, and has the greater troop-lift capacity. See the commentary on previous page.

Here is a direct acknowledgement that a Soviet weapon system is not yet deployed. But it is included in the chart on the previous page, as though it were already deployed.

Read carefully. We are not being told that the Soviets have a capability to which we have no counterpart. We are being told that they *may* have that capability. Equally, then, they may not. In effect, we are being warned that we have no counterpart to a capability which may or may not exist. Think of the possibilities this opens up! One need only imagine all of the capabilities to which we have no counterpart, even though they do not yet exist, and even though the record of the arms race shows that in almost every instance we have developed them first, as we shall probably do in this case as well. Yet on page 145, the authors no longer say that the HOCUM helicopter *may* give the Soviets such a capability. They say that it *will* give the Soviets this capability. Thus does propaganda slink from conjecture to certitude.

See the commentary on page 67.

Helicopters. To support ground operations, the Soviets are increasing and modernizing their helicopter forces. At division level, helicopter detachments are expanding to squadrons, and in some squadrons the number of HIND attack helicopters has increased. At army level, about 20 attack regiments have been formed, with up to 60 HIP and HIND attack helicopters in each. More than half are deployed opposite NATO forces. Attack helicopters are the heavily armed HIND D/E/F and HIP C/E/H versions. Soviet emphasis on a heavy-lift helicopter transport capability is reflected in the development and recent appearance of the HALO. It is the world's largest production helicopter and is capable of carrying internally 2 airborne infantry combat vehicles or more than 85 combat-ready troops.

The Soviets are now equipping their helicopters with infrared (IR) jammers and suppressors, IR decoy dispensers, and more armor, thereby increasing survivability. These additions are probably the result of lessons learned in Afghanistan. A new attack helicopter known as the HAVOC, similar to the US Army Apache, is expected to be deployed soon. Another new helicopter, the HOKUM, which has no current Western counterpart, may give the Soviets a significant rotary-wing air-to-air combat capability. The Soviets are also using helicopters as airborne command posts.

NSWP Support. The air forces of the USSR's Warsaw Pact allies provide important adjuncts to the Soviets' air and air defense capabilities in the Western and Southwestern TVDs. The non-Soviet Warsaw Pact countries have about 2,450 fixed-wing combat aircraft. Although the total number of these aircraft has remained fairly stable during the 1980s, modest qualitative improvement has taken place with the acquisition of aircraft such as the FLOGGER G, FROGFOOT, and FITTER K.

Air Operations

Key combined-arms theater-controlled campaigns in which the air forces will participate include the offensive air operation and a defensively oriented antiair operation. The former consists of a large strategic operation initiated at the outbreak of war, conducted without nuclear weapons. This joint operation is directed at attaining conventional and nuclear strike superiority within a TVD. It is accomplished by destroying or weakening the enemy air forces

and nuclear delivery means.

The Soviet Union envisions an air operation lasting several days that would involve two or three massed strikes on the first day and one or two on subsequent days. Ground forces would support the operation by conducting missile and artillery strikes against air and air defense facilities using conventional and possibly chemical munitions as well as airborne, air assault, and special operations forces.

The Soviets would also conduct an antiair operation. If they do not hold the initiative in the air, then their immediate priority would be to conduct an antiair operation to provide friendly forces freedom of movement while simultaneously causing maximum attrition of enemy air and air defense assets. The Soviets would attempt to gain the initiative through combined offensive and defensive actions of Frontal Aviation, the National Air Defense Forces, missile troops and artillery, and the antiaircraft defense elements of other branches of the armed forces. If the Soviets seized the initiative in the air through the preemptive execution of an air operation or were able to wrest the initiative from the West, the major focus of the antiair operation would be on defensive actions to protect friendly forces and installations from NATO's remaining offensive air capability.

Naval Force Developments

The Soviet Navy is headed by a commander in chief (CINC) who is also a deputy minister of defense. He functions as the equivalent of both the US Secretary of the Navy and the Chief of Naval Operations and is the chief adviser on naval policy to the minister of defense. Fleet Admiral Vladimir Chernavin has commanded the navy since 1985 and is assisted by several deputies who supervise the day-to-day operations of the navy, including the work of more than 10 staff directorates.

The Soviet Navy comprises four major fleets: Northern Fleet, Pacific Ocean Fleet, Baltic Fleet, and Black Sea Fleet. Fleet headquarters are located at Severomorsk for the Northern Fleet, Vladivostok for the Pacific Ocean Fleet, Kaliningrad for the Baltic Fleet, and Sevastopol for the Black Sea Fleet. In peacetime, the fleet commanders report directly to the chief of the Main Navy Staff and exercise operational control over all general-purpose forces afloat and ashore within their fleet ar-

The following paragraphs are the mirror image of NATO plans. NATO has the capability to carry them out. Soviet aircraft lack the range and load capacity, and their pilots lack the training. NATO's aircraft assigned to the war in the air would use their greater maneuverability and more lethal armament to maximum advantage, steadily eliminating aircraft flown by the Warsaw Pact until NATO had full control of the airspace over the battlefield.

Having shown most Soviet types of attack submarine, the authors here acknowledge that the U.S. has other types too, and assert that the single type shown is "for comparison purposes." This represents the new, "bold" approach to propaganda: admit what you are doing, and then go ahead and do it anyway. What sort of "purpose" does a "comparison" of this kind serve? It can serve only one: misrepresentation. Hidden here is the fact that the Soviets have been building their new submarines in very small numbers. As this edition is published, they have but one AKULA, one MIKE and two SIERRA Class boats. They have only 6 ALFAs and 3 OSCARs. The largest class shown here, the VICTOR III, is represented by 20 boats. The U.S., on the other hand, now has 36 LOS ANGELES Class submarines, and plans to build a total of 68 of them. It has another 35 STURGEON Class boats, and a total of 96 attack submarines of all types. While the Soviets currently keep 262 attack submarines in service, only 102 are in the modern classes shown here. The remainder are obsolete diesel boats, many of them more than 20 years old. Even if all the older Soviet boats were included in the worldwide balance of attack submarines, the U.S. and its allies would still retain a numerical edge in both the Atlantic and the Pacific. The specifications shown here reveal nothing of our qualitative advantage. Our LOS ANGELES Class submarine moves at 35 knots (65 km/hr) submerged, and can operate at depths of more than 3,000 feet, where the hull is subject to 1,338 pounds per square inch of pressure. Much has been rumored of the Soviet ALFA, but no evidence has been brought before the public to prove that it dives deeper or moves more quickly than this. Our submarines are quieter, and are likely to remain so for the forseeable future, despite allegations to the contrary. The typical Soviet attack boat creates more than 170 decibels of noise at the source, one meter from its propellers, while ours creates fewer than 120. At the same time, our submarines are equipped with much better acoustic detection equipment. The result of both these advantages is that, under average conditions, our boats can detect most Soviet boats in deep water at ranges of more than 100 km, while theirs cannot detect most of ours at ranges of more than 1 km. Our submarines are better armed. The current Soviet torpedo has a range of 8 km. Our Mk 48 has a range of 40 km, and a speed of 60 knots (110 km/hr). Our submarines are also equipped with the HARPOON antiship missile, whose range is 145 km, and the SUBROC antisubmarine rocket, whose range is 55 km. The only comparable Soviet weapon, the SS-N-16, has a range of 40 km. Some Soviet attack boats carry cruise missiles with ranges of up to 1,000 km. The cruise missiles aboard our attack submarines have ranges of up to 3,900 km.

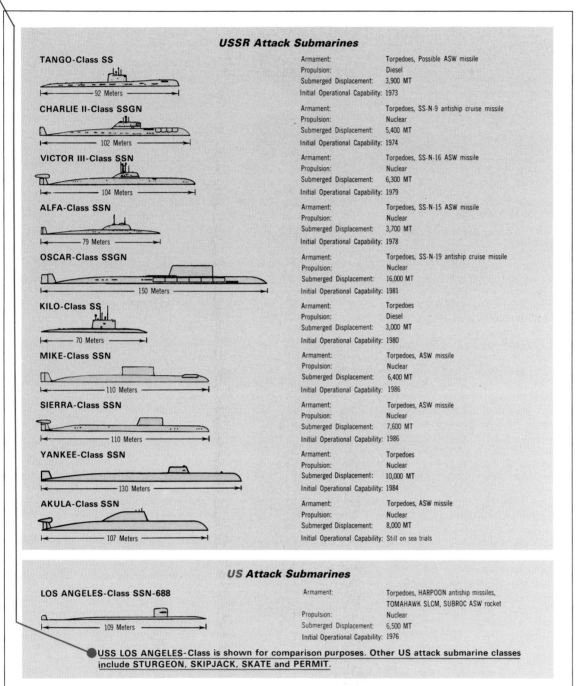

USSR Attack Submarines

TANGO-Class SS — 92 Meters
Armament:	Torpedoes, Possible ASW missile
Propulsion:	Diesel
Submerged Displacement:	3,900 MT
Initial Operational Capability:	1973

CHARLIE II-Class SSGN — 102 Meters
Armament:	Torpedoes, SS-N-9 antiship cruise missile
Propulsion:	Nuclear
Submerged Displacement:	5,400 MT
Initial Operational Capability:	1974

VICTOR III-Class SSN — 104 Meters
Armament:	Torpedoes, SS-N-16 ASW missile
Propulsion:	Nuclear
Submerged Displacement:	6,300 MT
Initial Operational Capability:	1979

ALFA-Class SSN — 79 Meters
Armament:	Torpedoes, SS-N-15 ASW missile
Propulsion:	Nuclear
Submerged Displacement:	3,700 MT
Initial Operational Capability:	1978

OSCAR-Class SSGN — 150 Meters
Armament:	Torpedoes, SS-N-19 antiship cruise missile
Propulsion:	Nuclear
Submerged Displacement:	16,000 MT
Initial Operational Capability:	1981

KILO-Class SS — 70 Meters
Armament:	Torpedoes
Propulsion:	Diesel
Submerged Displacement:	3,000 MT
Initial Operational Capability:	1980

MIKE-Class SSN — 110 Meters
Armament:	Torpedoes, ASW missile
Propulsion:	Nuclear
Submerged Displacement:	6,400 MT
Initial Operational Capability:	1986

SIERRA-Class SSN — 110 Meters
Armament:	Torpedoes, ASW missile
Propulsion:	Nuclear
Submerged Displacement:	7,600 MT
Initial Operational Capability:	1986

YANKEE-Class SSN — 130 Meters
Armament:	Torpedoes
Propulsion:	Nuclear
Submerged Displacement:	10,000 MT
Initial Operational Capability:	1984

AKULA-Class SSN — 107 Meters
Armament:	Torpedoes, ASW missile
Propulsion:	Nuclear
Submerged Displacement:	8,000 MT
Initial Operational Capability:	Still on sea trials

US Attack Submarines

LOS ANGELES-Class SSN-688 — 109 Meters
Armament:	Torpedoes, HARPOON antiship missiles, TOMAHAWK SLCM, SUBROC ASW rocket
Propulsion:	Nuclear
Submerged Displacement:	6,500 MT
Initial Operational Capability:	1976

USS LOS ANGELES-Class is shown for comparison purposes. Other US attack submarine classes include STURGEON, SKIPJACK, SKATE and PERMIT.

eas. In wartime, naval fleet CINCs would become the naval component commanders of the combined-arms high command in the appropriate TVD. Under each fleet commander are several major operational elements, including surface and submarine forces, naval base commands, naval aviation, and naval infantry. While the fleet commands provide administra-

Chapter IV Forces for Theater Operations

Who would deny what to whom? The Soviet SS-N-19 cruise missile has a range of only 460 km. The cruise missiles carried by US attack submarines have ranges of up to 3,900 km.

Wrong. The Soviets have 262 attack submarines, including 118 nuclear-powered and 144 diesel-electric boats.

The Soviets continue to build new diesel-powered submarines, including those in the KILO and TANGO Classes, but they are building them only in small numbers. Since diesel-powered boats have low speed and limited range, and could therefore be used only in territorial waters, these programs reflect a continuing Soviet commitment to defense of the homeland.

Even the newest Soviet submarines are very noisy. See the commentary on preceding page.

The SS-N-16 has a range of 40 km. The comparable US weapon, SUBROC, has a range of 55 km.

To date, only one boat in this class has appeared, though it was launched four years ago.

This is not exclusively a Soviet practice. We are probably moving ahead with plans of our own to refit five of our POLARIS ballistic missile submarines as attack submarines.

The OSCAR-Class SSGN, with 24 SS-N-19 antiship cruise missiles, would make a significant contribution to the Soviet Navy's sea-denial operations in wartime.

tive, logistics, and operational support to the strategic submarine force, operational control of Soviet SSBNs is at the national level.

Submarines

A significant part of Soviet naval strength lies in its general-purpose submarine force, the largest in the world. Today, this force numbers some 300 active units composed of some 35 classes of torpedo attack, cruise missile, and auxiliary submarines. About half the force is nuclear powered, and the percentage is expected to rise in the years ahead as heavy investment in submarine building programs continues to receive priority allocations of military resources.

Currently, the Soviets are producing or testing nine classes of submarines. Of these, almost all are nuclear powered. This program spans a wide range of undersea warfare applications, including torpedo and antiship cruise missile attack, land-attack submarine-launched cruise missile (SLCM) technology research, and specialized communications support. Backed by aggressive research and development, the newest Soviet submarine designs show evidence of an emphasis on quieting, speed, nuclear propulsion, weapon versatility, and incorporation of advanced technologies.

This emphasis has been greatly underscored since 1983, with the introduction of four

new classes of nuclear-powered attack submarines. The MIKE SSN, at almost 6,400 metric tons, will probably serve as a propulsion testbed. It is capable of firing a wide range of submarine-launched weapons, including the SS-N-15 nuclear depth bomb and the SS-N-16 ASW conventional and nuclear missiles.

The second nuclear-powered attack submarine launched in 1983 was the SIERRA. At 7,600 metric tons, the SIERRA is about 20 percent larger than the VICTOR III, which was introduced only 4 years earlier. In this era of rapidly developing technologies, the SIERRA is a clear demonstration of the high priority that submarine development programs receive in the Soviet Union. Technological advances are incorporated into designs as soon as practical, and while SIERRA differs little in hull form from the VICTOR III, it is believed to have a larger pressure hull and improved capabilities.

A third submarine development of 1983 typified another aspect of Soviet philosophy, which is to retrofit innovations into older designs, thus extending the service life and tactical utility of the submarine force. In one case, the ballistic missile tubes were removed from a YANKEE SSBN in a process that converted the unit to an attack submarine. This YANKEE SSN has probably been reequipped with updated fire control and sonar systems in addition

● Here the authors have used both visual distortion and selectivity. They have chosen only those Soviet ships with the highest tonnage, and have found smaller US ships to place next to them. When they could not find smaller US ships, as in the first two examples down the page, they have made the Soviet ships look larger. Thus, the new class of Soviet aircraft carrier looks heavier and almost as long as the US carrier, which displaces 26,500 more tons. The KIEV looks larger than the IOWA, even though the IOWA displaces 20,900 more tons. There is no indication here of how many of each type of vessel shown we and the Soviets have, nor of how many ships have been left out of this "comparison" entirely. In fact, the Soviets have only 3 KIEV, 2 KIROV, 1 SLAVA, 7 UDALOY and 6 SOVREMENNYY Class

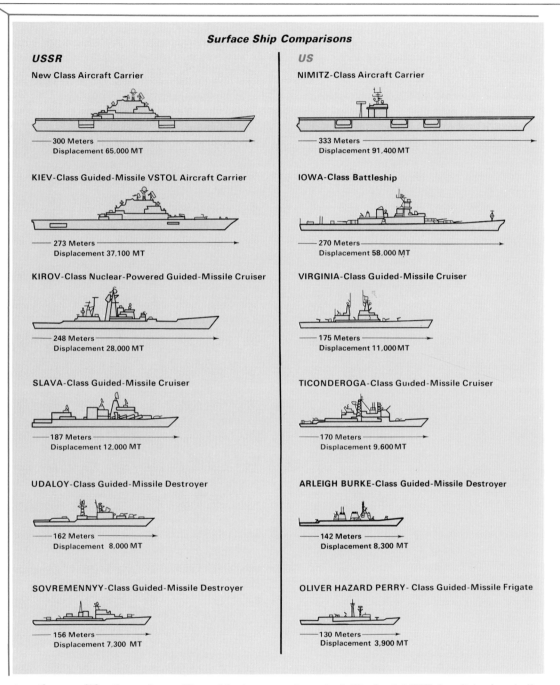

Surface Ship Comparisons

USSR

New Class Aircraft Carrier
—— 300 Meters ——→
Displacement 65,000 MT

KIEV-Class Guided-Missile VSTOL Aircraft Carrier
—— 273 Meters ——→
Displacement 37,100 MT

KIROV-Class Nuclear-Powered Guided-Missile Cruiser
—— 248 Meters ——→
Displacement 28,000 MT

SLAVA-Class Guided-Missile Cruiser
—— 187 Meters ——→
Displacement 12,000 MT

UDALOY-Class Guided-Missile Destroyer
—— 162 Meters ——→
Displacement 8,000 MT

SOVREMENNYY-Class Guided-Missile Destroyer
—— 156 Meters ——→
Displacement 7,300 MT

US

NIMITZ-Class Aircraft Carrier
—— 333 Meters ——→
Displacement 91,400 MT

IOWA-Class Battleship
—— 270 Meters ——→
Displacement 58,000 MT

VIRGINIA-Class Guided-Missile Cruiser
—— 175 Meters ——→
Displacement 11,000 MT

TICONDEROGA-Class Guided-Missile Cruiser
—— 170 Meters ——→
Displacement 9,600 MT

ARLEIGH BURKE-Class Guided-Missile Destroyer
—— 142 Meters ——→
Displacement 8,300 MT

OLIVER HAZARD PERRY- Class Guided-Missile Frigate
—— 130 Meters ——→
Displacement 3,900 MT

to other modifications that will enable it to launch a wider variety of weapons.

In 1984, another new class of nuclear-powered attack submarine — the AKULA-Class — was launched. The lead AKULA unit is also similar to the VICTOR III- and SIERRA-Classes.

The increased production of SSN designs that emphasize costly high-technology features un-

ships. We have, for example, 47 of the OLIVER HAZARD PERRY Class frigates with which the SOVREMENNYY is here compared. Not shown here are our 31 SPRUANCE Class destroyers, each weighing 7,800 tons, which might be compared with the UDALOY, or our LONG BEACH, which compared with the SLAVA displaces 17,350 tons. The KIROV should properly be compared with our IOWA Class battleships, of which there are three. The KIEV ought properly to be compared with our TARAWA Class amphibious assault ships, of which there are six. The new Soviet aircraft carrier shown here is not even yet deployed. The Soviets have only 138 ships which displace more than 2,000 tons. The US has 211 such ships, in addition to 14 aircraft carriers.

Wrong. 460 km.

derscores the Soviet determination to improve their antiship and antisubmarine warfare capabilities and the potential for torpedo tube-launched SLCM deployment. Other submarine missions have received emphasis as well. Patrols by the OSCAR-Class nuclear-powered

cruise missile submarine have become routine. At 16,000 metric tons, the OSCAR is fitted with 24 submerged-launched, 550-kilometer-range, nuclear-capable SS-N-19 antiship cruise missiles, targeted primarily against NATO carrier battle groups. In addition to continued OSCAR

84

production, the Soviets are proceeding gradually with a program to convert the older 1960s-era SS-N-3-equipped ECHO II SSGNs to carry the improved, 550-kilometer-range supersonic SS-N-12 antiship cruise missile.

In conjunction with other programs to produce specialized nuclear-powered submarines for research and development, weapons system evaluation, and fleet command and control, the Soviet Union maintains a diesel-powered submarine program with the production of the KILO-Class attack submarine.

Through an unwavering commitment to submarine development, the Soviet leadership has constructed a large, versatile, modern, offensive strike force capable of both conventional and nuclear operations throughout the world. Moreover, newer submarine classes are showing clear design improvements over their predecessors and are narrowing the technological lead long held by the West. This demonstrated capability to translate submarine research to production is a clear indication that the Soviet Union will strive to apply increasing technological pressure on the West in the years ahead.

Surface Forces

The surface forces of the Soviet Navy also continue to improve their ability to fulfill a broad range of naval operations, especially in waters distant from the USSR. In general, the afloat forces are modern and well equipped with both conventional and nuclear weapons.

The trend in Soviet major surface warship programs has been toward larger units with more sophisticated weapons and sensors. These ships can cruise for longer distances, carry more ordnance, and conduct a greater range of operations than their predecessors. This development has created a new flexibility for Soviet surface forces in carrying out deployed operations on a worldwide scale.

Currently, the largest combatant ship in the Soviet Navy is the KIEV-Class aircraft carrier. Its weapons suite includes a battery of 550-kilometer-range SS-N-12 antiship cruise missiles, which can be targeted beyond the ship's horizon by onboard HORMONE helicopters or information received from satellites or land-based long-range aircraft. This class also carries an array of other weaponry and support equipment, including over 100 long- and short-range surface-to-air missiles, air defense gun batteries, tactical sensors, electronic warfare

© Mitsuo Shibata

KIROV-Class nuclear-powered guided-missile cruisers now assigned to the Northern and Pacific Fleets contribute to the growing, global capabilities of the Soviet Navy.

The Soviet Navy, in time of war, could not operate throughout the world. Most of its vessels would not even be able to reach open ocean, because the US and its allies would deny them access to it. See the commentary on pages 8 and 9.

An important admission that this lead *is* held by the West. This is one more reason to question the speed and diving depth alarmists quote for the Soviet ALFA submarine. The US technology lead, according to the Secretary of Defense for Research and Engineering, is not "narrowing," but widening.

These are precisely the waters in which the Soviet Navy would *not* be able to operate.

US ships have far more sophisticated fire control, missile guidance, radar, antiaircraft, antimissile defense, and antisubmarine warfare systems than Soviet vessels do.

The Soviets have only three of these carriers. Each is less than half the size of most of our 14 aircraft carriers. Soviet carrier-based aircraft have a combat radius of only 250 km. Our carrier-based aircraft have a combat radius of 1,600 km. See the commentary on page 20.

These are the largest surface combatants the Soviet Navy has, and its only nuclear-powered cruisers. It has only two of them. Each of our three largest surface combatants, battleships of the IOWA Class, displaces more than twice as many tons as the KIROV. The US Navy has nine nuclear-powered cruisers.

As noted earlier, the Soviet Navy can be denied access to almost any area of ocean beyond the coastal waters of the USSR.

We already have 30 SPRUANCE Class destroyers equipped for the antisubmarine role. They are larger than the SOVREMENNYY, displacing 7,800 tons each.

Its combat radius is only 250 km. The combat radius of our own VSTOL aircraft, the AV-8B HARRIER, is 1,200 km.

It must have been frustrating for the authors to find an effective way of phrasing this. They could not say that the Soviets have the largest warships built by any nation. We have those. Each of our IOWA Class battleships weighs more than twice as much as the KIROV. If we had built these battleships in the 1950s, then the authors would have had to say the KIROV is the largest warship built since the 1960s. Since we have continued to build aircraft carriers three times as large as the KIROV throughout the period since the end of World War II, the authors have had to make an exception to these.

Wrong. 460 km.

A SOVREMENNYY-Class guided-missile destroyer, with its forward twin 130-mm guns elevated, on its transit to the Soviet Pacific Fleet.

© Mitsuo Shibata

systems, and advanced communications devices. The 180-meter flight deck accommodates both HORMONE and HELIX helicopters and the FORGER VSTOL aircraft, which is capable of daylight attack, reconnaissance, and limited air defense intercept missions.

A new era in Soviet warship development began in 1980 with the appearance of the initial units of the most technologically advanced classes produced in recent years. These included the first Soviet nuclear-powered surface warship — the KIROV guided-missile cruiser — and the UDALOY and SOVREMENNYY guided-missile destroyers (DDGs). In 1982, the first of a new class of gas-turbine-powered guided-missile cruisers — the SLAVA — entered the inventory. The SLAVA is equipped with 16 SS-N-12s, 64 SA-N-6 air defense missiles, 40 SA-N-4 point defense missiles, a 130-mm twin-barrel, dual-purpose gun, and the HORMONE surveillance helicopter.

Each of these classes is in series production. The KIROV, with a displacement of about 28,000 tons, is the largest warship, with the exception of aircraft carriers, built by any nation since World War II. Its principal armament is a battery of 20 550-kilometer SS-N-19 antiship cruise missile launchers, complemented by launchers for the SS-N-14 antisubmarine missile in the first ship of the class only. Three HELIX or HORMONE helicopters are included for ASW and missile targeting. The KIROV is outfitted with an array of air defense weapons, including 96 long-range SA-N-6 missiles and, on the second and subsequent unit, provisions for 128 SA-NX-9 shorter range SAMs. Medium-caliber-gun mounts, a number

of Gatling-type guns for point defense, torpedoes, and ASW rockets complete the KIROV's modern armament. In 1984, *Frunze,* the second unit of the KIROV-Class, became operational. A third KIROV-Class ship is now fitting out, and a fourth is under construction.

Other new construction programs show similar evidence of Soviet concern for the multidimensional aspect of modern naval warfare. All new destroyers and larger surface combatants are equipped with surface-to-air missiles and sensors and weapons for antisubmarine warfare, in addition to helicopters and specialized weaponry. The eighth SOVREMENNYY DDG, for example, is estimated to carry 40 SA-N-7 short-range surface-to-air missiles, a HELIX or HORMONE helicopter, 53-cm torpedoes, and 120 antisubmarine rockets, as well as 8 SS-N-22 supersonic antiship missiles.

The Soviets' newest class of aircraft carrier, launched in December 1985 at Nikolayev in the Black Sea, is still fitting out. The ship is approximately 300 meters overall in length and is expected to displace about 65,000 metric tons. The ultimate flight-deck configuration of the new carrier is yet to be confirmed, and the aircraft for its air wing are still under development.

In support of the development of aircraft for future carriers, the Soviets have an active test and evaluation program underway at Saki naval airfield near the Black Sea. There, the Soviets have constructed a 295-meter flight deck outline, arresting gear, and aircraft barricades, and two catapults — one being tested and one under development. Two ski-jump ramps have been erected to test aircraft in short, rolling, ramp-assisted takeoffs. Several aircraft have been variously associated with these test facilities, including the FLANKER and FULCRUM. While candidates to fly aboard future carriers themselves, these aircraft could also be testing particular aspects of sea-based aviation for a totally new aircraft designed specifically for the stringent requirements of carrier air operations.

Although it will take years after launch and fitting out and training with an operational air wing to develop operational effectiveness, the new carrier will enable the Soviets to extend their operations beyond the umbrella currently provided by land-based aviation. Eventually, high-performance aircraft of the embarked air wing are expected to permit them to conduct

Next year's edition will probably have an artist's illustration of the "new Soviet carrier-based aircraft under development," which will look as much as possible like our F-14 TOMCAT.

Still only two-thirds the size of our large carriers. See the commentary on page 20.

An important acknowledgement. Moreover, it would take decades before the Soviets could build as many carriers as we have, and decades more to equip them with comparable aircraft. In the meanwhile, the US would have ample time in which to further expand its own capabilities. Let us hope that neither one of these developments takes place.

integral air defense of task groups, decrease the vulnerability of their deployed surface forces, and contribute to overall national air defense. Additionally, the Soviets have an active interest in improving their peacetime distant-area power projection capabilities to become more influential in the Third World. To achieve this goal, they seek enhanced capability to protect and assist ground forces operating ashore, as well as to provide air protection for naval forces. Thus, the aircraft on the new carrier are expected to have both air-to-air and ground-support mission capabilities. Sustained combat operations in Third World areas, however, would require underway replenishment ship support of a kind that the Soviets currently lack.

Naval Aviation

Although the emphasis on sea-based aircraft development will be increasing, Soviet Naval Aviation (SNA) will remain primarily a land-based force. Numbering over 1,600 aircraft, SNA alone is larger than most of the national air forces in the world today. Since the mid-1950s, when the force was first equipped with missile-carrying jet bombers, weapon systems and tactics associated with its principal anti-ship strike mission have been progressively upgraded. The Tupolev-designed variable-geometry-wing BACKFIRE bomber entered the SNA inventory in 1974 and is currently deployed in the Black Sea, Baltic Sea, and Pacific Ocean Fleets. The BACKFIRE can carry antiship missiles, bombs, or mines and exhibits marked improvements in performance, nearly doubling the combat radius of its BADGER and BLINDER predecessors. In 1986, the improved BACKFIRE C model became operational in SNA.

Swingwing fighter-bombers are also assigned to SNA. Its FITTER C aircraft, which can carry over 3,100 kilograms of ordnance, are well suited to such roles as the support of

The first UDALOY-Class guided-missile destroyer was transferred to the Pacific Fleet in 1985 as part of the USSR's continuing upgrade of forces in the Far East.

© Mitsuo Shibata

● An admission that these forces are now vulnerable.

● Wrong. 1,315.

● The struggle for hyperbole. Not larger than our own Navy's air force, which flies 2,032 aircraft.

● The BACKFIRE has a combat radius of 2,900 km, about the same as that of the BLINDER. However, its speed is Mach 2, while the BLINDER's is only Mach 1.4.

● Another acknowledgement of a serious limitation on Soviet power projection. The US has much greater replenishment capabilities. See the commentary on page 9.

● Here is an insight into how quickly this administration really believes the Soviets will build and equip new aircraft carriers.

Soviet amphibious forces and antiship attacks against fast and highly maneuverable small combatants. Naval FITTERs were first assigned to the Baltic Fleet, and a new naval unit was formed subsequently in the Pacific. The recent addition of the FENCER fighter-bomber/reconnaissance variant further enhances the reconnaissance capability and strike potential of SNA.

ASW is an important and growing mission for SNA as new and improved airborne sensors are deployed. A turboprop BEAR F variant, designed for ASW missions, was introduced in 1970 and has since been upgraded. With a 5,000-kilometer radius and a sophisticated sensor suite, it enables the Soviets to extend the range and quality of their ASW searches. For shipboard applications, a new ASW helicopter, the HELIX, became operational in 1980. Now widely deployed in the Soviet fleets, the HELIX has significantly greater range, speed, and payload than its HORMONE predecessor.

SNA aircraft are also employed for vital maritime reconnaissance missions. Intermediate-range MAY aircraft are continuously deployed to South Yemen and periodically deployed to Libya and Syria, primarily to conduct maritime surveillance operations. Additionally, BEAR D and F long-range aircraft conduct regular deployments to staging bases in Cuba and Angola and are continuously deployed to Vietnam. BEAR Ds also deploy periodically to Angola. Operations from these bases provide the Soviets not only with military intelligence but also with detailed information on

ship movements along critical Western sea lines of communication.

Naval Mine Warfare

The Soviet interest in mine warfare dates to czarist Russia. During World War II, the Soviet Union used mines extensively in both offensive and defensive operations in the Baltic and Black Seas.

In the early 1960s, Soviet interest in mine warfare suffered in comparison to higher priority systems such as nuclear ballistic and cruise missiles. During the past decade, however, interest in mine warfare has renewed. Today, Soviet stockpiles of mines include some 100,000 moored contact mines and as many as 200,000 modern magnetic and acoustic magnetic induction mines.

Although the Soviet Navy includes only three ships designed primarily for minelaying, the Soviets have ample numbers of properly configured surface ships, aircraft, and submarines to support large-scale mining efforts. They practice minelaying regularly and write about it frequently in their military journals.

Mine warfare is a major mission of the Soviet Navy and receives adequate priority and resource support. Soviet literature discusses the mission, placing great emphasis on mine usage early in a war to close enemy ports and harbors. Other offensive applications are the blocking of shipping lanes, the isolation of naval operating areas, and the denial of chokepoint transit routes or operating areas to enemy missile submarines. The large stockpile of

A chemical protection company can cleanse the vehicles of one regiment with one load of decontaminant. The TMS-65, shown here, uses a jet engine to dispense decontaminant.

In the same way, while each of the US military services manages its own special operations units, and while overall coordinating commands like our Intelligence Support Activity (ISA) and our Joint Special Warfare Operations Command have appeared from time to time, overall direction and coordination often seems to come from the CIA. The CIA used our Special Forces and other military assets in its Phoenix Program and other operations in Southeast Asia, and has certainly used such forces elsewhere. In fact, a clandestine operations group of considerable size which our government can at least claim acts without its authority, composed entirely of military and intelligence specialists which our government can at least claim it no longer employs, now appears to have been in existence since at least 1976. As testimony to the Congressional hearings on the sale of arms to Iran and the diversion of profits from those sales to the Con-

Soviet chemical units operate on the move with combat units, thereby preserving a rapid rate of advance even in chemically contaminated areas.

mines and the significant resources committed to developing and producing even more-lethal mines show the lengths to which the Soviets comprehensively plan for modern warfare.

Special Operations Forces (SPETSNAZ)

Soviet special operations forces are managed by the Main Intelligence Directorate (GRU) of the Soviet General Staff and are trained to conduct various sensitive missions, including covert action abroad. Numerous SPETSNAZ troops have been assigned to Soviet forces in Afghanistan, and their success has led the Soviets to increase the number of units deployed.

During peacetime, the GRU carefully coordinates reconnaissance programs designed to meet the intelligence requirements for Soviet forces in war. In wartime, SPETSNAZ forces would operate for extended periods far behind enemy lines, where they would conduct reconnaissance and sabotage on a wide assortment of military and political targets.

While the GRU manages these forces, the KGB is assessed to have overall responsibility, under Central Committee guidance, for operational planning, coordination, and political control of special forces that operate abroad in peacetime. This control was evident in the Soviet invasions of Czechoslovakia in 1968 and Afghanistan in 1979. The KGB maintains its own special operations capabilities in the form of clandestine assets dedicated to assassination and wartime sabotage.

Although organized into brigades, these forces infiltrate and fight as small teams composed of six to eight men. In wartime, naval SPETSNAZ teams would be transported to a target area by aircraft, submarine, or surface ship and would be inserted immediately before hostilities. In a war, each brigade can be expected to field about 100 SPETSNAZ teams.

Once deployed, the teams conduct reconnaissance and tactical operations against a wide variety of targets, such as ship and submarine bases, airfields, command and intelligence centers, communications facilities, ports and harbors, radar sites, and — of prime importance — nuclear weapon facilities. Although a small force, SPETSNAZ has the potential to achieve results disproportionate to its size against critical, yet often vulnerable, targets.

Chemical Warfare

The USSR has the most extensive chemical warfare (CW) capability in the world. The Soviets can deliver chemical weapons with almost all of their conventional weapon systems, from mortars to long-range tactical missiles, available to land, air, and naval forces. Soviet plans for offensive CW operations become even more credible when viewed with their efforts to protect their own troops through the use of specially trained and equipped units that enable continuous operations through contaminated regions. This force has been reorganized

The existing stockpile of US chemical weapons holds 40,000 tons of lethal agents, enough to kill everyone in the world 5,000 times over. See commentary on page 91.

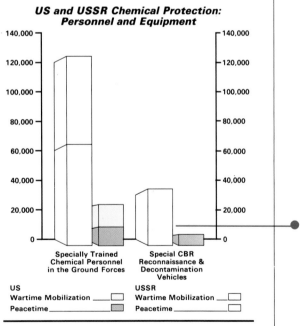

US and USSR Chemical Protection: Personnel and Equipment

Specially Trained Chemical Personnel in the Ground Forces

Special CBR Reconnaissance & Decontamination Vehicles

US
Wartime Mobilization
Peacetime

USSR
Wartime Mobilization
Peacetime

Wrong. Fewer than 10,000.

tras shows, this group is capable of hiring and equipping whole armies. Within our regular military structure, our Army has eight Special Forces groups, two Special Operations battalions, a Delta Force, three battalions of Rangers, thirteen Psychological Warfare battalions and one Civil Affairs battalion. Our Navy has four Special Warfare Groups, six SEAL Teams, two SEAL Delivery Vehicle Teams, two Special Boat squadrons, two Light Assault squadrons, and three Dry-Deck Shelter-Capable submarines for covert delivery and recovery of personnel. Our Air Force has a Special Operations Wing at Eglin Air Force Base, Florida, equipped with 20 AC-130H *Spectre* gunships, 14 MC-130E *Combat Talon Blackbird* transport aircraft, 9 UH-1H and 9 HH-53H *Pave Low* helicopters. The original doctrine for special forces envisioned them in the counterguerilla role, but this administration's Defense Guidance calls for their use in regions the US would enter "without invitation," or in situations where the use of regular forces would be "premature."

Another mirror image. This is roughly the size and shape of the dispersion pattern anticipated from the release of one of the BIGEYE nerve gas bombs our military wants to build.

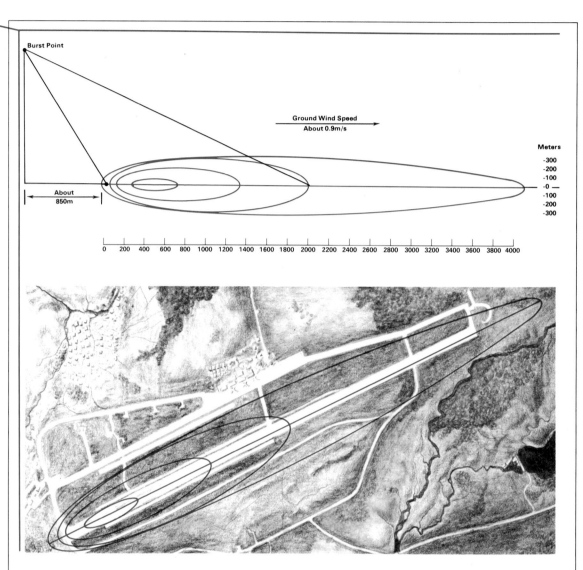

Burst Point

Ground Wind Speed
About 0.9m/s

About
850m

Meters
-300
-200
-100
-0 —
-100
-200
-300

0   200   400   600   800   1000   1200   1400   1600   1800   2000   2200   2400   2600   2800   3000   3200   3400   3600   3800   4000

A SCUD-B ground contamination pattern is shown superimposed on a military runway. Operational flights from contaminated runways are extremely hazardous. In a Soviet chemical attack against a NATO airbase, many SCUD missiles would be used to ensure coverage.

and reequipped in recent years to enhance its abilities. These specialized units, serving in all five branches of the armed forces, are known as the Chemical Service at division level and below and as Chemical Troops at army level and above. Chemical units have the mission of

Wrong. Fewer than 10,000.

protecting Soviet forces from chemical, biological, and radiological (CBR) contamination.

Since the late 1970s, there has been a proliferation and specialization of CW units at all echelons of the Soviet Armed Forces — primarily in the ground forces. Such units range from chemical protection platoons in support of regiments to independent chemical protection brigades that would support a wartime front. Proliferation of units has been most extensive above division level. Each army previously assessed to have a composite chemical defense battalion now fields a variety of independent battalions and companies. Increasing numbers of units also reflect greater specialization. Operationally, each unit or constituent subunit is designed to accomplish specific tasks. Those performing ground and aerial reconnaissance or locating the sites of nuclear bursts, detect areas of contamination, mark the boundaries of the contaminated zones, and measure the levels of the hazard. This information is processed and given to the operations staff. Attacking forces are maneuvered to avoid contaminated regions or decontaminated by equipment or personnel decontamination units as necessary. Additionally, special units are responsible for smoke generation and the use of light and heavy flamethrowers.

Because of organizational expansion, the peacetime strength of the Chemical Troops in the Soviet Ground Forces alone now totals more than 60,000, and this number would double in wartime by mobilizing reservists. More than 30,000 specialized vehicles would be available for use by these troops. Expansion and modernization of equipment have aided in building the capacity for widespread and prolonged CW operations. For example, the decontamination squads of a regimental chemical protection platoon can completely decontaminate eight companies with one load of special decontamination solution.

The types of chemical agents that the Soviets could be expected to employ in war, and in turn would themselves have to encounter, include the following:

- nerve agents (sarin, soman, and a V-series agent);
- blister agents (mustard, lewisite, and a mixture of the two);
- a choking agent (phosgene); and
- one other agent not specifically identified that causes unconsciousness for an hour or more and has been widely reported as being used in Afghanistan.

The Soviets stock both persistent and non-persistent agents. Persistent agents stay on the target from hours to days, depending on weather conditions, unless removed by decontamination. Non-persistent agents will clear from the target relatively quickly. The Soviets are also investigating binary weapon systems. In the binary concept, two relatively harmless chemical compounds are carried in separate compartments inside the munitions. In flight the two compounds mix, producing a lethal chemical agent. This type of system, in addition to its inherent safe handling and storage characteristics, expands the possibilities for newer agent combinations. Complete protection from Soviet chemical weapons requires special clothing and masks as well as rapid treatment for any exposed personnel.

Many CW units, manned to a large extent by reservists, responded to the disaster at Chernobyl. The long-term cleanup allowed the Chemical Troops to practice mobilization procedures; evaluate the ability of units to locate contamination and conduct complete decontamination of personnel, vehicles, terrain, lines of communication, and buildings; and correct whatever shortcomings were noted. Although the forces were deployed because of the accident at the civilian atomic energy station, the fielding of large forces for such a long time demonstrates the Soviet military capability to operate in a contaminated environment.

NATO and the Warsaw Pact

In 1984, the North Atlantic Treaty Organization published the second edition of the NATO and the Warsaw Pact Force Comparisons study. Some charts from the 1984 NATO study were published in *Soviet Military Power 1986.*

The following charts and tables present a US estimate of updated data. Not included in the data are forces of France and Spain. Although both nations are members of the North Atlantic Alliance, they do not participate in its integrated military structure. In an invasion of Western Europe by the Warsaw Pact, France and Spain would defend their national sovereignty with the following forces: approximately 20 divisions, 2,000 tanks, 3,000 artillery pieces and mortars, 1,000 antitank launchers, 8,000 combat vehicles, 450 helicopters, 900 aircraft, and 100 warships.

This is a bit of publicity for the binary chemical weapons, including the BIGEYE bomb, that our military, with the enthusiastic support of this administration, wants to build. These weapons are not as "safe" as advertised. In tests, the BIGEYE has exploded prematurely and leaked. In June, 1986, the General Accounting Office released a report highly critical of the BIGEYE's reliability and usefulness.

Chemical and radioactive contamination of an environment are two very different problems. Most chemicals can be neutralized. Radioactive materials must be physically removed, placed in secure containers, and buried. If radioactive elements are released into the air, a decision must be made as to how large an area to clean. Fallout beyond that area will remain, and no one knows what its long-term consequences will be. A long series of nuclear weapons tests, and numerous accidents at nuclear weapons assembly sites and nuclear power plants, have given the US a good deal of experience of its own with the dangers and difficulties of radioactive contamination. No simple solutions have been found.

A poor excuse for not including the equipment listed here in force comparisons. If these nations would merely defend their national sovereignty, why does France have more than 50,000 troops in West Germany today? They are not there as tourists. Both nations are full military partners in NATO.

The US chemical arsenal utilizes two types of nerve gas, GB and the more persistent VX, as well as mustard gas. Our current stockpile includes 500,000 4.2 inch mortar shells filled with mustard gas, 500,000 105 mm howitzer projectiles with mustard gas, 900,000 105 mm howitzer projectiles filled with GB, 250,000 155 mm howitzer projectiles with mustard gas, 200,000 155 mm and 203 mm howitzer projectiles with GB, 300,000 155 mm and 203 mm howitzer projectiles with VX, 3,500 500 lb bombs with GB, 9,500 750-lb bombs with GB, 900 160-gallon spray tanks filled with VX, and several hundred thousand M-55 medium-range rockets filled with GB and VX.

This represents a fallback position. The administration had originally told the world that the Soviets were using nerve gas in Afghanistan and critics pointed out that, if this were true, the administration quickly would have gained custody of the bodies as evidence, had autopsies performed on them by an international team of experts and taken the results to the World Court. The administration did none of these things. So it now reports use of a nonlethal gas which has only temporary effects, and then wears off without a trace. If there is no trace, perhaps there is no gas.

● Wrong. NATO does not have only 3,260 combat aircraft in place. It has 5,234. When fully reinforced by US carrier-based aircraft and additional US land-based aircraft, NATO would have a total of 7,718 combat aircraft, not the 5,125 shown here. The chart more honestly shows a total of 6,650 Warsaw Pact combat aircraft after full reinforcement from the USSR, but creates the false impression that this reinforcement would consist of only 340 aircraft, and that 6,310 of the Pact's aircraft are already in place. In fact, about 4,500 Warsaw Pact combat aircraft are in place, including those in four Soviet Tactical Air Armies, as well as Soviet medium-range bombers. Soviet reinforcement, therefore, would consist of 2,150 aircraft. This still would not match NATO's total.

Retired submarines, coastal ● and fast patrol boats which cannot operate in the open ocean, and frigates and corvettes which displace only a fraction of the tonnage of their NATO counterparts are all included here to create the false impression that the Warsaw Pact has higher numbers of naval vessels. For the correct naval balance in the Atlantic and Mediterranean, see the commentary on page 8. See also the commentary on pages 81 and 83.

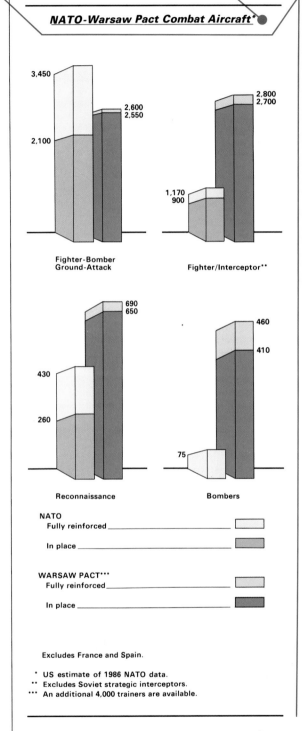

NATO-Warsaw Pact Combat Aircraft*

Fighter-Bomber Ground-Attack: 3,450 / 2,100 / 2,600 / 2,550

Fighter/Interceptor**: 1,170 / 900 / 2,800 / 2,700

Reconnaissance: 430 / 260 / 690 / 650

Bombers: 75 / 460 / 410

NATO
Fully reinforced _____
In place _____

WARSAW PACT***
Fully reinforced _____
In place _____

Excludes France and Spain.

* US estimate of 1986 NATO data.
** Excludes Soviet strategic interceptors.
*** An additional 4,000 trainers are available.

NATO and Warsaw Pact Maritime Forces in the North Atlantic and Seas Bordering Europe 1986*

Category	NATO	Warsaw Pact
Aircraft Carriers VSTOL Carriers	11	—
KIEV-Class Ships	—	2
Helicopter Carriers	6	2
Cruisers	16	22
Destroyers, Frigates, Corvettes	310	201
Coastal Escorts and Fast Patrol Boats	267	586
Amphibious Ships – Ocean-going	57	24
– Other Ships/ Coastal Craft	71	188
Mine Warfare Ships/Craft	270	330**
Total Submarines (All Types)	206	258
– Ballistic Missile Submarines	35	44
– Long-Range Attack Submarines	68	145
– Other Types	103	69
– % Submarines Nuclear Powered	50%	51%
Sea-based Tactical ASW and Support Aircraft Including Helicopters	832	205
Land-Based Tactical and Support Aircraft Including Helicopters	389	527
Land-Based Anti-Submarine Warfare Fixed-Wing Aircraft and Helicopters	462	209

Excludes France and Spain
* US Estimate of 1986 NATO data
** Excludes minesweeping boats and drones

92

The administration's insufficient excuse for omitting Spain's contributions to these figures is that Spain did not join NATO until 1982. Its excuse for excluding French contributions is that "France withdrew its forces from NATO's international command in 1966." France, however, remains a full member of NATO. That is why it has 3 armored divisions in West Germany today. These insupportable exclusions affect all of the figures on this and the preceding page, and are part of the reason why so much exception is taken to them. The authors have tried to cover themselves for this little bit of cheating by announcing it in advance on page 91.

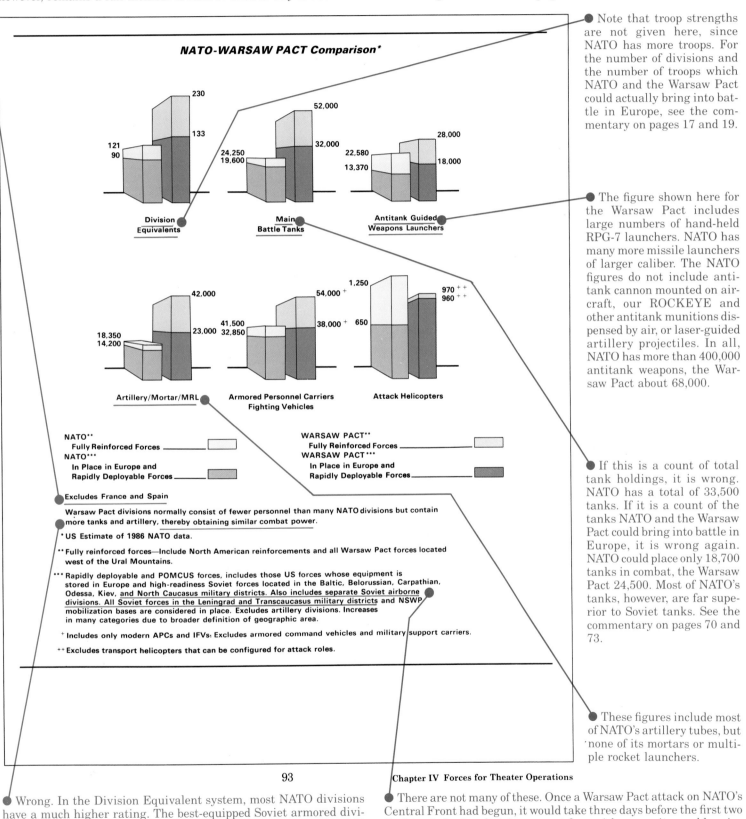

NATO-WARSAW PACT Comparison*

Division Equivalents: 121, 90, 230, 133

Main Battle Tanks: 24,250, 19,600, 52,000, 32,000

Antitank Guided Weapons Launchers: 22,580, 13,370, 28,000, 18,000

Artillery/Mortar/MRL: 18,350, 14,200, 42,000, 23,000

Armored Personnel Carriers Fighting Vehicles: 41,500, 32,850, 54,000 +, 38,000 +

Attack Helicopters: 1,250, 650, 970 ++, 960 ++

NATO**
Fully Reinforced Forces _____
NATO***
In Place in Europe and
Rapidly Deployable Forces_____

WARSAW PACT**
Fully Reinforced Forces _____
WARSAW PACT***
In Place in Europe and
Rapidly Deployable Forces_____

Excludes France and Spain

Warsaw Pact divisions normally consist of fewer personnel than many NATO divisions but contain more tanks and artillery, thereby obtaining similar combat power.

* **US Estimate of 1986 NATO data.**

** **Fully reinforced forces—Include North American reinforcements and all Warsaw Pact forces located west of the Ural Mountains.**

*** **Rapidly deployable and POMCUS forces, includes those US forces whose equipment is stored in Europe and high-readiness Soviet forces located in the Baltic, Belorussian, Carpathian, Odessa, Kiev, and North Caucasus military districts. Also includes separate Soviet airborne divisions. All Soviet forces in the Leningrad and Transcaucasus military districts and NSWP mobilization bases are considered in place. Excludes artillery divisions. Increases in many categories due to broader definition of geographic area.**

+ **Includes only modern APCs and IFVs; Excludes armored command vehicles and military support carriers.**

++ **Excludes transport helicopters that can be configured for attack roles.**

Note that troop strengths are not given here, since NATO has more troops. For the number of divisions and the number of troops which NATO and the Warsaw Pact could actually bring into battle in Europe, see the commentary on pages 17 and 19.

The figure shown here for the Warsaw Pact includes large numbers of hand-held RPG-7 launchers. NATO has many more missile launchers of larger caliber. The NATO figures do not include antitank cannon mounted on aircraft, our ROCKEYE and other antitank munitions dispensed by air, or laser-guided artillery projectiles. In all, NATO has more than 400,000 antitank weapons, the Warsaw Pact about 68,000.

If this is a count of total tank holdings, it is wrong. NATO has a total of 33,500 tanks. If it is a count of the tanks NATO and the Warsaw Pact could bring into battle in Europe, it is wrong again. NATO could place only 18,700 tanks in combat, the Warsaw Pact 24,500. Most of NATO's tanks, however, are far superior to Soviet tanks. See the commentary on pages 70 and 73.

These figures include most of NATO's artillery tubes, but none of its mortars or multiple rocket launchers.

Wrong. In the Division Equivalent system, most NATO divisions have a much higher rating. The best-equipped Soviet armored division has 325 tanks and 9,500 troops. A US armored division has 360 tanks and 18,500 troops.

There are not many of these. Once a Warsaw Pact attack on NATO's Central Front had begun, it would take three days before the first two Soviet reinforcing divisions, apart from airborne units, could arrive in the region. It would take another 10 days before an additional five divisions could mobilize and reach the front. See the commentary on pages 17 and 19.

The purpose of this illustration is to dramatize the suggestion made in its caption that Soviet ballistic missile submarines will be able to fire their missiles and then reload at sea during a nuclear war. According to the Defense Intelligence Agency, reloading missiles at sea would be "unlikely, if not impossible, during a nuclear war."

Chapter V

Readiness, Mobility, and Sustainability

The large numbers of weapon systems that the Soviets have amassed do not alone describe the extent to which the USSR has comprehensively built up its military power. Soviet forces are not equipped and trained as a home-based defense force; rather, they are designed for offensive operations in the enemy's homeland. To support this objective, the Soviets have developed an extensive offensive military support structure, including storage depots that stock some 27,000 meters of bridging equipment, 13 million metric tons of arms and ammunition, and 60 million metric tons of petrol (fuel), oil, and lubricants — enough war materials to support intense offensive operations for 60 to 90 days. The threat inherent in Soviet military power is indeed a result of the commitment made to meticulous planning for military operations.

The Soviets have not overlooked any aspect of military power. They devote considerable resources to their logistics support structure, to refining training programs to maintain a high degree of readiness, and to improving their strategic mobility. This facet of the USSR's military might is less visible than the warships and fighter aircraft, and less eye-catching than a show of firepower. Nonetheless, Soviet forces could not be sustained in combat without a well-planned and highly developed infrastructure tailored to support offensive operations.

The **ALEXANDER BRYKIN,** *lead unit of a new class of strategic ballistic missile submarine tenders, is preparing to join the Soviet fleet. The survivability and sustainability of the Soviet SSBN/SLBM force will be further enhanced with missile-reloading operations in protected waters. Such operations demonstrate a growing Soviet capacity to engage in protracted nuclear war.*

Military forces are equipped in precisely the same way, whether they are intended for offensive or defensive operations. Most are also trained for offensive operations, whether or not there is any intention to use them in that role, since taking the offensive is the most "spirited" form of defense. It is we who read the offensive intent into Soviet military forces. Had the US not amassed so much military power of its own, and continued to multiply its military advantages over the Soviet Union, one might believe these words were written with at least a degree of real concern.

Not enough time, then, to last until Soviet reserve formations could be mobilized. See the commentary on page 19.

Their readiness is not very high. See the commentary on page 19.

More repetition. It's the only way to drive the point home.

Not likely. See the commentary on opposite page.

How can any nation develop such a capacity, when its leaders will never know whether they can survive the first weapons to detonate? This is sheer fantasy. But it is a dangerous fantasy, and when our leaders cultivate it they are dangerous men.

Wrong. Many of these divisions have only half their required equipment and much of that equipment is obsolete.

Since training and mobilization are so important, why does this book take up so much space exaggerating numbers?

Wrong. Most of these divisions would take up to four months.

For a more precise understanding than is given here of Soviet readiness and mobilization capabilities, see the commentary on page 19.

Yes, many Soviet forces are at "not-ready" levels.

These divisions would be filled by Soviet reservists. It would take at least six months before they were ready for combat.

The Soviets leave little to chance, even in peacetime. They are aware that their high numbers of forces and equipment alone are insufficient to achieve national objectives unless the troops are properly trained and can be mobilized, moved, and sustained.

Soviet military power rests on a comprehensive and increasingly sophisticated mobilization and support structure designed to focus the nation's resources on waging war. Soviet military planners emphasize that the armed forces must be prepared to participate in a broad spectrum of conflicts, ranging from short local engagements to protracted global wars. As a result, the Soviets have developed detailed plans, established procedures, and undertaken wide-ranging preparations to mobilize the nation's resources and to sustain their forces under a variety of wartime contingencies.

Readiness

Soviet military doctrine holds that the initial period of war is critical in determining the overall course of a conflict. Thus, the Soviets are continually enhancing the combat readiness of their armed forces to ensure that large, well-equipped forces can be rapidly fielded and committed. This emphasis on combat readiness is applied to all branches of their military and to all theaters of military operations (TVDs). In support of this doctrine, Soviet Air and Aerospace Forces are at high readiness. Some pilots of late-model aircraft are being trained to handle secondary roles. Less-experienced pilots, flying older model aircraft, probably will continue to be limited to single roles because of low flying-time opportunities and because of aircraft limitations. The Soviet Navy normally has less than 10 percent of its major combatants deployed out of area at any time but has the readiness capability to deploy up to 50 percent on short notice. The ground forces have the lowest peacetime manning levels of the major force components. They are highly dependent on the mobilization of manpower and equipment from the civilian economy to reach wartime status. Overall, the Soviets have developed a posture in which the most ready forces are deployed in the area of the greatest perceived threat, backed by the capability to mobilize and move their entire force structure as required.

The Soviets maintain their ground forces at so-called ready and not-ready levels. Ready divisions are manned with a high percentage of their planned wartime personnel and equipment requirements. These forces are trained extensively during peacetime. Not-ready units are divided into active cadre divisions, with less than 50 percent of required manpower, and inactive mobilization divisions, which are unmanned equipment sets. The ready divisions constitute about 40 percent of Soviet forces, including all the forces stationed in Eastern Europe, and can begin combat operations after a brief period of mobilization and preparation. The not-ready cadre divisions can be assembled in about a week, and the mobilization divisions require longer. An extensive period of training would be required before these units were ready for offensive combat. Although the Soviets emphasize the rapid mobilization of their entire force structure, recent enhancements have stressed the mobilization responsiveness of the not-ready forces.

Since the late 1970s, the Soviets have converted some 30 unmanned mobilization divisions into low-strength cadre-level units staffed at less than 5 percent manning. This process has involved the assignment of experienced personnel, some expansion and modernization of equipment holdings, and the construction or expansion of garrison facilities. These enhancements improve the mobilization capability of these divisions and make them available for earlier commitment as more effective formations.

The Soviets are strongly emphasizing the rapid mobilization capability of all their ready and not-ready ground forces because most units are manned at less than war-authorized levels. Elaborate mobilization plans are drawn up and continually refined. Drilling in alert and mobilization procedures is a constant element of unit training, and timed mobilization exercises are frequently practiced.

Mobilization System

The USSR has developed a comprehensive manpower and materiel mobilization support system. Soviet doctrine calls for two levels of mobilization — general and partial. General involves all the armed forces and pursues a full, rapid transition of political, economic, and manpower resources to a wartime posture. Partial involves selected military districts using limited numbers of military units and installations, as seen in preparations for the

Wrong. The Soviets do not have this level of strength. To achieve it, they would have to mobilize all 2,100,000 of the reservists the authors later acknowledge would be required to bring their forces up to full "wartime" strength. But this is not wartime. The Soviets currently have 3,700,000 active uniformed military personnel. Accord-

ing to the Center for Defense Information, the entire Warsaw Pact alliance has only 4,800,000 active uniformed military personnel, while NATO has 5,900,000. Even if the Soviets were able to mobilize so many reserves, and NATO activated all of its reserves, the Warsaw Pact would then have a total of 6,900,000 active personnel in all

---

invasions of Czechoslovakia and Afghanistan.

At the heart of the system is the network of about 4,200 military commissariats (voyenkomaty) located throughout the USSR. Commissariats — subordinate ultimately to the General Staff — are found at local and regional administrative levels throughout the USSR. They serve as draft boards, armed forces reserve centers, and the veterans administration.

Military Manpower Base

From May through June, and from November through December, more than 2 million Soviet males are inducted into the armed forces. Conscripts are about 18 years old and serve for 2 years or, in the case of naval personnel aboard ship, 3 years of active duty. They are then discharged into the reserves.

Soviet Armed Forces personnel strength currently exceeds 5.8 million. Of these, the career officer corps comprises more than 1 million, or about 20 percent. Reserve officers would be called up in wartime. The reserve system has over 55 million people, of whom more than 9 million have been discharged from active duty within the past 5 years. Although many reservists do not receive annual training, and although callups are of uneven quality and frequency, the pool of recently discharged conscripts is sufficient to meet mobilization needs. About 2.1 million reservists would be required in order to bring the armed forces up to full wartime strength, leaving an enormous manpower base available to provide replacements and create units.

Within the Soviet military, women serve mainly in enlisted ranks in auxiliary and specialist support roles. Military law subjects women to conscription during wartime. This practice not only releases men for combat duty but also provides a reservoir for expanding forces, as in World War II, when some 800,000 women served in the Soviet Armed Forces.

Mobility

The USSR has always maintained formidable forces suited for combat on the Eurasian landmass. During the past 2 decades, however, the Soviets have bolstered their overall military force posture by steadily increasing the size and capability of all their forces. Through advancements in airlift, sealift, and command-and-control structures, the Soviets can project powerful armed forces into areas contiguous to

the USSR and sustain them. With the enhanced capability to deploy light, well-armed, mobile forces in support of political goals and foreign policy objectives, the Soviets are also expanding their ability to exert influence in the Third World.

Sealift

The military sealift capability of the USSR is based primarily on its large merchant fleet. This military-adaptable fleet has grown steadily during the past 2 decades, and it now includes more than 1,700 ships whose combined deadweight tonnage exceeds 22 million.

Nearly half the cargo ships are equipped with cranes capable of lifting the heaviest military armor and vehicles, thereby reducing the dependence on prepared port facilities. The inventory includes numerous modern ships, such as barge carriers, roll-on/roll-off cargo ships, and roll-on/float-off ships. All these ships have direct military applications. Soviet merchant ships are frequently used to transport arms and the forces of client states in support of Soviet foreign policy objectives.

All of the important merchant ship designs produced over the past 2 decades have probably been prepared to military standards. Key features include chemical-biological-radiological protection; increased endurance and surface speeds; improved capability in handling-gear and self-servicing features; and advanced communications, navigation, and electronics systems, such as identification-friend-or-foe systems, that in the West are restricted to naval ships.

Merchant marine operations are closely coordinated with the Soviet Navy. Part of the logistics support required by the navy in peacetime, mainly in distant areas, is provided by Soviet merchant ships. This flexibility allows these ships to obtain supplies for naval use from ports where Soviet warships are denied access. In a crisis, the highly organized, centrally controlled merchant fleet can provide military support quickly and effectively, particularly for amphibious operations, troop movements, and arms shipments.

Augmenting the oceangoing merchant fleet is a river and sea fleet consisting of numerous tankers and dry-cargo carriers. These ships, which operate in coastal sea areas and in the Soviet and European inland waterway system, provide an added wartime capacity to transport

The US has the much larger sealift capability. The combined deadweight tonnage of our smaller fleet of 740 merchant marine vessels exceeds the Soviet Union's at 24 million. The Soviets do rely heavily on their merchant fleet, because their military sealift capability is so small. Our Navy's 53 largest replenishment ships displace a total of 1,413,000 tons. The 85 largest replenishment ships in the Soviet Navy displace a total of only 570,000 tons.

As we have learned, US merchant ships and foreign merchant ships hired by the US do the same.

branches of military service, while NATO would have 8,200,000. According to the International Institute for Strategic Studies, the Soviet reserve system has fewer than half this number of people. Few of these have had recent training. According to the Institute for Foreign Policy Analysis, the Soviet Army relies upon "over 2,000,000

trained reservists." Most of them would be used to fill out the many divisions acknowledged on the previous page to be "not ready." They would not be ready for combat for up to four months. The remaining trained reservists would be used to create some additional divisions, but these would not be ready for combat for at least six months.

The US has the higher airlift capacity. The largest Soviet transport aircraft shown here, the CONDOR, is not yet in service. Only three have been produced to date. We have had 78 of our largest transport aircraft, the GALAXY, in service for several years and we plan to build 16 more. We have 733 HERCULES transport aircraft, while the Soviets have only 260 CUB transport aircraft. The combined lift capacity of all of the Soviet transport aircraft shown here is currently 16,150 tons. The combined lift capacity of all of our GALAXY, STARLIFTER and HERCULES transport aircraft is currently 35,900 tons. Note that most of our transport aircraft have greater range than their Soviet counterparts, and that our aircraft, as the authors quietly acknowledge in a footnote at the bottom of the chart, can be refuelled in midair, whereas the Soviet aircraft cannot be.

- Wrong. 45 MT.
- Wrong. 4,000 km.
- Wrong. 35 MT.
- Wrong. 3,250 km.
- Wrong. 5,600 km.
- Wrong. 4,900 km.
- Wrong. 310.
- Wrong. 50.

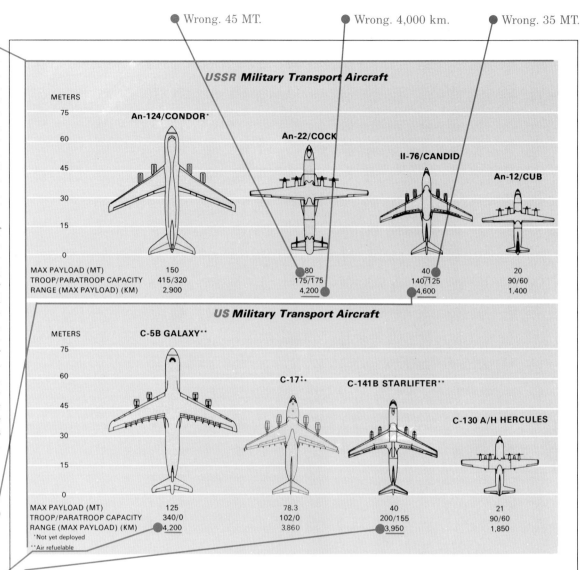

USSR Military Transport Aircraft

	An-124/CONDOR*	An-22/COCK	Il-76/CANDID	An-12/CUB
MAX PAYLOAD (MT)	150	80	40	20
TROOP/PARATROOP CAPACITY	415/320	175/175	140/125	90/60
RANGE (MAX PAYLOAD) (KM)	2,900	4,200	4,600	1,400

US Military Transport Aircraft

	C-5B GALAXY**	C-17*	C-141B STARLIFTER**	C-130 A/H HERCULES
MAX PAYLOAD (MT)	125	78.3	40	21
TROOP/PARATROOP CAPACITY	340/0	102/0	200/155	90/60
RANGE (MAX PAYLOAD) (KM)	4,200	3,860	3,950	1,850

*Not yet deployed
**Air refuelable

supplies and materiel to continental military theaters of operations.

Airlift

The most visible of the USSR's military mobility assets is Military Transport Aviation (*Voyenno-transportnaya aviatsia,* abbreviated VTA). In wartime, VTA forces would support airborne operations and provide logistics airlift to the armed forces. In peacetime, VTA aircraft make arms and military equipment deliveries, including materiel to Third World clients.

This organization has nearly 600 aircraft, and its worldwide presence and missions are growing. Marked in civilian Aeroflot colors,

VTA aircraft provide famine relief to Ethiopia; arms deliveries to Angola, Libya, Syria, Iraq, and other countries; as well as airlift support to combat forces in Afghanistan. The force continues to acquire aircraft with improved range, speed, and cargo capacity.

VTA's 4-engine, turboprop-driven CUB is being replaced by the long-range CANDID jet transport, of which about 340 are in the VTA inventory. The USSR's heavy-lift capability, currently consisting of 55 COCK aircraft, will be upgraded by new CONDOR heavy-lift jet transports in 1987 or 1988. The CONDOR, comparable to the US C-5B Galaxy, can carry 150 metric tons — almost twice the capacity of

98

It will probably turn out that the CONDOR's lift capacity is smaller than our GALAXY's, since that is the way almost every one of these predictions has turned out for almost forty years. The GALAXY can carry 345 fully equipped combat troops, or 2 M-60 main battle tanks and 16 ¾-ton trucks, or 3 M-41 tanks and 16 ¾-ton trucks, or 1 M-60 tank and 2 UH-1B helicopters, or 3 CH-47 helicopters or 6 M-113A1 armored personnel carriers, or 10 LANCE missiles with towing and launch vehicles. We currently have more than double the Soviet airlift capacity, and we continue to build new GALAXYs. Moreover, a new US military transport aircraft, the C-17, will soon be deployed. A total of 210 C-17s is planned. In the foreseeable future, the Soviets are not likely to be able to match our growing airlift and sealift capabilities.

The An-124/CONDOR transport, which has a greater heavy-lift capability than the US C-5B Galaxy, may be deployed this year. CONDOR's visor nose and clamshell rear doors enable rapid drive-through loading and unloading.

the COCK. This increase in heavy-lift capacity will enhance the Soviets' ability to support their commitments abroad. In wartime, the large lift capacity of the CONDOR will aid the rapid movement of critical reserve stocks to forward areas, as well as outsized weapons such as tanks, helicopters, missiles, and other important equipment where needed.

The civilian airline, Aeroflot, is the USSR's strategic air transport reserve. On mobilization, the total armed forces aircraft capacity for military passenger transport would be increased significantly. These long- and medium-

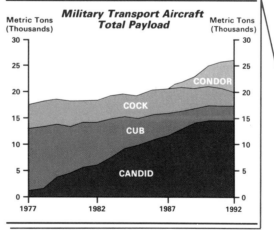

Military Transport Aircraft Total Payload

Metric Tons (Thousands)

CONDOR
COCK
CUB
CANDID

1977 1982 1987 1992

While this falls far short of the US military airlift capacity, it is still an exaggeration. The Soviets currently have a military airlift capacity of 16,150 tons. See the commentary on the preceding page.

The AirLand Battle doctrine changes nothing for Soviet planners. They have been threatened by our deep-strike capabilities ever since the NATO alliance was formed.

range transport aircraft, numbering over 1,600, provide the Soviets with an immediate source of strategic air transport. Aeroflot and the Ministry of Civil Aviation maintain a close working relationship with the military. Aeroflot is headed by a chief marshal of aviation, most Aeroflot aircrews are reserve military officers, and its organization mirrors the military structure.

Logistics and Sustainability

The rapid Soviet force modernization, the evolving concepts for the conduct of theater-wide operations, and the development of US-NATO forces and doctrines intended to counter the USSR's growing military strength have presented Soviet planners with demanding logistics support requirements. Therefore the planners have focused increasing attention on developing a logistics force structure and management system capable of simultaneously sustaining strategic offensives by coalition armed forces in multiple theaters of military operations. One effort has been the establishment of echeloned reserves of critical supply items and equipment throughout the Warsaw Pact. Another has been the introduction of increasingly capable logistics transport means, mobile repair shops, pipeline-laying vehicles, materiel handling equipment, and other specialized rear service items.

In addition to such extensive peacetime investments in rear service resources, the Soviets have developed an innovative program to improve the operations of theater logistics formations and systems in war. One of the most important developments in this effort has been the Pact-wide restructuring of logistics support units and groupings tasked to provide ammunition, fuel, repair parts, food, clothing, and other materiel to theater forces. Another important development was the creation of powerful theater-level rear service control and planning headquarters within the High Commands of Forces in continental theaters of military operations.

The restructuring of logistics support units has taken place concurrently with other modernization programs. These programs are designed to configure Soviet combat forces and concepts for effective execution of theater operations. Soviet planners strive to ensure that the mobility, responsiveness, and overall capabilities of logistics formations keep pace with

the demands generated by modern coalition combined-arms forces engaged in offensive operations. Soviet planners also recognize that US concepts, such as Airland Battle, and new generations of US-NATO deep-strike weapon systems could threaten the Warsaw Pact rear area and thus the success of their theater-wide operations. Soviet logisticians are particularly concerned about increasingly accurate and powerful non-nuclear strike systems that they believe could be targeted against rear service units and facilities.

To deal with these perceived force improvements, the Soviets have formed materiel support units within combined arms organizations from tactical to front levels. Within the divisions and regiments, materiel support battalions and companies, respectively, have been organized to combine formerly fragmented transport, supply, and servicing functions under one materiel support commander at each level. These new rear service units constitute a substantial improvement in tactical logistics capabilities as a result of a 30-percent increase in motor transport assets and a streamlined command structure. Soviet planners believe that a divisional materiel support battalion would be more survivable and better able to support the fast-moving maneuver units envisioned for future battlefields.

Simultaneously, a similar reorganization of logistics assets at army and front level has resulted in the creation of materiel support brigades. These brigades incorporate transport, supply, and associated servicing functions under the centralized control of materiel support brigade commanders. They replace the loosely organized and jointly controlled logistics bases that were assigned to provide ammunition, fuel, parts, and other supplies to army and front forces. Each combined-arms and tank army could now have a materiel support brigade. Each front could have one or more brigades in addition to a large relocatable front supply base complex. The development, refinement, and training of these new units is still underway, and variants are likely to be fielded. Materiel support units of regimental size, for example, have been included in the composition of the new corps-type organizations being formed.

Non-Soviet Warsaw Pact forces are also forming materiel support units in line with the Soviet model. The eventual standardization of

Hardly any innovations here. A separate logistics command has long been part of the permanent structure of each of the US military services, as well as those of most other NATO nations.

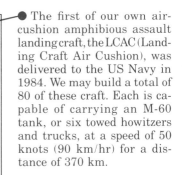

The first of our own air-cushion amphibious assault landing craft, the LCAC (Landing Craft Air Cushion), was delivered to the US Navy in 1984. We may build a total of 80 of these craft. Each is capable of carrying an M-60 tank, or six towed howitzers and trucks, at a speed of 50 knots (90 km/hr) for a distance of 370 km.

Aside from the immense stocks of ammunition, lubricants and fuel which NATO has pre-positioned in Europe, the United States has pre-positioned full sets of equipment for six divisions, an armored cavalry regiment and several corps-level support units in Europe. Moreover, 18 pre-positioning ships now sit in the Indian Ocean, loaded with $8.5 billion worth of additional sets of divisional and other unit equipment and supplies for the US Central Command and US Marine Corps.

The new POMORNIK-Class air-cushion landing craft, 57 meters long and 350-tons displacement, marks an important advance in the USSR's ability to conduct amphibious operations.

these key rear service units throughout the Warsaw Pact will reduce the command-and-control problems associated with logistics support for coalition warfare.

Overall, the extensive restructuring of tactical and operational-level supply units will increase the staying power of divisions, armies, and fronts tasked to achieve theater objectives in wartime. Additionally, tailored mobile materiel support unit elements are particularly well designed for supplying forces isolated from main combat formations.

During a war, supplies from strategic stockpiles in the Soviet Union will be sent forward to supplement the large pre-positioned stocks already in place for each theater. These supplies will be carried over a road and rail network that in the Western TVD is highly developed

and affords a number of alternate routes necessary in wartime. Besides the fuel and ammunition supplies established in forward logistic depots and in the Soviet interior, materiel of all types has been stockpiled throughout the USSR. This hardware includes tanks, armored personnel carriers, field artillery, and air defense systems. In the past decade, the amount of pre-stocked military supplies has substantially increased. Today, more than 3 million metric tons of ammunition is pre-stocked by the Pact in the Western TVD. This ammunition, along with over 9 million metric tons of petrol (fuel), oil, and lubricants (POL), is sufficient to support Warsaw Pact military operations against NATO for 60 to 90 days. Additional supplies would be provided by strategic reserves dispersed throughout the USSR.

This would not allow sufficient time for reinforcement. Half the Soviet Army would still be mobilizing, training, or just beginning its journey to the front.

The Far Eastern Theater of Military Operations (FETVD) ranks second in importance only to the Western TVD. During the past decade, the Soviets have increased considerably the sustainability of their forces in this vital military region. Moscow has realized that the lines of communication (LOC) to the FETVD are vulnerable and that more support is needed for the large, modernizing forces stationed opposite China and Japan.

Nowhere else is this support more evident than in the buildup of storage capacities for ammunition and POL. This buildup reduces the dependence of Soviet FETVD forces on logistics supplies coming from Strategic Reserve stockpiles in the Soviet interior. The armed forces can sustain conventional defense operations in the FETVD for more than 100 days.

Soviet planners have provided for theater-level rear service integration and direction through the establishment of logistics management and planning bodies within the High Command of Forces in the various TVDs. In creating theater-level logistics commanders and staffs, the Soviets have drawn on the lessons of history.

In a future war, TVD logistics staffs, headed by deputy commanders for rear services and armament, will exercise great authority over vast transportation, materiel, and technical support resources slated for the theater forces. In peacetime, these Soviet-directed staffs in each theater opposite NATO further centralize the formulation of rear service plans predicated on the use and control of facilities and resources in the Warsaw Pact. This preparation for theater-wide military operations is comprehensive. It includes the creation of military supply depots echeloned and dispersed throughout each theater. In wartime, some of these supplies will be under the direct control of the theater commander and his rear services deputies.

Besides these military resources, Warsaw Pact national transportation routes and systems critical to the movement and supply of theater forces have been designated and constantly improved. To deal with potential wartime destruction, stocks of bridging, rail, road, and airfield repair construction material and equipment have been pre-positioned. Civilian factories and industrial facilities of the Warsaw Pact have been designated to serve as military repair facilities in wartime. Large parts of the civilian hospital system in each country will also be incorporated into the military medical system during war.

Wartime operational control of both Warsaw Pact military logistics assets and substantial resources of the members' national economies already has been assigned to the commander of the High Command of Forces in the various TVDs. These resources will be managed by TVD rear service staffs, in accordance with overall operational plans, to sustain Warsaw Pact strategic offensive operations.

This approach underlines the Soviet view that rear service support is a continuation of the process — which begins in the production sphere — of managing the economy for war. That is, all national assets are to be focused on waging and winning war, a concept now being applied within each theater opposite NATO under more direct Soviet control.

With these resources and the authority that transcends issues of non-Soviet Warsaw Pact (NSWP) national sovereignty, Soviet commanders of the theater forces facing NATO can influence theater operations directly and independently of NSWP national command authority. They would do so by allocating and shifting war-sustaining resources among strategic or operational axes, as dictated by the situation. Thus, the extensive and continuing Soviet efforts to ensure that the logistics support base is capable of meeting future battlefield requirements can be seen in the following activities: the restructuring of rear service units, the establishment of theater-level logistics planning and management bodies, and the more direct control of Warsaw Pact military and civilian resources by Soviet TVD High Commands.

Logistics also plays a major role in the deployment of the Strategic Rocket Forces (SRF). Soviet decisionmakers have given high priority to efforts to ensure reliable supplies of nuclear weapons. During peacetime, missiles, propellants, and spare parts for strategic ballistic missiles are normally moved from production factories to rear missile depots, and from there to rail transfer points located near operational launch sites. In times of conflict, provisions probably exist to deliver necessary equipment to resupply SRF units. Additionally, Soviet planners recognize that rail interdiction could threaten the success of SRF logistics operations; therefore, extra missiles, additional

---

Of course. That is where we have more Communists on our side than the Soviets have on their side.

The mirror image of every nation's plans for war.

Our Defense Department has estimated that "reloading a significant fraction of the ICBM force" would take the Soviets "up to several weeks." Even if the launcher and the missile survived the first moments of a nuclear war, it isn't likely that surviving command centers would have the information to redirect them to a remaining secondary target, let alone the means to communicate with them.

This passage describes the typical logistical problems faced by an invading army trying to cope with a popular uprising. These problems are identical to those the US faced in Vietnam. The passage is here primarily to remind us that the Soviets are in Afghanistan, and deserve the world's condemnation for being there. Since we are no longer in Vietnam, and US military forces, so far as the general pub-

Soviet forces stockpile more than 27,000 meters of bridging equipment to support river crossings during offensive operations.

propellants, and spare parts are pre-positioned at a number of sites to minimize the effectiveness of LOC interdiction. Newer missile systems such as the road-mobile SS-25 and rail-mobile SS-X-24 have significantly enhanced chances of survival because of their high mobility. Their mobility also greatly increases the opportunity for ballistic missile refire. Logistics support, particularly for force reconstitution, has a high priority in the SRF.

Logistics Support in Afghanistan

The Soviet rear service system is organized to sustain large-scale, high-intensity operations. In Afghanistan, however, the Soviet logistics establishment has been required to support small, widely dispersed combat units in a protracted low-intensity conflict. Although the scope of this logistics effort is limited by Soviet standards, the difficulties posed by geographic and operational factors have been substantial. The absence of a rail system in Afghanistan has limited the movement of supplies to air and road transportation as well as to fuel pipelines. Although Military Transport Aviation aircraft and helicopters are being used extensively to bring supplies into Afghanistan, and to transport them within the country, the overall resupply effort in the country has relied more on motor transport and tactical pipeline. Nonetheless, these logistics complications have not greatly impeded the Soviets' ability to prosecute the war.

Large quantities of supplies are being brought from military districts and central depots in the USSR by rail, truck, barge, and pipeline to transshipment points just inside the

Afghan border. Much of the fuel is then shipped by Soviet-constructed and Soviet-maintained tactical pipelines or tanker trucks to key locations in Afghanistan. Most other supplies, however, are transported by convoys to storage complexes or to the depots of tactical units. The Afghan road network is poorly developed, extremely restrictive, difficult to maintain, often impassable, and heavily used by assorted military and civilian vehicles. As a consequence, routes dedicated to resupply operations have not been established.

Among the most vexing problems the Soviets face in Afghanistan is security for LOCs and rear area assets. Since the invasion more than 7 years ago, Soviet transport columns, equipment, facilities, and garrisons have been subjected to continuing harassment and attack. Convoys, pipelines, and depots have been struck. Convoy duty is so dangerous that the Soviets award pennants for "Courage and Valor" to truckdrivers who complete a specified number of trips.

This security issue has focused Soviet attention on a problem that has implications beyond those of logistics support in Afghanistan. Soviet planners are now closely studying the problem of providing security for logistics units tasked to support combined arms operations in a major war. This effort is reflected, for example, in expressed concerns about training now being given to new commanders and personnel from materiel support units in the skills needed to repel attack by enemy special operations forces or diversionary units. Route and rear area security would be especially critical for forces operating on isolated axes. Soviet planners are also using the Afghanistan experience to review procedures for field maintenance of equipment in adverse geographic and climatic conditions as well as medical support for combat and non-combat casualties.

Soviet logistics operations in Afghanistan have been hindered by environmental constraints and combat activity. Nonetheless, the Soviets have maintained a logistics support system that has been able to sustain a sizable military presence and active counterinsurgency war for more than 7 years. The continuing incorporation of new procedures into overall logistics support concepts will help to improve the capabilities of the critical rear service component of Soviet military operations.

lic knows, are not now stationed anywhere else in the world without invitation, it may seem a good time to adopt a posture of moral outrage over the Soviet presence in Afghanistan. A settlement must be reached in Afghanistan and the Soviets must withdraw. But the crusade to achieve those objectives cannot be led by a government which has intervened in the affairs of other nations and peoples so many more times than the Soviet government has, which declares itself to

be Moscow's implacable foe, which systematically lies to its own people about Soviet military capabilities, global ambitions, and atrocities in Afghanistan, using this propaganda to justify a needless, wasteful military buildup of our own, and which has continued a covert relationship with the Afghan rebels ever since it began sending arms to Mohammed Daud in 1973—six years *before* the Soviet intervention began.

So far, the USSR has been able to build four of these aircraft. The US has 34 E-3A AWACS (Airborne Warning and Control System) aircraft, which first became operational in 1981. An earlier prop-driven version of the Soviet airborne radar system, the Tu-126 MOSS, first entered service in 1970. The USSR has seven of these. Our own prop-driven airborne radar system, the E-2C HAWKEYE, first entered service in 1966. Our Navy flies 64 HAWK-EYEs today. Our E-3A aircraft has an effective target detection range of more than 400 km. Its radar can track 600 targets simultaneously, successfully distinguishing them, at altitudes below its own, from what radar operators call "ground clutter," and its computer and data processor can identify and fully interpret over 240 targets simultaneously, determining the size, speed, altitude and directional bearing of each. According to our Department of Defense, the Soviet Tu-126 system is "ineffective" in distinguishing objects from ground clutter over land and only "marginally effective" over water. Once again, the US has the better technology, has had it longer, and deploys it more extensively.

Chapter VI

Research, Development, and Production

● More misplaced hyperbole. We are still outspending them. In Fiscal Year 1988, we plan to spend a total of $44 billion on military research alone.

● The US began sea trials of an amphibious air-cushion vehicle more than a decade earlier. See the commentary on page 101.

To support their drive for technological dominance, the Soviets have established the largest national research and development (R&D) resource base in the world, far outstripping those of the US and other nations. The USSR spends between 40 billion and 50 billion rubles a year on R&D, about half of which is dedicated to military projects.

The results of this wide-ranging R&D effort can be seen in all areas of Soviet weapon systems. To cite one example, during the past year the Soviet Navy, which is currently building nine classes of submarines and eight classes of major surface combatants, began sea trials of a revolutionary new class of amphibious air-cushion vehicle.

The POMORNIK-Class landing craft, with its 21-meter beam and 350-ton displacement, is the largest military air-cushion vehicle ever built. At 57 meters in length, it is 10 meters longer than the AIST-Class air-cushion craft it is designed to supplement. The POMORNIK-Class units will also be faster and have greater lift capability than the AIST-Class, and its 30-mm Gatling guns appear designed to improve direct fire support. The rapid production of the POMORNIK-Class, which went from building ways to sea trials in less than a year, illustrates the Soviet Navy's concerted effort to introduce new ship types into the fleet.

The Soviet naval air R&D effort has continued its pursuit of wing-in-ground (WIG) tech-

The MAINSTAY airborne warning and control system (AWACS) aircraft will provide Soviet Air Forces with a battle management capability for their new FLANKER and FULCRUM aircraft. An effective Soviet AWACS capability could advance the Soviets' drive for theater air superiority and would help to maximize the combat potential of their numerically superior ground forces.

Of these, 118 are nuclear-powered boats, 144 are diesel-electric. A comparable chart of US attack submarines would show that almost all were nuclear-powered.

Of these, the Soviets currently have 23,322 T-54 and T-55 tanks, 14,085 T-62s, 7,500 T-64s and 9,370 T-72s (including the "T-80" variant), for a total of 54,277 tanks of all types. Even the newest Soviet tanks are no match for modern US and NATO tanks. See the commentary on page 73.

This claim will have to be rapidly developed if it is to play a role in justifying greater expenditures for our own "Stealth" aircraft program, which we have pursued since at least 1979, when its existence first became known to the public.

We don't yet know how much of an improvement, if any, the MAINSTAY is over its predecessor, the MOSS. For an official evaluation of the MOSS, see the commentary on page 104.

The US has more than twice the Soviet airlift capacity, and its aircraft have much greater range. See the commentary on page 98.

Not yet deployed. See the commentary on page 80.

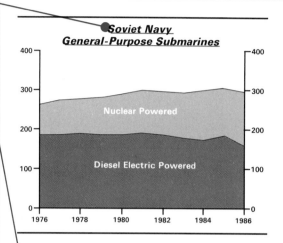

**Soviet Navy
General-Purpose Submarines**

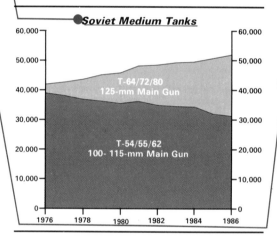

Soviet Medium Tanks

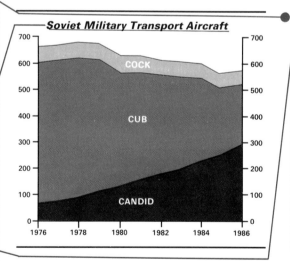

Soviet Military Transport Aircraft

nology for amphibious vehicles. WIGs are designed to cruise efficiently at altitudes of less than 15 meters, riding on the cushion of air formed between the wing and the ground during low-altitude flight. This factor greatly increases the craft's ability to carry heavy loads over long distances, especially over water, making it well suited for amphibious warfare.

Although the initial WIG design seems to have been abandoned, two new versions, are under development. The smaller version, designated the ORLAN-Class, is designed for amphibious operations. The larger version appears to have greater range, and with six missile launch tubes, it evidently has a dedicated antiship mission.

The Soviet aircraft industry, especially the military aircraft industry, is in the midst of a technological revolution. Most of the new military aircraft incorporate much more complex and sophisticated electronic subsystems and armaments than did their predecessors, and evidence suggests the Soviets have made progress in developing aircraft that may have a low-observable radar signature. The Soviets probably have at least one totally new fighter in design or development, and several variants of existing Soviet fighters — particularly the newer ones — can be expected to enter production over the next several years.

The Soviets also are bringing in a new airborne warning and control system (AWACS) aircraft, the MAINSTAY, for early warning and air combat command and control. Now in production, this modified Il-76TD has a true over-land look-down capability. In addition to a new identification-friend-or-foe system, this aircraft may have a comprehensive electronic countermeasures complement.

Two new Soviet attack helicopters, the HAVOC and the HOKUM, remain in prototype testing; both may become operational this year. The HAVOC, a ground-attack helicopter similar in appearance to the US Apache helicopter, is expected to feature similar advances in performance, survivability, armament, and night/adverse weather capability. Its primary armament will probably include a 23- or 30-mm cannon and up to 16 antitank guided missiles (ATGMs). Its two primary targets will be tanks and antitank helicopters, and it has probably been built to meet the threat presented by NATO weapons using thermal imaging systems.

● Wrong. The Soviets have been producing tanks at an average rate of 950 per year.

● Not yet deployed. See the commentary on page 80.

● The Soviets are producing self-propelled artillery pieces at a rate of about 60 per year.

● The engine in the T-72, and consequently in its "T-80" variant, produces about 780 horsepower. A new engine could always be fitted into the T-72, but that would not make it a new tank. It would make it an upgraded tank. By contrast, the US M-1 ABRAMS tank has an engine producing 1,500 horsepower. That is why our M-1 has a top speed of 70 km/hr, while the T-72, and its "T-80" variant, have a top speed of only 60 km/hr.

The HOKUM, a unique special-purpose helicopter, features a distinctive coaxial rotor system; a streamlined fuselage with a tapered nose, resembling a jet aircraft; and retractable landing gear. It has a lightweight performance design with swept rotor tips and no observable ATGM hardware. It can travel at speeds estimated at up to 350 kilometers per hour. Based on preliminary data, the HOKUM is thought to be a fighter helicopter with a primary air-to-air role. It is expected to be capable of employing air-to-air missiles and a rapid-fire cannon in day, night, and adverse weather conditions as a low-level, tactical counterair system. HOKUM's prime targets would be close air support aircraft, including antitank helicopters.

Evidence suggests the Soviets are also pursuing development of tilt-rotor type aircraft, most likely for use as troop carriers. If development of these aircraft proves successful, tilt-rotor models could eventually replace the HIND/HIP family of helicopters in the 1990s.

The Soviets continue to be the world's largest producer of ground force equipment, turning out some 3,000 tanks, 3,000 light armored vehicles, and 2,800 artillery weapons each year. The already huge tank fleet was enhanced by the recent addition of the T-80 medium tank, a probable follow-on to the T-64 and T-72. Roughly the size of the T-72 but significantly faster, the T-80 is powered by a gas-turbine engine producing 1,000 horsepower. It has greater mobility, more firepower, and better fire control than its predecessors, and its automatic loader has enabled the Soviets to reduce their crew size from four to three. The T-80 also has a passive night-vision system and a collective protection system for use in biological-radiological environments.

Military Expenditures

The Soviets have made a huge commitment of the nation's best resources to sustain their military buildup over the past 2 decades. Enormous expenditures for military programs have been a major factor behind slowing economic growth rates, as the most valuable and productive resources were channeled to the Soviet military program at the expense of living standards and investment in industries essential for economic growth.

The magnitude of Soviet military programs is revealed in a comparison with those of the US. Cumulative Soviet military costs from 1977 ●

*Soviet Navy Surface Warships**

Missile Equipped

Non-Missile Equipped

*Reserve units are not included.

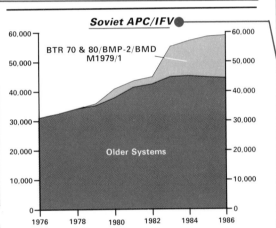

Soviet APC/IFV

BTR 70 & 80/BMP-2/BMD M1979/1

Older Systems

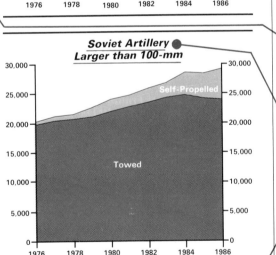

Soviet Artillery Larger than 100-mm

Self-Propelled

Towed

● A comparable chart of US surface warships would show that all were missile equipped.

● The automatic loader on the T-72 gives its gun a theoretical rate of fire of six rounds per minute. Several serious injuries, however, have been suffered by Soviet crewmen attempting to use the loading system, whose power rammer tends to load the gunner's arm into the gun breach. Consequently, Soviet crews have not used the automatic loader since 1979. The gun must be manually loaded, and would be so loaded in combat. This reduces its rate of fire to a maximum of two rounds per minute.

● This correctly shows about 20,000 fewer armored vehicles than the chart on page 71 does.

● Wrong. All T-72s, including the "T-80" variant, have the same 125 mm main gun.

● Fewer than 4,000 of these guns are self-propelled.

● The authors clearly understand, then, what military expenditures are doing to living standards and economic growth here in the United States.

(continued on next page) 107   Chapter VI Research, Development, and Production

● The first of these statements is a flat lie. The second is a bland acknowledgement of the method used to make that lie seem plausible. The "estimated dollar cost" of the Soviet military program estimates what it would cost to pay the entire active Soviet military establishment at current US military pay rates and what US manufacturers would charge, with profits and cost overruns included, to produce Soviet military equipment. The Soviets pay their personnel only a fraction of what we pay ours. Soviet military equipment is produced, needless to say, at a cost far lower than what US manufac-

turers would charge. The "dollar cost" estimate, therefore, is a deliberate method of inflating the actual level of Soviet military spending. Ruble estimates of Soviet military spending are also made. According to the CIA, these show that the Soviet Union is currently spending the equivalent of about $100 billion a year on its military. We are curently spending $300 billion a year on ours. In the decade cited through 1986, the US spent approximately $600 billion more on its military than the Soviets spent on theirs. See the commentary to the Preface, and on page 10.

(continued from page 107)

Wrong. See the commentary on page 105.

Wrong. See the commentary on page 10.

This passage describes how the Soviet Union organizes its resources for military research and development and for the design and production of weapons. It is not a perfect system. Neither is ours. In 1983, a Presidential commission found that, of $390 billion in US defense outlays over the preceding two years, $92 billion had been wasted. In 1984, the 10 largest military contractors in the United States averaged profits of 35 percent. In 1985, no fewer than 45 of our nation's leading defense contractors were under criminal investigation for overpricing and fraud. Senior citizens now face the prospect of giving up more of their Social Security benefits so that this administration may buy more combat aircraft we don't even need, while defense industry profits go to building summer homes for executives who already have homes.

to 1986 greatly exceeded those of the US. During this period, the estimated dollar cost of the total Soviet military program is 25 percent higher than comparable US defense outlays, and weapon procurement costs are 30 percent higher. Increased US defense spending has narrowed these differentials, but in critical areas such as R&D, the Soviet costs continue to exceed those of the US.

Moreover, Soviet major weapons procurement has shown consistent growth since the early 1980s, after several years of high acquisition activity.

Estimates of Soviet military spending in current rubles reflect a significant increase from the early 1970s to the early 1980s — at a rate substantially faster than their overall economic growth. The Soviet military effort now consumes 15 to 17 percent of their Gross National Product (GNP). As a result of this increased commitment, the defense industrial ministries absorb almost 60 percent of the output of the vital machine building branch of industry.

The heavily armed, nuclear-powered KIROV-Class cruiser Frunze carries three HORMONE (seen here) or HELIX helicopters, which provide ASW reconnaissance and target acquisition capabilities.

R&D Organization

Direction of the R&D effort is carried out through the Party hierarchy as well as government organizations. The military R&D sector has a more streamlined chain of command than its civilian counterpart. Requirements for new or modified systems to provide needed operational capabilities are formulated by staff orga-

nizations of the Ministry of Defense working in close collaboration with the R&D community. These new capabilities are proposed to top echelons of the Party and government and, if accepted, are implemented by a joint resolution — a one-time, multiyear commitment by both the Party and government to research, design, test, and serially produce the weapon. For major new weapons, the Defense Council, headed by the General Secretary, participates in this decision. The fulfillment of the joint resolution is the responsibility of the appropriate industrial ministry, with constant oversight by Ministry of Defense representatives. To ensure that weapons development proceeds as efficiently as possible, the Military Industrial Commission — which coordinates the development and production of military systems — has the authority to overcome bureaucratic obstacles and bottlenecks.

Soviet R&D programs and institutes are subordinate to one of three organizations, depending on their primary functions. The academies of sciences are charged with conducting basic, exploratory research in the natural and social sciences. Composed of the national-level USSR Academy of Sciences and 14 republic academies, this segment controls more than 350 research facilities and 300,000 scientists.

The higher education institutions subordinate to the Ministry of Higher and Secondary Education play an important but comparatively small role in Soviet R&D by undertaking exploratory R&D and by providing educations to all prospective scientists and engineers. Both the academies and higher education institutions are called on to solve technical problems in all segments of the national economy. As modern weapons become more complex, and as the Soviets assimilate more advanced technology in their weapons, these segments of the R&D community are becoming increasingly involved in military-related research.

Applied R&D falls within the purview of the industrial ministries. Each has scientific research institutes, design bureaus, and test facilities supporting development of their products working in collaboration with production plants. Nine defense industrial ministries conduct most of the applied R&D for new Soviet military capabilities. Their scientific research institutes provide design support research in their assigned areas of technology.

Personnel in the design bureaus are often the

● Here is a good example of the use of emphasis in propaganda. In describing the purposes of Soviet research into life sciences, the authors have chosen categories so broad as to include virtually every possibility but the one they want to emphasize. Obviously, such research will *either* "contribute to the solution of critical economic and industrial problems," *or* may provide "a military advantage." Merely by placing "a military advantage" first in the sentence, the authors give the impression that the Soviets themselves place special empha-

sis on this goal.

● In international diplomatic circles, the much larger issue has been over the Geneva Protocol of 1925, which banned the use of chemical and biological weapons in war. The Soviet Union formally agreed to comply with this Protocol in 1928. The United States did not sign and ratify it until 1975. The issue has been this: why did it take the United States so much longer?

---

best known members of the development team and serve as the system integrator and project office managers for the new product. They oversee the entire development process and are supported by subsystem and component design bureaus. About 50 design bureaus are involved in developing major military systems that are in turn supported by almost 250 subsystem and component design bureaus. Each defense industrial ministry has its own test facilities to evaluate the performance of its products, and these facilities are complemented, and in some cases replicated, by test facilities of the Ministry of Defense.

The Ministry of Aviation Industry (MAP) is in many ways prototypical of the defense industrial ministries. It designs and builds aircraft and aerodynamic missiles for all branches of the Ministry of Defense and Ministry of Civil Aviation. It supervises an impressive array of research organizations, including the Central Aerodynamics Institute and the Central Scientific Research Institute of Aviation Motor Building.

MAP has eight active aircraft design bureaus and seven air-breathing-missile system design bureaus. These are supported by 16 component and accessory design bureaus and 10 design bureaus that develop air-breathing powerplants. MAP's test facilities include flight and static test capabilities at Ramenskoye Air Base near Moscow, diversified liquid- and solid-rocket-propellant test stands, rocket sled tracks, and wind tunnels.

Reflecting the continuing high priority of its products, MAP's facilities have grown by more than 25 percent during the past decade. The results of that investment are reflected in a number of impressive new weapons such as the FULCRUM and FLANKER fighters; CONDOR super transport; BLACKJACK bomber; HAVOC, HOKUM, and HALO helicopters; numerous air-to-air, air-to-surface, surface-to-air missiles; and cruise missiles.

Biological Research

Most Soviet life sciences research has focused on disciplines that will allow them to establish and maintain a military advantage or contribute to the solution of critical economic and industrial problems. The Soviets recognize the virtually limitless potential of biotechnology, including use as a source of new biological warfare (BW) agents.

The Soviet Biological Warfare Capability. The Soviet offensive BW program has been monitored by the US for decades. When the Biological and Toxin Weapons Convention (BWC) of 1972 went into force in 1975, the issue became one of whether the Soviets were in compliance. Although the BWC bans the development, production, and stockpiling of biological agents and toxins for hostile purposes, no reduction in Soviet offensive BW activity has been observed. Thus, the conclusion arises that the Soviets are still capable of developing and producing BW agents.

Scientific personnel at a number of Soviet microbiological research institutes are capable of performing R&D with highly infectious disease agents and very potent plant, animal, and microbial toxins. Likewise, considerable Soviet work has been noted in aerobiology, cloud physics, airborne infections, and disease agent stabilization that has direct application to BW. Much of the knowledge and expertise at these institutes is funded and utilized by the Soviet Ministry of Defense for offensive BW as well as for defensive/protective aspects.

A number of installations capable of producing disease agents and toxins on a large-scale basis and placing them in munitions and delivery/dissemination systems have also been identified. These installations have been established by the Ministry of Defense and are under its control. One such facility is in the city of Sverdlovsk and has a long history of biological warfare R&D and production with emphasis on the causative agent of anthrax. In addition to anthrax, we believe the Soviets have developed tularemia, plague, and cholera for BW purposes, as well as botulinum toxin, enterotoxin, and mycotoxins.

Biological Warfare Agent Production. The production of large quantities of disease agents by the Soviets for BW purposes can be accomplished by various fermentation processes. In a strict sense, industrial fermentation processes are concerned with the products from multiplying microorganisms. However, a fermentation process can also be used to produce large numbers of microorganisms that themselves become the desired end-products. Thus, an infectious agent grown in large numbers and then placed in a weapon/dissemination system becomes a BW weapon. Production of a toxin agent is usually accomplished using fermentation processes except that the toxin produced by the

● The Soviets also agreed to comply with the Biological and Toxin Weapons Convention, which bans the development and production of biological warfare agents. They are certainly still "capable" of developing and producing such agents, just as we are. But if we can only conclude that they have the capability, and not the agents themselves, then what sort of "activity" are they engaged in, of which we claim to observe "no reduction"?

● Another effort to suggest that a capability may be an activity. If there were any evidence of such activity, it would be featured here in place of the innuendo and doubletalk.

● These are included on this list because the administration, during its first few years in office, waged an intensive propaganda campaign to persuade the world that the Soviets had used mycotoxins in Southeast Asia, pointless and inefficient though the use of such agents would be. Again, however, no victims were produced, and Harvard biochemist Matthew Meselson found that the "yellow rain" which the administration claimed the Soviets were using to disperse these agents was, in fact, bee excrement.

Standard Soviet equipment is a heavy rubberized suit that cannot be worn for more than four hours, or at temperatures above 60 degrees fahrenheit. Our standard equipment is a light protective suit weighing 4 lbs, which may be worn at temperatures of up to 78 degrees for as long as 24 hours.

microorganisms during the growth process is the end-product rather than the microorganism itself. A viral or rickettsial agent, unlike a bacterial agent, requires living metabolizing animal cells for growth, thereby requiring large-scale use of embryonated eggs or tissue cell culture systems to produce quantities of viruses or rickettsia for BW weapons.

Continuous fermentation can also be used for BW agent production. The anthrax agent can be produced from start to finish in 96 hours since bacteria can multiply very quickly. Both systems can be computer controlled.

During the growth cycle of anthrax, the microorganism is in the shape of a rod, its vegetative form. Toward the end of its growth cycle, it can be made to convert into spores by heat or chemical shock. It is the spores that are harvested and placed into delivery/dissemination devices. The spores are very resistant to heat, disinfectants, sunlight and other environmental factors. When the spores are inhaled, they convert again to the vegetative form, establish an infection, and as they multiply in the host, produce a highly lethal toxin. Anthrax causes a high mortality rate when the infection results from ingestion (up to 70 percent fatal) or inhalation (almost 100 percent fatal) if treatment is not begun promptly. Besides penicillin, other antibiotics may be effective. Although anthrax bacteria are penicillin sensitive, successful treatment of the disease depends upon killing the microorganisms before a lethal concentration of anthrax toxin is produced. The skin form of infection can also be lethal if it invades the bloodstream and therapy is not started quickly.

Anthrax spores can be disseminated in either a liquid or dry form. Although highly resistant in the environment, they can be killed with strong disinfectants or high temperature. Anthrax is a noncontagious agent. The number of anthrax spores required to kill 50 percent of exposed individuals (lethal dose 50 or LD50) is between 8,000 and 10,000. Even though such high concentrations of anthrax are required to be delivered over a target population, the Soviets have no technical difficulties in achieving this.

The Soviets have vaccines or antidotes for many of the diseases that they might use in a BW attack. These include those for anthrax, tularemia, plague, and botulism. Immunization is essential for those personnel who produce,

Neither do we. We have extensively tested a variety of techniques for the dispersal of such agents. Since many of these tests were conducted in US cities, they were conducted in secret. In the early 1960s, the US Army used the New York subway system for one of its tests.

handle, and deliver BW agents and weapons as well as for those who would move into an area where BW agents had been disseminated. Standard Soviet protective suits and masks, together with sanitary and disease control measures, would be sufficient to protect most Soviet soldiers from the effects of their BW agents.

The Sverdlovsk Biological Warfare Facility: Events of 1979. During early April 1979, an accidental release of anthrax occurred in Sverdlovsk that caused many casualties and most likely a very high death rate among Soviet citizens who were exposed. The government at that time admitted only to some public health problems, which it said were caused by the illegal sale of anthrax-contaminated meat. Soviet leaders have never acknowledged the existence of the Sverdlovsk facility. The US Government has often requested an explanation of what happened in Sverdlovsk, but the Soviets persist in blaming contaminated meat for the anthrax epidemic.

Our analysis shows that the following events occurred:

- Early in April 1979, an accidental release of anthrax occurred within the Microbiology and Virology Institute in Sverdlovsk City. The Institute is a military facility located in the southwestern outskirts of the city. While bulk quantities of anthrax spores in dry form were probably being prepared, a pressurized system most likely exploded.
- As much as 10 kilograms of dry anthrax spores were released from the Institute.
- The bacterial aerosol contaminated an area with a radius of at least 3 to 5 kilometers.
- Within 2 weeks, which is within the time frame expected for the disease to develop, a significant number of deaths occurred.
- Residents and workers within the contaminated area contracted pulmonary anthrax through inhalation. Additionally, some may have contracted anthrax by skin contact and, over time, a number may have contracted anthrax by consumption of food contaminated by the fallout of spores.
- Initial disinfection and decontamination procedures were largely ineffective.
- Mass immunizations with the Soviet anthrax vaccine were partially effective at best.

110

● This is a belabored effort to revive an accusation we first made in 1980, when we circulated reports that an outbreak of anthrax in the city of Sverdlovsk was the result of an accident at a bacteriological warfare laboratory. The Soviets said it was the result of infected meat supplies. According to the International Red Cross, the type of anthrax suffered in Sverdlovsk was gastric—the wrong kind to result from release of a bacteriological agent, which would have been in-

haled, causing pulmonary anthrax. In this updated version of our accusation, the authors have tried to explain the presence of gastric anthrax by suggesting that "over time, a number may have contracted anthrax by consumption of food contaminated by the fallout of spores." So it seems there was contaminated meat after all, just as the Soviets said. Nor has the US offered any evidence of pulmonary anthrax

- Vaccinations and antibiotic treatment were administered too late as an initial response.
- Containment procedures were effective in confining the problem to the southwest area of Sverdlovsk City.
- Strict censorship as to the true nature of the incident served to neutralize early panic and to limit the fears of the Sverdlovsk population.
- Containment procedures continued into July 1979. Some inspection procedures were conducted until fall 1979.

In summary:
- A major outbreak of anthrax occurred at a closed military installation.
- The Soviets have persisted in claiming that a routine outbreak of anthrax among animals caused intestinal anthrax among people who consumed the bad meat.
- The extraordinary efforts to "clean-up" are inconsistent with the Soviet explanation.
- Reports surfaced that hundreds of Soviet citizens died from inhalation anthrax within 7 to 10 days of the outbreak despite heroic efforts by Soviet doctors to save their lives.
- Other reports stated that in subsequent weeks, 1,000 or more cases may have developed. These figures are about 100 or more times the annual incidence of inhalation and intestinal anthrax throughout the USSR in recent years.
- Heavy military involvement and early military casualties immediately after the accident, total military control within 2 weeks, plus rooftop spraying of decontaminating solutions from aircraft are not consistent with public health control measures for dealing with anthrax acquired by eating bad meat.
- The reported aerial spraying activity and disinfection with steam and hypochlorite solution around the military facility were clearly intended to decontaminate surfaces affected by an infectious aerosol.

Collectively, these events are a very strong contradiction of the Soviet position that the anthrax outbreak was just a public health problem resulting from the sale of contaminated meat.

Biotechnology and the Soviet Union. The Soviet Union has been combating and controlling disease epidemics for many years. As a result, the Soviets have developed expertise in biomedical research, identifying the focuses of infections and controlling diseases. They have made significant contributions to the literature on infectious diseases and have had an impact in the international arena on public health matters. Their knowledge of the behavior of bacteria, viruses and rickettsia is voluminous and has been used to address domestic and international problems of disease control.

The Soviets have also been interested in industrial biotechnology since World War II. During the siege of Leningrad, single-cell protein (SCP) derived from wood shavings was used as food. Since that time, the Soviet SCP industry has grown to be the largest in the world, with over a million tons produced annually and used for fodder. Estimates are that 1 ton of SCP frees up about 6 tons of feed grain that otherwise would have to be imported and paid for in hard currency. The Soviets are also dependent on their microbiological industry to produce vitamins, antibiotics, vaccines, and advanced diagnostics and therapeutics for legitimate use in their military and civilian populations.

The Soviets now recognize the potential of modern biotechnology and genetic engineering, particularly since the USSR has a greater need for advancements in agriculture and public health than does the West. As such, the Soviets made the development of a biotechnological industry a top priority in 1974 and reaffirmed their commitment in 1981. Since that time, they have made remarkable progress in developing their biotechnological capabilities.

These same technologies are being used by the Ministry of Defense to develop more effective BW agents. With this biotechnological capability, naturally-occurring microorganisms can be made more virulent, antibiotic-resistant, and manipulated to render current US vaccines ineffective. Such developments would greatly complicate our ability to detect and identify BW agents and to operate in areas contaminated by such Soviet biological agents.

Key Military Technologies

The large-scale, continuous infusion of resources into other R&D areas reflects the determined effort of the Soviets to improve their technological capabilities. Although the technological gap between the USSR and the West is constantly narrowing, the West still holds

See commentary on next page.

to any recognized body of international experts for independent verification. This new version of our story is also heavy-handed. If we are going to assert that "as much as 10 kilograms of dry anthrax spores were released" to contaminate an area with a radius of "at least 3 to 5 kilometers," then why cite the "extraordinary" Soviet efforts to "clean up" the area afterwards, as though this were evidence to support what we claim we already know? Why coyly refer to "reported" aerial spraying and other clean-up activities, as though we were reluctant to declare we had observed these activities ourselves? The hesitant, "scholarly" tone the authors seek here is not consistent with their initial flat contention that dry anthrax spores were released into the air.

an overall technological lead. This lead will continue to diminish unless the West maintains strong safeguards against sophisticated Soviet efforts to acquire Western military and dual-use technology.

also using some East European countries, which are developing their own computer industries, to help meet their needs. Even with these efforts, the Soviets remain an average of 10 years behind the West in civil/industrial technology applications.

Aerodynamics

The Soviets have built the world's largest wind tunnel and are accumulating very sophisticated aerodynamics research facilities. Through the use of empirical techniques, they are pursuing novel developments that have no military equivalents in the West, such as the previously described WIG effect vehicles. While the Soviets have tended to mimic Western aerodynamics research, they deserve recognition for engineering effective weapons for their aerodynamic systems. Even so, most of the important aerodynamic principles have been developed in the Free World. The US maintains its advantage in aerodynamic computational capabilities.

Chemical

The chemical industrial sector includes a broad range of technologies with direct and indirect effects on Soviet military capabilities. The Soviets have made significant strides in areas such as chemical explosives and chemical warfare, to which they give high priority. The research effort in new chemical explosives is several times larger than any such Western program and has given them a significant lead over the West. Conversely, Soviet fuels, lubricants, and industrial fluids fall short of Western standards, and the USSR remains dependent on the West for sophisticated diagnostic equipment.

Computing

Soviet computer technology continues to be based on Western developments. Although the Soviets have a solid understanding of basic principles, they have lingering problems in applying this knowledge to computer production. Reliability and quality control difficulties have not yet been resolved, and the Soviets have been unable to develop the peripherals and software to meet their requirements. Improving their computing capabilities remains one of their most pressing technological requirements. The Soviets are increasing the use of their diplomatic missions, intelligence services, and academic and scientific foundations to acquire Western computer technology. They are

Directed Energy

Lasers. The USSR has established a very large and well-funded multi-ministerial program to develop strategic and tactical laser weapons, and it maintains R&D efforts in all the technologies critical to the evolution of laser weapons. The Soviets have built high-energy laser devices to the 10-megawatt level and generally place more emphasis on weapon applications of lasers than does the West. In doing so, they have concentrated on gas-dynamic and electric discharge lasers. They have not attained the high-power outputs for chemical lasers as has the West.

The tactical laser program has progressed to where battlefield laser weapons could soon be deployed with Soviet forces. The Soviets have the technological capability to deploy low-power laser weapons — at least for antipersonnel use and against soft targets such as sensors, canopies, and light materiel. Even low-power lasers, as in rangefinders, can have weapon applications. Recent Soviet irradiation of Free World manned surveillance aircraft and ships could have caused serious eye damage to observers.

Radio Frequency. Recent Soviet developments in the generation of radio-frequency (RF) energy have potential applications for a fundamentally new type of weapon system that would degrade electronics or be used in an antipersonnel role. The Soviets already have or are working on much of the technology needed for such a system. In their research the Soviets have generated single pulses with peak power exceeding 1 billion watts and repetitive pulses of over 100 million watts. If they choose to develop such a system, no significant technological obstacles stand in the way of a prototype short-range tactical RF weapon.

Particle Beam. Soviet research in technologies applicable to particle beam weapons is extensive, and military interest and support has been evident since the early 1960s. Work in certain necessary technologies, such as powerful accelerators, is at the forefront of the state-of-the-art. The Soviets, however, have probably

● A good example of emphasis. Western naval vessels have even more powerful laser devices, and have used them to irradiate Soviet patrol aircraft.

The electro-optic sensor/laser device (at lower right) on the SOVREMENNYY-Class destroyer has been used by the Soviets to irradiate Western patrol aircraft. Such laser irradiation, depending upon the distance, could permanently blind.

not demonstrated the feasibility of actual propagation of a particle beam for any meaningful distance and probably have not moved from research to system development.

Electronics

The Soviets have demonstrated capabilities in electronics that are comparable to those of the West in their theoretical understanding as well as in most areas of circuit design and systems engineering. They continue to be plagued, however, by problems in translating their R&D results to production.

Chronic production problem areas include ion implantation, masking, lithography, and testing equipment for microelectronics. The USSR also lags behind the West in specialized solid-state component technologies such as photosensitive, magnetic bubble memory, acoustic wave, and Josephson Junction devices. This situation could become even more pronounced because of the US effort to produce a very-high-speed integrated circuit. In military electronics applications, the Soviet Union has developed strong technological capabilities in millimeter wave devices as well as in over-

● See commentary on next page.

● Probably not. Particle beams would be useless for ballistic missile defense. For such a defense to be even theoretically feasible, attacking missiles would have to be caught as they move through the atmosphere in their boost phase, before separating into a mass of individual warheads and decoys. The atmosphere charges neutral particle beams by coupling their neutrons with air molecules. Once a particle beam is charged it cannot be aimed, because its particles are steered off course by the earth's magnetic field. If it were based above the atmosphere, a particle beam might be an effective antisatellite weapon. But there are much simpler and less costly ways to build antisatellite weapons.

● Poorly reproduced here is a European commercial SPOT satellite photograph of the Chernobyl area. The SPOT satellite images are capable of resolutions of ten meters. Imagine the difference between this and the US military satellite photographs of the Chernobyl area shown to members of Congress at a classified briefing held by Pentagon officials on April 30, 1986, four days after the accident occurred. At this briefing, chairman of the Joint Chiefs of Staff Admiral William J. Crowe described one photo which "showed a soccer game going on in the area of the plant."

● Initial US propaganda claimed that reactors of this type were dangerous, and lacked a containment structure. We now circumspectly acknowledge, as the authors do here on page 114, that the Chernobyl reactor had a "1,200-ton upper biological shield." By contrast, the US has eight military and research reactors managed by the Department of Energy which have no containment at all: one at Hanford,

(continued from page 113)

● The steels we use for our submarines, HY-100 and HY-130, and our titanium, Ti-100, are second to none.

● See the commentary on page 27.

● One of the largest advantages the West holds over the USSR in ASW (Antisubmarine Warfare) capabilities is that the US and its allies control most of the coastlines of both the Atlantic and the Pacific Oceans. Consequently, the West can maintain a vast array of hydrophones, including our Navy's SOSUS underwater surveillance system, off the continental shores, to identify and track Soviet submarines.

● In what areas does bigger mean better? Not in missiles. Not in submarines.

● They may have the theoretical understanding, but in practice the Soviets have been unable to miniaturize the components of their nuclear weapons to the extent we have, or to achieve as efficient a ratio of fissionable materials to explosive yield.

● According to Soviet scientist Zhores Medvedyev, a much larger accident may have taken place when a nuclear waste site exploded at the city of Kyshtym, 800 miles east of Moscow, in 1957. Medvedyev has shown that both the Soviet and US governments kept the incident secret, for fear of stirring resistance to their nuclear power programs.

the-horizon and phased-array radars.

Electro-optics

In general, the West is slightly ahead of the USSR in electro-optics technologies that have wide-ranging military applications in reconnaissance, communications, navigation, and target designation. The West is ahead in basic R&D, material quality, and fabrication aspects of the more advanced electro-optics technologies. The Soviets, however, are strong in some of the older, less-sophisticated technologies such as certain detector materials and solid-state glass lasers, in which they have heavily invested their R&D efforts.

Environmental Sciences

The Soviet Union has developed environmental modification techniques that could be used in wartime, primarily in tactical situations. They have published the results of their R&D on fog dispersal situations at airfields, precipitation enhancement in areas near the Black Sea, and hail suppression in regions subject to crop damage. Experimental programs have been conducted in ionospheric heating, with implications for improving long-range communications.

Coincident with this research, the Soviets are signatories of the Environmental Modification Convention, drawn up to ban the hostile employment of such techniques. They are clearly aware of the political consequences of such programs as well as the military advantages. Their oceanographic research program is the largest in the world, and it has undoubtedly played an important role in the Soviet ASW R&D program.

Manufacturing

The Soviets have strong technological capabilities to transform raw materials into final military products. They are highly capable in areas where bigger means better, having built the world's largest forging and extrusion presses. The Soviets have excellent electroslag and plasma arc remelt capabilities for producing high-quality alloys, and they match world standards in sheet metal forming and metal removal. In welding, they are international innovators in electroslag, friction, electrogas, electron beam, and pulsed arc welding. They are knowledgeable in all aspects of computer-aided industrial production and are the equal

of the West on a theoretical basis. Nonetheless, in hardware for computers and electromechanical devices, and in fielding experienced teams of designers and programmers, the Soviet Union lags the West.

Materials

Soviet R&D in materials and associated processing is comparable to that of the West, and in some areas leads the world. The Soviets are especially strong in all areas of metallic materials. Their innovative work in light metal alloys based on aluminum, magnesium, and titanium gives them a major asset in designing and producing aircraft and missile systems as well as some naval and ground forces equipment. They have a strong ferrous metallurgy program and an extensive, continuing effort to improve steels in their inventory as well as to develop others. In leading edge technologies such as refractory and superalloys, powder metallurgy, ceramics, and composites, their R&D efforts are extensive. Overall, they probably trail the West by a small margin.

Nuclear

For many years, the USSR has been highly active in nuclear R&D for industrial and military applications. Until February 26, 1987, the Soviet underground nuclear test program remained inactive under a self-imposed moratorium since August 1985. From 1970 to 1985, the Soviets conducted more than 200 tests. Of these, over three-fourths were probably for weapons design and effects purposes, while the remainder were for their Peaceful Nuclear Explosion program. Among the former, they have carried out weapons effects tests on intercontinental ballistic missile (ICBM) reentry vehicles and electronics. Soviet theoretical understanding of nuclear weapons physics is probably on a par with that of the West. Their nuclear reactor R&D program has been aggressive and has developed the full range of needed technologies — from isotope separation, to reactor design, to fuel reprocessing. The Soviet nuclear power industry has not been without its setbacks and problems, however, as evidenced by the recent disaster at Chernobyl.

Chernobyl. The accident at the Chernobyl Atomic Power Station on 26 April 1986 was the worst of the atomic age. Two large explosions ripped through Reactor No. 4, displacing the 1,200-ton upper biological shield, heaving ra-

(continued from above)

114

Washington; one near Idaho Falls; two near Oak Ridge, Tennessee; and four along the Savannah River near Aiken, South Carolina. The N Reactor at Hanford has a graphite core, exactly like the reactor at Chernobyl. According to the CIA, Chernobyl's containment was stronger than that of approximately one-third of the reactors in the US. It could withstand pressures of up to 57 pounds per square inch, whereas the Shoreham containment on Long Island, New York, can withstand pressures of up to only 30 pounds per square inch.

● Chernobyl's effects may be mild compared with the cumulative toll in deaths, disease and human suffering caused by a long series of accidents and deliberate experiments, many of them kept secret from the public for years, at nuclear power and nuclear weapons assembly plants across the United States over the past four decades. Little known are the three fires, in 1957, 1965, and 1969 at the Rocky Flats plutonium processing plant near Denver, Colorado. The first of these released more than a quarter ton of plutonium. A tenth of that was enough to administer a radiation dose one million times the permissible lung burden to every one of the 1,400,000 people then living in the Denver area. There were three releases of enriched uranium from the Getty Oil Company's top-secret Nuclear Fuel Services Plant at Erwin, Tennessee in 1979 and 1980. In July, 1959, a meltdown began at Atomics International's Sodium Reactor in Santa Susana, in the heart of the San Fernando Valley and 35 miles north of downtown Los Angeles. Seven hundred thousand people lived within 10 miles of the plant. At least 10,000 curies of highly radioactive materials were released into the air they breathed. This incident was kept secret for 23 years. In 1949, our government deliberately released a radioactive cloud of 5,000 curies of Iodine 131 from the Hanford Nuclear Reservation in Washington state. From 1955 to 1965, we conducted open-air tests of nuclear reactor core meltdowns in the Nevada desert, releasing more than a billion curies of uranium dioxide, plutonium and other fission products into the air. The public did not

Reactor No. 4

Commercially Acquired From the CNES SPOT Image Corp. and EOSAT Inc., 1986

The destruction of Chernobyl Reactor No. 4 has not altered Soviet emphasis on research and development of nuclear power as their main source of electricity for the future.

● Nor has it altered the US emphasis, more's the pity. When state and local officials refused to cooperate in a test of evacuation plans for the area surrounding the Shoreham plant on Long Island, Shoreham officials urged the Nuclear Regulatory Commission to drop the regulation requiring that state and local authorities participate in such plans.

● Since this completes a list of clearly undesirable developments, the authors presumably feel that the "organized expression" of "antinuclear fears and sentiments" is undesirable too—even though it may be what saves us. They also continue the practice of implying that nothing undesirable is given organized expression in the Soviet Union. *Glasnost*, then, must be very painful for them, and they predictably deal with it by denying that it will make any difference.

dioactive materials into the atmosphere, and starting numerous local fires around strewn bits of the reactor's graphite core. The many deleterious effects of the explosion include 31 direct fatalities, hundreds of injuries, contamination of the food chain in European USSR and Eastern Europe, and low-level radiation exposure in the Scandinavian countries. In addition, thousands of cancer deaths in the

Military variants of the Mi-26/HALO heavy-lift helicopter were used in the 1986 Chernobyl nuclear reactor clean-up operation.

Soviet Union are expected over the next 50 to 70 years. Another development is likely to be felt not in the Soviet Union, but in the West, where antinuclear fears and sentiments are already present and given to organized expression.

The Soviets have played down the fact that Chernobyl-type reactors are capable of providing not only nuclear power to the civilian economy but weapon-grade plutonium for the military. The Chernobyl accident has not dampened the Soviet resolve to increase their reliance on nuclear power, including the completion of more reactors of the Chernobyl dual-purpose type. In addition to the Chernobyl-type and pressurized water reactors, the Soviets are building fast-breeder and another dual-purpose type of reactor to produce both electric power and heat for industrial needs.

Power Sources (Non-Nuclear)

The Soviets have a significant R&D effort committed to developing specialized power systems for military applications, including all

● Wrong. US propaganda tried to play up this fact, even though our government had to acknowledge that the reactor at Chernobyl was not being used to produce weapon-grade plutonium.

learn about this for 17 years. The public still hasn't learned about Three Mile Island. Figures from the State of Pennsylvania show that the infant mortality rate within 10 miles of Three Mile Island rose 300 percent in the months following the accident there. The international community will be keeping a close watch on the long-term effects of radiation released at Chernobyl. No official studies have been released to the public on the long-term effects of any of the incidents cited here at home, just as no official reports have been released about the health effects upon those living downwind from the Nevada test site during the open-air weapons test in the 1950s, or on the soldiers exposed to those tests, or on the 42,000 sailors who helped clean up Bikini 40 years ago. Yet, in some of the towns downwind of the Nevada test site there are streets where every member of every family in every house on every block has cancer.

Their technology is slowly catching up.

types of directed-energy weapons, high-power radars, and jamming systems. They are probably world leaders in magnetohydrodynamic power generation and have attained power levels of several tens of megawatts from their portable devices. Soviet physicists have made major accomplishments in magnetocumulative generation R&D as well as in areas such as thermionics and inductive stores. Their research in several supporting technologies, however, tends to lag behind the state-of-the-art in the West; for example, in certain switches and in electrochemical sources.

Propulsion

The USSR has comprehensive, effective R&D programs in all forms of propulsion technologies for military systems, often taking approaches different from those of the West. Soviet aircraft engines have shown marked technological advances, although they continue to reflect design simplicity and manufacturing ease. The principal shortcomings have been in cooled blade fabrication, electronic engine controls and, until 1984, a large high-bypass-ratio engine. The D-18T turbofan, which powers the CONDOR super transport, fills this gap.

We filled this gap more than 20 years ago.

The Soviets also have an aggressive R&D program in ramjet propulsion and have fielded missile systems using ramjets. They were the first to develop the combined-cycle rocket-ramjet on an operational missile.

Today, the Soviets are the acknowledged world leader in liquid-propellant missiles, owing in part to the West's emphasis on solid-propellant motors. Liquid propellants continue to be the main propulsion system on most Soviet operational ICBMs, submarine-launched ballistic missiles (SLBMs), medium-range missiles, and space launch vehicles. Concurrently, the Soviets have been devoting increasing emphasis on developing solid-propellant rocket motors of all sizes. Applications now include systems ranging from ICBMs such as the SS-X-24 and SS-25 to tactical missile developments. Although the Soviets have usually lagged the

This, too, is meant to suggest a stunning new military development. But this propulsion system is also unlike any *desired* in the West. See the commentary on opposite page.

The Frunze, a KIROV-Class nuclear-powered guided-missile cruiser, is powered by a new hybrid propulsion system unlike any seen in the West. The KIROV is one of eight classes of major Soviet surface combatants currently being produced.

West in solid propellants, their technology is rapidly catching up.

Soviet application of advanced technologies to naval propulsion systems continues at an impressive level. They were the first to build a

As dishonest and misleading a statement as any in this book. In their struggle for hyperbole, the authors have tried to make a serious Soviet military weakness sound like a major military advantage. The only reason the Soviets continue to use liquid propellants is because they have had a great deal of trouble developing modern solid fuels. If you are forced to use obsolete technology, this hardly makes you "the acknowledged world leader" in that technology. The US abandoned the use of liquid propellants 20 years ago because they were unreliable, volatile, and dangerous. For an example of the rewards of using liquid propellants, see the photograph and commentary on page 34, as well as the commentary on page 30.

class of gas-turbine-powered warships. One of the more recent precedent-setting Soviet efforts is the KIROV-Class cruiser hybrid propulsion system, which uses nuclear reactors operating in parallel with oil-fired boilers.

The West continues to lead the USSR in the general area of automotive technology. The Soviets, however, have demonstrated the effective application of their technology to military equipment, such as off-road missile

The oil-fired boilers are the backup system, in case the reactors have to be shut down. They are a measure of Soviet faith in their design for reactors large enough to power a ship of this size, which displaces 28,000 tons.

© Mitsuo Shibata

An old chestnut of alarmist rhetoric is that the Soviets can incorporate new technology into their weapons more quickly than we can, because of their "centralized management" and firmer "control over resource allocation." Our weaknesses are always said to be our "market-oriented" economy and our concern for "consumer goods." The invariable prescription is to make our society more like theirs, so that we no longer suffer this "disadvantage." One day, an administration may come along which tries to do this. The current administration is certainly doing its best. But in fact, the "market-oriented" segment of our society is in a shambles. Our consumer goods no longer

Many leading Western scientists have their own covert agendas too.

transporters. Although many Soviet engines produce less power than state-of-the-art Western engines of equivalent weight and displacement, it is a result of Soviet preference for durability, reliability, and simplicity rather than a lack of capability.

Technology Acquisition and Applications

The Soviet leadership is very pragmatic about technological deficiencies in relation to the West. Even their most optimistic prediction does not call for attaining technical ascendency over the West before the 21st century. They are, however, concerned about the qualitative edge in weapons that Western technologies now provide. They are seeking to neutralize the West's advantage in basic technologies by deploying relatively advanced and technologically sophisticated weapons in large numbers. At the same time, they are working very hard to improve their indigenous capabilities in order to catch up with and surpass those of the West in basic weapons technologies. The Soviets seek to accomplish this goal by investing heavily in their own R&D base and by aggressively obtaining the best possible technology from any source and applying it to their military effort as quickly as possible — often much faster than their Western counterparts. Their centralized management uses its control over resource allocation to ensure that the most modern technology is obtained and channeled directly into military R&D rather than into consumer goods, as is often the case in the market-oriented economies of the West.

This centrally coordinated effort to obtain the most advanced technology began to take shape in the mid-to-late 1960s. Virtually all Soviet research projects with military applications continue to benefit, in varying degrees, from know-how acquired elsewhere.

A major responsibility of the Military-Industrial Commission (VPK) is to act as the prime coordinator for technology acquisition to support the defense industrial ministries. It seeks unique military or civilian hardware, documentation, or techniques to improve the technical levels and capability of Soviet weapons, military equipment, and associated industrial machinery. The Ministry of Foreign Trade and the intelligence services administer a trade diversion program to obtain significant numbers of manufacturing and supporting equipment for direct use on Soviet military-industrial production lines. The purpose of this program is to improve Soviet capabilities to produce reliable modern weapons.

Hardware, designs, and production techniques are not the only targets of the Soviet acquisition program. A goal in Soviet-Western scientific exchanges, for example, is to gain access to Western technological know-how. Soviet participation in scientific exchanges enables the Soviets to acquire and exploit Free World technologies.

Even this process of scientific exchanges is highly centralized and serves the military sector. Among the agencies charged with fulfilling collection requirements established by the Military Industrial Commission are not only the KGB and GRU, but also the USSR Academy of Sciences and the State Committee for Science and Technology, both of which are the official — "above board" — partners in scientific exchanges with the West. Soviet scientists are, with few exceptions, selected and assigned to participate in exchanges according to covert collection priorities.

These successful programs concentrate on the US and the other advanced industrial nations of the Free World. As these countries improve their technology security, however, the Soviets have had to vary the means by which they acquire information. They have entrusted more collection responsibilities to their allies to mask their efforts to acquire militarily critical technology. They have put more emphasis on acquiring technology that is advanced but less than state-of-the-art, as in automated production control technology. In the continuing top-priority area of microelectronics, the Soviets apparently rely on more cumbersome, more expensive, and less reliable illegal methods.

The Soviets have shown increasing interest in the newly industrialized nations that are emerging technological powers as well as in countries undergoing technological modernization that may be recipients of Western technology or serving as transshipment points. In the area of dual-use technology for direct application to Soviet military-industrial production lines, the Soviets are increasingly able to look beyond the US — where acquisition is more difficult — to satisfy their requirements.

Soviet efforts to divert dual-use technologies continue to target microelectronics fabrication

(continued from above)

compete with foreign imports. We have a war economy, which incorporates new technologies so quickly that we cannot even be sure that they will be effective. Nevertheless, this procedure fattens the profit margin most quickly for defense manufacturers, and that is why it is followed. Lacking the same incentives, the Soviets will continue to incorporate new technology more slowly. Alarmists must continue to say the reverse is true, of course, since that is so essential a part of their mission of threat enhancement. But we will no doubt continue to take the initiative in the arms race, as we have done for more than 40 years.

● The purpose of these charts is to dramatize the administration's claim, elaborated in the accompanying text, that the Soviets have been stealing our technology. This is the myth of the rape of the West. The cunning barbarian steals our knowledge and uses it to destroy us. But when will he be able to destroy us? If one takes the figures given here to be true, then it seems that the Soviets, having stolen so much in recent years, have had even more to steal in subsequent years. Will they have to steal even more than that in future years? Are they catching up, or falling behind? It isn't really clear, is it? One gets the impression that the West is producing new technology at such a rapid pace that the Soviets cannot handle the flow. The truth of the matter, of course, is that nations acquire most of each other's technology by open and legitimate means, that the worldwide flow of technical information is so broad and constant that it has grown ever more difficult to deny certain nations information of certain kinds, and that if information must be acquired by covert and

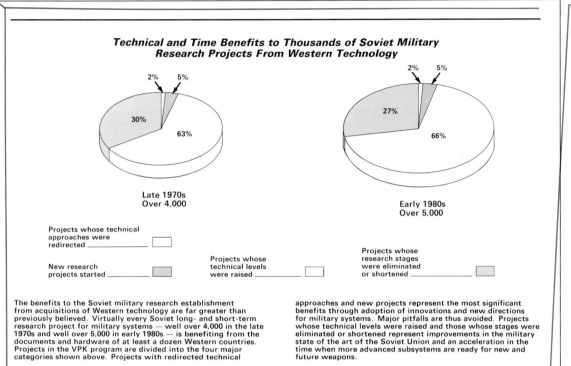

Technical and Time Benefits to Thousands of Soviet Military Research Projects From Western Technology

2%   5%
30%
63%

**Late 1970s
Over 4,000**

2%   5%
27%
66%

**Early 1980s
Over 5,000**

Projects whose technical approaches were redirected _____ ☐

New research projects started _____ ▨

Projects whose technical levels were raised _____ ☐

Projects whose research stages were eliminated or shortened _____ ▨

The benefits to the Soviet military research establishment from acquisitions of Western technology are far greater than previously believed. Virtually every Soviet long- and short-term research project for military systems — well over 4,000 in the late 1970s and well over 5,000 in early 1980s — is benefiting from the documents and hardware of at least a dozen Western countries. Projects in the VPK program are divided into the four major categories shown above. Projects with redirected technical approaches and new projects represent the most significant benefits through adoption of innovations and new directions for military systems. Major pitfalls are thus avoided. Projects whose technical levels were raised and those whose stages were eliminated or shortened represent improvements in the military state of the art of the Soviet Union and an acceleration in the time when more advanced subsystems are ready for new and future weapons.

● If *Soviet Military Power* is still being published four to six years from today, rest assured that it would still give the West the lead in microelectronics, with a new "estimate" of the number of years by which it led the USSR. The beauty of prediction is that the exact point in time when dire events will occur is subject to infinite revision by those who warn of its eventuality.

equipment and computers. Nearly half the detected trade diversions fall into these categories. Using unscrupulous Western traders who employ false licenses, deceptive equipment descriptions, dummy firms, and false end users for illegal purchases; smuggling; and assistance from Soviet and allied intelligence operations, the USSR has acquired several thousand pieces of major microelectronics fabrication equipment. This equipment is largely responsible for advances the Soviet microelectronics industry has made thus far. This progress has reduced the overall Western lead in microelectronics from 10 to 12 years in the mid-1970s to 4 to 6 years today.

Although the Soviets are not exclusively dependent on Free World finished technology to upgrade their military systems, they have reaped major benefits from their legal and illegal technology acquisitions. Innovation, higher technical levels of research, accelerated development of more sophisticated weapons, and avoidance of major pitfalls are among the benefits the Soviet military derives from US and Free World R&D projects. Western technology gives the Soviet designer another option, often better than his own research establishment can produce, from which to choose. The Soviet practice of eclectically incorporating technology permits the efficient, rapid assimilation of equipment and knowledge obtained in the West into the military sector.

Soviet requirements for militarily related foreign technology are not expected to decrease. The problem of technology transfer may actually intensify because of the requirements that will be generated by the planned modernization of the Soviet economy. Economic modernization is the centerpiece of General Secretary Gorbachev's domestic policy. Ultimately, overall economic revitalization will have a profound effect on the Soviet Union's military capability as well. Soviet leaders have no doubt taken this factor into account and see it as a further incentive to pursue their modernization campaign.

An important secondary objective of this modernization program is the reduction of technological dependency on the West by producing equal or superior technology. Ironically,

(continued from above)

illegal means, then the USSR is not the only nation doing this. The US has its own espionage services, and one of their major missions is to ensure that we avoid technological surprise. But the propagandist is not concerned with logic or the truth. As Joseph Goebbels said, "we speak only for effect." If the Soviets hold any lead in technology, then the propagandist will say so, because this enhances the Soviet threat. If it is we who hold the lead in technology, the propagandist will not say so. He will say, as he does here, that the Soviets are trying to steal our technology, because that is the simplest way to enhance the Soviet threat. He professes outrage at Soviet spying, even though he knows we spy ourselves, because this dramatizes the threat. It doesn't matter to him that we are widening the technology gap, that our lead in technology places the heavier moral burden on us not to take new initiatives in the arms race, or that the more nations share such information the safer the world will be. But these considerations should matter to us.

This chart serves exactly the same purpose served by the chart on the preceding page. See the commentary on that page. An interesting project for the student of propaganda would be to request the data on which the administration presumably based this chart and, if the administration provides any documentation, go through it to see how genuine and complete it is. How many pieces of such equipment do the documents actually show the Soviets acquired? How many times can the transfer of such equipment really be traced through bonafide shipping and customs records from their points of origin to the Soviet Union? How many times were these transfers truly "illegal," as the fine print below this chart asserts? How many times did the government represent in court that the equipment involved was classified? How many times were convictions sustained against officers or employees of firms involved in the transfer of this equipment for false licenses, false end-use certificates, or illegal purchases?

The quality of the Soviet radar required to provide this capability is still highly in doubt. See the commentary on page 58.

After 120 pages of this book, we still await news of Soviet weapons whose capabilities "exceed their Western counterparts."

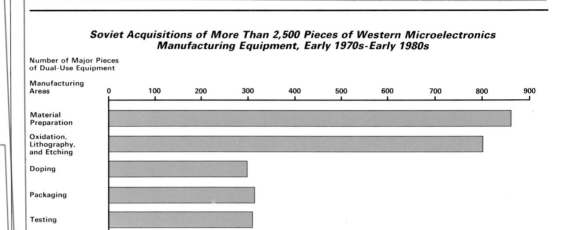

Soviet Acquisitions of More Than 2,500 Pieces of Western Microelectronics Manufacturing Equipment, Early 1970s-Early 1980s

Number of Major Pieces of Dual-Use Equipment

Manufacturing Areas

Material Preparation

Oxidation, Lithography, and Etching

Doping

Packaging

Testing

Over the past few years the Soviets have virtually completed their entire building construction program for manufacturing military microelectronics components. To equip many of these buildings with advanced production equipment, they acquired more than 2,500 pieces of major Western controlled and uncontrolled microelectronics fabrication equipment covering the entire spectrum of manufacturing operations. They acquired this equipment from the US, Japan, and Europe, and diverted it through many parts of the world. Years of illegal acquisitions of large numbers of dual-use products through worldwide trade diversions have enabled the Soviets to narrow the microelectronics technological gap with the west from 10 to 12 years a decade ago to about four to six years today.

This means that it can strike within no fewer than 1,312 feet of its aimpoint. Not an impressive level of accuracy.

Yes, but can it be launched from a mobile transporter? In pictures and in text throughout this book, the authors have repeatedly implied that it can be, yet they have carefully worded each of their statements to avoid clearly confirming that this is so.

We first deployed terminal guidance with our PERSHING II in 1983. When our TRIDENT II D-5 becomes operational, it will probably use reentry vehicles with terminal guidance, too.

reaching this objective will require greater infusions of Western production-enhancing controlled technologies, including microelectronics, computers and software, communications, and robotics, as well as advanced machinery and testing equipment.

The ability of the Soviet military-industrial complex to develop and deploy weapons with capabilities that often match or exceed their Western counterparts, and yet are beyond the generally assumed Soviet technological baseline, is both impressive and ominous. Their overall technology base is below that of the West. Nonetheless, the comparative technological level of deployed systems demonstrates a serious effort to upgrade those systems.

The Soviets have made significant incremental improvements in the operational capabilities of their weapons across the entire spectrum of military missions. The following examples illustrate this point:

- The product improvement in fighter aircraft is evident in comparing the latest generation FULCRUM with the FISHBED, which entered service in the early 1960s. Both aircraft have air-superiority/intercept missions. The FULCRUM, has a 15-percent increase in speed and about a 40-percent increase in combat range. It can carry a much wider load of ordnance, including three types of air-to-air missiles. Perhaps most significant, however, the FULCRUM is the first Soviet tactical fighter to have all-aspect look-down/shoot-down capabilities.
- The SS-25 ICBM, which reached initial operational capability in 1985, is 5 times more accurate than the SS-13, the USSR's first solid-propellant ICBM. It has twice the throw-weight, and is both road mobile and capable of being silo-launched.
- Soviet leaders believe that the range, accuracy, and speed of missile weaponry have revolutionized warfare, as shorter range ballistic missile forces are expected to have a key role in any land-based military conflict involving Soviet interests. Therefore, they place a high priority on keeping pace with advancing technology to maximize missile effectiveness. The Soviets are expected to introduce terminal guidance systems, which provide significant accuracy improvements, and to incorporate various nuclear and non-nuclear warheads. The improved

The SS-21 and SS-23 are capable of striking within no fewer than 1,000 and 1,150 feet of their aimpoints, respectively. Not sufficient to use conventional munitions against theater targets.

Since this is a fantasy tank, descriptions of it vary a great deal from passage to passage in this book. Now we hear, for the first time, that it combines "some features" of the older T-64 tank with those of the T-72, though we are not told which features these are. The claims of a "better" powerplant, "improved" armor protection, and "more advanced" fire control are all repeated here, but this time the claim

of "greater firepower" has been dropped. All of the features mentioned are those of the T-72.

How much added speed? They don't say. See the commentary on page 117.

The frequencies and band-widths of the KIROV's air search and tracking radars have already been programmed into the memories of the jamming and other electronic warfare equipment aboard our Navy's strike aircraft, and are routinely updated when changes in frequency and band-width are monitored.

---

accuracy of the SS-21 and SS-23 probably provides the Soviets with non-nuclear capabilities to attack theater targets.

The recently deployed T-80 tank continues the developmental pattern epitomized by the T-64 and T-72 tanks in the past 2 decades. Combining some features of both, the T-80 incorporates a better powerplant, improved armor protection, and more advanced fire control.

The KIROV-Class nuclear-powered guided-missile cruiser is a major improvement over earlier Soviet guided-missile cruisers. The KIROV, which has a 28,000-ton displacement, is a heavily armed ship with a nuclear power propulsion system that gives it virtually unlimited range. It also incorporates oil-fired boilers to give the ship added speed. The cruiser carries a wide range of weapons as well as three helicopters. The KIROV has excellent air search radars, a much-improved antiair warfare missile fire control system, and significant electronic warfare and command, control, and communications capabilities. It carries five types of surface-to-surface and surface-to-air missiles. It is also fitted with medium-caliber guns, antiaircraft Gatling guns, antisubmarine warfare rockets, and torpedoes.

The Soviets have also successfully incorporated technological advances including extensive automation, into their submarine programs. Improved control of magnetic, electromagnetic, and acoustic signatures have rendered newer Soviet submarines far less detectable than older units. Titanium has been used in the pressure hulls of some units, probably to achieve deeper operating depths.

Soviet Industry

Military Production

The Soviet Union has the world's largest active military-industrial base producing virtually every type of military equipment in large quantities not only for its own forces but for export. Despite recent increases in US output, Soviet output in the 1980s continues to lead the US in overall military production.

The output of ground force and general-purpose equipment continues at the high over-

all rates that have characterized Soviet production for a quarter of a century. The production of the most modern tactical fighters and the most modern naval surface combatants and nuclear-powered attack submarines, on the other hand, is below the levels sustained in previous years.

From 1982 through 1986, declines have also been noted in tactical materiel equipment such as some artillery-type weapons — but not the newer self-propelled models — minor naval ships, helicopters, and tactical ballistic missiles. The drop in fighter output, for example, reflects new high technology models that are more costly and difficult to produce. At the same time, the output of systems such as bombers, long- and short-range cruise missiles, submarine-launched cruise missiles (SLCMs), and AWACS was on the increase. ICBM output rose for the second straight year and is now at the 1982 level. Further advances in both liquid- and solid-propellant models are expected.

In the midterm, no great changes are expected. Output of materiel for the ground forces will not change much except for helicopters. In that category, production will continue to decline slightly until series manufacture of the HAVOC and HOKUM are well underway.

Fluctuations in naval production are expected over the short term because ships are built in small numbers at great cost over long construction periods. Future production of small surface combatants will increase, considering

US and Soviet Procurement of Major Weapon Systems 1977-1986

	US	USSR
ICBMs and SLBMs	850	3,000
IRBMs and MRBMs	200	1,000
Surface-to-Air Missiles *	16,200	140,000
Long- and Intermediate-range Bombers	28	375
Fighters **	3,450	7,150
Military Helicopters	1,750	4,650
Submarines	43	90
Major Surface Combatants ***	89	81
Tanks	7,100	24,400
Artillery	2,750	28,200

* Includes naval SAMs
** Excludes ASW and combat trainers
*** Excludes auxiliaries

Wrong. 3,496. This includes the entire production to date of our PERSHING II missile, and of our long-range Air-Launched, Ground-Launched and Sea-Launched Cruise Missiles.

Wrong. 1,186.

Wrong. 880.

Wrong. 310.

Wrong. 2,948.

Wrong. 1,450.

Wrong. 59.

Wrong. 44.

Wrong. 9,370.

Wrong. 5,625.

Wrong. 84,000.

Wrong. 2,043.

Wrong. 45.

Wrong. 12,655.

Soviet submarines are still much noisier than ours, and much easier for us to detect than ours are for them. See the commentary on page 81.

Only in some categories of equipment. In others, we are out-building the USSR.

The corrected figures given here are for weapon systems procured by the US and Soviet governments for their own military services, as the title to this table specifies, and do not include export production. The figures given by the authors for Soviet fighter aircraft and helicopters nearly match the total numbers of those weapon systems in service with Soviet forces today, many of which were produced prior to this period. In their figure for major Soviet surface combatants, the authors probably included ships displacing fewer than 2,000 tons. The corrected figures do not include these. See the commentary on page 9 for good reasons why.

Let us reflect for a moment on the credibility of the claim made in this chart that the Soviets are producing tanks at a rate of 3,000 per year. Had they been producing tanks at this rate for the past four decades since the end of World War II, they would have 120,000 tanks today. Instead, we find that they have fewer than half that amount. Have they suddenly stepped up production, then? Not according to previous editions of this book. The 1981 edition had them producing 3,000 tanks in 1979, and 3,000 in 1980. If anything, subsequent estimates were revised upwards. The 1983 edition had the Soviets producing 3,500 tanks in 1979, and 3,100 in 1980. Well then, have they completely reequipped their armored forces with new tanks? No, it seems not. More than 23,000 T-54 and T-55 tanks, along with more than 14,000 T-62s, are still assigned to Soviet line divisions. Had they wished, they certainly could have equipped more units with their newest tank, the T-72. But it seems they have been in no hurry to do this. Since the T-72 has been in production, more than 2,000 have been exported. Nor are the Soviets engaged in any major force expansion. Give or take a division or two, the number of active and inactive

(continued on next page)

The figures given here exaggerate Soviet ICBM production by 200, and understate NATO ICBM production by 9. They understate LRINF production, which should include the production of Ground-launched Cruise Missiles, by about 800, and exaggerate Soviet SRBM production by about 200 per year. While a note explains that the category of SLCMs includes both short-range and long-range systems, it does not explain that all of the short-range systems are Soviet, while all of the long-range systems are US Cruise Missiles. It also exaggerates the number of Soviet SLCMs produced in this period by more than 1,000. The figures for SLBMs are almost correct, but do not include 16 French MSBS M-4/TN70 missiles. The category of air-launched Cruise Missiles has been excluded here, since all would be US long-range systems adding to the NATO balance.

Production of Ground Forces Materiel USSR/NSWP and NATO*

Equipment Type	USSR	NSWP	USSR	NSWP	USSR	NSWP	NATO		
	1984		1985		1986		1984	1985	1986
Tanks	3,200	450	3,000	700	3,000	700	1,600	1,800	1,000
Other Armored Fighting Vehicles	3,800	1,200	3,500	1,200	3,000	1,200	2,500	2,700	2,400
Towed Field Artillery	1,900	250	2,000	200	1,300	150	450	550	225
Self-Propelled Field Artillery	1,000	300	1,000	350	1,000	500	250	300	225
Multiple Rocket Launchers	900	100	700	100	500	75	75	75	500
Self-Propelled AA Artillery	50	0	100	10	100	50	50	25	0
Towed AA Artillery	0	225	0	225	0	200	25	0	0

* Revised to reflect current total production information. Includes United States; excludes France and Spain.

Missile Production USSR and NATO*

Missile Type	USSR			NATO		
	1984	1985	1986	1984	1985	1986
ICBMs	75	100	125	0	0	10
LRINF	125	125	25	80	175	125
SRBMs	500	450	400	0	0	0
SLCMs**	700	700	1,100	1,100	800	700
SLBMs	50	100	100	70	75	25

* Revised to reflect current total production information. Includes United States; excludes France and Spain.
** Short- and long-range sea-launched cruise missiles.

Aircraft Production USSR and NATO*

Aircraft Type	USSR			NATO		
	1984	1985	1986	1984	1985	1986
Bombers	50	50	50	0	2	25
Fighters/Fighter-Bombers	800	650	650	550	550	550
Transports	250	250	200	250	300	300
ASW	5	5	5	10	5	5
Military Helicopters	600	600	500	720	525	350
Utility/Trainers	10	0	55	305	300	250

* Revised to reflect current total production information. Includes United States; excludes France and Spain.

Naval Ship Construction USSR and NATO*

Ship Type	USSR			NATO		
	1984	1985	1986	1984	1985	1986
Submarines	9	8	8	12	8	7
Major Combatants	9	8	9	19	16	11
Minor Combatants	50	50	50	34	30	25
Auxiliaries	5	5	6	11	5	5

* Revised to reflect current total production information. Includes United States; excludes France and Spain.

the new facilities online or coming online at shipyards that traditionally build small combatants. Over the longer term, the Soviet ship-building industry, reflecting a more global outlook, will produce units of greater capability and generally greater size. These larger ships will permit the Soviet navy to better operate in broad ocean areas.

For aircraft, bomber production, which has increased significantly during the 1980s, is believed to have peaked. A moderate decline is expected at least until series production of BLACKJACK begins. BACKFIRE output will probably be unchanged for the next several years. Production of the FULCRUM and FLANKER is expected to rise notably in the next several years. The output of FROGFOOT and FOXHOUND is likely to grow only slightly. Transport aircraft production is expected to decline further during the next several years.

An acknowledgment that the Soviet Navy's current ships of smaller size do not operate well in broad ocean areas.

These figures are roughly correct. Nor is their presentation misleading, since the authors here make the distinction between major and minor combatants, a distinction they have usually obscured elsewhere in the book.

These figures exaggerate Soviet fighter-bomber production by about 900, Soviet transport aircraft production by about 500, and Soviet helicopter production by about 1,100. Figures for NATO fighter-bomber production are higher than usual, but only because production of several new aircraft, including the *Jaguar*, the *Tornado*, and the US F-15, F-16, and A-10 peaked at the same time.

divisions in the Soviet Army's order of battle has not changed appreciably for some time. What has not changed for a very long time is the number of Soviet divisions stationed in Eastern Europe. From a simple inspection of current equipment stocks and export records, it is clear that the Soviets have been producing, on average, about 1,150 tanks per year, about 950 of them for their own use, as the corrected records on the preceding page reflect, and the balance for export. As the bulk of new production reequips front line divisions, and older equipment is reassigned to other units, more of the oldest equipment

becomes available for export, along with a fraction of the new. The Soviets may decide, of course, to build up their tank inventory to a higher level, in order to fully equip inactive and reserve divisions. But so far, the equipment needed to accomplish this continues to be exported abroad in pursuit of foreign policy goals that have always held higher priority. Most of the other Soviet and Warsaw Pact production figures in this chart are exaggerated as well. The other nations of the Warsaw Pact produce, at most, 150 tanks per year. Most of their tanks are from Soviet stocks. Romania produces a variant of

The mobile SS-21 is one of a growing number of improved short-range nuclear missiles available to Soviet divisions opposite NATO.

Production of strategic and tactical missiles should rise during the next few years. Substantial increases in ICBM production are expected by the end of the decade as the SS-X-24 enters series production and as the new liquid-propellant ICBM, a replacement for the SS-18, completes testing and enters production. LRINF production should also rise in the next few years as the improved version of the SS-20 begins deployment. Annual output of tactical missiles will also grow as the SS-23 reaches peak production. High levels of SAM

and cruise missile production are expected to continue for the next few years as new systems are phased into production. In the longer term, the Soviets' ability to provide their military forces with the modern high-technology materiel required in the 1990s will depend on the success of Gorbachev's program to reinvigorate the military-industrial base.

● Lest there be any confusion here, which seems quite likely, the SS-18 presumably being replaced by a "new liquid propellant ICBM" uses liquid propellants, too. The "new" ICBM therefore does not represent, as this passage seems intended to suggest, some sort of advance in propellant technology.

the Soviet T-55 which NATO calls the M-77, and has about 200 of these. All produce much fewer artillery pieces and armored vehicles of other types. The Soviets have been producing fewer than 500 self-propelled artillery pieces per year. Figures for NATO production, on the other hand, have been significantly understated. The years cited are those in which the British began production of their new *Challenger* tank, the West Germans continued production of their *Leopard 2* both for their own use and for export, the French continued

production of their AMX-30, the Italians continued licensed production of the M-47 and M-60 tanks, and the US produced the M-1 *Abrams* and the M-60A3, both types for our military services but the latter type for a vigorous export program of our own as well. In at least this period, the combined tank production of all NATO nations came close to the level the authors have fabricated here for the USSR. NATO production of multiple rocket launchers and self-propelled antiaircraft artillery was also much greater than shown.

● The Soviet SA-5 shown here has a speed of Mach 2.6 and a range of 250 km. Our PATRIOT air defense missile has a speed of Mach 3.9 and a range of 400 km. SA-5 missiles were one of the types of air defense missile rendered inoperable when their radars and other associated equipment were destroyed with antiradiation missiles fired by US Navy aircraft during operations in the Bay of Sidra and over Libya in March and April, 1986. The administration openly declared that the latter operation, which involved the bombing of Libyan leader Muammar Quaddafi's living quarters in Tripoli, was in retaliation for Libya's alleged involvement in the terrorist bombing of a West German discotheque on April 5. Privately, administration officials, so long as their names were not used, confirmed that the purpose of the Tripoli bombing raid had been to kill Quaddafi. It killed more than 100 other people, presumably including two US servicemen whose F-111 aircraft was reported missing. The bombing raid against Tripoli was not launched until after the administration had repeatedly announced to the public that it had found "irrefutable" evidence linking Libya to the discotheque bombing. The administration did not immediately offer to explain what this evidence was—as though it felt itself under no obligation to provide the American people with any of the facts upon which it based policies for which it expected their full support. It was not until a journalist inquired about this oversight that a White House spokesman described the evidence as "radio intercepts." How likely was this to be? If the Libyans really had been involved in the bombing of the discotheque, which police and intelligence agencies in West Germany and every other major West European country very much doubt, how likely would it have been that they would communicate with each other by radio in planning the event? Wouldn't they know that they might be monitored and caught? Yes, they would.

They would know this, because this is what the US periodically tells the world that it does. We intercept radio communications all over the world. In case the Libyans forgot that we had this capability, their most recent reminder of it came in the fall of 1983, when at the United Nations the US played tapes of radio traffic it had intercepted

between Soviet ground controllers and Soviet interceptor pilots pursuing Korean Air Lines Flight 7. To communicate by radio, then, would have been about the last thing the Libyans would do, if they had any role in this affair and wanted to keep it hidden. In retrospect, the Tripoli raid is not only an example of a major power making arbitrary and wrong decisions about whom to blame for frustrating events over which it has no control; it is also an example of conditioning. The public was being told to accept as an article of faith that the Executive Branch of government had good reasons to do what it did, and that there were no checks, no balances in this system. The public was also being told that punitive military actions of any type, on any scale, including the assassination of a foreign head of state, fell within the framework of legitimate policy.

Chapter VII

Political-Military and Regional Policies

Under Gorbachev, the Soviet Union is pursuing a dynamic foreign policy. To the General Secretary and his colleagues, economic revitalization, foreign policy activism, and enhanced military power are not mutually exclusive, but rather are inextricably linked. Gorbachev is trying <u>to shake Moscow's foreign policy out of the drift and lethargy of the past several years.</u> He has stressed that Soviet policies abroad should be based on more imaginative thinking, greater tactical flexibility, more sophisticated propaganda and diplomacy, and greater emphasis on the East-West struggle.

<u>Although the style and rhetoric have changed, the ultimate goals have not.</u> Expansion of influence and consolidation of gains remain the basic goals of the Soviet Union's activity worldwide.

To energize Soviet foreign policy and to overcome the impression that the influence of the USSR abroad is based solely on its military prowess, Gorbachev has restructured the upper echelons of the country's foreign affairs apparatus. Eight of 11 first deputy and deputy foreign ministers, in addition to Foreign Minister Shevardnadze, are Gorbachev appointees. More than 30 ambassadors have been replaced, including those in most major Western and Asian capitals. Gorbachev's three top foreign policy advisers have extensive experience with the West. Anatoliy Dobrynin, who spent 24 years as Ambassador to the US, now heads

SA-5 surface-to-air missiles for Libya are among thousands of tons of weaponry shipped by the Soviet Union to its client states each year. In return for military and political support to countries such as Libya and Syria, the Soviets have advanced their political-military objectives and have gained access to military facilities in the region.

After five chapters devoted to the exaggeration of Soviet military capabilities, the authors here return to the theme of Soviet intentions which dominated the opening chapter of this book. As reflected in Soviet political, military and regional policies, or at least in the interpretations of those policies attempted here, Soviet intentions are effortlessly simple to understand. They are hostile, and they are unchanging. The single purpose of all of this is to perpetuate the threat. Should the military balance too clearly favor the West, so that efforts to draw a threatening picture of Soviet military capabilities fail, the skillful propagandist can still justify a program of defense expenditures of staggering proportions by warning that while the military balance may change, Soviet intentions will not.

It is only in retrospect, of course, that we hear about "drift and lethargy" in Soviet policies. In every one of the same "past several years" alarmists warned of clear and resolute Soviet global ambitions, just as they do today.

Predictably, the "ultimate goals" of Soviet policy are presented here as unchanged. Even if that were the case, there have been no "gains" to consolidate in a period when Soviet influence, far from expanding, has eroded. See the commentary on page 13.

● The increasing number of interviews with Soviet spokesmen in Western news media may become an important test of how effective our anti-Soviet propaganda has been. Many Western news managers undoubtedly feel confident that their audience is trained well enough to distrust anything a Soviet spokesman says, no matter how much sense he makes, so that these interviews become mere exercises in inuring ourselves to reason. Other news managers may hope to see reason prevail, subverting our propaganda effort. But the most significant subversion may be of the democratic process itself. US news media, in particular, have increasingly chosen Soviet spokesmen to substitute for powerful voices of domestic opposition which challenge official policy here at home. This creates the false impression that no such domestic opposition exists, at a time in our history when that opposition is massive; that there is no need for broader debate on issues of national security; and that the only real differences of opinion over such matters are those between the US and Soviet governments.

● The authors here articulated a viewpoint which they know repre-

This chapter will be filled ● with accusations of this kind, which cannot be supported by example.

An important seed of in- ● nuendo is delicately planted here. We are to believe that the funding of US defense programs in current years cannot be complicated by growing public outrage over the monumental levels of waste incurred in funding every prior year of US defense programs, or about the perfect, unbroken record of 40 years of official misrepresentations of the balance of power, from the bomber gap to the missile gap, intended to justify that waste. We are to believe, instead, that funding of current US programs can only be threatened by "well-targeted" Soviet propaganda.

On the contrary, it is the ● White House which manipulates Congressional funding decisions, by submitting its major military funding requests before each new round of arms talks is scheduled to begin, so that members of Congress inclined to withhold support for major new weapons systems may later be accused of lacking "bipartisan" spirit, of weakening our negotiating hand, and of abandoning our leadership in its hour of need.

We claim this whenever we ● want to pretend we cannot agree among ourselves about an arms treaty we have no intention of signing anyway.

the Central Committee's International Department, the major coordinating body for Soviet foreign policy decisionmaking. Aleksandr Yakovlev, Ambassador to Canada for 10 years, is now in charge of the Central Committee's Propaganda Department. Anatoliy Chernyayev, who came from the International Department, has become Gorbachev's personal foreign affairs adviser.

In the Ministry of Foreign Affairs, regional divisions have been realigned and several new departments have been established — cultural relations, information, arms control, nonaligned nations, and atomic energy — to respond better to the realities of the foreign environment. The new appointees are sophisticated men with backgrounds in Party work and international relations as well as knowledge ● of or experience in dealing with the news media. A significant part of their jobs is to court foreign leaders and the news media, stressing global interdependence and the flexible, pragmatic nature of Soviet foreign policy.

Arms control diplomacy is a major tool in the ● Kremlin's policy toward the West. The Soviets are trying to wrest concessions from the US through superficially tempting but one-sided offers, weaken Alliance resolve through pro- ● tracted negotiations and well-targeted propaganda, and complicate the funding of US defense programs. In the wake of the 1986 Reykjavik meeting, Moscow sought to win support in the US and Western Europe through Gorbachev's misleading portrayal of the Strategic Defense Initiative (SDI) as the only obstacle to the resolution of a number of arms control issues, including significant reductions and eventual elimination of nuclear arms.

After years of occasionally strident diplomacy, Moscow is trying to improve relations with several US allies, particularly Japan. Gorbachev's July 1986 Vladivostok speech signified the USSR's renewed interest in Asia. Soviet-North Korean ties are on the upswing, and Moscow has offered minor concessions in an effort to improve relations with China. Some Western observers believe the USSR might want to lessen its burdens in the Third World, but the Kremlin has continued to provide heavy military support to its beleaguered clients in Sub-Saharan Africa, give moral and materiel support to Libya, and maintain the flow of arms to Cuba and to the Sandinistas in Nicaragua. In exchange for the establishment of a strategi-

cally located forward military base, the Soviets have continued to provide significant military and economic aid to Vietnam. While calling for peace in Afghanistan and offering a troop withdrawal plan, they replaced the leadership in Kabul, introduced better equipment and different tactics in that country, and stepped up the campaign to intimidate Pakistan.

The USSR and Arms Control

Soviet regional policies, particularly those directed toward the West, are complex, interrelated, and largely revolve around military issues. The policies of the USSR on arms control, US and NATO force modernization, and the campaign against SDI are central to its dealing with Western Europe. Soviet arms control policy goes well beyond the narrow goal of reaching an agreement with the West. The USSR believes that the negotiating process itself can produce important military and political dividends, even without actually reaching an agreement. Moscow realizes benefits can be derived from carefully negotiated agreements that lock-in existing military advantages, set limits on the threat environment for economic and military planners, and confirm its superpower status. Moreover, it also sees arms control negotiations as a way of furthering Soviet military objectives and undermining public support for Western defense policies and programs.

The Soviets are using several strategies to ● derail US defense programs. They seek to influence congressional funding decisions by engaging in arms talks, hoping that Congress might be reluctant to appropriate funds for systems that could be bargained away later. They also believe that arms talks can stimulate public pressure for defense cutbacks. Moscow ● frequently tries to stir up discontent in the US and in NATO Europe by arguing that US intransigence at the arms control talks, particularly its unwillingness to negotiate on SDI, is blocking any agreement and will lead to a new arms race.

The USSR hopes that over time, well-orchestrated campaigns involving public relations efforts, propaganda, and active measures can aggravate tensions in the Western Alliance ● and undercut cohesion on strategic issues. Ultimately, the Soviets manipulate arms control talks to get their opponents to negotiate with themselves rather than with Moscow.

(continued from above)

sents the thinking of a great many people in the United States, and throughout the world. However, by calling it Moscow's idea, they hope to subtly discredit it, so that many readers, long trained to be suspicious of any ideas from Moscow, will find themselves questioning its validity—even though its truth is self-evident. At work here, in the propagandist's arsenal, are the principles of association and discreditation. A good example of both is Ronald Reagan's remark that if a bilateral nuclear freeze is a Soviet idea, "then there must be something wrong with it." Discreditation is most effective when it recog- nizes the inconsistencies and deceptions in the propagandist's own position, articulates these observations, and calls them all the ideas of its adversary. The propagandist's target, usually a loyal public, then has more difficulty seeing simple facts for what they are. This is how certain ideas about the US government, for example, are made almost unthinkable. How could the US show "intransigence" in arms control negotiations?

Once again, the authors are unable to define what Soviet military ● "advantages" these proposals would "lock in." But a review of our own proposals shows that we have repeatedly tried to "lock in" major military advantages of our own, and that "equitability" is the last thing this administration has ever taken any interest in. In 1981, our "Zero Option" proposal asked the Soviets to dismantle or withdraw all of their SS-20 and other nuclear missiles of intermediate range targeted on Western Europe, without proposing that comparable British POLARIS, American POSEIDON, and French M-20 and SSBS-2 missiles targeted against Eastern Europe, be dismantled or withdrawn, too. Soviet refusal to accept these terms was used to jus-

tify deployment of a new generation of Cruise and Pershing II missiles, now stationed in Europe along with all of the other ones. In 1982, the administration's START (Strategic Arms Reduction) proposal asked for what seemed equivalent reductions in Soviet and American nuclear arsenals to the same level of ballistic missile warheads each. Less publicized behind the "great fanfare" was the fact that it also asked the Soviets to achieve their reduction by eliminating 75 percent of their force of SS-17, SS-18 and SS-19 missiles, the most modern weapons they had developed, while it did not include the

Since gaining power, General Secretary Gorbachev has offered a number of arms control initiatives in rapid succession and with great fanfare. Moscow has tried to project an image of a peace-loving superpower stymied by an inflexible US determined to gain military superiority. Although Gorbachev is the first Soviet leader to propose significant arms reductions, these current proposals would lock-in Soviet military advantages while frustrating Western efforts to achieve deep, equitable, and effectively verifiable arms reductions.

Domestic Affairs and Arms Control Policy

Soviet arms control strategy is shaped primarily by the Kremlin's perception of the military and foreign policy benefits to be gained from Soviet participation in the negotiations process. Domestic political and economic pressures, although important, are secondary. Gorbachev and other Soviet leaders are well aware that the potential economic savings from arms control would be marginal at best. No significant opposition is apparent within the strategic leadership to Gorbachev's arms control approach. Many who comprise this leadership team are Gorbachev appointees.

Gorbachev's accession to power coincided with the resumption of the Geneva talks in March 1985. Since then, the new General Secretary has imparted a certain pace and style to Soviet arms control policy. He must still seek consensus on major foreign policy issues, but he clearly holds the dominant position within the strategic decisionmaking team. Moreover, broad agreement seems to exist in the Soviet leadership on the overall goals of arms control strategy. Indeed, Soviet strategy to constrain the US defense modernization program, particularly SDI, was formulated before Gorbachev became General Secretary.

Policy To Undermine SDI

The USSR, as part of its arms control strategy, is orchestrating a worldwide campaign to undermine US domestic and foreign support for SDI. The Soviet program against SDI consists of diplomacy, propaganda, and deceptive operations. These efforts are designed to bring pressure on SDI simultaneously from several sources: US critics, the NATO countries, and the Third World. One of the least appreciated aspects of Moscow's efforts to derail SDI is the active measures campaign, which is probably

broader in scope than any other such effort ever mounted by the USSR.

The Soviets are intent on sabotaging SDI primarily because they perceive it as having the potential to limit their ability to achieve their offensive strategic objectives. Although the Soviets recognize the grave consequences of a nuclear war, they nonetheless make their plans on the assumption that any conflict between the USSR and the US could escalate to such a level. Contrary to the Western theory of mutual vulnerability, Soviet nuclear doctrine is based on the premise that the USSR could fight and survive a nuclear war. The Soviets believe they could prevail in such a conflict by destroying enemy nuclear targets with offensive strikes while employing defensive operations to blunt the effects of retaliatory nuclear strikes.

Moscow is concerned that SDI will lead to an effective US strategic defense system that could undermine the Soviet ability to launch a successful preemptive strike, which is the linchpin of their strategic doctrine. The Soviets are also greatly concerned about potential SDI technology spinoffs. Such technologies will impact on future weaponry and on a wide range of scientific endeavors.

Political Influence Operations

Moscow has made extensive use of political influence operations to discredit SDI. The Soviets have tried to induce professional groups such as journalists, scientists, businessmen, academics, and physicians to come forth with supposedly unofficial criticism of SDI based on scientific, economic, medical, or other criteria. By establishing private and professional contacts with members of Western groups, the Soviets are seeking to generate pressure against SDI among influential individuals who might not come in contact with, or who would consciously avoid, Soviet propaganda or diplomats.

The Soviets have looked to the Western scientific community as a key professional group against SDI ever since the late General Secretary Andropov suggested in April 1983 that Soviet and US scientists should meet and explore the consequences of SDI. Considering the importance of the scientific element in the SDI program, the extensive Soviet effort to influence Western scientists is understandable. Moscow has drawn heavily on its own scientists and scientific institutions to inject its views into Western political forums. The Sovi-

● There is no greater single source of potential economic savings for any industrialized nation than arms control. This is one of the more disturbing sentences in this book. The authors would here cold-bloodedly bury the truth of the arms race as deeply as possible. In fact, the arms race has already battered our economies into very fragile condition, and is directly responsible for rising inflation, rising unemployment, severe shortages of irretrievable resources, a steady depletion of engineering and scientific skills, and a growing failure to compete in the international market. More and more members of our society live at the margins of tolerance. The US infant mortality rate is now higher than that of Singapore or Hong Kong. In short, merely by continuing to prepare for war, the arms race is killing us without a shot being fired.

● If the authors could prove that Soviet nuclear doctrine was based on such a premise, they would document that premise here. They do not. How, in any case, is such a premise "contrary" to Western theory? Anyone so naive as to believe that the US would be unwilling to strike the first blow should read the commentary at the top of page 18.

● Wrong. Moscow is concerned that SDI will lead to an effective US antisatellite system which could support the US ability to launch a successful preemptive strike.

most modern weapons we had developed, long-range Air-Launched Cruise Missiles, or the very large arsenal of nuclear gravity bombs our strategic aircraft also deploy, even though these two categories of weapons perpetuate a sizeable numerical and qualitative US lead in strategic power over the Soviet Union. In 1985, in response to a Soviet proposal to reduce *all* strategic warheads to a common level, the administration responded by trying to exclude nuclear gravity bombs and short-range attack missile warheads from the negotiations. These are not sincere efforts to negotiate on an "equitable"

basis. Nonetheless, hiding its own intransigence, the administration likes to come away from the bargaining table saying that it did its best to negotiate "in good faith," but that Soviet intransigence always made agreement impossible. Characteristically, this states the reverse of the truth.

● Here is another example, and a fairly nasty one, of the principle of association utilized in an effort to discredit a wide variety of professional groups across the country which have come out in strong opposition to SDI. It is presumably, also, an example of the campaign of

(continued from page 127)

"active measures" the authors have promised to describe. None of the groups in question needed any inducement of any kind to oppose SDI. What was wrong with SDI, and what was dishonest in President Reagan's presentation of it, were patently clear at the outset. See the commentary on pages 44 and 45. The reaction of all of these groups was immediate and comprehensive. It did not result from Soviet influence, as the authors would here have readers believe. It resulted from good, old-fashioned American moral outrage at the largest pork barrel the US taxpayer has yet seen. The opposition to SDI is native, and massive. All of this is deeply frustrating to an administration whose instincts are so clearly totalitarian, and which has done all it could to constrain or penalize free speech. It has a very low threshold of tolerance for massive public opposition, and can generally be relied upon to respond with some updating, like the present one, of the red-baiting techniques of the 1950s. The authors may hope that this sort of discreditation will intimidate some critics into silence. But they also hope, for other Americans, to provide a "reinterpretation" of why there is so much opposition to SDI. There are,

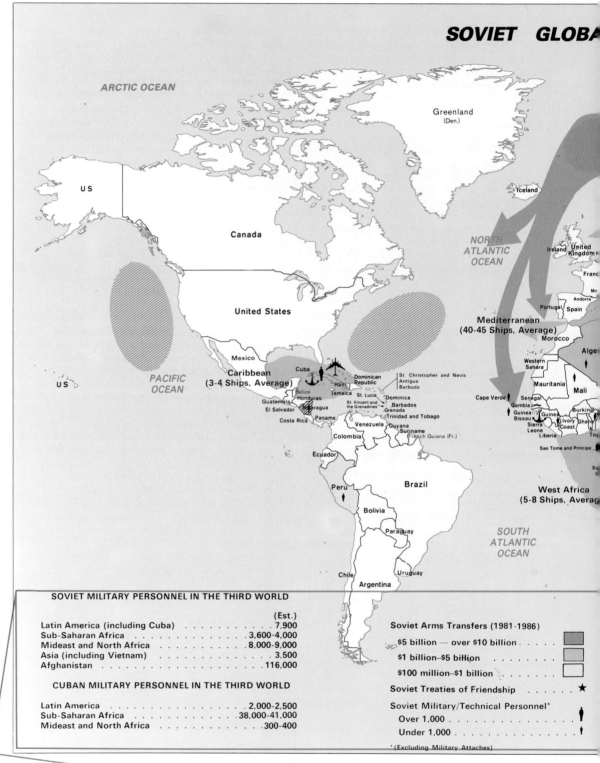

SOVIET MILITARY PERSONNEL IN THE THIRD WORLD

	(Est.)
Latin America (including Cuba)	7,900
Sub-Saharan Africa	3,600-4,000
Mideast and North Africa	8,000-9,000
Asia (including Vietnam)	3,500
Afghanistan	116,000

CUBAN MILITARY PERSONNEL IN THE THIRD WORLD

Latin America	2,000-2,500
Sub-Saharan Africa	38,000-41,000
Mideast and North Africa	300-400

Soviet Arms Transfers (1981-1986)

$5 billion — over $10 billion	
$1 billion–$5 billion	
$100 million–$1 billion	
Soviet Treaties of Friendship	★
Soviet Military/Technical Personnel*	
Over 1,000	
Under 1,000	

* (Excluding Military Attaches)

(continued from above)

after all, a number of Americans who don't want to hear any criticism of official policy. They will wrap themselves in the flag, and call all critics KGB agents. By that token, all of the housewives, professionals, students and businessmen who voted for a bilateral nuclear freeze in the November, 1982 elections, a clear majority of the electorate, were KGB agents. The administration wishes these were not the majority, and that the frightened Americans were. The frightened Americans seem more afraid of opposing their government than they are of nuclear war. We must try to understand their fear, and help them to see that you do not best serve your country by keeping silent and loving America, right or wrong. You only serve politicians momentarily in power that way.

● The USSR maintains or has access to 80 military bases beyond its national borders. Only 13 of these are outside the Warsaw Pact area. Beyond our national borders, the US maintains or has access to 967 military bases, 730 of which are outside the NATO area. We also have access to 1,300 other military installations. The Soviet inter-

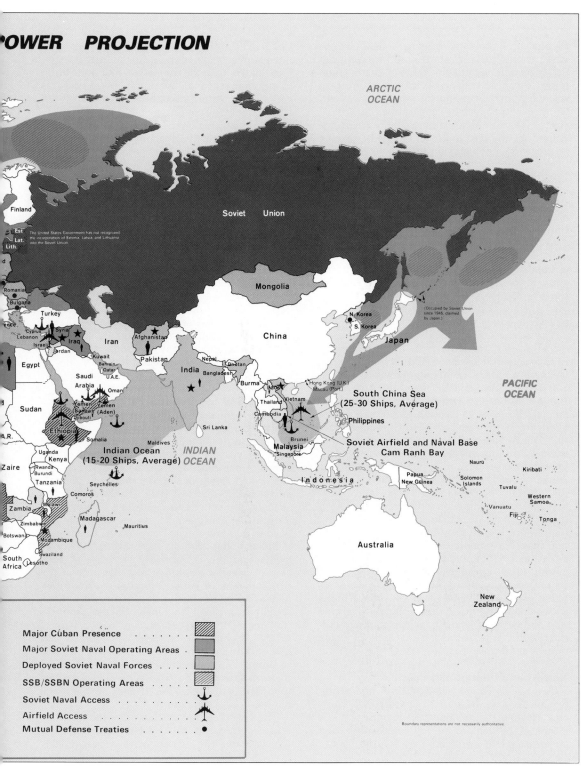

OWER PROJECTION

ARCTIC OCEAN

Soviet Union

The United States Government has not recognized the incorporation of Estonia, Latvia, and Lithuania into the Soviet Union.

Finland

Est.
Lat.
Lith.

Romania
Bulgaria

Turkey

Cyprus
Lebanon
Syria
Israel
Jordan

Iraq

Iran

Afghanistan

Mongolia

China

N. Korea
S. Korea

Japan

(Occupied by Soviet Union since 1945, claimed by Japan.)

Kuwait
Bahrain
Qatar
U.A.E.

Egypt

Saudi Arabia

Oman

Pakistan

Nepal
Bhutan

India

Bangladesh

Burma

Laos
Thailand
Vietnam
Cambodia

Hong Kong (U.K.)
Macau (Port.)

South China Sea
(25-30 Ships, Average)

Philippines

PACIFIC OCEAN

Sudan

Yemen (Sanaa)
Yemen (Aden)
Djibouti

Sri Lanka

Maldives

Indian Ocean
(15-20 Ships, Average)

INDIAN OCEAN

Brunei
Malaysia
Singapore

Soviet Airfield and Naval Base
Cam Ranh Bay

Nauru

Kiribati

Ethiopia

Somalia

A.R.

Zaire

Uganda
Kenya
Rwanda
Burundi

Tanzania

Seychelles

Comoros

I n d o n e s i a

Papua
New Guinea

Solomon
Islands

Tuvalu

Western
Samoa

Zambia
Malawi

Madagascar

Mauritius

Vanuatu

Fiji

Tonga

Zimbabwe

Botswana
Mozambique

Swaziland
South Africa
Lesotho

Australia

New Zealand

Major Cuban Presence	
Major Soviet Naval Operating Areas .	
Deployed Soviet Naval Forces	
SSB/SSBN Operating Areas	
Soviet Naval Access	⚓
Airfield Access	✈
Mutual Defense Treaties	●

Boundary representations are not necessarily authoritative.

vention in Afghanistan involves 118,000 Soviet troops. Our intervention in Vietnam involved more than 500,000 US troops. Apart from its troops in Afghanistan, and those in support of the Warsaw Pact and Mongolia, the USSR has 22,650 military personnel stationed in 28 countries as combat troops, technicians or advisers. The US, apart from its troops in support of NATO, has 168,590 military personnel stationed in 62 countries as combat troops, technicians, or advisers. The US conducts military maneuvers in support of mutual defense

pacts with 43 nations around the world. In this administration's first five years, the US government sold a total of $61.3 billion in arms and approved another $6 billion in commercial sales. It provided $34.4 billion in International Security Assistance in the same peiod. Soviet arms sales and military aid in this period amounted to just over half the combined US total. For the current balance of naval power in the Atlantic and Mediterranean, and in the Pacific and Indian oceans, see pages 8 and 9 respectively.

● Since we are a democracy, it is difficult to achieve the degree of control this administration would like to have over the flow of information. The list of ideas which occur only too naturally, but which require discreditation, grows too long, and the task becomes too great. Here's an example of an idea which did not even have time to originate in Moscow, but which appeared spontaneously throughout the US news media, large portions of which remain deaf to the message that any criticism of SDI is a challenge to official policy.

● The US carries some influence with certain political parties abroad, too. We have found that money often works best. So, from 1948 through 1968, the US taxpayer unknowingly spent an average of $30 million a year in payments to political and labor leaders to support anti-communist candidates in the Italian elections. The CIA judged that this helped prevent the Communist party from coming to rule in that nation. Today, under Project Democracy, we are spending even more money in this way, and spending it more openly than ever before.

● We never needed any help seeing that. See the commentary on pages 44 and 45.

ets have used their scientists _to disseminate the view among their Western counterparts that SDI is technically unachievable or easily countered_. They have also pointed out to Western scientists that one result of pursuing SDI will be an eventual end to cooperative, "peaceful" space research. _Meanwhile, some of these scientists are engaged in Soviet efforts to develop advanced technologies for missile defense._

USSR. _The USSR is believed to exert some influence over more than 70 Communist parties._ The Soviets manage the network of non-ruling Communists through overt and covert contacts run by the International Department of the CPSU Central Committee.

Activities against SDI by pro-Soviet non-ruling Communist parties have included a joint communique issued in September 1985 by French Communist leader Georges Marchais and General Secretary Gorbachev declaring that the "Star Wars" project, "far from ending the arms race, spreads it to outer space."

● The ostensible inconsistency is false. Scientists in both nations continue research. This requires that they keep an open mind, but it does not mean that any of them believes a missile defense will ever become achieveable.

Forgeries and Front Organizations

The Soviet Union's "active measures" (influence) program is based largely on the creation of forgeries and the maintenance and exploitation of front organizations. Soviet forgeries constitute a method of disinformation produced and surfaced by the KGB. In 1986, the Soviets circulated a wide variety of forgeries, _including a forged speech purported to have been made by the US Secretary of Defense, which reflected false themes_ that the Soviets hope would support their policy to undermine SDI.

The Soviet Union has also enlisted its front organizations, particularly in Western Europe, in the campaign against SDI. It controls 10 primary front groups, including the widely known World Peace Council (WPC) and the Afro-Asian Peoples' Solidarity Organization. Several examples illustrate the activities of such fronts against SDI. In January 1986, Gorbachev told the World Federation of Scientific Workers Congress in Moscow that "peaceful space is an important precondition for banishing the war danger from the life of the people." The following May, _the Generals for Peace and Disarmament, an organization indirectly linked with the WPC,_ held its fourth meeting in Vienna. Representatives sharply denounced SDI, asserting that it destabilizes the military-political situation and whips up the arms race. The same month, an Asian and Pacific countries' trade union seminar sponsored by the Vietnamese affiliate of the World Federation of Trade Unions was held in Hanoi. A news release declared that the struggle against "plans for space militarization" was an important task of trade unions in all countries.

Non-Ruling Communist Parties

The Soviet Union has mobilized non-ruling foreign Communist parties against SDI. Moscow frequently uses local Communists as a means of influencing foreign electorates and governments to adopt policies favored by the

---

News Media Campaign

Moscow has aggressively used a number of ploys in the news media to discredit SDI. For example, it wasted no time in directing Soviet and other nations' news media to challenge the effectiveness of SDI by linking it to the January 1986 explosion of the US space shuttle _Challenger_. Moscow claimed that the tragedy showed that a space-based defense system such as SDI is too dependent on complex technologies and that US technology is unreliable. It asserted that an accident could "plunge the world into an unintended nuclear war."

The USSR has tailored many aspects of its anti-SDI campaign to play on the concerns of individual countries and regions. In an effort aimed at Canada, the Soviets have tried hard to portray the plans to modernize the North American Air Defense Command as a US Trojan Horse in the SDI program. In news media reports directed at Japan, the Soviets unsuccessfully sought to capitalize on Japanese antinuclear sentiment by exaggerating the SDI need to conduct nuclear explosions in space.

Moscow has also claimed through its news media that the US military facilities at Pine Gap, Australia, are important elements of the SDI program. In Western Europe, Soviet diplomats and news media representatives have sought to mislead audiences on the ramifications of SDI by presenting an array of arguments. Moscow, for example, has claimed that SDI will be a severe drain on resources needed to permit NATO to mount a conventional defense in Europe. The Soviets have also argued that SDI will make the British and French nuclear forces obsolete.

The Soviet campaign has also included extensive efforts at the United Nations. The UN provides the Soviets with a particularly

● If the KGB is circulating any forgeries, then it engages in no practice unfamiliar to US intelligence agencies. Between 1962 and 1964, the CIA used forgeries in its successful campaign to overthrow the government of Brazil's João Goulart. In 1981, after several of the documents gathered together by our State Department as "incontrovertible proof" of a flow of arms from Nicaragua to El Salvador were judged forgeries, the State Department officer responsible for compiling them admitted they had been "embellished."

● Or was it a genuine speech, which the administration had not foreseen might be leaked?

● Here again, is the standard practice of discreditation by association. The authors do not even have to explain how the two organizations are "indirectly linked," if they were ever linked in any way at all. They merely assume they are writing for an audience which will take their word for it that there is something suspicious about the World Peace Council, and consequently something suspicious about any organization _they_ say is linked to it. But in fact, the Generals for Peace and Disarmament has no relationship with the Council in any case. There was nothing suspicious about the timing of its meeting in May; it has been meeting every May. Its membership includes many distinguished high NATO commanders, including West German General Gert Bastion, Dutch General Herman von Meyenfeldt, and British General Michael Harbottle. By the most generous standards, what they have to say is far more important than anything the authors of this book have to say. Obviously, that is why they are a target here.

useful forum from which to influence other industrialized and Third World nations against SDI. Soviet delegates have told representatives of the nonaligned countries that "imperialist intrigues in space" would divert economic resources needed by the developing countries. The Soviets also have tried to gain passage of a treaty against the militarization of space and have proposed establishing an international space organization. In addition, they have engaged in political lobbying, including Foreign Minister Shevardnadze's "Star Peace" proposal made to the General Assembly in September 1985 and Premier Nikolay Ryzhkov's program for "peaceful exploitation of space" proposed in June 1986.

The USSR and Low-Intensity Conflict

The Soviet Union has long supported revolutionary leftist forces conducting insurgencies in the Third World, many of which have brought Marxist-Leninist regimes to power. In the last decade, however, Moscow has learned that the tide of socialism can ebb as well as flow. Several key Soviet clients are now fighting insurgencies against their own repressive regimes, and the Kremlin is now supporting these clients against those "counterrevolutionary" forces. Soviet advisers and surrogate combat troops are assisting beleaguered clients in Ethiopia, Angola, and Nicaragua, and 116,000 Soviet troops are battling the Mujahideen in Afghanistan. In Cambodia, the Soviets finance a Vietnamese occupation of some 150,000 men.

Third-World Strategy

As the Soviet Union emerged as a global power in the 1970s, the nation's military doctrine evolved to match a more activist foreign policy. A stronger, more adventurous Soviet Union had begun to view conflict in the Third World as an avenue for furthering Soviet interests through military assistance and intervention. That view heralded an era of extraordinary and continuing Soviet activism — the 1975 Soviet-Cuban intervention in Angola, the 1977 intervention in Ethiopia, the support for Vietnam's 1978 invasion of Cambodia, and the 1979 invasion of Afghanistan. Early optimism gave way to a less positive view, however, as a number of Moscow's clients faced significant insurgencies. Soviet ideology offered no explanation for these setbacks, and the Kremlin had trouble understanding how an emerging socialist state could find itself subject to a popular rebellion.

At the same time, Soviet military thinkers struggled to deal with the new realities and to develop a coherent doctrine defining a possible role for the Soviet Armed Forces in countering these insurgencies. By the end of the Brezhnev era, military writers were labeling the fight against the new insurgencies "wars in defense of socialism" by nations on the "path of socialist development." While this rationale served to justify Soviet actions in support of a friendly state, the Kremlin ideologues still could not acknowledge the possible legitimacy of such opposition. Instead, they blamed it on resurgent imperialist meddling in support of counterrevolutionaries and "bandits" in former colonial states.

Soviet military leaders have been slow to adapt to the requirements of counterinsurgency campaigns. The war in Afghanistan has become a proving ground for new equipment and tactical developments. For the most part, however, these military adaptations have been ad hoc modifications to conventional doctrine and have not found their way into the mainstream of Soviet military thought. The Soviet Army has had little previous experience with fighting counterinsurgencies. The best example came shortly after the 1917 revolution, when the Bolsheviks acted to suppress a widespread uprising in Central Asia. Called *basmachi* by the Bolsheviks (from a Turkish word for bandit), the Muslim insurgents were defeated only after a long and bitter campaign under the direction of General Mikhail Frunze.

The Afghan Insurgency

Moscow clearly recognizes that the Mujahideen can only be defeated by a systematic approach comprising military action tailored to the Afghan environment in combination with coordinated social, economic, and political policies intended to undermine the insurgent cause and its popular support. One endeavor that has produced mixed results was the replacing of Babrak Karmal with Najibullah, which was accompanied by significant political infighting.

Thus far, however, most of Moscow's non-military measures have consisted of token gestures and have been largely ineffective. Several domestic reforms were announced at the beginning of Babrak Karmal's regime, and other measures were taken to give the appear-

According to Barney Rubin of Amnesty International, "no one has ever seen any of these booby-trapped items," even though many mines and other explosive devices are routinely found and displayed. Rubin adds that the booby-trapped doll purportedly found in Afghanistan, whose photograph appears in full-page advertisements sponsored by the Afghanistan Relief Committee in *The New York Times* and other major newspapers across the country, was created "in a New York photo studio."

Moscow is unlikely to make much progress here. The major obstacle to sovietization is Islam. Over 99 percent of all Afghans are Muslim. Our State Department recently concluded that the Soviets were "far from integrating Afghanistan's economy into their own."

Apparently not a sham. See the commentary on opposite page.

ance of a wide base of popular support for Karmal. Land reform and agricultural improvements were proclaimed, although only sporadically implemented, and monetary incentives are widely offered to persuade individual groups to fight on the government side or at least declare neutrality. Soviet propaganda publicizes alleged insurgent atrocities against the population, while asserting that the Mujahideen are under foreign direction.

Along with these policies, Moscow has pursued a ruthless military campaign to suppress the insurgency and subjugate the population. Relocation of the populace in some regions, coupled with bombing and mining of civilian centers, has devastated many areas and reduced vital local support to the Mujahideen. Recently published reports from Amnesty International and the UN Commission on Human Rights document the widespread and systemic terror inflicted on the civilian population. Three examples are provided below:

- Some 1,000 civilians were killed by army elements during reprisal operations against 12 villages in March 1985. Women were summarily executed, children were locked up in a house and burned to death, and livestock holdings were decimated.
- Over 700 civilians were massacred during a large-scale operation against villagers in the Kunduz Province.
- Greater use is being made of booby-trapped items resembling harmonicas or pens, as well as bombs shaped like birds.

Soviet military and political pressure has increased against neighboring Pakistan, where approximately 2.5 million Afghan refugees have fled. Moscow has also made some progress in the sovietization of Afghanistan. Thousands of young Afghans have been taken to the USSR for education and indoctrination in the Soviet way of life. This policy has backfired somewhat, however, as many Afghans quickly become disillusioned with the Soviet system and with the racial prejudice they encountered in the USSR. Deepening penetration of the Afghan economy, and increasing dependence of many urban areas on the USSR's largesse, further Soviet domination. Moscow has also achieved some success in developing a credible, and equally brutal, Afghan equivalent of the KGB, known as the KhAD.

Nonetheless, the military dimension of the

During the Soviets' removal of some forces from Afghanistan, young Afghans were assembled to witness the sham withdrawal.

counterinsurgency has received the greatest attention in Moscow's campaign against the Mujahideen. Since the December 1979 invasion, the Soviet 40th Army in Afghanistan has concentrated on five basic military counterinsurgency objectives:

- Establish control in cities and towns;
- Deny outside aid and sanctuary;
- Protect lines of communication;
- Isolate insurgents from popular support; and
- Eliminate resistance combat forces and coopt rebel leaders.

These objectives are similar to those set forth by the principal author of Soviet military doctrine, Mikhail Frunze, 60 years ago, but they have not produced the same results. Neither the Soviets nor their puppet regime in Kabul control the Afghan countryside, and the insurgents operate freely in many towns. External support and sanctuary, despite Moscow's concerted efforts to intimidate Pakistan, continue to play a key role in Mujahideen operations. Moreover, world attention remains focused on the insurgents' struggle.

The mixed success of the Soviets in attaining their basic military objectives is due largely to their inability to build the Afghan Armed Forces into an effective, independent fighting force. Other factors contributing to poor Soviet performance include insufficient available forces, difficult terrain, the nature and tactics of the opposing forces, and the Soviets' desire to minimize their losses. Another critical shortcoming has been an adherence to traditional Soviet concepts of centralized command and control, which stifle low-level initiative and reduce the small-unit flexibility necessary to

Afghanistan Withdrawal

General Secretary Gorbachev announced during his late-July 1986 televised speech from Vladivostok that he intended to withdraw a "limited number" of Soviet forces from Afghanistan. He promised that six regiments would be pulled out before year's end.

Moscow quite likely calculated that infantry units should be included for any withdrawal package to be credible, but the Soviet leadership was unwilling to degrade the military effectiveness of its forces in Afghanistan. To accommodate these contradictory goals, the Soviets brought in two infantry units from Central Asia expressly for the purpose of being able to remove them.

Half the units in the withdrawal effort were for air defense. Since the Mujahideen have no air force, the three antiair regiments scheduled to be pulled out were of marginal value to the Soviet military effort, reflecting the shallowness in the Soviet proposal.

The tank regiment stationed in Afghanistan was also of limited military value. It was severely understrength and was not involved in much combat. Shortly after the Gorbachev speech, this unit was expanded to full strength with newly arrived tanks from the USSR. Journalists at the withdrawal ceremonies remarked how the vehicles showed few signs of wear. Brief interviews with Soviet soldiers of the units to be withdrawn further revealed that they had never seen any insurgents. The two new infantry regiments brought in from the Soviet Union were readily identifiable since the equipment contrasted markedly with that of units deployed in Afghanistan. The new units included truck-mounted infantry with towed artillery, whereas the standard equipment for motorized rifle regiments in Afghanistan includes armored personnel carriers and self-propelled artillery. Truck-mounted elements are normally associated with low-strength units from military districts within the USSR. The trucks of the new motorized rifle regiments were replaced immediately by armored personnel carriers borrowed from local Soviet units to give the regiment a more "normal" appearance for the ceremonies. The equipment was then returned to the local units after the ceremony.

The Soviets gave great fanfare to their late October 1986 removal of three antiair, two motorized rifle, and one armored regiment from Afghanistan. Close examination of the episode, however, reveals the deception behind the action.

The Soviet military campaign generally consists of cautious, carefully planned, tactical operations. Most of these operations lack the boldness and emphasis on momentum and speed found in their conventional doctrine. Their efforts are largely focused on securing the urban centers, lines of communication, and military installations. This task is accomplished through an extensive network of garrisons and strongpoints, linking secured cities with protected highways and supported by mobile reaction forces and artillery firebases. Convoys are provided ground escort and air cover, and they generally move only during daylight. Minefields are also widely employed to secure cities, roads, and installations.

Over the past year, the Soviets have emphasized small-unit raids and ambushes, along with increased use of artillery and air strikes. Regular ground units are conducting fewer large operations. The number of special operations forces, or SPETSNAZ, has been increased to conduct small-unit operations against the insurgents. Some of the latest equipment in the Soviet inventory is being deployed to Afghanistan not only for testing but also for improving the firepower, mobility, and survivability of Soviet forces. The Kremlin's philosophy is clearly aimed at increasing firepower rather than manpower.

Moscow is steadily tightening its pressure on Pakistan in an effort to force Islamabad to deny sanctuary to the Mujahideen and to halt the flow of outside aid to the insurgents. This pressure includes an increased number of border violations by Afghan forces as well as terrorist bombings by KhAD agents in Pakistan's western provinces. Although the incursions have generally consisted of brief air raids or artillery barrages only a short distance across the Pakistani border, both Kabul and Moscow have warned that they reserve the right to engage in hot pursuit of retreating insurgents.

Soviet military writers have focused on the lessons learned in Afghanistan solely in terms of their application to conventional doctrine. The armed forces leadership does not consider the operation there as distinctive or one that requires the development of a specialized counterinsurgency doctrine. The adjustments appear to be merely ad hoc adaptations to specific conditions in Afghanistan, without consideration of similar conflicts facing other Soviet clients in the Third World. The components

conduct a successful counterinsurgency. An inability to conduct many counterinsurgency operations hinders most Soviet soldiers. Regular Soviet infantry training lacks emphasis on small-unit tactics, such as patrolling and ambushes, particularly useful in such operations. Specialized training, except for elite units, is also inadequate.

of such a counterinsurgency doctrine exist in Soviet military art, but the military has not drawn them together into a coherent form applicable to other counterinsurgencies. After 7 years of experience in Afghanistan, the ability of the Soviets to wage a counterinsurgency has improved gradually, although the application of their experience to such conflicts elsewhere has not been demonstrated.

Sub-Saharan Africa

Soviet involvement in Sub-Saharan Africa in 1986 remained at high levels, and the USSR's assistance to client states in the region continued to be firm and significant. Arms deliveries and training for military personnel from many African countries continued at 1985 levels, while support for Angola remained a Soviet priority. Involvement in Ethiopia was also significant, as Moscow encouraged Chairman Mengistu's efforts to develop a constitution and to create the first authentic Communist state in Africa. Soviet involvement in counterinsurgency efforts in Southern Africa was not as salient in 1986 as in the previous year. The Soviets may be reassessing the costs and effectiveness of their counterinsurgency support in Mozambique.

Ethiopia

Recognizing the strategic importance of the Horn of Africa, the USSR has repeatedly shown willingness to pursue its interests in the region through substantial military assistance. Forced out of Sudan and Somalia in the 1970s, the Soviet Union found a ready client in Marxist Ethiopia. The provision of more than $4 billion in military hardware, together with substantial Soviet logistics and advisory support, has enabled Ethiopia to develop the largest army in Sub-Saharan Africa. In turn, Addis Ababa permits Soviet military access to key ports and airfields, providing logistics and reconnaissance support for Soviet operations in the Indian Ocean. The Soviets maintain a small naval support base in the Dahlak Islands in the Red Sea — the first of its kind in East Africa.

Despite the largest Soviet military assistance program in Sub-Saharan Africa, Ethiopia has been unable to contain its primary internal threat — insurgencies in northern Eritrea and the Tigray Regions. The Marxist Eritrean People's Liberation Front and the Tigrayan People's Liberation Front have been fighting the central government since 1962 and 1975, respectively. In spite of 25 years of inconclusive conflict that has severely drained national resources, Mengistu continues to seek a military solution.

Because neither side has the capability to defeat the other decisively, the insurgents are likely to persist for the near term. The counterinsurgency effort will continue to consume the government's resources and military strength, and Ethiopia will remain almost totally reliant on Soviet military support. About

Major Soviet Equipment Delivered to the Third World 1981-1986 *

	Near East and South Asia	Sub-Saharan Africa	Latin America	East Asia and Pacific	Total
Tanks/Self-propelled Guns	3,720	585	500	660	5,465
Light Armor	6,975	1,050	200	660	8,885
Artillery	3,350	1,825	800	530	6,505
Major Surface Combatants	22	4	4	4	34
Minor Surface Combatants	28	18	39	37	122
Submarines	9	0	1	0	10
Missile Attack Boats	10	8	6	2	26
Supersonic Aircraft	1,060	325	110	210	1,705
Subsonic Aircraft	110	5	0	5	120
Helicopters	635	185	130	75	1,025
Other Combat Aircraft	235	70	50	90	445
Surface-to-Air Missiles	11,300	2,300	1,300	375	15,275

* Revised to reflect current information.

134

The authors seem to know all about the "greatly increased capabilities" of the RENAMO guerilla movement. Small wonder. Support for RENAMO, in direct violation of the Nkomati Accords of 1984, now comes not only from South Africa but also from the US. Like the Contras in Central America and Jonas Savimbi's UNITA force in Angola, RENAMO has no popular support, and would not exist had a major foreign power not specifically created it for no other purpose than to challenge the legitimacy of a government otherwise recognized throughout the world. South Africa has even acknowledged creating RENAMO for this purpose. What we have in Mozambique is

1,700 Soviet military advisers assist the Ethiopian military. On the other hand, Moscow will continue to urge Mengistu to seek a political solution, and will try to guide Addis Ababa toward development along Soviet lines. Programs such as forced resettlement are used to control the population and to deny support to the insurgents.

Mengistu is providing training and Soviet-supplied weapons to the Sudanese People's Liberation Army in its attempt to overthrow the new democratically elected Sudanese Government. This effort increases instability in this strategically important region of the world.

Mozambique

Moscow has not provided Mozambique with the type and amounts of assistance necessary to conduct an effective counterinsurgency. Maputo has expressed dissatisfaction with the support it has received from Moscow. Despite relatively large arms deliveries and the presence of about 850 Soviet military advisers, the Mozambique Armed Forces were much less effective in 1986 than in earlier years against the National Resistance of Mozambique (RENAMO). Considering the greatly increased capabilities of RENAMO's force and the continued failure of the Soviets to provide training and equipment specifically geared to a counterinsurgency effort, RENAMO is a serious threat to the survival of the regime. If the security situation deteriorates to where the new Mozambique Government decides it has no recourse but to call for major Soviet assistance, the Soviets would probably demand substantial concessions, such as permanent air and naval basing rights in the country.

Angola

Direct Soviet support, as well as that of 36,000 Cuban military surrogates, continues to impede progress toward a negotiated settlement between the Luanda government and Jonas Savimbi's National Union for the Total Independence of Angola (UNITA). UNITA now has extended its operations into all provinces. The regime's counterinsurgency strategy is marked by the same ad hoc adjustments characteristic of the Soviets' war against the Mujahideen.

Angola has taken some political and social measures to enhance its legitimacy. Locally organized militias and a network of neighborhood informants have been enlisted to expand government control and to impede UNITA expansion. Some forced resettlement is used both to control the population and to deny support to the insurgents.

As in Afghanistan, Soviet propaganda portrays the insurgents as puppets of another power — in this case, South Africa — and as perpetrators of massacres and other abuses against innocent civilians. Guerrillas who defect from ineffective insurgent fringe groups receive extensive publicity and are used with government troops in the pacification of particular areas of the country. Political education in military units has also received a high priority. On the other hand, UNITA has proved to be a fairly cohesive organization, unlike the Afghan insurgent groups. Thus far, it has been quite immune to government efforts to foster rivalries between factions or coopt local leaders.

The Soviets have developed no specific military doctrine to deal with the insurgency in Angola. Government forces have enjoyed little success against UNITA. They have focused on securing the few cities, towns, and economically productive extraction industries such as oil and diamonds. Their campaigns have mostly been large, slow-moving sweeps during the dry season aimed at destroying UNITA bases. As in Afghanistan, a major effort is being made to interdict external support to the guerrillas. This procedure requires dedicating a disproportionate amount of resources to air defense in an effort to cut off South African supplies believed to be coming in by air.

In 1986, Soviet arms support continued with the delivery of additional FLOGGER aircraft; HIP H helicopters; SA-3 and SA-8 surface-to-air missiles; and numerous tanks, artillery pieces, and BMP armored vehicles. Soviet advisers also participated in the continued dry-season operations against UNITA — albeit somewhat reduced in scope from that in 1985 but supported by enhanced Soviet logistics assistance. At the same time, Soviet and Cuban advisers have not been able to develop the Angolan Armed Forces into a military organization dependable and effective enough to permit withdrawal of the Cuban forces now propping up the unpopular regime.

Asia

Gorbachev drew fresh attention to Soviet policy in Asia in his July 1986 Vladivostok

In this case, the portrayal is quite accurate. Savimbi and his UNITA force would not last long without any support from South Africa and the US.

The authors, of course, have no desire to point out that a US firm, Gulf Oil, draws the bulk of Angola's oil from Cabinda province, where Cuban troops protect US pipelines and other equipment from attack by guerrillas funded by the US taxpayer.

A poor effort. The Luanda regime has been officially recognized by the United Nations and the Organization of African Unity since its inception in 1975. It has grown in popularity. It does far more trade with the West than with the USSR today. US firms would like to expand trade with Angola. But this administration is determined, of course, to force Angola into greater dependence on the USSR, and so complete the self-fulfilling prophecy that no socialist government can be a friend to the West. So the bloodshed will go on.

No progress is needed toward a "negotiated settlement" between the Luanda government and UNITA. That settlement was reached, and recognized by virtually every nation in the world save the US and South Africa, when the forces of the MPLA defeated UNITA forces on the field of battle in the Angolan Civil War in 1975, and established the Luanda government. Cuban forces were invited in by the new government to protect Angola from repeated South African attacks which began as soon as the Civil War concluded. The Cubans remain, and will certainly not leave, until the US and South Africa cease their support for UNITA.

a textbook exercise in low-intensity warfare, whereby powerful nations, with a combination of threats, promises, economic sanctions, and paramilitary operations, steadily wear down and demoralize impoverished nations to the point where they must reconsider their political alignment. The West may win this one. The authors seem to understand this. Mozambique has resisted fuller dependency on the USSR. The USSR, in turn, seems to understand this, too, and is not placing pressure on Mozambique in what the authors would have us believe is their characteristic manner.

speech. He emphasized that the Soviet Union is a Pacific nation with important interests in the region. The speech reflected Gorbachev's long-term effort to improve economic relations with the Asian nations, particularly Japan, in an effort to bolster the Soviet economy. Moscow believes that improved economic relations with these nations will lay the groundwork for gradual political gains. Nonetheless, Moscow's principal goal remains the achievement of superior military power in the region through the quantitative and, increasingly, qualitative improvement of Soviet forces in the Far East. As in its policy toward the West, the Kremlin remains more willing to alter style than substance.

The Vladivostok speech contained unprecedented conciliatory gestures toward Chinese security concerns. The most significant overture to Beijing was the pledge to withdraw some Soviet troops from Mongolia. In mid-January 1987, the Soviets announced that one of five divisions would be withdrawn from Mongolia. Gorbachev also renewed a Soviet offer to discuss "concrete steps aimed at a proportionate lowering" of ground force levels, gave the appearance of flexibility over Sino-Soviet border issues, and highlighted additional areas for economic cooperation. He did not, however, offer to compromise over Soviet support to Vietnam, which the Chinese regard as the greatest obstacle to improved relations.

In an effort to revive Japanese interest in the economic development of the Soviet Far East, the General Secretary proposed establishing joint ventures in the region, as well as research on the ocean's resources and programs for the peaceful study and use of space. Gorbachev avoided mentioning Soviet occupation of the Northern Territories, the primary obstacle to improved Soviet-Japanese relations.

China

At the time of the Vladivostok speech, Sino-Soviet relations had shown little substantive progress since the renewal of normalization talks in 1982. Improvements were mainly in the economic realm. Building on the 5-year agreement signed in July 1985, First Deputy Premier Ivan Arkhipov's March 1986 visit to Beijing further enhanced Sino-Soviet economic and technological collaboration. The September trip by Soviet GOSPLAN Chairman Talyzin sought to institutionalize this collaboration.

In the diplomatic realm, agreement was reached last June to establish a Soviet consulate in Shanghai and a Chinese consulate in Leningrad, the first two to be reopened since the 1960 Sino-Soviet split. Normalization talks continue to be held every 6 months. The October 1986 round was less perfunctory, discussing at length Soviet support to Vietnam. Moscow consistently seeks to portray Sino-Soviet relations as advancing steadily, while Beijing maintains a more skeptical view.

North Korea

The improvement in Soviet-North Korean relations since mid-1984 has been among the most significant recent developments in Soviet policy in Asia. Its major manifestations have been a rudimentary air-navy training exercise and the expansion in Soviet intelligence overflights of North Korea that until last year were limited to southbound flights. Soviet strike aircraft based at Cam Ranh Bay, Vietnam, are now allowed to overfly North Korea on their northbound journey to the Soviet Union. During these two-way flights, Soviet bombers conduct simulated missile strikes as well as reconnaissance. These flights are targeted against US and South Korean forces, Okinawa, Japan, and probably Chinese naval facilities. Apparently in return, Pyongyang has now received the equivalent of at least one FLOGGER regiment and part of a second, as well as SA-3 surface-to-air missiles.

Moscow and Pyongyang also have made extensive use of joint celebrations to certify their improving relations. The 4 through 8 July ceremonies honoring the 25th anniversary of the Soviet-North Korean Mutual Assistance Treaty were highlighted by aircraft and naval visit exchanges. A Soviet Pacific Ocean Fleet squadron led by the KIEV-Class aircraft carrier *Minsk* called at Wonsan harbor, the second such visit by Soviet naval combatants in as many years. The North Korean Navy made a reciprocal visit to Vladivostok for Soviet Navy Day later that month. In October, an unprecedented joint naval exercise took place off the east coast of North Korea. The further expansion in ties was confirmed by Kim Il-song's October state visit to Moscow.

Japan

Gorbachev's efforts to portray a new image of flexibility in Asia have been apparent in relations with Japan. Both countries'

136

foreign ministers made reciprocal visits last year, affirming the reestablishment of bilateral foreign ministerial exchanges after a 10-year hiatus. Gorbachev and Prime Minister Nakasone may hold a summit in 1987. While these visits have improved the opportunities for dialogue, neither side is likely to yield on the two major issues dividing them — the Soviet military buildup in Asia and the Northern Territories dispute. Notably, Soviet bombers have on a number of occasions flown attack profile missions into the Japanese Air Defense Zone. Moscow will continue to claim control of the illegally occupied four islands, as reflected in the buildup of Soviet forces there since 1978.

The shift in Soviet tactics has been motivated partly by the desire to revive Japanese investment in Soviet Far East development. A new 5-year trade agreement was signed last year, including provisions for talks on further Siberian development. A joint commission on science and technology, inactive since the Soviet invasion of Afghanistan, was revived, and a new commercial pact on coastal trade was signed. New Japanese participation in development of the petrochemical industry has been cancelled and further cooperation in the joint Sakhalin offshore gas project is stalled.

Japan's 9 September 1986 statement strongly endorsing SDI as potentially beneficial to strengthening Western deterrence, the US-Japan security treaty, and Japan's conventional self-defense capability have drawn stiff criticism from the Soviet Union.

Vietnam

Cam Ranh Bay remains the largest Soviet naval forward-deployment base outside the USSR, servicing the 25 to 30 Soviet ships routinely deployed to the South China Sea. The installation includes a naval base, a composite air unit, and a growing communications, intelligence collection, and logistics support infrastructure. Moscow's commitment to maintain this former US facility was demonstrated by the completion of a seventh pier, which increased dock space by 20 percent, and by the USSR's utilization of Cam Ranh Bay as if it were sovereign Soviet territory by and large off limits to the Vietnamese. Significantly, Soviet naval and naval air assets at Cam Ranh Bay in February 1986 participated in the first coordinated anticarrier warfare exercise in the South China Sea.

The Soviet military presence in the South China Sea highlights the increasing reach of Moscow's military power and the potential political influence of the USSR on regional issues. The dramatic expansion of Soviet influence in Southeast Asia is primarily the result of vastly increased Soviet support for Vietnam as well as Laos and Cambodia. Since 1978, Moscow's military aid to Hanoi has totaled almost $9 billion. A military advisory group of over 2,500 Soviet military personnel in Vietnam supports this program. Additionally, more than $8 billion in Soviet economic assistance has been provided to Vietnam through 1985. This Soviet aid has been the primary reason for Hanoi's ability to maintain its occupation of Cambodia and has encouraged continued Vietnamese intransigence in negotiating a peaceful settlement of the Cambodian problem.

India

Gorbachev's November visit to India, his first trip to the Third World as General Secretary, reaffirmed the "special relationship" between Moscow and New Delhi. The well-orchestrated visit, complete with extensive Soviet attempts to prepare the Indian news media and the careful sidestepping of sensitive issues, produced a warm reception. Gorbachev's visit demonstrated the wide variety of tactics the Kremlin can use to widen its influence in developing countries in general and India in particular.

The Soviets view India not only as critical in the USSR's rivalry with China but also as an influential member of the Nonaligned Movement, whose support for nuclear disarmament is essential to the Soviet initiatives to undermine SDI. The composition of the entourage of Soviet advisers accompanying Gorbachev underscored the importance of the Indo-Soviet relationship. These included Georgiy Arbatov, the Kremlin's senior US specialist; Marshal Sergey Akhromeyev, the Chief of the General Staff; and Foreign Minister Shevardnadze.

Moscow extended a 1.2-billion-ruble line of credit for the modernization of India's steel, energy, and oil-exploration sectors. Substantial public relations benefits were gained for the Soviet Union from a joint Gandhi-Gorbachev announcement — since dubbed the Delhi Declaration — which enumerates 10 principles for building a world free of nuclear weapons.

Despite the rhetoric of a joint call for disarmament and the focus on economic cooper-

Surely, support for nuclear disarmament comes not merely from the Nonaligned Movement. Even Ronald Reagan supports nuclear disarmament. At least, so he said at Rejkyavik. Surely, then, support for nuclear disarmament need not undermine SDI. Or should we look at the Nonaligned Movement in a new way? Should we wonder why so many of its leaders, among them Indira Gandhi, Samora Machel and Olaf Palme, all died under such very unusual circumstances?

See the commentary on page 69. For the number of bases to which the US and Soviet Navies have access worldwide, see the commentary on page 128.

A classic example of emphasis. The authors are making all they can of Soviet use of the naval base created and abandoned by the US at Cam Ranh Bay. It is the only naval base the Soviets have in this area of the world. See the commentary on page 69. For the number of bases to which the US and Soviet Navies have access throughout the world, see the commentary on page 128.

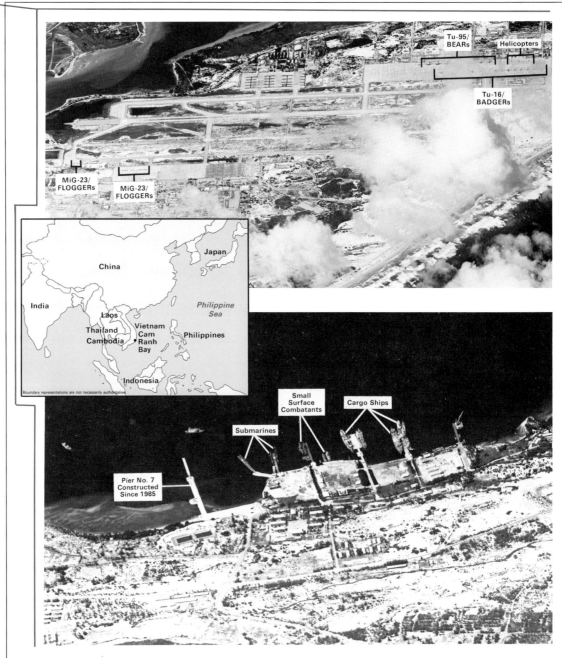

The Soviets are improving the capability for extended naval and air operations in Southeast Asia by expanding their military base at Cam Ranh Bay, Vietnam. BEAR D/F reconnaissance and ASW aircraft, BADGER strike aircraft fitted with antiship cruise missiles, and FLOGGER fighters routinely patrol from the airfield. CHARLIE-, ECHO-, and KILO-Class submarines, as well as KASHIN-Class destroyers and NANUCHKA-Class guided-missile patrol combatants, are among the Soviet ships supported by the naval facilities.

ation, Moscow continues to be the dominant supplier of military hardware to India. In one of the most significant deliveries of the year, India received its first shipment of the much-heralded FULCRUM fighter aircraft. As part of the deal, New Delhi will not exercise its option to coproduce the French-designed Mirage 2000. However, Moscow is not participating in Indian efforts to build its proposed Light Combat Aircraft. Other significant deliveries of Soviet-produced military equipment include a KILO-Class submarine, 2 CANDID and 12 CLINE transport aircraft, and SS-N-2c surface-to-surface missiles.

ASEAN

Moscow has persisted in its efforts to improve relations with the states of the Association of Southeast Asian Nations (ASEAN) through expanded trade and cultural ties as well as by stressing issues of regional concern. Economic ties may become increasingly attractive to these states, especially Indonesia and Malaysia, as they seek to boost non-oil exports to improve their trade positions. Thailand has been a target for new Soviet overtures through political influence operations and expanded cultural ties. ASEAN has reacted coolly to Soviet efforts to expand their influence in Southeast Asia, in part due to continued Soviet support to Vietnam's occupation of Cambodia.

In the Philippines, Moscow suffered a setback during the election of 1986 by supporting Ferdinand Marcos until his abdication of power to opposition presidential candidate Corazon Aquino. After initial reluctance to recognize the new government, Moscow has undertaken to expand its influence in the Philippines through increased diplomatic, economic, and cultural contacts.

South Pacific

The Soviets are relying on commercial and scientific programs to gain influence and access in the South Pacific. Moscow continues to exploit its August 1985 success in signing a 1-year fishing access agreement with the Pacific island state of Kiribati. Although it was not renewed, this agreement could set a precedent for additional pacts with other island states, which could permit Soviet access to a wide area of the mid-Pacific. In early 1987, Vanuatu negotiated an agreement that permits Soviet access to that island state's ports and possibly

airfields. The Soviets attempted to make a propaganda gain in December by signing the protocols to the South Pacific Nuclear-Free-Zone Treaty, but their statements of reservation did nothing to further security in the region.

Middle East-Southwest Asia

The past year has brought a renewed activism in Soviet policy toward the Middle East and Southwest Asia. Moscow has shown its determination to capture a major role in regional politics through visits to the area by high-ranking Kremlin officials, as well as through several "new" initiatives on subjects ranging from Cyprus and the Arab-Israeli dispute to increasing involvement in the Gulf War. These initiatives include a concerted effort to reunify the PLO into a cohesive, pro-Soviet organization, and proposals such as the convening of a "preparatory committee" for an international conference on Middle East peace. These efforts have been supported by a number of high-level visits to the region. In August, for example, First Deputy Foreign Minister Yuliy Vorontsov visited Syria, Jordan, and Algeria; Deputy Foreign Minister Vladimir Petrovskiy went to Tunisia, Iraq, and Egypt; and candidate Politburo member Petr Demichev attended the celebration of the 17th anniversary of the Libyan revolution.

For the most part, the initiatives have been repackaged versions of the standard Soviet line intended to reinforce Moscow's efforts to become a major player in regional affairs. This goal remains Gorbachev's key objective in the Middle East. Soviet policy is aimed at supplanting the US as the leading external power, expanding military access, improving ties to Arab moderates, and further increasing the dependence of Moscow's clients on Soviet arms and assistance.

The Kremlin's efforts to gain influence in the Middle East continue to rely on exploitation of the Arab-Israeli conflict. The principal means for this effort remains the sale of Soviet arms of increasing numbers and sophistication. Recent agreements included an estimated $2-billion deal with Algeria and continued deliveries to Syria and Libya. Libya has received more SA-5 strategic surface-to-air missiles, the sophisticated SENEZH air defense command-and-control system, and one KONI-Class frigate. Libya's eighth NATYA-Class minesweeper has also arrived. Syria will soon

● No vigorous expansion of Soviet influence here, then.

● Neither did major US covert-action programs in Palau and Fiji, designed to ensure that the region *not* become a nuclear-free zone.

● Wrong. Soviet policy is not to supplant the US role, but to guarantee a Soviet role, in settling this region's affairs.

Should Moscow fail, not to worry. Baghdad has been receiving military equipment from Great Britain, West Germany, France, Italy, and the US, as well as US satellite intelligence. Meanwhile, we all know what the US has done to rebuild its relationship with Teheran.

For an analysis of the evidence linking Libya with the act in question, see the commentary on page 124.

To keep these figures in perspective; the US to date has sold $26.2 billion in military equipment and services to Saudi Arabia, and has extended credit to Israel for the delivery of another $21.4 billion in US military equipment and services. Of the latter amount, the US has waived repayment of $11.1 billion. That means this equipment is being paid for by the US taxpayer.

---

take delivery of the FULCRUM, one of the most advanced Soviet fighters.

In return for their military and political support, the Soviets have gained greater access to military facilities in the Mediterranean, notably in Libya and Syria. Port calls have increased in frequency, and deployments of Soviet Naval Aviation antisubmarine warfare and reconnaissance aircraft have expanded.

Libya

Soviet support to Libya is a clear measure of the lengths to which Moscow will go in order to expand its presence and influence in the Middle East. Despite evidence linking Tripoli to direct support for terrorism, the Kremlin continues to supply vast quantities of advanced arms and to offer public support. Moscow has denied Libyan involvement with terrorism, and Soviet active measures campaigns have even tried to blame the US for the Berlin disco bombing that led to the April 1986 retaliation against Tripoli. The Soviets claim the CIA planned and executed the incident in order to fabricate a pretext for attacking Libya. Following the US response to that Libyan terrorist act, Moscow provided intelligence information to Tripoli on the movements of US forces in the Mediterranean and helped to replace or to repair some damaged equipment. The Kremlin also gave Muammar Qadhafi substantial propaganda support that continues to portray him even now as an innocent victim.

On the other hand, Soviet support is tempered by a clear understanding of the dangers inherent in a relationship with the unpredictable Libyan leader. Moscow may even have cautioned Qadhafi not to provoke the US by conducting or sponsoring others to conduct terrorist acts. The USSR has not granted the treaty of friendship and cooperation long sought by Tripoli, thereby providing the clearest indicator of Soviet reluctance to cultivate an even closer relationship with the regime. Qadhafi apparently was dissatisfied with the degree of Soviet support after the US airstrike, but Moscow is not likely to give the Libyans a security guarantee that would link the Soviet Union too closely with Libyan adventurism. Only recently, however, Moscow bowed to Libyan pressure and criticized US military support of Chadian President Hissein Habre's resistance to Libyan aggression in northern Chad.

Iran-Iraq

While maintaining official neutrality in the Gulf War, the USSR provides extensive military assistance to Iraq and, at the same time, continues efforts to gain leverage in Iran. Relations with Tehran remained strained in 1986, mainly over Moscow's occupation of Afghanistan and support to Baghdad. However, the Soviets continued to probe for openings, as with the February 1986 visit to Tehran of Deputy Foreign Minister Georgiy Korniyenko. His delegation was the highest level group to visit Iran since Khomeini came to power in 1979. In return, Iranian Deputy Foreign Minister Muhammad Larijani visited Moscow in August.

In keeping with their desire to maintain some contact with Tehran, however limited, the Soviets signed several economic cooperation accords encompassing the renewal of a joint economic commission and the exploration for Caspian Sea oil. The tenuous character of bilateral relations was highlighted in September when Iran detained a Soviet merchant ship loaded with arms for Iraq in the Persian Gulf. Following a sharp diplomatic protest by Moscow, the vessel was released and the Soviets began to provide military escorts for the arms carriers that have come to symbolize their relationship with Iraq. That relationship is secured by continued arms sales and military assistance. In 1985 and 1986, Iraq received $3.5 billion in Soviet arms and equipment, as well as the continued services of almost 1,000 military advisers. Moscow will quite likely continue to provide Baghdad with the arms necessary to sustain its involvement in the war with Iran.

The Yemens

Soviet-North Yemeni relations have remained tense following the January 1986 coup in South Yemen. Moscow's efforts to help the new hardline Marxist regime consolidate its power have aroused suspicion and concern in North Yemen, and President Salih has provided sanctuary and support for the deposed South Yemeni leader and his remaining forces. Nonetheless, North Yemen has extensive ties to Moscow, which Sanaa would find difficult to sever. The USSR remains North Yemen's primary source of military aid, having supplied more than $2 billion in arms, training, and logistic assistance since 1962.

Moscow's support to the Marxist regime in

140

South Yemen has been a major focus of Soviet efforts to expand its influence on the Arabian Peninsula. South Yemen has received more than $3.5 billion in military equipment from the Soviet Union, and some 1,000 military personnel provide maintenance, training, and support for Soviet military activities. In return, Moscow has ready access to the port facilities in Aden, which are used to deliver military and economic aid and to support Soviet naval forces and commercial ships.

In the brief civil war between rival Marxist factions in South Yemen in 1986, Moscow provided direct support to the hardliners, who eventually emerged on top. This support included Soviet pilots flying combat missions on behalf of the hardliners. Also, a battalion of Cuban troops, airlifted by the Soviets from Ethiopia, spearheaded the drive in Abyan Province that led to the expulsion of President Al-Hasani's main force across the border. Since the January 1986 coup, Soviet involvement in South Yemen's military and civilian sectors has been greater than at any time in the past to shore up the Al-Attas regime and to ensure Soviet military access. Moscow recognizes that chronic political instability jeopardizes Soviet military access to Aden and complicates efforts to establish normal ties to and curry favor with conservative countries on the Persian Gulf.

Latin America

Latin America presents the Soviet Union with unique opportunities to expand its influence and indirectly weaken the US strategic position. The USSR and its willing ally, Cuba, try to exploit the severe economic, social, and political problems that undermine the region's stability and those policy differences existing between the US and individual nations of Latin America. Soviet objectives in Latin America are diverse. The Soviets have, to some extent, been successful in portraying themselves as wanting peace and in turn continue to portray the US as warlike. Moscow seeks to undermine Washington's influence in an area vital to US interests. The Soviet Union is attempting to divert US resources and political energies away from other regions and issues of more direct importance to the USSR. Other objectives include spreading "socialism," securing access to agricultural products, gaining support for the USSR's positions on such issues as arms control, and improving its geostrategic options

in the region. Soviet activity in this area has been highlighted by a number of recent diplomatic firsts, including Shevardnadze's October 1986 visit to Mexico, the first by a Soviet Foreign Minister to a Latin American country other than Cuba.

Cuba

The continuing flow of large amounts of military and economic aid highlights the importance Moscow attaches to Cuba, the focal point of Soviet policy in Latin America. Since 1960, Moscow has provided Havana with about $9 billion in military equipment at no cost to Cuba, emphasizing Havana's importance to Soviet planners. After very large deliveries from 1981 to 1985, Cuba in 1986 received modest quantities of new equipment, including FLOGGER aircraft, HIP helicopters, T-62 tanks, T-54/55 tanks, and BM-21 rocket launchers. The Soviets continue to support Cuba's military with 2,800 military advisers.

During the 1980s, the USSR has furnished Cuba with over $4 billion in economic assistance and subsidies per year. However, Soviet subsidies declined somewhat in 1986, primarily reflecting the lower market price of oil, some of which the Cubans re-export for hard currency. Soviet financial help in 1986 was not sufficient to solve Cuba's hard currency shortage. The Soviet Union continues to provide most of Cuba's oil supplies, either directly or through swap arrangements with third countries. Moscow has agreed to provide Havana with 2.5 billion rubles in new credits between 1986 and 1990, an increase of 50 percent over the 5-year period ending in 1985. One project that Soviet credits will fund is completion of the first phase (two of four reactors) of the Cienfuegos nuclear power station.

In return for its investment, the Soviet Union continues to reap substantial benefits. Cuba supports revolutionaries in Latin America with training and materiel and assists pro-Soviet states such as Nicaragua, Angola, and Ethiopia. For example, 2,000 to 2,500 Cuban military and security personnel are in Nicaragua. Cuba also provides the USSR with military and intelligence-collection benefits. At least nine deployments of BEAR D naval reconnaissance and five of BEAR F antisubmarine warfare aircraft were made to Cuba in 1986. The 26th deployment of a Soviet naval task force to the Caribbean began in October. The task force,

Since he first came to power in 1959, Castro has repeatedly sought better relations with the US. It is we who force Cuba into dependency on the USSR.

It isn't clear how "pro-Soviet" any of these nations is really inclined to be. All have sought better relations with the US. We turn them away, persisting in our effort to create the false impression that no leftist regime can live in harmony with the West. Yet there is the example of Zimbabwe. There is the rather large example of the People's Republic of China. On this scale, the propagandist cannot sustain a consistent interpretation of reality. But neither has this ever worried him very much.

This is one of the harbors our CIA mined, in violation of our own Neutrality Act, and of Article 2(4) of the United Nations Charter, which our government signed, and United Nations General Assembly Resolutions 2131 (XX) of 1965 and 2625 (XXV) of 1970, which our government approved, along with other articles of international law respecting the sovereignty of nations and condemning unilateral acts of war.

Our Navy conducts similar exercises from our own naval base in Cuba—at Guantanamo.

Our National Security Agency has a network of 4,120 intercept sites around the world.

The propagandist's purpose here is to obscure recent history by creating the impression that the Sandinista revolution merely follows a Soviet agenda. Readers who do not know any better might assume from this that the Sandinista revolution was inspired by the Soviet Union, or could not have taken place without Soviet help.

The massive US troop exercises regularly held in Honduras are clearly intended to threaten the Sandinistas with the prospect of a US invasion. Here, the authors try to blame Soviet propaganda, not US troops, for this threat.

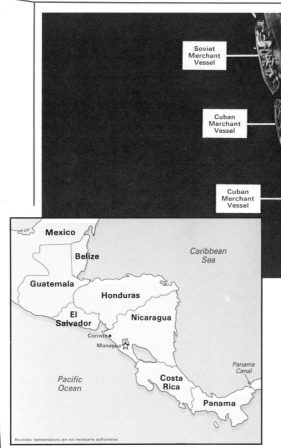

Soviet delivery of military equipment to Nicaragua set a record in 1986, with numerous seaborne deliveries to Corinto. The 23,000 metric tons included six HIND helicopter gunships, three patrol boats, and numerous armored personnel carriers.

which consisted of a KARA-Class guided-missile cruiser, a KASHIN-Class guided-missile destroyer, a FOXTROT-Class submarine, and a BORIS CHILIKIN-Class oiler, conducted antisurface, antisubmarine, and antiair exercises with Cuban naval units during the month-long deployment. The Soviet-manned intercept site at Lourdes, the largest outside the USSR, enables Moscow to monitor sensitive US maritime, military, and space communications as well as US domestic telephone calls.

The first session of the 3d Congress of the Cuban Communist Party and the 27th Congress of the Communist Party of the Soviet Union last February highlighted a renewed closeness in Soviet-Cuban political relations. Yegor Ligachev, the second most powerful Kremlin leader, headed the Soviet delegation to the 3d Congress, and President Fidel Castro led the Cuban delegation to the 27th Congress. In Moscow,

Castro had his first two meetings with Gorbachev. Despite manifestations of close relations at the two congresses, Soviet-Cuban relations continued to be plagued primarily by economic differences. Cuba's hard currency shortage has forced Havana to seek even more financial support from Moscow, but the USSR may not be willing or able to satisfy its partner.

Nicaragua

The Soviet Union's primary objective in Central America is to consolidate the Sandinistas' control of Nicaragua without taking the risk of provoking the US. To this end, the USSR devoted considerable political, economic, and military resources in 1986. Shortly after the US Congress voted to provide $100 million to the Nicaraguan guerrillas, the Soviet Union sent Deputy Foreign Minister Viktor Komplektov to Peru and Venezuela, where he criticized US policy in Central America. The Soviets also launched a propaganda campaign claiming that the US is preparing to invade Nicaragua.

During 1986, the continuing decline of Nicaragua's economy and of non-Communist financial support for the Sandinistas forced the

Some of the $600 million in Soviet military equipment shipped to Nicaragua in 1986 was on display in the 25th Anniversary Parade of the Sandinista Party in Managua. Howitzers, antiaircraft guns, and shoulder-fired missiles were among the newly acquired weaponry.

Soviets and East Europeans to provide additional economic aid. About $500 million in economic assistance was furnished during the year, of which some $300 million came from the USSR. However, that aid did not fully replace the assistance lost from non-Communist sources and has not halted the deterioration of Nicaragua's economy.

The most visible form of Soviet support to the Sandinistas in 1986 was the substantial increase in military deliveries. The USSR and Eastern Europe delivered more than 23,000 metric tons of military and military-related equipment worth approximately $600 million. This amount compares with 13,900 metric tons worth $115 million for all of 1985. Warsaw Pact deliveries in 1986 included 6 HIND helicopter gunships, 24 HIP helicopters, 4 CURL transport aircraft, 3 ZHUK-Class patrol boats, and more than 1,200 vehicles for probable military use.

Peru

Throughout South America, the Soviets patiently persist in their efforts to develop economic, political, and military relations while engaging in anti-US propaganda and covert activities. Moscow's relations, however, are mostly limited to economic activity. Peru is the only South American country to have pur-

chased large amounts of Soviet military equipment. The Soviets have supplied nearly half of the army's and air force's equipment, trained over 200 officers and 2,000 enlisted men, and stationed advisers (currently about 115) with nearly every army and air force unit. Since 1973, the value of military assistance to Peru has totaled about $1.5 billion. In addition, Peruvian ports support more than 200 Soviet fishing vessels in South American waters, resulting in $120 million in revenues. Peru also provides the Soviet state airline, Aeroflot, one of its few points of entry into South America.

Outlook

With the coming to power of General Secretary Gorbachev, Soviet foreign policy has taken on a seemingly more open and vigorous style. Initiatives in such diverse realms as arms control, public diplomacy, counterinsurgency, and increased presence abroad have been launched. Despite the variety of these overtures, the USSR's ranking as a world power — a result of its powerful armed forces — does not depend on a network of well-developed commercial, diplomatic, social, and economic relationships. In the near term, Soviet global ambitions will quite likely remain unchanged as the USSR's foreign policy activities remain buttressed by military strength.

● Wrong. A network of well-developed commercial, diplomatic, social, and economic relationships is precisely what a nation must depend on for its achievements in the world today. Little can be accomplished any longer through the use of military power, as the Soviets should be learning in Afghanistan, and as the US already should have learned in Vietnam. Determined to overlook the lesson of Vietnam, the Reagan administration called at the outset of its tenure for a massive and needless expansion of US military power. It is doubtful the Soviets will make the same mistake. They are building only to meet the level of the Western threat, but not to project additional military power abroad. The arsenal they have built has done little to "buttress" Soviet foreign policy activities. For the most part, Soviet foreign involvement has been shaped by local conditions over which Moscow has had little control. Their military involvement in most areas of the world has been quite restrained, as in Vietnam and Mozambique. Over the past few decades, the Soviets have lost considerable influence in the world. See the commentary on page 13. This is not the sort of record to encourage "global ambitions" in the Soviet leadership, as the authors here try to suggest.

● The purpose of this chapter is to create the impression that US defense programs are merely a response to Soviet initiatives. Yet, it has always been the US that has held and never relinquished the initiative in the arms race for the past 40 years. It is the US which deployed the first intercontinental strategic bomber in 1948, the first carrier-based nuclear-capable aircraft in 1950, the first tactical nuclear weapons in Europe in 1952, the first nuclear-powered submarine in 1955, the first strategic reconnaissance aircraft in 1956, the first forward land-based missile in 1958, the first operational intercontinental ballistic missile in 1959, the first supersonic bomber in 1960, the first strategic reconnaissance satellite in 1960, the first operational submarine-launched ballistic missile in 1960, the first high-speed reentry vehicle in 1965, the first onboard computer for missile guidance in 1960, the first solid propellant for an ICBM in 1960, the first forward-based strategic submarine in 1961, the first operational antisatellite system in 1964, the first operational MIRV (Multiple Independently Targetable Reentry Vehicle) on an ICBM in 1970, the first operational neutron bomb in 1981, and the first operational long-range cruise missile in 1982. It is the Soviets who have always had to respond. After we first placed ballistic missiles at sea in 1960, they placed theirs at sea in 1968. After we first placed MIRVs on ICBMs in 1970, they placed MIRVs on their ICBMs in 1975. Now that we have deployed long-range cruise missiles, the Soviets are

According to the caption for ● this illustration, the new Soviet attack helicopter shown here will "give the Soviets a significant rotary-wing air-to-air combat capability for which no Western counterpart exists." It is difficult to imagine why the West would *want* a counterpart to it, when modern, fixed-wing aircraft, of which the West finds itself in no short supply, will always have a *more* significant air-to-air capability. They are much faster and more maneuverable. A helicopter cannot engage in a dogfight with a fixed-wing aircraft. It could not close range with its target. It could not position itself to fire before it had already been fired upon. The only other aerial targets for helicopters would be other helicopters. It is simple enough to give helicopters an "air-to-air combat capability." Arm them with air-to-air missiles. If two helicopters, with top speeds of no more than 300 km/hr, face off with air-to-air missiles whose average speed is Mach 2.5, neither party to the encounter is likely to survive, no matter how sophisticated their use of chaff, flares and infrared plume suppressors. The primary role of attack helicopters is against ground targets. Surely, this will turn out to be the case for this one, if and when it ever appears.

struggling to deploy them too. In retrospect, we have always looked back and regretted each of these developments, but only because the Soviets had caught up with us. Never once have we considered slowing the pace of our own military research and development. We have given technology the lead, and let it take us as far as it can go. In 40 years, our "defense" planners have never taken up the simple question of what we really need for the defense of our nation. There has never been an objective assessment of our security interests, of precisely what forces we need to protect them, and of whether the US needs to build additional forces or already has more than sufficient force at hand. An objective assessment of US security needs would find that we do not require any force expansion. It would acknowledge that the US has always held, and probably always will hold, the significant military advantages over the USSR, and that the Soviets are far more afraid of us than we need to be of them. It would cut the current US military budget by more than 60 percent, and it never would have allowed the Reagan administration to obtain the funds it said it needed to "rearm America." Those who wonder where all the money went must remember that the US military-industrial complex has no more than a marginal interest in arming America, just as it has only a marginal interest in Soviet military power. Books like this one are needed merely to justify continued funding.

Chapter VIII

The US Response

● To meet the threat posed by the continuing buildup of Soviet military power, the US, in coordination with allies and friends who share common security interests, is following a dual approach. The US has established strategies, policies, and programs to improve our forces and those of our allies and friends to deter Soviet aggression in all its forms. At the same time, we seek to secure a more stable military balance through the negotiation of significant, verifiable force reductions.

This chapter provides a brief overview of US defense policy and strategy designed to deter the threat of Soviet military power, as well as the aggressive designs of other states and groups hostile to our interests. There is also discussion of the forces and programs we have deployed or initiated to enable us to meet our defense strategy.

US defense policy is guided by the necessity to maintain nuclear deterrence while pursuing research into strategic defenses. It seeks to maintain deterrence against conventional attacks while combating the more ambiguous forms of aggression characteristic of low-intensity conflict. The US is enhancing military stability, where possible, through negotiated arms reductions and by utilizing enduring US strengths to exploit long-term Soviet weaknesses through competitive strategies.

More detailed accounts of these programs can be found in the Fiscal Year 1988 *Annual Report to the Congress* by the Secretary of Defense and the *United States Military Posture FY 1988* prepared by the Joint Staff.

The new HOKUM attack helicopter, now in flight-testing, will give the Soviets a significant rotary-wing, air-to-air combat capability for which no Western counterpart exists. Deployment of the HOKUM and HAVOC (lower right) attack helicopters will further underscore the capabilities and the challenge of Soviet military power.

● Here is a clue to how little the authors would like to say in this chapter about US military programs, lest they spoil the effect this entire book is meant to have. Previous editions of *Soviet Military Power* were criticized for giving only one side of the picture. It was only with the greatest reluctance that this chapter was added. Since it is a most uninformative chapter, the authors get themselves off the hook by referring the reader to other publications.

A reference to our proposed antiballistic missile defense system based in space. If such a system "threatens no one," why did Defense Secretary Caspar Weinberger say that he found the idea of a Soviet system of such weapons based in space "one of the most frightening prospects" imaginable?

Nuclear Deterrence

We seek to preserve the US and our allies as free nations with our fundamental institutions and values intact. Since World War II, we have sought to accomplish this objective by maintaining military forces capable of deterring Soviet and other military aggression and of frustrating their efforts to use military strength for political intimidation. And while we believe that, as President Reagan has stated, "a nuclear war cannot be won and must never be fought," the most effective means of avoiding such a catastrophe is through an effective deterrent. This strategy requires that we be able and prepared to defeat armed aggression, should deterrence fail. For the longer term, we hope to be able to move toward a more defense-reliant deterrence based on the increasing contribution of defensive systems, which threaten no one.

Simultaneously, the US is committed to negotiating real arms reductions — agreements that provide for equitable and effectively verifiable arms reductions. Such agreements, if complied with, could strengthen deterrence and enhance stability while reducing the numbers of weapons and total destructive power of Soviet and US nuclear arsenals. Our proposals to the Soviets at the Nuclear and Space Talks in Geneva reflect that commitment.

Nuclear Forces Modernization

Strategic Forces

Neither the promise of strategic defense nor the brightening prospects for deep arms reductions obviates the need to keep our nuclear deterrent strong. For the foreseeable future, we must maintain a modern and credible nuclear deterrent — a requirement that mandates not only adequate forces and effective plans for their use, but also effective command, control, communications, and intelligence, as well as reliable, safe warheads. In 1981, President Reagan committed the US to reversing the potentially dangerous erosion of the credibility of our strategic nuclear deterrent. This erosion resulted from the Soviets' expansion and modernization of their strategic forces during the 1970s, as well as the USSR's plans to press ahead with development and deployment of new generations of ICBMs, submarine-launched ballistic missiles, and strategic aircraft.

This Soviet modernization effort, which in-

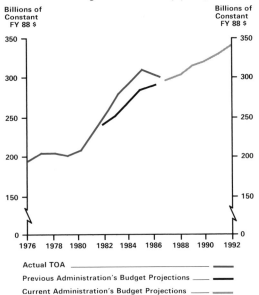

Actual and Projected DOD Budgets

Expressed in Terms of
Total Obligational Authority (TOA)

Actual TOA ———————————————

Previous Administration's Budget Projections ————

Current Administration's Budget Projections ————

cluded the hardening of ICBM silos and other key military assets, combined with our restraint in upgrading our strategic offensive nuclear forces, significantly eased the problems for Soviet nuclear planners. They could begin to envision a potential nuclear confrontation in which they could threaten to destroy much of our land-based force in an attack while retaining overwhelming nuclear forces to deter any subsequent retaliation on our part.

This condition also threatened to destabilize the deterrent link between our strategic nuclear forces and our forward-deployed conventional and nuclear forces. Additionally, by increasing their emphasis on advanced defenses against ballistic missiles, the Soviet leadership might come to believe that they could emerge from a major conflict with their forces, command-and-control systems, and other support systems damaged but still functioning.

During the past 6 years, however, the US has begun to make significant improvements in our strategic nuclear deterrent which, if carried to completion, will greatly increase our deterrent capability. The program's purpose is not to achieve strategic superiority over the

Another direct denial. Yet, military superiority over the Soviet Union was precisely what the Reagan electoral team promised during the 1980 Presidential campaign. It is now less desirable that this be remembered, at a time when the administration seeks credit for the strong interest it professes in arms control. Yet the nature of the weapons it continues to develop indicates that nothing has changed.

This is one of the favorite myths in the Reagan administration's litany. For the record, during the period in which the Soviets "modernized" and we let our strategic forces "erode", we added multiple warheads to 550 MINUTEMAN and 496 POSEIDON missiles, replaced 900 MINUTEMAN warheads on 300 missiles with a more powerful warhead, replaced 192 POSEIDON missiles with the TRIDENT missile, delivered the first TRIDENT submarine, and added to our bomber force 65 FB-111 and 356 F-111 bombers, 1,140 short-range attack missiles and, most significant of all, the first of more than 3,400 long-range cruise missiles. We also completed a $1.4 billion dollar Silo Upgrade program for the MINUTEMAN missile. This, according to Representative Les Aspin, directly contradicting concurrent charges of MINUTEMAN vulnerability, "Delayed MINUTEMAN vulnerability for at least six years." Aspin asked: "Is cost necessarily proportionate to effectiveness?" Even if the Soviets did spend what they are said to have spent on improving their ICBMs, "our ICBM improvements" he pointed out, "have been more than six times as cost effective."

Soviet Union but to frustrate its efforts to shift the strategic balance in its favor. Our strategic modernization program consists of five key elements:

- We are replacing a limited number of Minuteman missiles with Peacekeeper missiles to balance the threat posed by Soviet fourth-generation deployments and to counter Soviet efforts through hardening to undermine the effectiveness of a US retaliatory response. We are beginning advanced development on the small ICBM and on a survivable rail garrison basing mode for the second 50 Peacekeeper missiles. Both these systems are designed to counter improved Soviet ICBM accuracy.
- We are building Trident submarines at the rate of one a year to replace our aging Poseidon nuclear-powered ballistic missile force, which will face block obsolescence in the 1990s. Deployment of the D-5 missile in the Trident, beginning in late 1989, will strengthen deterrence, since it will be able to hold at risk even the most valued hard targets.
- The usefulness of our B-52 bombers — the newest of which was built 25 years ago — has been extended for a few more years, owing to the standoff capability of the air-launched cruise missile being deployed on more than 130 B-52s.
- We introduced the B-1B in 1986. The B-1B will ensure a continued penetration capability against Soviet defenses, at least until the deployment of a new advanced-technology bomber in the 1990s.
- In addition to fielding more effective forces, we are improving the endurance and effectiveness of our command, control, and communications systems. This enhancement adds to stability by making the systems more survivable and therefore less attractive targets should the Soviets contemplate a preemptive attack against them. Additionally, these improvements will ensure our capability to manage our strategic forces effectively.

Non-Strategic Forces

The growth over the past decade of Soviet theater nuclear capabilities — in particular, SS-20 deployments — poses a unique challenge to the US and its allies. These weapons affect our vital national security interests by significantly increasing the threat to friends and allies, as well as our own forces, in Europe and Asia. A collective Western response is therefore necessary to deal with this threat. Together, we and our NATO Allies are meeting the challenge. In accordance with its 1979 dual-track decision, NATO has completed deployment of 108 Pershing II missiles. Deployment of ground-launched cruise missiles (GLCMs) continues on schedule, with 208 GLCMs deployed as of the end of 1986. At the same time, the US, in close consultation with our NATO Allies, is seeking to negotiate an agreement with the Soviets at Geneva that would eliminate or greatly reduce the entire class of longer range intermediate-range nuclear forces (LRINF) missiles.

NATO is also following through on the 1983 Montebello decision to withdraw 1,400 nuclear weapons from the NATO stockpile within the next few years. Taken together with the 1,000 warheads already withdrawn, the number of nuclear warheads in the Alliance stockpile will be reduced to their lowest point in 20 years. The USSR has not exhibited comparable initiative.

Strategic Defense

The US Strategic Defense Initiative (SDI) research program is designed to determine whether advanced defensive technologies could contribute to a future in which nations could live secure in the knowledge that their national security did not rest solely upon the threat of nuclear retaliation but increasingly on the ability to defend effectively against ballistic missile attacks. The SDI program is being conducted in a manner fully consistent with US obligations under the ABM Treaty.

At a minimum, the SDI is a prudent response to the very active Soviet efforts in offensive and defensive forces. If the Soviets were to have a monopoly on advanced defenses against ballistic missiles, in addition to their large and growing offensive and defensive forces, they might come to believe that they could launch a nuclear attack against the US or our allies without fear of effective retaliation. Most important, the SDI offers the promise of a far more stable and secure strategic order over the long term — one based on the increasing contribution of defensive forces.

We see the potential merit of advanced technologies providing for a layered defense de-

- Obviously we would not unilaterally withdraw these warheads if doing so placed us at a disadvantage. What finally happens, however, will depend on what happens at the negotiating table. Meanwhile, the USSR has exhibited much more initiative than we have: it has offered to withdraw all nuclear warheads of all types from Europe, if we would do the same.

- How can the Soviets cease to fear "effective retaliation"? Even if they were as interested as we are in building a defense against ballistic missiles, they know as well as we do that no defense can guarantee complete protection. Without that guarantee, however, they immediately face what planners call "unacceptable levels of damage." These are the same unacceptable levels of damage they faced throughout the period when we pretended they had exposed us to a "window of vulnerability." The only way we have been able to solve this problem in the past has been by creating a double standard. We would imply that the Soviets were more barbaric, and that a Soviet leader would be willing to take risks no US leader could ever take.

Chapter VIII The US Response

- How does the SS-20 significantly "increase" the threat to the West, when it reduces the total megatonnage aimed at Western European cities to less than half of what it was in all of the 18 years prior to the SS-20's deployment, throughout which time all of the same cities were threatened by the SS-4 and SS-5?
- It is precisely because the D-5 will be able to hold such targets at risk, including military command and communications centers, that its deployment, far from "strengthening deterrence," will be dangerously destabilizing.

- This is the MIDGETMAN. It will violate SALT II.
- According to our Congressional Budget office, 75 percent of the B-52s we flew to the Soviet Union would not need to rely on their standoff capability, but could penetrate Soviet air defenses and deliver their weapons to their targets. Most of the B-52s have been fully rebuilt and refurbished. They will remain in inventory for some time. But if that won't do, then reopen the B-52 production line. The Soviets continue to build new models of their old prop-driven BEAR bomber, and we take these to be a serious threat.

Why agree to adhere to the ABM treaty only until 1996? This is placing a time limit on adherence. As the agreement stands, it can be adhered to in perpetuity. Then, this is really an attempt to phase the ABM treaty out.

rived from the possibility of destroying a ballistic missile or its warheads at various points after launch. Because our security remains indivisible from that of our allies, we are working on technologies with applications for defense against both long- and short-range ballistic missiles that threaten our allies and our own forces.

Our SDI research program is fully consistent with our objective to achieve deep, equitable, and effectively verifiable reductions in Soviet and US offensive nuclear forces. Because effective defenses would deprive ballistic missiles of much or even all of their military utility, they would provide the basis for deep reductions in those offensive weapons. The US hopes that we and the USSR could jointly manage a transition to a more defense-reliant deterrence. We have proposed "open laboratories" that could enable each side to reassure itself concerning the other's strategic defense research. As the President stated on 6 August 1986:

SDI is no bargaining chip; it is the path to a safe and more secure future. And the research is not, and never has been, negotiable. As I've said before, it's the number of offensive missiles that needs to be reduced, not efforts to find a way to defend mankind against these deadly weapons.

In summary, the SDI seeks to move us toward a safer world — one with reduced levels of arms and deterrence based on defending against an attack, rather than retaliating after an attack. We will continue to try to convince the USSR to join us in working out a stable transition toward this realistic, achievable goal.

Arms Control

We are seeking to build upon the progress made at the October 1986 meeting in Reykjavik between President Reagan and General Secretary Gorbachev and their agreement in principle for:

- a 50-percent reduction in strategic offensive arms, which would be appropriately applied over the next 5 years, to be implemented by reductions to 1,600 strategic nuclear delivery vehicles and 6,000 warheads on those delivery vehicles; and
- a reduction to a global limit of 100 warheads on LRINF missiles, with none in Europe.

To enhance stability at these lower levels of

strategic forces, the US has proposed sublimits of 4,800 ballistic missile warheads, of which 3,300 can be ICBM warheads. No more than 1,650 of the ICBM warheads can be on ICBMs other than silo-based light and medium ICBMs with 6 or fewer warheads. These reductions would be carried out in a phased manner and be completed by the end of 1991. The US proposal regarding continued adherence to the ABM Treaty until 1996 in the context of elimination of offensive ballistic missiles is also on the table in Geneva. We have made clear that at the end of the period, either side could deploy advanced defenses against ballistic missiles unless the parties agreed otherwise. Further, the US put forward ideas on verification that were discussed and agreed to in principle in Reykjavik. These call for a comprehensive and accurate exchange of data, onsite observation of the elimination of these systems down to agreed levels, and effective monitoring of remaining inventories and associated facilities, including onsite inspection.

Another area in which we are making progress in arms control is that of lowering the risk of conventional war. Last fall, agreement was reached at the Conference on Confidence and Security Building Measures in Europe on measures providing for an exchange of military information among the 35 nations involved. They agreed to provisions concerning the forecast, notification, and observation of military exercises, as well as inspection for the purpose of verification. Further, we continue to seek enhanced stability and security in Central Europe through the Mutual and Balanced Force Reduction Talks in Vienna, although Soviet refusal to exchange basic data and discuss the verification procedures hinders an acceptable agreement. In an effort toward further stability in Europe, the NATO Ministers issued the Brussels Declaration on 11 December 1986. It expressed willingness to open discussions on enhancing conventional stability in Europe from the Atlantic to the Urals. At the Geneva Conference on Disarmament as well as in US-USSR discussions, we are engaged in negotiations to ban chemical weapons. Currently, verification procedures constitute the greatest hurdle to progress because the Soviets have been unwilling to engage in serious discussion on this issue. In US-Soviet confidence-building measures, our initiatives have led to the modernization of the "Hotline" between our heads

One wonders why the Soviets, who have been putting so much pressure on the US in the diplomatic arena, and making so many positive proposals that have favorably impressed the world community, would behave so badly at these meetings. But who can check to find out if this is true or not? Only the delegates who attended these meetings know how the Soviets behaved. Those who work for this administration are unlikely to contradict what is said here. Those from other nations are unlikely even to see this book. So, these are easy shots to take.

148

of government and a common understanding to the 1971 Accidents Measures Agreement designed to facilitate communications in the event of a possible terrorist nuclear incident. We also are negotiating with the Soviets on the establishment of "Nuclear Risk Reduction Centers" in Washington and Moscow.

Conventional Forces Modernization

To help deter non-nuclear aggression, US strategy emphasizes the role of conventional forces. This emphasis is in preference to reliance on nuclear weapons, whose deterrent value eroded as the Soviet Union matched or exceeded US capabilities in key areas of our nuclear posture. A robust conventional posture provides us with the safest, most reassuring deterrent at the lowest feasible risk of nuclear war, indeed of any major war. The conventional forces of the US are structured and deployed primarily to counter, in cooperation with our allies, our most serious global threat — Soviet military power. However, they must also be designed to operate in conjunction with our special operations forces to counter less ominous threats at the lower end of the conflict spectrum, and to complement diplomatic and economic measures supporting our security.

Land Forces

US land forces, our Army and Marine Corps, contribute to deterrence and defense through their presence abroad and by our capability to deploy them from the continental US to crisis areas worldwide. Our forces are more complex and widely deployed than those of any other nation. They reflect our global commitments and the variety of missions to which they may be assigned. The increased capability of our land forces bolsters deterrence by helping to convince adversaries that they cannot capture and hold terrain whose loss would be counter to US interests. Our force objective is to attain a fully modernized, sustainable, deployable, and ready 28-division Army, as well as a 4-division Marine Corps manned with quality personnel.

Procuring new systems in numbers adequate to modernize our active and reserve land forces, at the same time that we are developing new ones, is an expensive but necessary undertaking. A rapidly modernizing threat and our own limited resources dictate a prudent and well-balanced approach toward our own mod-

ernization. We must be ready to fight today and at the same time invest in our future capability. Moreover, new systems must add to our capabilities in proportion to their cost. To ensure balanced modernization, no one system can consume a disproportionate share of our total resources.

The M1A1 tank, M2/3 Bradley Fighting Vehicle, and AH-64 Apache antitank helicopter are examples of the mature and modern systems that are now entering the Army in significant numbers. At the same time, the Army is continuing research on a future family of armored vehicles, improved air defense systems, antiarmor missiles, helicopters, and command, control, communications, and intelligence systems. The Forward Area Air Defense initiative and Light-Helicopter Family are examples of systems at the forefront of research and development that are needed for the future battlefield.

As in the Army, the Marine Corps has modernized in the face of the worldwide proliferation of modern weapons. It is improving its tactical mobility with the light-armored vehicle and improved assault amphibious vehicle (AAV7A1). It has fielded the CH-53E Super Stallion to provide heavy tactical lift and is upgrading the AH-1T attack helicopter fleet to the more capable AH-1W Super Cobra. The MV-22 Osprey holds promise as an advanced tilt-rotor aircraft to perform assault transport missions at greater speed and range than current conventional helicopters. It will also permit direct deployment from CONUS as well as maneuverability on the battlefield.

Naval Forces

Over the past 6 years, impressive progress has been made in restoring the maritime strength required to maintain our global defense responsibilities. We have substantially increased both the size and quality of our forces. Since 1980, the fleet has grown from 479 to 555 deployable battleforce ships. If our program is fully funded, the Navy will achieve its goal of 600 ships by the end of the FY 1988–FY 1989 budget period. This growth in numbers reflects corresponding increases in naval capabilities in all major mission areas. All our naval improvements bolster deterrence by showing our adversary that he cannot control the sea, nor prevent our maritime support of US forces and interests worldwide.

We have especially improved our power-

The deterrent value of a nation's nuclear weapons does not "erode" because another nation matches or exceeds its nuclear capabilities. If the Soviets, for example, were ever able to match or exceed our nuclear capabilities, this would do nothing to eliminate the risk they would face of US retaliation to a Soviet first strike. But when and how *did* the Soviet Union "match or exceed US capabilities in key areas of our nuclear posture?" Is this an effort to back up President Reagan's claim that the Soviets have "a definite margin of strategic superiority?" The administration has never provided any evidence to support that statement. Nothing in this book supports it. The US has always had more reliable nuclear weapons. The US has always had more accurate nuclear weapons. The US has always been able to deliver almost twice as many nuclear weapons to their targets in the USSR as the USSR could deliver to targets in the United States. According to the Department of Defense, the number of deliverable strategic nuclear warheads a nation possesses is "the most significant measure" of its strategic power. The authors will have to make some effort to clarify what they mean, if they want to be taken seriously here.

Reminders that Soviet military power is not primarily what we have built our forces to deal with.

projection forces. Our 14th deployable aircraft carrier has joined the fleet, to be followed by the 15th carrier at the end of the decade. Three reactivated battleships have already augmented our carrier force. A fourth will join the fleet next year. Large numbers of Harpoon cruise missiles have been deployed, and we are introducing new Tomahawk missiles aboard our surface ships and submarines, giving our forces a vastly improved capability to strike targets at sea and on land over long distances. To modernize and expand our amphibious forces, we have begun construction of three new types of assault ships and procurement of air-cushioned landing craft able to transport troops and equipment from ship to shore from over the horizon.

Our antiair warfare capabilities have also grown considerably. Seven CG-47 Aegis cruisers have now joined the fleet, providing a major leap forward in the surveillance range and defensive firepower of our battle groups. The Aegis weapons-control system has already demonstrated its effectiveness under combat conditions during deployments to the Mediterranean in support of our antiterrorism operations. Our 5-year program provides the fleet with more Aegis-equipped ships through continued procurement of CG-47 cruisers and DDG-51 destroyers.

Our antisubmarine warfare forces have grown in number, and we have extended their effective range. The attack submarine force has been modernized through the addition of SSN-688 submarines, up from 10 in 1980 to 36 today. The number of nuclear-powered attack submarines has grown from 73 in 1980 to almost 100 today. Additionally, we are developing a new attack submarine, the SSN-21 Sea Wolf, that will offer quieter operation, increased speed, better under-ice capability, as well as more weapons.

The range of antisubmarine systems deployed aboard surface ships is being greatly extended by new sonars and antisubmarine helicopters. Four squadrons of the new SH-60B LAMPS (light-airborne multipurpose system) helicopter are now operational, enabling our surface ships to engage submarines detected dozens of nautical miles from our forces. With new MK-48 ADCAP (advanced capability) and MK-50 torpedoes, our forces will be able to attack and destroy Soviet submarines that are quieter, faster, deeper diving, and harder to damage than their predecessors.

Tactical Air Forces

Over the past 7 years, we have greatly improved our tactical aviation capabilities. The overall US fighter/attack aircraft force structure — aircraft operationally assigned to combat units — has increased by about 10 percent. Significant modernization has also taken place. With continued fielding of F-14, F-15, F-16, and F/A-18 aircraft, we are well on the way to replacing completely our less capable F-4s. The number of F-4s in combat units has declined by 50 percent since FY 1980. We are also acquiring additional AV-8Bs, which are unique because of their ability to take off and land without prepared airstrips.

In tactical command, control, and communications, we have several programs, such as the Joint Tactical Information Distribution System, underway. Sophisticated tactical weapons such as the imaging infrared Maverick are now in full production, and revolutionary missiles such as the AIM-120A (AMRAAM) are being tested. These modernization programs have enabled us to increase the quality of equipment in our tactical aviation forces relative to that of our principal adversary.

We continue to exploit our technological advantages by adding to our target acquisition, surveillance, and warning capabilities. Improvements are being made to our E-3 (AWACS) aircraft, while concurrently we are developing more advanced systems such as the Joint Surveillance and Target Attack Radar System to keep us technologically ahead in this vital area.

Improvements are also being made in the area of defense suppression, with specialized aircraft such as the F-4G, EA-6B, and EF-111 being updated. Our high-speed antiradiation missiles are also being improved to keep pace with the threat.

We plan to fund advance procurement of the Air Force Advanced Tactical Fighter (ATF) beginning in FY 1992. The ATF is intended to incorporate entirely new engines, avionics, and airframe design approaches, giving greatly increased air-to-air capability over the F-15 or F-16. The Navy also has an entirely new aircraft in development, the Advanced Tactical Aircraft (ATA).

Our planned modernization program also includes our important reserve forces, which are a significant portion of our tactical aviation assets. National Guard as well as Air Force,

Soviet BEAR H bombers have routinely flown training missions against North America during which they have been intercepted by US F-15s.

Navy, and Marine Reserve units are programmed to be equipped with the latest aircraft and weapons.

Readiness, Mobility, and Sustainability

Readiness, sustainability, modernization, and force structure are essential components of military capability. In the past 6 years, substantial progress had been made in all four areas. Major investments have been made in both manpower and materiel to bring our readiness and sustainability up to a reasonable level.

Readiness. Our strategy is defensive; therefore, we determine our requirements based on the need to be able to deter or defeat Soviet aggression. Since our forces in the US are far from their probable theaters of operation, we must maintain higher relative readiness levels than the Soviets to ensure a timely response to their actions and those of their surrogates.

The readiness of our forces has improved significantly. For example, reenlistment rates for all personnel and the number of recruits having a high school diploma rose during the past 6 years. Because our forces enjoy better equipment, better training, and have highly motivated personnel, our military is better prepared to accomplish its peacetime and war-fighting tasks.

Mobility. In response to the growing global Soviet threat, the US has improved its ability to project forces worldwide using a combination of airlift, sealift, and pre-positioned materiel. This capability allows us to deploy our forces rapidly when and where needed.

Since 1980, we have expanded our airlift capability by 35 percent, giving us the means to move troops and equipment by air that is unmatched by any country. The current Military Airlift Command force includes 72 C-5 and 234 C-141 long-range cargo aircraft, designed primarily to transport materiel to or between theaters of operations, and 45 KC-10 dual-role airlift and aerial-refueling aircraft. The Army, Navy, and Marine Corps can provide more than 700 helicopters (CH-46s, CH-47s, CH-53s, and CH-54s) to move troops and supplies within theaters. The civil fleet would contribute 247 passenger and 74 cargo aircraft through the Civil Reserve Air Fleet program.

There have also been increases in government-controlled sealift. Most of these increases have been achieved by acquiring ships from the commercial sector. Many of these ships, which previously were available for requisitioning in time of war, would otherwise have been sold or scrapped, owing to the economic decline of the privately owned US-flag merchant fleet.

Approximately 103 dry-cargo ships and 30 tankers are now under control of the Military

● An important acknowledgement of a capability that was not apparent from the charts on page 98.

Sealift Command or the Maritime Administration in the Ready Reserve Force. Other government-owned ships, those in the National Defense Reserve Fleet, are a valuable but aging asset, containing about 100 ships to meet sustainability requirements.

Our military sealift forces would be augmented in a major deployment by ships drawn from the civil fleet as well as from NATO shipping. This US-flag fleet could supply approximately 180 dry-cargo ships and 110 tankers.

The US looks to pre-positioning, whether ashore or at sea, to reduce sharply the response times in the critical early stages of a deployment. Pre-positioning programs are in effect for Europe, the Pacific, and Southwest Asia.

Sustainability. Adequate logistics support — munitions, fuel, equipment, and repair parts — is important to deterrence as well as to defense. Our objective is to provide full support to our conventional forces from the beginning of a conflict to its successful termination. To do this, we need sufficient war reserve stocks to support our forces until a mobilized industrial base can meet our requirements.

Since 1981, we have substantially improved our sustainability with gains in all four services. We have reduced the maintenance backlog, increased medical support, increased war reserve stocks and special munitions, and expanded the availability of spare parts. Although improved, the current level of sustainability is still inferior to that of the Warsaw Pact. As with readiness, sustainability cannot be purchased quickly because of the lead times required to produce and deliver many of these items. But together with our allies, we will seek to build on our recent gains to ensure deterrence.

Alliance Security Structure

Since World War II, Soviet actions have provided a clear, enduring picture of the threat the Soviets pose to peace and freedom. Their actions in Eastern Europe, Afghanistan, Vietnam, and Angola, as well as those of their surrogates in Central America, Africa, and Southwest Asia, continue to promote conflict and destabilization.

To deter the Soviets and their surrogates, the US relies on an alliance strategy that includes a system of defensive alliances. We participate in and support a number of formal alliances established to protect common interests. The US is a signatory member to 7 security agreements, with some 40 allies. By pursuing a coalition strategy with them and by maintaining close working relations with other friendly states, we are able to marshal the forces of the Free World to deter aggression. These alliances allow each of us to share the burdens of defense rather than each having to bear the burden alone. This strategy also promotes regional security by demonstrating to potential aggressors that they would face a determined and united opposition. To support this strategy, we seek to strengthen our allies and friends so they can provide or help provide for their own defense while resisting the increasing threats of low-intensity conflict, including terrorism, subversion, and insurgency, from the Soviet Union and its surrogates.

Our alliance relationships require our constant attention in order that we may effectively counter increases in Soviet capabilities and aggressive activities. We seek to achieve a balance among the diverging and often conflicting interests of our partners.

The North Atlantic Treaty Organization is involved in a continuing effort to counter the threat to vital interests in Europe and North America posed by the USSR and its Warsaw Pact allies. For nearly 40 years, NATO has helped keep the peace in Europe by maintaining strong groups of standing forces that are forward deployed to protect against incursions into NATO territory, and establishing other forces that can rapidly reinforce the forward area in any crisis. The Alliance is committed to deterring intimidation and aggression and, should deterrence fail, to mounting a strong defense of a member's territory. NATO's strategy of flexible response is designed to produce an appropriate response to aggression by drawing on a spectrum of conventional, non-strategic nuclear, and strategic nuclear forces.

Two key force improvement programs are progressing in NATO. One involves strengthening conventional forces through the Conventional Defense Improvement program. The other consists of responding to Soviet deployment of SS-20 missiles by stationing 108 Pershing II missiles and by completing the deployment of 464 ground-launched cruise missiles by 1988. Cooperation among NATO Allies in the development and production of new conventional weapon systems, involving emerging and new technologies, is an important element in the effort to improve the organization's conventional force capability.

East Asia and the Pacific are vital to our economic well-being and security. More than 35 percent of US trade is conducted with this region. Five of our seven mutual security treaties link us with East Asian or Pacific nations. We therefore maintain a strong and visible presence to deter the Soviet Union, North Korea, and Vietnam from encroaching upon our friends and allies.

Over the past 6 years, we have strengthened our ties in this region. Our help to Thailand and South Korea, which are faced with continuing conflicts or threats, contributes directly to our own defense. In the Philippines, we have encouraged reforms and economic development and assisted the armed forces in their efforts to cope with a serious insurgency. In regard to Cambodia, the US provides moral, financial, and political support to the non-Communist Cambodian resistance forces opposed to Vietnam's continued occupation of their country. Japan has assumed a greater self-defense capability and pledged further efforts, including territorial, air, and sealane defense to 1,000 nautical miles. Requisite capability will be achieved with full implementation of its 1986 through 1990 defense program. While forced to drop our formal commitment to the security of one our oldest allies, New Zealand, we continue bilateral cooperation with Australia under the provisions of the ANZUS treaty.

Although we have no formal alliances in the Middle East and Southwest Asia, we remain steadfast in our commitment to protect Free World interests and to achieve stability in these regions. This task poses complex and dangerous challenges to US interests and policies because of the regions' political and military instabilities. To meet these challenges, we have continued to strengthen our relations with the nations of those regions. Our objectives are to deter Soviet aggression, promote a lasting Arab-Israeli peace, and ensure continued access to Persian Gulf oil for ourselves, our friends, and our allies. In addition to improving our readiness and mobility force capabilities for the regions, we have expanded our security relationships with regional states and increased cooperation with Egypt, Jordan, and Pakistan. We have also continued to solidify military cooperation with Israel.

In the Western Hemisphere, the Soviet Union and its proxies — Cuba and Nicaragua — are trying to take advantage of the social, political, and economic instability of the region. They are expanding their foothold in Central America and the Caribbean through low-intensity conflict and terrorism. Our objective in the region is to maintain the security of North America, the contiguous Caribbean Basin, and the sea and air approaches that link us to the rest of the world. Our policy seeks to foster democracy, reform, and human rights; economic development; dialogue and negotiations; and a security shield under which these elements can be nurtured. The Rio Treaty and the Canada-US Basic Security Plan reinforce our commitment to regional security. Despite Soviet efforts to undermine democratic development, the leaders of countries such as El Salvador have demonstrated their willingness to resist aggression with our security and economic assistance.

Africa is also faced with Soviet and Soviet proxy penetration, low-intensity conflict, and terrorism. This threat directly challenges our regional objectives of reducing violence, increasing stability, ensuring free access to critical resources, and lessening Soviet influence throughout the region. In Chad, which is resisting Libyan aggression, we have supported unification of the country, assisted economic development, and established our own military assistance program to augment the French program. We have made substantial progress in implementing security assistance in countries such as Guinea and Madagascar to encourage their shift away from the Soviets toward a more nonaligned posture. The administration also seeks to help the countries of the Sub-Saharan region raise their levels of food production and overcome the effects of economic stagnation and extended drought.

Third World Issues

Challenges to US security interests in the Third World usually are not apparent and their significance often not understood. Inattention to these problems frequently results in difficult to reverse crisis situations that can cause enduring harm to the interests of the US and our allies. Although the USSR is not solely responsible for the turmoil we must deal with in many Third World states, Moscow nonetheless often stands to benefit from such instability. Indeed, the Soviet Union has demonstrated a

● Where are Cuba and Nicaragua engaged in low-intensity conflict and terrorism? Only within the confines of their own territory, where we wage these forms of warfare against them. If there were a shred of evidence of Cuban or Nicaraguan involvement in the affairs of any other nation in the region, the Reagan administration would be parading it everywhere. This has not happened. Propaganda traditionally attributes to our adversaries the wrongs we know we commit ourselves. But only a major power, with considerable economic, political, and military resources, can place a nation in the grip of low-intensity war, closing off credit and trade, threatening military intervention, demanding austerity measures before rescheduling debt, calling for "free" elections, refusing to recognize or negotiate with the regime in power except on its own terms, and sustaining a worldwide barrage of propaganda against that regime. These measures are beyond the means of Cuba or Nicaragua.

Cuban airfields provide bases for long-range naval intelligence platforms as well as the BEAR F ASW aircraft, shown here being intercepted by an F-15 over the Caribbean.

willingness to actively support nations such as Libya and Nicaragua as well as to exploit an insurgency or subversive movement if prospects for expanding Soviet influence or diminishing US security present themselves.

The Soviet Union is actively challenging US security interests in many parts of the world today. An important part of its strategy involves supporting terrorism, subversion, and insurgency. Since World War II, Soviet support to ambiguous forms of aggression, popularly referred to as low-intensity conflict, has grown. As a result, we have had to devote increased attention and resources to combating these subtle forms of aggression that are increasing in destructiveness and frequency.

The expanding role of low-intensity conflict is a result of a number of factors. First, the recognition that nuclear war could exact incalculable costs has made the Soviet Union look for other means to advance its aggressive designs. Further, the success of our alliances in deterring nuclear and major conventional wars in Europe and the Pacific has driven the Soviets, and other hostile states, toward more subtle forms of aggression. <u>Also, many Third World states continue to experience serious economic, political, and social problems, making them ripe for internal upheaval and external exploitation. These same nations have difficulty opposing the Soviets and supporting Western interests because they are susceptible to overt forms of Soviet pressure.</u>

Low-intensity conflict is also useful to Moscow because it is relatively inexpensive and difficult to counter. <u>Since Soviet sponsorship of these forms of aggression is frequently difficult to trace, the Soviet role is often easily denied.</u> Additionally, the ambiguous and protracted nature of insurgency and terrorist warfare make it difficult for democratic governments to rally and maintain the long-term public support and national resolve necessary to counter the Soviets and those hostile movements that they support. Consequently, low-intensity conflict will remain the most likely and the most enduring threat to our security.

The core of our efforts to counter these forms of aggression is the economic and security assistance we provide to help Third World nations solve the problems of development while combating the threats to their security. Our conventional and special operations forces, however, are capable of providing direct assistance should the need arise, as has been demonstrated in Grenada and, more recently, in counterterrorist operations against Libya.

While insurgency and subversion pose the more dangerous threats to US security interests, terrorism has become a more visible and politically charged form of low-intensity aggression. Although still centered in the Middle East, the incidence of indiscriminate terrorist acts of violence has increased in Europe. In 1986, facilities and citizens of some 90 countries were victimized. Our citizens abroad are now

154

They are also susceptible to overt as well as covert forms of US pressure.

Equally, a Soviet role can be alleged when it was never present. Then, any form of internal upheaval can be explained as Soviet subversion, even though it may have been caused by any of the "serious economic and social problems" which the authors acknowledge exist, without external intervention. We are free to interpret these matters, of course, pretty much as we please. Then, if our only concern is to preserve the status quo and make sure the coffee beans continue to arrive in time, we will see no revolutionaries struggling for their freedom from hunger, poverty, or oppression. We will see only terrorists supported by Moscow.

● Indeed so. One of them is called the CIA.

targets for about 25 percent of all international terrorist incidents. To meet this challenge to international order and the rule of law, the US continues developing its active defenses against terrorism and urging all nations to cooperate in sharing intelligence and developing appropriate counterterrorism measures.

● <u>Our security is also threatened by illegal narcotics traffic. In some instances, drug trafficking networks have developed into shadow governments with paramilitary or military forces of their own.</u> They not only threaten the internal stability of the countries in which they operate, but also poison the societies into which the drugs are smuggled. Indications are that drug trafficking is also being used to finance leftist insurgencies in Latin America, thus posing a threat to regional stability.

We are meeting this threat with a cooperative program of assistance to foreign governments. Military helicopters and training related to the eradication of illegal crops and production facilities and the interdiction of drug supply routes have been made available to selected states in support of their efforts to halt the illegal flow of drugs. Additionally, DOD is providing support to US law enforcement agencies consistent with national security requirements and the availability of resources. We have flown surveillance and transport missions, loaded equipment, towed or escorted seized boats, and provided advisory assistance to local governments.

Humanitarian aid has also proved effective in Third World countries faced with low-intensity threats. Through the Department of State's Agency for International Development, these efforts include the transportation of humanitarian cargo from private donors when space is available, and providing excess, non-lethal US property worldwide. This assistance, such as that given to the Sudanese and the Afghan peoples, has been expanded since 1984. We also are increasing our capacity to provide timely and effective civic assistance. These activities are performed in conjunction with authorized military operations, provided they promote our security interests and specific readiness skills.

Special Operations Forces

Fully capable special operations forces (SOF) are essential to our national security. They provide us with a unique culturally and geo-

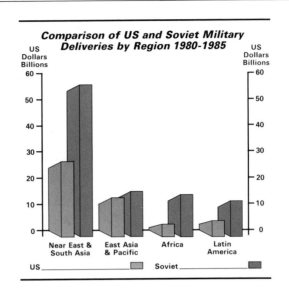

Comparison of US and Soviet Military Deliveries by Region 1980-1985

graphically oriented capacity to assist others in defending themselves as well as a potent force for conventional war.

In 1981, we undertook a long-overdue revitalization of these forces, with the objective of completing the process before FY 1991. Our goal was the restoration of a global SOF capability to deter the escalation of violence encountered in low-intensity conflict and to operate with conventional forces in a war. The following developments are taking place:

Army: A fifth Special Forces Group, a second aviation battalion, and the Special Operations Command's first communications and support battalions will be activated by 1991.

Navy: An additional SEAL (Sea/Air/Land) team to meet the goal of three teams per fleet as well as a Naval Special Warfare Unit in the Mediterranean will be activated. Naval Special Warfare Group and Unit staffs will be expanded to provide necessary command and control, and the Naval Special Warfare training organization will be expanded.

Air Force: Our program corrects major special operations airlift shortfalls by procuring or modernizing aircraft needed to support contingency and wartime SOF taskings. This program includes procuring additional MC-130 Combat Talon II aircraft and MH-53 Pave Low helicopters to support infiltration, exfiltration, and resupply missions; AC-130 Spectre gunships to provide precise, day/night, adverse weather fire support; and navigation and avion-

● The Soviets have fewer than 30 of these aircraft at present. Eventually, they will have more, of course. But that is not going to "increase" the air-superiority threat to the West. You can't "increase" a threat that doesn't exist in the first place. An entire generation of US aircraft, including the F-14 TOMCAT and F-15 EAGLE, is superior to the MiG-29 in speed, range, maneuverability, load capacity, avionics, weapons guidance, and every other significant respect.

ics upgrades for the AC-130H and MC-130E aircraft in the inventory.

Security Assistance

Security assistance is an integral component of our worldwide alliance strategy. Our goals are to help our friends and allies better defend themselves, while at the same time contributing to the collective security effort that benefits us all. Security assistance helps the US to retain access to foreign bases and training areas for our forward-deployed forces and to gain critical overflight privileges.

Our security assistance programs respond well to Soviet-supported or other radical challenges around the world. The Soviet Union, in conjunction with its military buildup, has increased its military aid and arms sales ties to several Third World countries. Moscow supports a policy of opportunism and influence expansion that emphasizes military aid over economic aid, preferring to use its military production and logistics system to create and to exploit vulnerabilities around the world. These military priorities have created a wealth of military equipment to supply to their surrogates who, in many cases, use these arms to heighten tensions and exploit regional instabilities.

The military element of US security assistance comprises the following:

- Foreign Military Sales Credit Financing, which provides direct credits to countries at prevailing interest or concessionary rates, allowing the purchase of equipment or services from the US Government or directly from US contractors;
- The Military Assistance Program, which furnishes on a grant basis defense articles and services to eligible governments; and
- The International Military Education and Training Program, which allows DOD to provide training support to foreign military personnel as grant assistance.

We have made considerable progress in Central America, the Middle East, NATO's southern flank, and other regions of US interest. We have worked closely with friendly countries to expand dialogue, to aid the planning and execution of programs in ways that respond to countries' defense needs, and to address any economic difficulties caused by those needs. This effort has produced military and economic assistance programs tailored to each country's situation. The number of countries receiving aid grew — from 63 in 1981 to 103 in 1986 — as did the number of students receiving US military training.

This administration worked closely with Congress to develop an effective security assistance program through a number of new funding instruments and other legislative changes. A reinvigorated Military Assistance Program (MAP), a small support program for non-US manufactured equipment, forgiven-debts for Israel and Egypt, and streamlined procedures have enhanced the security assistance program. The administration has used these funding, legislative, and management improvements to bolster relations with recipient countries. For example, we have established a program in Pakistan; augmented programs in Central America, Tunisia, NATO's southern tier, Israel, and Egypt; and expanded planning to ensure balanced programs and the best use of funds.

Additionally, we have pursued specific initiatives to stretch our dollars through more careful management and better terms. Legislatively, we have obtained more flexibility by obtaining more MAP funding and concessionary credits. Such efforts help to lessen future debt problems for many countries. Our policy initiatives include continued pursuit of improved management efforts as well as some creative approaches and alternatives to country financing to help ease their debt burden.

The administration developed an austere but responsible continuity budget for security assistance framed within an overall budget responding to the requirements of the Gramm-Rudman-Hollings Act. Recent congressional appropriations, however, have not realized the administration's assessment of the security assistance need.

Without continuity, many of the advances of the past few years, which serve to strengthen deterrence and contain any aggression, are threatened. And other advances in key areas — such as base rights and access — may be severely impaired. These gains were acquired with great effort and would be very difficult to reestablish if insufficiently funded.

Technology Security

One of our most important endeavors is to safeguard those technologies that contribute to the efficient and effective operation of our weapons and support systems.

By consolidating all the technology security

responsibilities of the Office of the Secretary of Defense, we have entered a new phase in controlling the transfer of militarily significant technology to the Soviet Union and its allies. As part of this consolidation, we are pursuing management objectives of efficiency, predictability, and openness, while providing expertise in the identification of military applicability of proposed dual-use exports.

Efficiency and predictability in export licensing strengthen the competitiveness of US industry and, in turn, contribute to a healthy defense industrial base. We are developing an export case precedent decision-aid system based on an export case history and policy data base. The data base will contain guidance that will enable DOD export license application officers to identify key current policy considerations relevant to the applications they are processing. This flexible system will keep guidance and licensing criteria up to date and will ensure consistent treatment.

Another means of increasing the predictability of export licensing is to track the capability of all technologically sophisticated countries worldwide in terms of the years they are ahead or behind the US, as well as the parameters of equipment that give the country its state-of-the-art capability. This approach enables the foreign-availability aspect to be included in the export license decision process. It should decrease the flow of militarily critical technology to potential adversaries.

A major step in slowing the Western technological subsidy of the Soviet military is to increase both government and private sector awareness of the problem. We conduct this information campaign through briefings, seminars, publications, and technical meetings presented to private and government groups.

Internationally, we are trying to raise the awareness of the need for technology security and export control programs. Export control personnel exchange programs have included visits from officials of a dozen countries. Additionally, the countries associated with the Coordinating Committee for Export Controls (COCOM) are seeking comprehensive trade security agreements with friendly, non-COCOM nations that produce militarily critical goods or are the site of potential diversion attempts.

We must continue to encourage our allies and friends to strengthen their programs of technology security. We hope that many of them will place greater political emphasis on export controls, set tougher penalties for violators, and tighten enforcement procedures. The US must work with COCOM and other governments to gain more information on how the Soviets are trying to acquire our technology and to plan joint strategies to stop them.

Our SDI technology security approach builds on established DOD procedures for transfer of technical data, classifying material, and the competitive procurement process. Further, for the first time we have integrated technology security with technology cooperation objectives at the outset of a major program.

Heightened awareness of technology security is essential as we cross new frontiers in our defense partnerships. We are ensuring that control over Western technology is an integral part of every agreement being entered into within the framework of the President's Strategic Defense Initiative, in other cooperative ventures in military technology, and in civilian technologies with military application.

Conclusion

The US, together with our allies and friends, must maintain the military capabilities required to deter and, if necessary, defeat Soviet aggression against our vital interests. Realizing that the perceptions of the Soviets, our allies, and other nations are affected by the military global balance, we cannot accept a position of military inferiority. Maintaining a strong military capability over the long term requires that each year we fund an adequate defense program, one that is grounded in a clear understanding of the nature and character of the threats posed to our national interests.

The purpose of this publication has been to document the realities of Soviet military power. It is clear that the Soviet Union, together with Soviet-backed forces, is fully capable of simultaneous aggression in multiple regions of the world and of threatening our vital interests. US national security strategies and the capabilities we acquire to execute them must take into account this, the reality of Soviet military power.

If that's all we need, why do we have so much more? Why has President Reagan authorized the production of 17,000 new nuclear warheads? Only 6,000 of these are scheduled as replacements for warheads already existing. This means that the already swelling US arsenal is scheduled for a net expansion of 11,000 additional warheads. What purpose do they serve? What purpose does the PERSHING II serve? What purpose will the TRIDENT II D-5 serve? Both of these weapons, capable of destroying hardened Soviet military command and communications centers in Moscow and other cities, are designed only for use in a first strike. They are not needed to deter Soviet aggression. All they can do is force the Soviets to rely on automatic warning systems, thereby making the world an infinitely more dangerous place. This is a reckless, myopic, and suicidal way to protect our vital interests. As noted at the beginning of this chapter, a defense program "grounded in a clear understanding of the nature and character of the threat" posed to our national interests, would cost about one-third of what the US spends on its military budget today. Instead, we spend much more for a program grounded in a series of distortions and lies, and based on a hidden agenda.

Titles of Related Interest From VINTAGE BOOKS